HAROLD HARVEY
Painter of Cornwall

AF394529

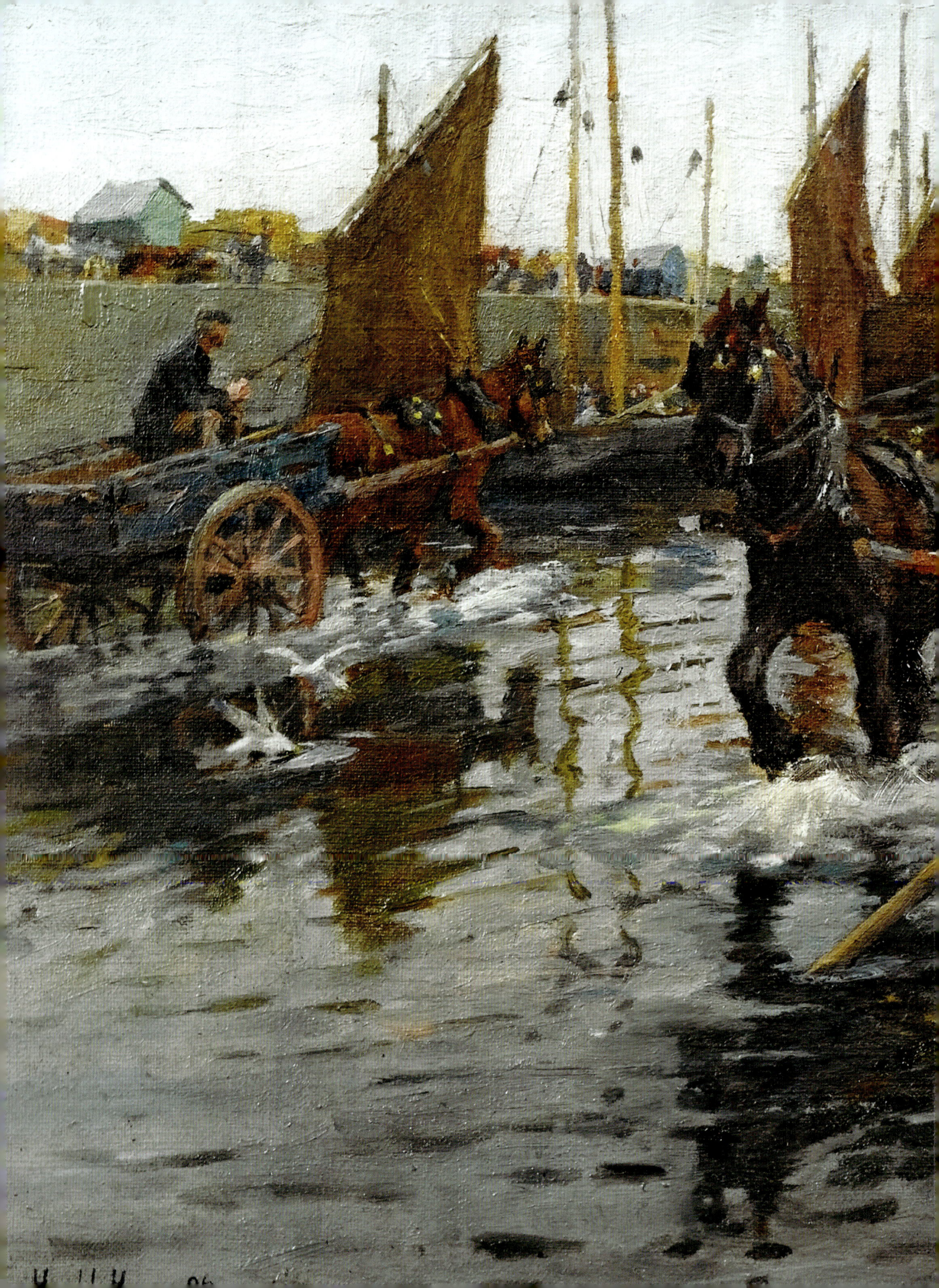

HAROLD HARVEY
Painter of Cornwall

**PETER RISDON
AND
PAULINE SHEPPARD**

with an introduction by
KENNETH McCONKEY

Sansom & Company

PENLEE HOUSE
Gallery & Museum
PENZANCE

First published in 2001 by Sansom & Company,
a publishing imprint of Redcliffe Press Ltd,
81G Pembroke Road, Bristol BS8 3EA
www.sansomandcompany.co.uk | info@sansomandcompany.co.uk

This revised edition published in 2024 on the occasion of the exhibition
'The Exceptional Harold Harvey', Penlee House Gallery & Museum, Penzance
1 May–29 September 2024

Publication sponsored by

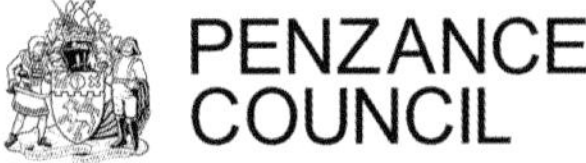

Penlee House Gallery & Museum is owned and operated by

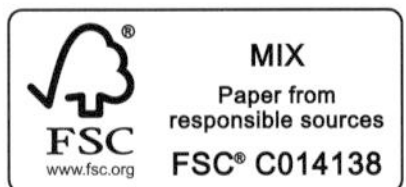

Text © Peter Risdon and Pauline Sheppard
Introduction © Professor Kenneth McConkey
Catalogue raisonné © Peter Risdon

ISBN 978-1-915670-13-7

British Library Cataloguing-in-Publication Data
A catalogue record for this book is available from the British Library.

All rights reserved. Except for the purpose of review, no part of this book may
be reproduced, stored in a retrieval system, or transmitted, in any form or by
any means, electronic, mechanical, photocopying, recording or otherwise,
without the prior permission of the publishers.

Design and typesetting by E&P Design, Bath
Printed and bound via Akcent Media

Sansom & Company is committed to being an environmentally publisher.
This book is made from Forest Stewardship Council® certified paper.

cover
Mousehole [detail]
1922 | oil on canvas | 40.5 x 60 cm
PRIVATE COLLECTION; IMAGE COURTESY DAVID MESSUM FINE ART

frontispiece
Unloading the Boats, Newlyn Harbour
1906 | oil on canvas | 30.5 x 46 cm
BONHAMS

Contents

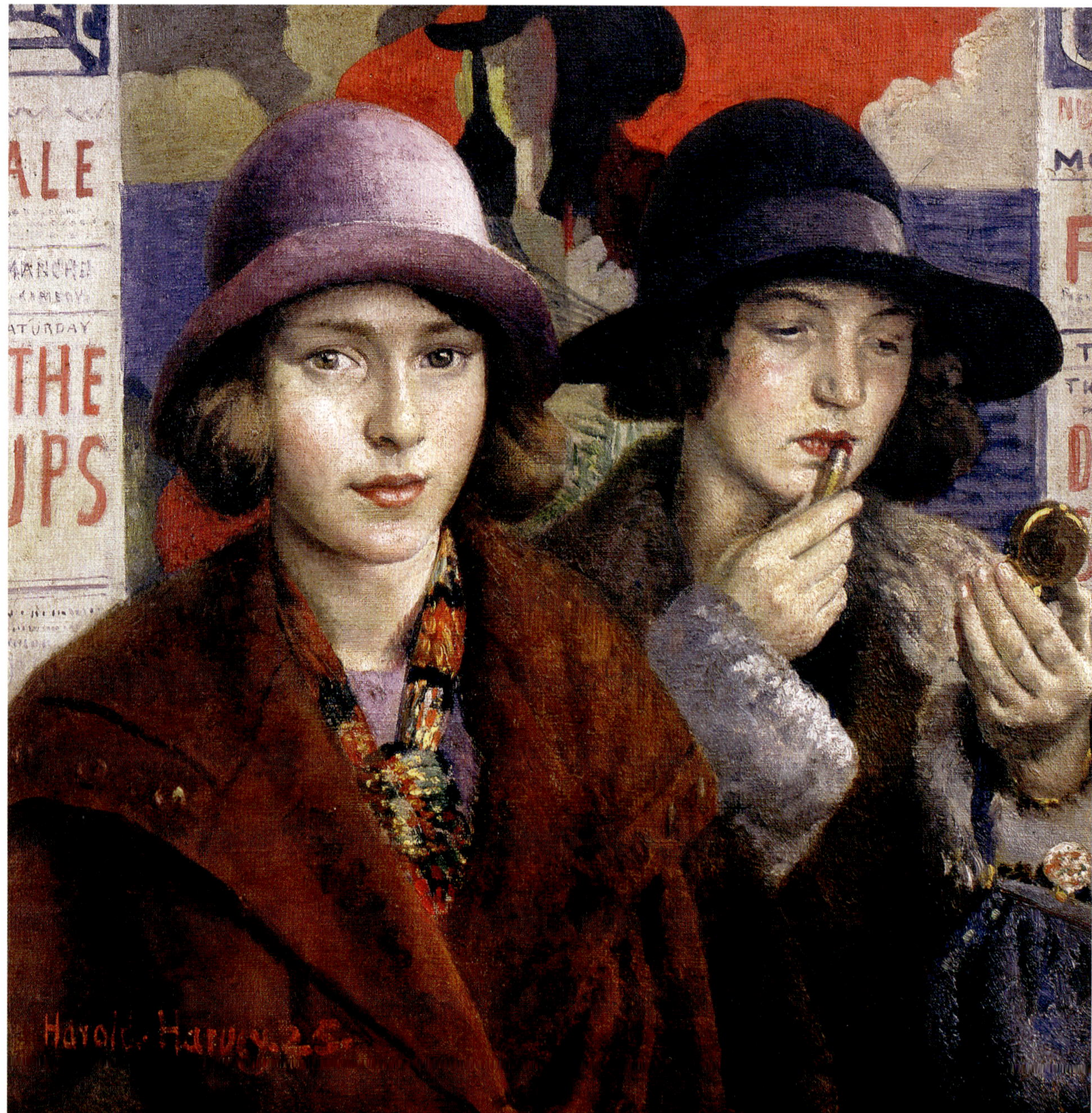

Girls Outside the Gaiety Cinema, Newlyn
1925 | oil on canvas | 46 x 46 cm
PRIVATE COLLECTION

Foreword

This revised edition of the 2001 publication, featuring a new selection of full-colour illustrations and greatly updated catalogue raisonné, accompanies a major new exhibition of Harold Harvey's paintings curated by Penlee House Gallery & Museum. 'The Exceptional Harold Harvey' commemorates the 150th anniversary of the birth of this inspiring Cornish-born artist, whose work continues to be a firm favourite with visitors to the Gallery.

In his introductory essay Kenneth McConkey sets Harvey in the context of the art movements of the time and shows how his early genre paintings of rustic and marine life, so characteristic of the early Newlyn artists, gradually gave way to more sophisticated subject matter – Harvey was noted for his sumptuous interiors – and a flatter and more decorative style of painting.

This complements a comprehensive biography of Harvey, written and researched by Peter Risdon and Pauline Sheppard, which is in turn illuminated by Risdon's painstakingly compiled catalogue raisonné of over 800 paintings. Harvey's output was prodigious, and the illustrations feature many of his favoured subjects: the Cornish at work, children at play, intimate interiors and conversation pieces.

Harvey's early work might be compared with that of Stanhope Forbes, while his later paintings show clear affinities with those of fellow painters such as Laura Knight and Dod Procter. Many of his contemporaries in Newlyn were visiting observers, but for Harvey, who rarely left the county even though a regular exhibitor at the Royal Academy, the Cornish world was his subject 'because it was there'.

Katie Herbert
Curator/Deputy Director
Penlee House Gallery & Museum

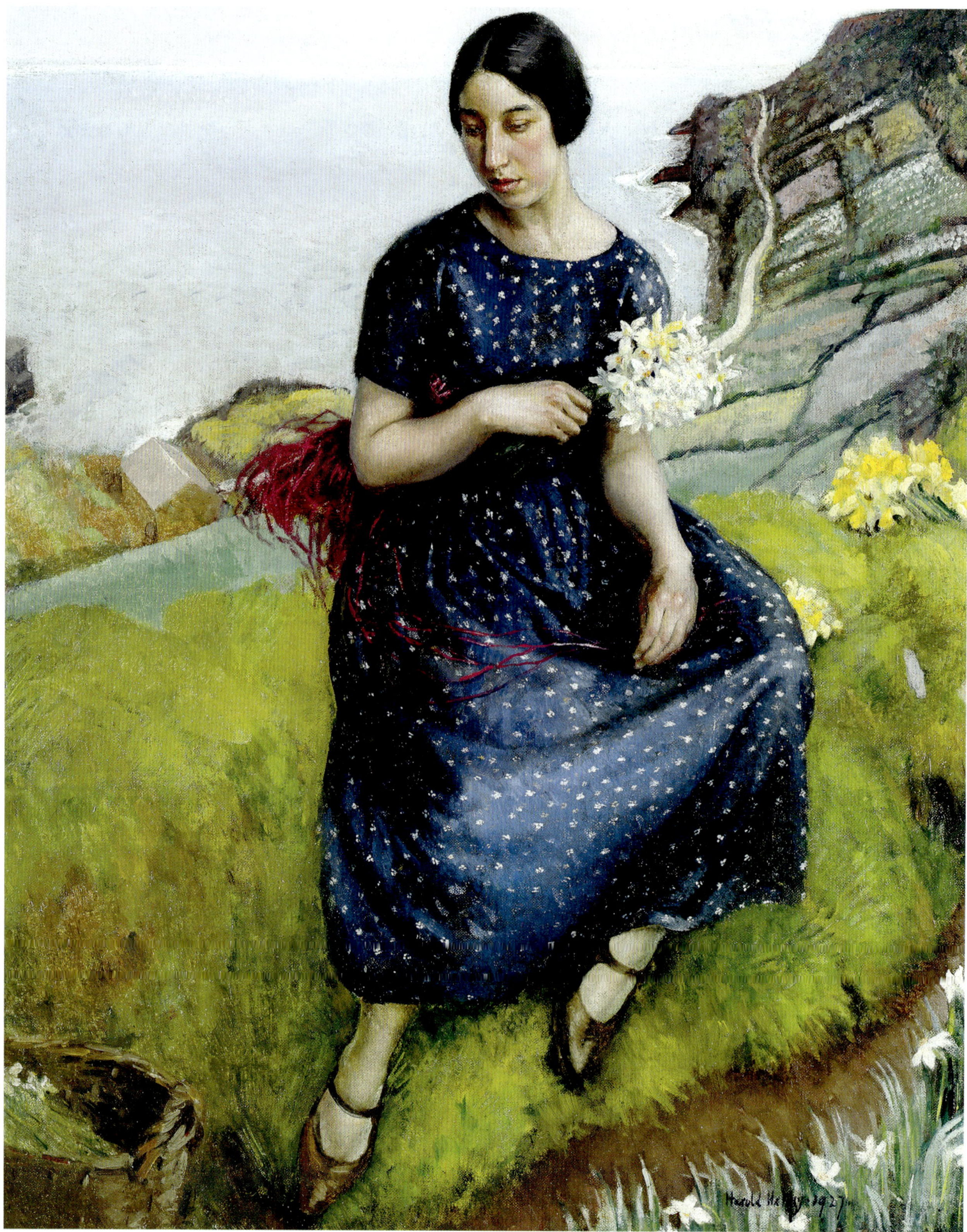

Daffodils
1927 | oil on canvas | 61 x 51 cm
DAVID MESSUM FINE ART

Introduction
Time and place in the art
of Harold Harvey

Kenneth McConkey

In 1901 Stanhope Forbes exhibited a genre painting in the Royal Academy. It showed the familiar Cornish cottage interior with a family grouped around the table, its aged patriarch reading the newspaper. Further description would be unnecessary were it not that the title of the work – *22nd January 1901* – indicates something more portentous than the daily ritual of reading the news.[1] This was the day the world changed; when everyone realized that the Victorian age had come to an end. The moment of the reporting of the Queen's death was something even a child would remember. All at once a routine potboiler is transformed by the stroke of the pen. We begin to register that three generations are represented.[2] The newsreader and his wife look back through the era which had passed. The young couple are those who will have to bear this change, and their three year old son may live to fight for his country in the new century. The whole group has come round into the light to see the paper and hear the report, leaving an empty chair in the shadows on the right. Empty chairs had signified absent presences in Victorian painting.

Throughout the early years of his career, Forbes resisted the temptation to engage in moralizing. Where others like Frank Bramley looked increasingly for 'symbolic purpose', Forbes stuck for the most part with 'realistic truth'.[3] He was, he consistently claimed, seeking for objectivity.[4] The comparison of *22nd January 1901* with Bramley's *A Hopeless Dawn* (1888), the picture which more than anything else lodged the Newlyn school in the public consciousness, is worth making, if only for the obvious point that a newspaper has replaced the Bible. National sadness has replaced personal tragedy. However, the insistence upon a meaning beyond the literal which links both paintings opened the way to wider possibilities in the interpretation of Forbes' work in the Edwardian years. The seamen in *The Seine Boat* (1904) and women and children in *The Fleet in Sight* (1911) have to be viewed differently. These characters have become archetypes in an age in which land and sea, and the activities associated with them, were enfolded in a national rhetoric.

1. For further reference see Caroline Fox and Francis Greenacre, *Painting in Newlyn, 1880–1930* (London: Barbican Art Gallery, 1985), p. 111. See also Caroline Fox, *Stanhope Forbes and the Newlyn School* (David and Charles, 1993), p. 85. Forbes had treated the theme of the empty chair in a slightly earlier work, *The Fireside*.

2. Ibid. Fox and Greenacre identify the setting as Primrose Cottage, the home of Stephen and Hannah Hichen and their three-year old son. The elderly man was Willie Hichens (*sic*), a frequent model for Forbes. He was not actually related to the young couple, although in this context, it might be implied that he was.

3. These terms are borrowed from D.S. MacColl's criticism of Henry Herbert La Thangue's *The Man with the Scythe* (London: Tate Gallery); see Kenneth McConkey, *A Painter's Harvest, Henry Herbert La Thangue, 1859–1929* (Gallery Oldham exhibition catalogue, 1978), p. 33.

4. See for instance Stanhope A. Forbes, 'The Treatment of Modern Life in Art', in *Transactions of the National Association for the Advancement of Art and its Application to Industry, Birmingham Meeting*, MDCCCXC, 1891 (22 Albermarle Street, London), p. 124.

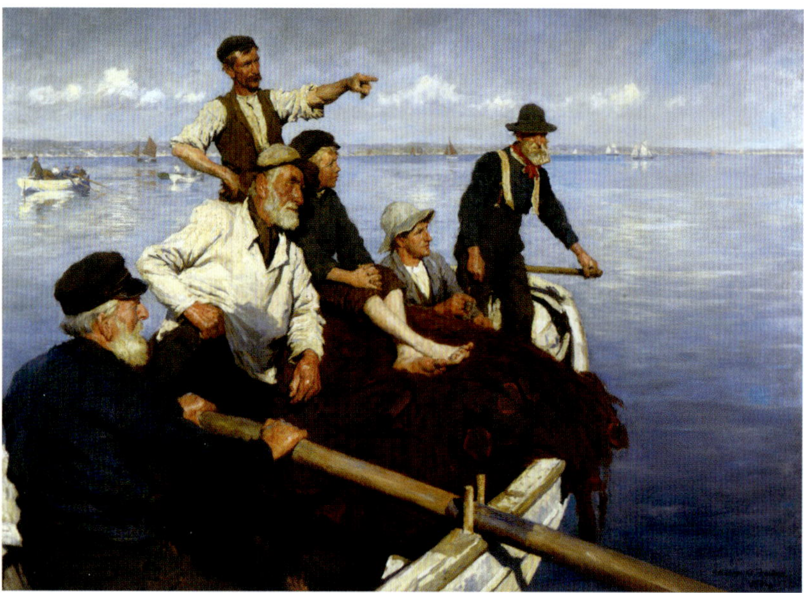

Stanhope Forbes
The Seine Boat
1904 | oil on canvas | 114.5 x 157.5 cm
PRIVATE COLLECTION

Although the Newlyn School initially defined itself in terms of coastal genre, it was never exclusively such, and by the mid-nineties, many of its adherents had turned their backs upon the fishermen, in order to represent scenes of Cornish rural life. Forbes had led the way in this regard, and with the new century rural subject matter for him was just as prevalent as coastal.[5] In this, the early work of Harold Harvey is in keeping with the general shift away from coastal genre. In 1897, he announced himself with a large canvas entitled *The Dinner Hour* showing a plough team at rest in the spring sunlight in a field over-looking the sea.[6] Having trained in Paris, Harvey had returned to Newlyn with a mission to portray the area whence he came. Unlike William Rothenstein and Charles Conder, he had apparently not been drawn to the low life of the *café-concerts*, or the charms of artist colony life at Giverny. *The Dinner Hour* is a thesis picture in an earlier mode, but one which still had currency in Britain. It summarises the concerns of painters in the previous twenty years, looking back to Jules Bastien-Lepage. With his hobnail boots jutting forward, the young man in the foreground sits staring out of the picture in the manner of Bastien-Lepage's exhausted peasant woman in *Les Foins* (1878) or the field work in Peter Henry Emerson's naturalist combination print, *In the Barley Harvest* (1888). Harvey's picture goes further than these in its representation of all of the generations of the peasant family. In mediating the potential harshness of the labourer's exhaustion, his work draws more upon the pictorial language of George Clausen and Henry Herbert La Thangue than upon mainstream Newlyn subject matter. The young woman who has brought the food for men and horses to this high field, holds her side after what must have been a steep climb. Duty and charity lie beneath her proud profile.

5. His first essay on gypsy life, *Their Ever Shifting Home* (Art Gallery of New South Wales), had of course been painted in 1887. In the Edwardian years, predominantly rural pictures by Forbes were selected to illustrate Mary R. Mitford, *Sketches of English Life and Character* (Edinburgh: TN Foulis, 1909).
6. For reference to this work see David Messum, *British Impressions* (exhibition catalogue, 1994), no. 8. The picture is dated 1897, although it may have been worked between that date and 1901. Harvey later simplified and reworked this composition in a small canvas entitled *Crowst* (*c.*1906).

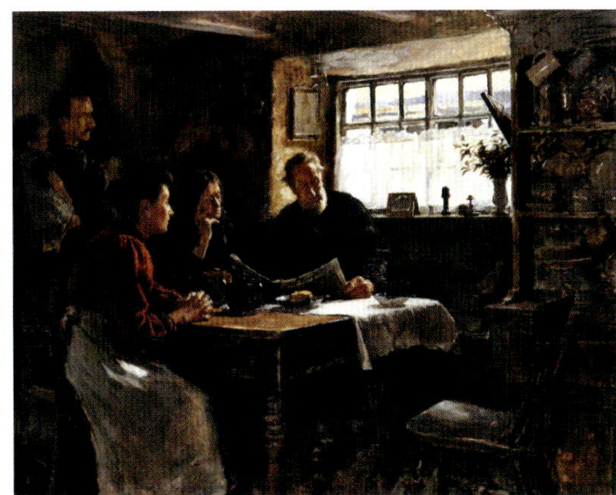

Stanhope Forbes
22nd January 1901,
Reading the News of the Queen's Death
1901 │ oil on canvas │ 96 x 124 cm
ROYAL ALBERT MEMORIAL MUSEUM, EXETER

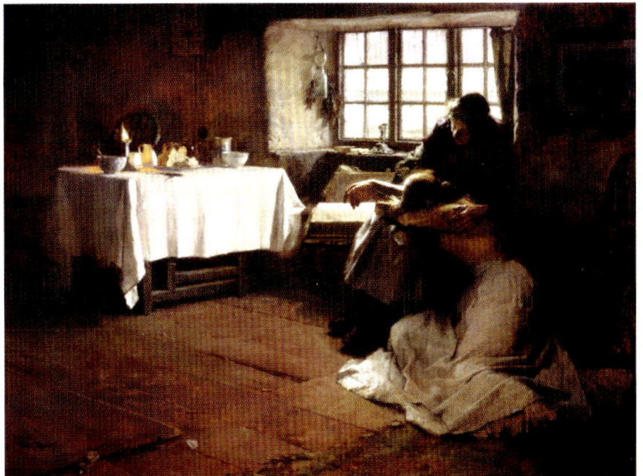

Frank Bramley
A Hopeless Dawn
1888 │ oil on canvas │ 112 x 167 cm
© TATE, LONDON, 2024

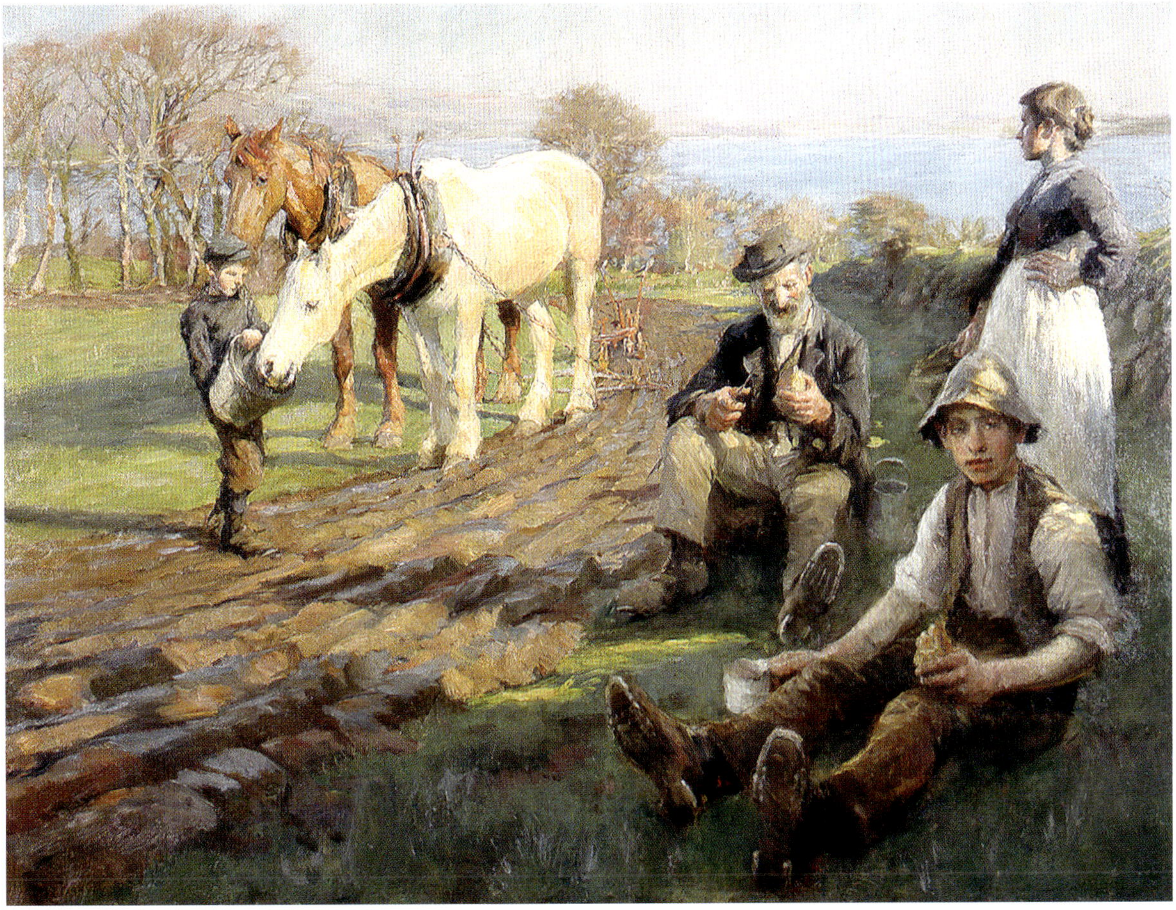

The Dinner Hour
1897 │ oil on canvas │ 94 x 122 cm
PRIVATE COLLECTION

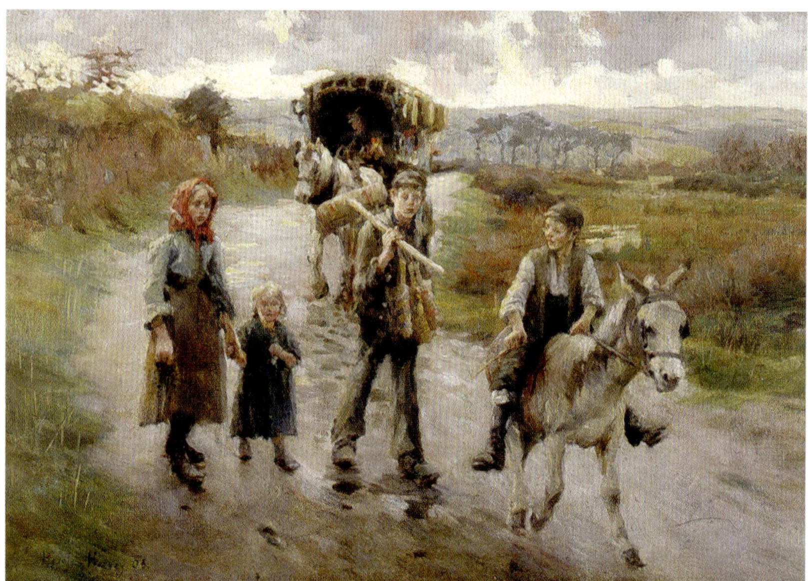

The Wayfarers
1906 | oil on canvas | 30.5 x 46 cm
PRIVATE COLLECTION

It is but a few years since Walter Langley's *Charity* (1897) had been extravagantly praised for its exemplification of Christian virtues in Tolstoy's *What is Art?*[7]

Charity remains as the undercurrent of the encounter described in *The Pedlar* (1902), in which the protagonist is graciously received and his wares diligently inspected by a mother and her children at the cottage door. Like *The Dinner Hour*, the picture was a reframing of earlier prototypes dating back to Bastien-Lepage's *Le Mendiant* (1881).[8] In the British context, Harvey's general theme refers to the problem of vagrancy in rural communities, now that parish councils have surrendered many of their powers to the counties. The pedlar is a survival from the past, his age and general dilapidation indicating that for such types there can be few future prospects.

The sense of crisis in the countryside, of fundamental change in the life of the rural poor, continued as a sub-plot in Harvey's work for the next four or five years. It is re-engaged in two small processional works, *The Wayfarers* and *Off to Market* (both 1906). Both are dependent upon Alfred Munnings' *The Wayfarers*, a major Academy piece of 1902.[9] The downtrodden poor, travelling field workers and gypsies were not an uncommon feature of life in East Anglia and Cornwall. Unlike Munnings, however, Harvey's handling is uncertain and it suggests that ultimately he felt uncomfortable with social subjects of this type. He may have intuitively realised that in the period of high imperialism, of public confidence and visual bombast, such themes, although continuing in currency, were no longer in fashion. They referred to a residuum, a nineteenth-century legacy which many, on the threshold of a new age, wished to forget. The economy of the area in which

7. Leo N. Tolstoy, *What is Art?* (Macmillan, 1898; Library of Liberal Arts edition, 1960), p. 137.
8. Fox and Greenacre, p. 83, compare this picture with Forbes' *The Letter* (1898) (The Box, Plymouth).
9. For further reference see Kenneth McConkey, *An English Idyll, Works by Sir Alfred Munnings* (Sotheby's London, exhibition catalogue, 2001), pp. 11, 56–7.

Harvey had grown up was shifting dramatically towards the new social phenomenon of tourism with its associated 'place-myths'.[10] The later harbour scenes such as *On the Quay at Newlyn* (1905), *Carrying the Oars* (1906), *Mousehole Harbour* (1907) and *Mousehole* (1908) reveal a casual approach to the rigours of the fishermen's life.[11] Such works sit comfortably alongside Forbes' *Old Pier Steps* (1911) and *Fitting Out, Mousehole Harbour* (1919), confirming the temporary shift away from Newlyn to the more picturesque village a mile or two down the coast. However, where Forbes tends to centre his composition around a single motif, there is a seeming randomness about Harvey's assembly of the mise-en-scène. And while balancing motifs help to retain the strength of the composition, the figures appear uncoordinated and there is a profound sense of disjuncture. In *Mousehole* for instance, a woman lifts her hand to her brow as if looking out to sea, but the action lacks the conviction that we would find in the early work of Langley. The heroic fisher family of the early Newlyn years now confronts a growing sense of diffusion and purposelessness in the face of the new economy. A contemporary tourist visiting Mousehole would, by 1905, be accosted by fishermen offering to take him round the local caves and coves on a pleasure cruise.

Simultaneously Harvey was diversifying into softer subjects. Groups of boys are observed in rowing boats 'whiffing' in the harbour on sunny days. These are not the same sophisticated young men, clad in tailored oilskins, racing their well-trimmed yachts along the south coast, as are found in the work of Charles Napier Hemy. Joseph Conrad castigated this particular pastime as a 'form of social idleness ministering to the vanity of certain wealthy inhabitants of these isles …'[12] Harvey's lads, by contrast, are local 'sons of the sea', dabbling in the friendly waters of a familiar bay. The 'old salts' of *The Seine Boat* have been pensioned off and are now to be found ruminating by the harbour wall in his *Three Fishermen* (1909). This formidable study of *ouvriers* links Harvey to a long tradition stretching back to the Le Nains, and his search for deep visual and cultural roots was a common preoccupation of contemporary observers. At Mousehole, for instance, C. Lewis Hind found himself 'trying to detect in the faces of the battered fishermen who leaned idly over the railings, showing a long sinuous line of weathered garments, any trace of their traditional Spanish ancestry'.[13] W.H. Hudson mused at length upon the Cornish Celt, failing to find 'the hidden vein of romance' and 'poetic feeling' which still persisted elsewhere in the English peasantry. Druidical, pagan and early Christian myths had died out in the previous thirty years, despite the current efforts of artists and intellectuals to revive them.[14] Deprived of his past, and facing an uncertain future, the Cornishman seemed to Hudson 'nearer mentally to the child'.[15] Harvey's figuring of the 'old salt' therefore addressed deeper levels of consciousness. His handling is clean and his figures, strongly delineated. They become racial types like those in William Orpen's *Old John's Cottage, Connemara* (1909) suspended in a kind of limbo, when viewed by the metropolitan artist.[16]

10. See for instance: anon, 'In old Penzance', *Cook's Traveller's Gazette*, March 1906, pp. 12–13, commends the town to 'the jaded Londoner', the artist, the antiquary, the botanist, the ornithologist, the geologist and 'one and all in search of a holiday resort'. For a general consideration of the opening up of west Cornwall see Ella Westland (ed.), *Cornwall: The Cultural Construction of Place* (Patten Press, 1997).

11. *On the Quay at Newlyn* (1905) was sold Sotheby's, London, 12 Nov 1986, lot 42; *Carrying the Oars* (1906) was sold Phillips, London, 11 Nov 1986, lot 48; *Mousehole Harbour* (1907) was sold Phillips, London 21 Nov 1995, lot 60 and *Mousehole* (1908) was shown in Richard Green, *Modern British Paintings* (exhibition catalogue, 1985), no. 5.

12. Joseph Conrad, *The Mirror of the Sea, Memories and Impressions …* (1906; J.M. Dent & Sons edition, 1946), p. 23.

13. C. Lewis Hind, *Days in Cornwall* (Methuen & Co., 1907), p. 186. Mousehole had been destroyed by the Spanish in 1595.

14. The most important instance in this regard is of course Elizabeth Forbes; for reference see Judith Cook, Melissa Hardie and Christiana Payne, *Singing from the Walls, The Life and Art of Elizabeth Forbes* (Sansom & Co., 2000).

15. W.H. Hudson, *The Land's End, a Naturalist's Impressions in West Cornwall* (Hutchinson & Co 1908; Wildwood House edition, 1980), pp. 178, 183; Hudson's was based upon articles which had appeared in *The Saturday Review* and *The Speaker*. For the contemporary, c.1905, revival of interest in Cornish myth and legend see, Philip Payton, 'Paralysis and Revival: the Construction of Celtic-Catholic Cornwall 1890–1945', in Westland (ed.), 1997, especially, pp. 27–8. Youth and age has of course particular resonance in Cornish painting dating back to Thomas Cooper Gotch's *Mental Arithmetic* (1883) (National Gallery of Victoria, Melbourne) and Stanhope Forbes' *A Son of the Sea* (1894) (private collection).

16. Harvey was as Cornish as Orpen was Irish. Their respective return to roots, indecisive in Orpen's case, is nevertheless a complex phenomenon involving re-invention more than reengagement. In this sense Harvey's schooled sensibility plays against his local connections and places him in an international, rather than sub-national context.

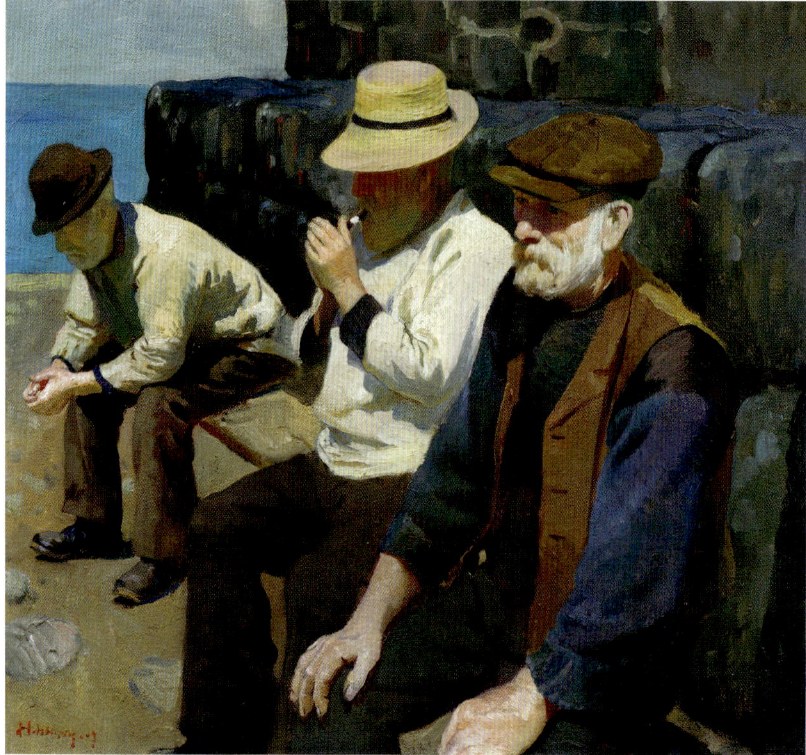

Three Fishermen
1909 | oil on canvas | 44.5 x 55 cm
PRIVATE COLLECTION; IMAGE COURTESY RICHARD GREEN GALLERY, LONDON

It is Harvey's image of the young healthy farm-hand and fisherboy
which advances current thinking and fuses it with the now almost
universal imagery of the seaside holiday. The peninsula in the Edwardian
years became a place of endless sunny days. The grey weather favoured
by Forbes at the beginning of his career has been blown away, to be
replaced by a warm, sultry playground. This is the new Cornwall
described in Arthur Symons' 'Cornish Sketches'. At Fowey, it was
a dream which recalled Arles, Posilippo or the coast of Spain, 'the air
was full of sleep; the faint noise of the water flapping on the rocks, the
sound of voices, of oars, something in the dull brilliance of the water,
like the surface of a mirror, reflecting all the heat of the sky came
up to one drowsily.'[17] Such words could act as the accompaniment
to the images such as *A Test of Strength* (*c.*1910) and *A Quiet Paddle*
(1913).[18] Harvey's children potter and play quietly among the rock
pools. His naked boys, like those of Henry Scott Tuke, lounge
in the sun, an innocent anticipation of the nudism which was to
emerge as a more coherent social force in the inter-war period.
As Symons implies, we remain emphatically in the lotus land
of Tennyson. Paradoxically this is reinforced by the sensuality
of Harvey's paintings. He had taken heed from the debates about
Impressionism and was preoccupied with enveloping light. He was
alive to the potential of vivid colour and an active paint surface, even
though this was consistently restrained, and in *Three Fishermen* moves
to a clear marquetry of shapes and colours.

17. Arthur Symons, 'Cornish Sketches
– 1. At Fowey', *The Saturday Review*,
1901, p. 297.
18. For reference to *A Test of Strength
(Tug of War)* (*c.*1910), see David Messum,
British Impressions (exhibition catalogue,
1988), no. 100; *A Quiet Paddle* (1913)
was included in Kenneth McConkey,
Impressionism in Britain, 1995 (Barbican
Art Gallery, exhibition catalogue, 1995),
no. 96.

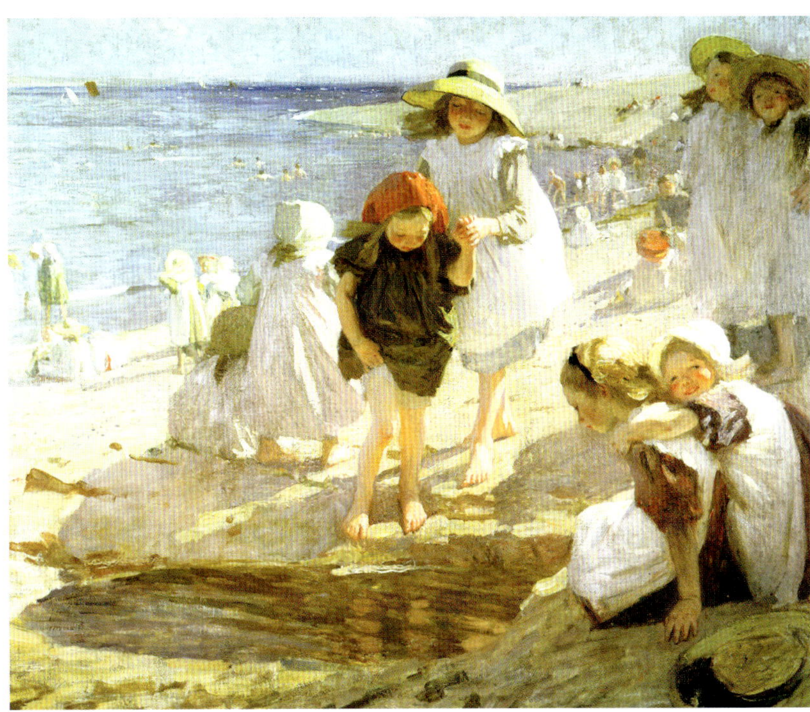

Laura Knight
The Beach
1909 | oil on canvas | 127.6 x 153.2 cm
LAING ART GALLERY, NEWCASTLE UPON TYNE · BRIDGEMAN IMAGES

19. Norman Garstin, 'The Art of Harold and Laura Knight', *The Studio*, vol. 57, 1912, p. 195.

20. For a discussion of the current understanding of the term 'envelope' in connection with impressionism and with particular reference to George Moore see Kenneth McConkey, 'A Walk in the Park: Memory and Rococo revivalism in the 1890s', in David Peters Corbett and Lara Perry (eds), *English Art 1860–1914, Modern Artists and Identity* (Manchester University Press, 2000), pp. 100–115.

21. Gertrude Harvey, for instance, borrowed a favourite cardigan from Laura Knight in which to pose for her husband. See Laura Knight, *Oil Paint and Grease Paint* (1936; Penguin edition, 1941), vol. 2, p. 219.

22. Clearly the fact that these pictures of women on headlands coincide with or closely follow those of Orpen and John is not without significance. Orpen's 'Howth' series (*c.*1910) and John's Provence series of the same date carry the same essential combination of decorative and symbolic elements within the iconography of the solitary emblematic figure on a rugged headland landscape, which appears in Knight and Harvey.

At this point new artistic dependencies emerge with the influx of new painters, some attracted to the Forbes school. The most important of these connects Harvey with Laura and Harold Knight who arrived in Newlyn in 1907. The Knights were drawn to west Cornwall by what Norman Garstin described as 'a riot of brilliant sunshine, of opulent colour, and of sensuous gaiety'.[19] Laura Knight immediately began her first ambitious painting, *The Beach*, and although she claimed that it merely extended the work she had been doing at Staithes, it is clearly situated within the ambience of Harvey's studies of Cornish children. It shares in the desire, in an Academy-piece, to create a sense of 'envelopment', a concept now widely accepted as one of the hallmarks of Impressionism.[20] However around 1909, contours, as we have observed, become harder, and the humidity evaporates leaving crisper, more shape-conscious forms standing out against the uniform backdrop of the south western approaches. For the next few years Knight's and Harvey's work is directly comparable.[21] Both paint figures parading in front of the immensity. The reasons which lie behind this complex visual phenomenon – and which extends to Charles Sims, Gerald Moira, Orpen, Augustus John and others – are manifold.[22] The now ubiquitous 'new woman' ethos and the health and degeneracy debates provide one kind of meaning for what artists and commentators often sought to mystify as a 'vague desire' for the infinite. 'One would stand on the brink,' wrote Garstin, 'looking over the frontiers of space, gazing into the unknowable. It is the suggestion of illimitableness conveyed by the limit that fires our fancy, what is distant grows vast

through some trick of the imagination.'[23] It is more than tricks of
the imagination that convert Knight's London models into *Daughters
of the Sun* (1912; destroyed), in praise of nudity.[24] Or, more than vague
desire, which makes these modern heroines, garbed in new libertarian
fashions, in jumpers, cardigans, short skirts and cube-heeled shoes,
in *Wind and Sun* and *Two Girls on a Cliff*, assert their freedom.[25]

Although there were great stylistic affinities between Harvey and
Laura Knight, there were occasions when the fluency of his sketches
more accurately recalls Munnings, whose Lamorna interlude contains
farm studies close to those of Harvey. Indeed throughout the period
up to the First World War, Harvey continued to produce small genre
pictures of rustic life, consistently reworking successful motifs such as
that of the mounted farm hand watering his horse or labourers resting
or the harvesting of marigolds. Occasionally, in emulation of Arnesby
Brown, he and Munnings painted scenes of cows returning to the
byre at sunset.[26]

By 1913, a vital new area of subject matter opened up with a series of
paintings of interiors. The conventional view of these pictures is that
they derive from the curtailment of the painter's activities in time of
war. Coastlines could not be represented since, it was thought, pictures
of them could assist an invader. However Harvey was undoubtedly
aware of the sophisticated interiors of John Singer Sargent and John
Lavery. He must also have seen the suave, stylish modernist rooms
of Orpen, Clausen, Philip Connard and William Nicholson distilled
in Newlyn in the work of Harold Knight. Knight's pictures often play
what Whistler would have referred to as 'old games', that is, they play
the game of balancing shapes and rectangles. Harold Knight's *Morning
Sun* (1913), for instance, shown at the Royal Academy, ostensibly a study
of sunlight falling into a room in which a woman sits calmly reading,
is in fact, strictly formalist.[27] The figures and the back wall are ranged
parallel to the plane of the picture and the window rectangle mimics
the proportions of the canvas. The curtain is pulled to the right to
balance the girl on the left and the clock in the upper left corner holds
composition taut. References to Whistler's *Arrangement in Grey and
Black No. 1, The Painter's Mother* (1872) would not be inappropriate.
Knight's woman even uses a footstool.

When he came to these subjects Harvey looked beyond Knight and
Whistler to important contemporaries. The broadly mounted print,
the dado and circular table in *Winding Wool* (1914) and the ornate
convex mirror, containing a self-portrait, in *Laura and Paul Jewill Hill*
(1916) tell us for instance, that he was aware of Orpen and Rothenstein.
For all their obvious referencing – and a piece of furniture cannot be
viewed as if it, or its replica, had not first been seen by others – it is
clear that such pictures, modernising past precedent, appealed to
Harvey. Although not averse to quotation, his initial studies of
Gertrude reading strike a more meditative tone than similar works
by his immediate mentors. Two interiors titled *Woman Reading* (c.1914)

23. Norman Garstin, 'West Cornwall
as a Sketching Ground', *The Studio*,
1909, vol. 47, p. 109. See also: anon,
'Cornish Cliffs', *The Saturday Review*,
vol. 105, 8 Feb 1908, p. 171. Garstin's
own work in this regard is noteworthy.
In the early 1890s he and Brangwyn
produced canvases depicting cliff-top
trysts and single figures looking out
to sea.
24. Laura Knight, *Oil Paint and Grease
Paint* (1936; Penguin edition, 1941),
vol. 2, p. 182. See Ysanne Holt, 'The
English Landscape: Modernity and the
Rural Scene, 1890–1914', unpublished
PhD thesis, University of Northumbria,
1998, pp. 111–116.
25. These works were of course produced
in the context of the fight for women's
suffrage and the general debates about
women and the professions which stalled
during the war, until the passing of the
Sex Disqualification (Removal) Act
of 1919. Popular expression of the new
freedoms continued to express themselves in ever more liberated fashions
into the twenties.
26. See for instance Harvey's *Feeding the
Calves* (1906), *Cows* (1908) and *Summer
Milking* (1916) (all private collections).
27. RA 1913 (358), sold Phillips, London,
21 Nov 2000, lot 11.

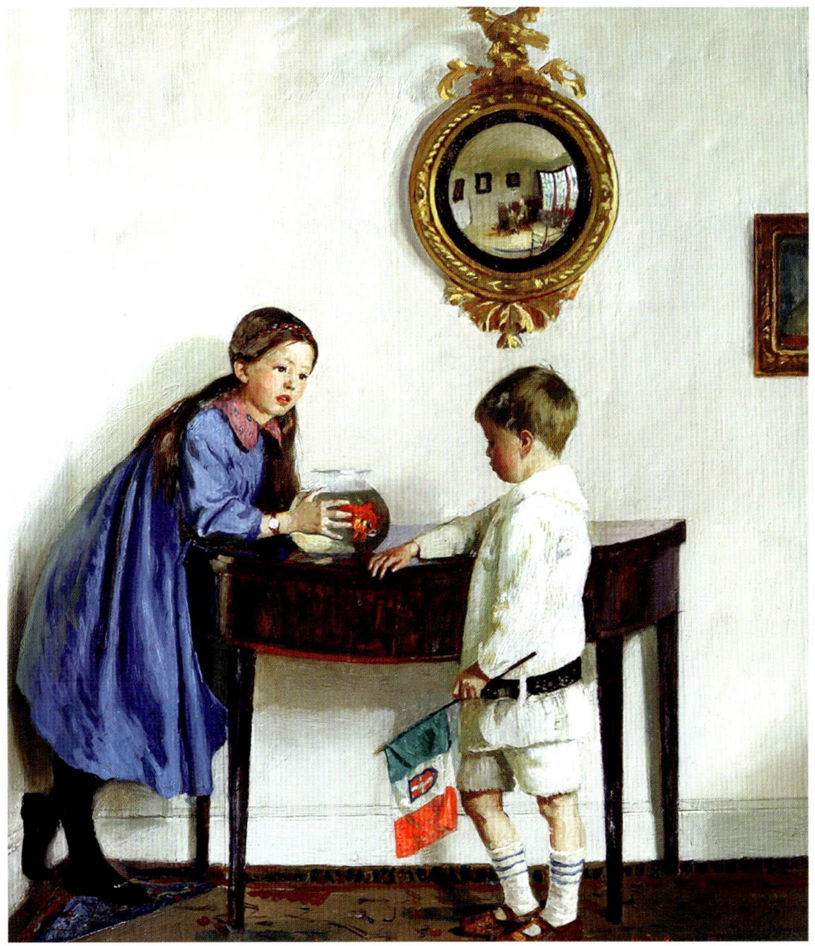

Laura and Paul Jewill Hill
1916 | oil on canvas | 48 x 43 cm
PENLEE HOUSE GALLERY & MUSEUM

and *Woman in an Interior, Sewing* (1917) demonstrate the restricted range of Harvey's interests.[28] One takes the viewer into the space of the sitting room at Maen Cottage using the steep perspective of the wall on the right to lead the eye to the figure, while the other engages more closely with his subject as she sits in the corner by the fire. One is rigorously formal, the other *intimiste*.

Thereafter an inner compulsion drove the series. Whitewashed parlours, containing a few common bits of Edwardian Hepplewhite, replace the humble cottages of fisherfolk. Sunlight strikes the wall in the background and the simple objects of a dressing table radiate their presence to the spectator. Gertrude Harvey poses again and again, trying on her gloves or reading a letter. She is dressed more for the mirror than for the street. She tries a new headscarf, a new shawl; she moves a little to the side and it is enough to give a new picture. This describes *Reflections* (1916; see p. 61), the resplendent *Blue Gown* (1917) and *Woman by a Sideboard* (1917) pictures roughly 20 x 16 inches, which in each case show Gertrude full length.[29] The first two are *contre jours*. Sunlight streams in from the bedroom window, casting the painted

28. See Pyms Gallery, *Edwardian Impressions* (exhibition catalogue, 1981), no. 12, and *Woman Reading*, sold Sotheby's, 21 May 1986, lot 86.
29. See Pyms Gallery, *Autumn Anthology* (exhibition catalogue, 1983), no. 22, and *Woman by a Sideboard*, sold Sotheby's, 9 November 1988, lot 35.

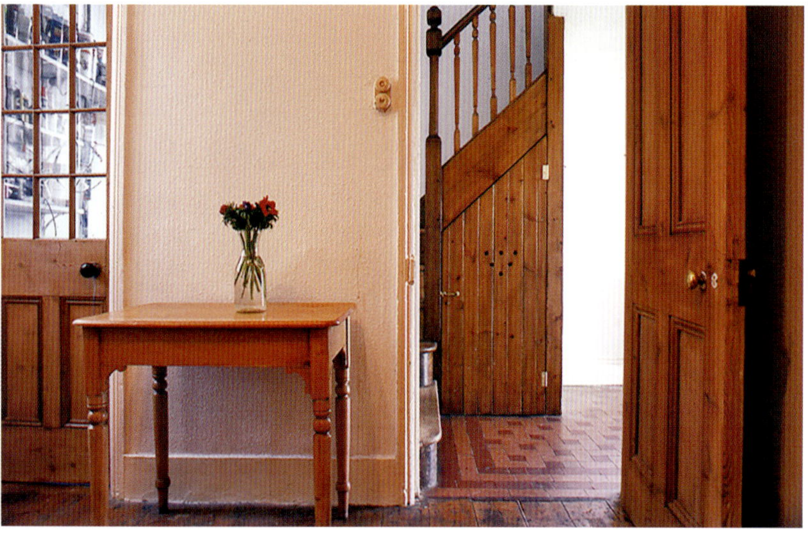

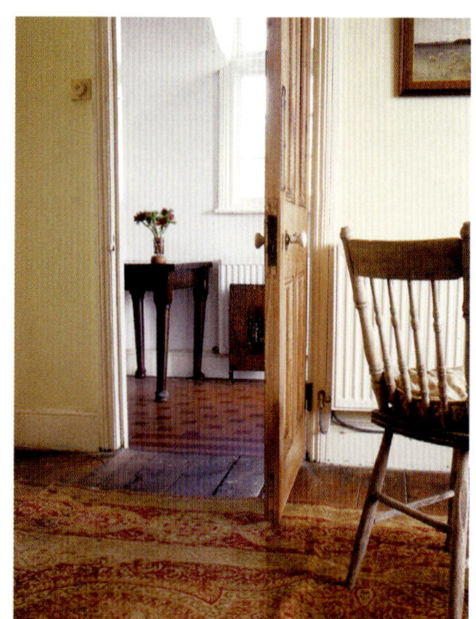

Interiors at Maen Cottage, settings for *The Critics* (p. 93) and *Titbits* (p. 69)

Victorian chest of drawers into shadow and wrapping the figure with its patterns. But what do these pictures mean? Is their retreat to domesticity a re-affirmation of the values of private life at a time when its values are threatened? Are they a subtle encoding of provincial mores among the 'arty' types? Posing the questions in this way in a sense devalues the enterprise and denies the rigour of works which strike the viewers like a Vermeer, a Metsu or a Terborch. It does however alert us to the shifts of emphasis which occur in the 1920s.

Harvey entered an uncertain world against which even the comfort and security of Newlyn could not protect him. During the inter-war period he wavered between naturalism and artifice. In *The Critics* (1922; p. 93) for instance, the viewer is taken into the world of the Harvey-Procter School which had been established in 1920. Ella Naper and Gertrude Harvey are seen examining the drawings of an anxious art student. The event occurs at a moment of relaxation, over coffee and port wine.[30] At the same time he produced a number of kitchen interiors which are more stiffly formal, converting his models into strong sculptural forms and using chequerboard floorscapes to map spatial relationships.[31] In these Harvey documented the rapid turnover in women's fashions during the twenties. Coats, skirts and hats changed with the time of day. Thus the women in *Titbits* (1929; see p. 69) are dressed in day-wear skirts to the knee; those in *Fête Champêtre* (1934) wear calf-length skirts for formal afternoon wear.[32] Throughout the early twenties, Harvey's women are trying to look boyish, and only after 1925 does hair styling, nail enamel and the use of lipstick pull the spectator away from the colourful 'modern primitive' archetype.[33] This was a time when beauty parlours, hairdressers and chemists proliferated and when the ubiquitous Woolworths began to sell cosmetics, but what is the place for modishness, for the eye witness and social commentator?[34]

30. The picture confirms Gertrude's role as aesthetic partner, which Harvey celebrated in *The Flower Painter* (1930) (private collection). She exhibited alongside her husband at the Leicester Galleries exhibitions of 1918 and 1920 as well as showing at the Royal Academy in the 1930s and '40s. The watercolours and gouaches being examined seem to be stage designs in the manner of Gordon Craig.

31. See for instance, *My Kitchen* (1923) (Gallery Oldham); see also *The Tea Table*, sold Christie's, 5 March 1987, lot 46.

32. For reference to this work see Richard Green Galleries, *Modern British Paintings* (exhibition catalogue, 1986), no. 20.

33. Thus for instance, one of the two *Girls Outside the Gaiety Cinema, Newlyn* (1925) (private collection), holds up a powder 'compact' to put on her lipstick. Here we witness the democratization of cosmetics, formerly elite, decadent embellishments, as described in Max Beerbohm's 'The Defence of Cosmetics', *The Yellow Book*, vol. 1, pp. 65–82. The cinema, the recently opened Newlyn picturedrome, signifies the arrival of the new popular form of entertainment.

34. Robert Graves and Alan Hodge, *The Long Week-End, a Social History of Great Britain, 1918–1939* (Faber and Faber, 1950), pp. 39–42, 278.

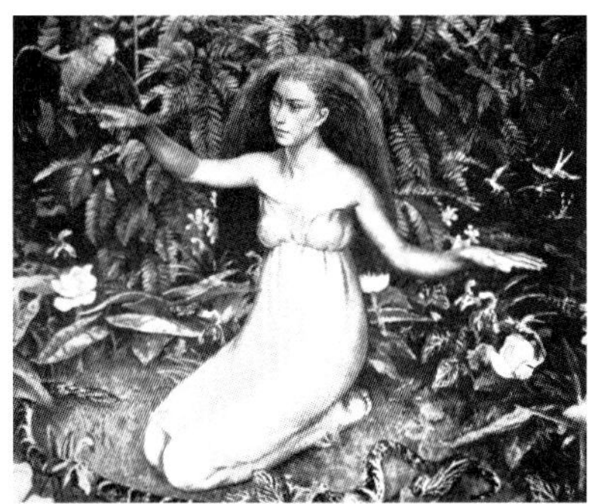

Rima
1926 | oil on canvas
unlocated | image from *Royal Academy
Illustrated 1926* (Walter Judd Ltd), p. 112

The painter was a keen observer of these and other changes. He remained responsive to the remaking of the image of rural England during the inter-war period. In a number of notable works he turned to the currently fashionable gypsy subject matter.[35] Deeply affected by the revival in Cornish Pre-Methodist religious belief, Harvey converted to Catholicism in 1926. While avoiding the extreme Teutonic classicism of Ernest Procter, he was nonetheless interested in the current fascination for mural painting. He consorted with Bernard Walke, the bohemian Anglo-Catholic priest of St Hilary, painting three of the panels of saints in the choir stalls. And in 1925 he decided to produce a memorial to the writer and naturalist W.H. Hudson, who had spent his last years in Penzance, and had died in 1922.

Rima (unlocated), was taken from Hudson's first and most successful novel, *Green Mansions: A Romance of the Tropical Forest*, published in 1904. It tells the story of a young Spanish-American who, after a failed attempt to overthrow the corrupt Venezuelan regime, is forced to flee to the upper reaches of the Orinoco river where, in a forest paradise, he meets and falls in love with the ill-fated Rima, a beautiful woodland dryad. After many adventures, Rima is tracked down and killed by the local tribe. She is first encountered in a sunny glade, surrounded by exotic plants, with her hands raised towards a small brown bird. In Harvey's rendering of this scene, the bird is translated into a parrot, with dragonflies, a serpent, orchids and lilies surrounding the goddess. An unusual work for Harvey, it attracted little comment when shown in the Royal Academy in 1926. This is surprising given the public controversy which had greeted Jacob Epstein's *Rima*, which had been unveiled in Hyde Park by the Prime Minister, Stanley Baldwin, in May of the previous year. Epstein was vilified and his Hudson Memorial regarded as an 'atrocity'.[36] We cannot assume that Harvey's work was anything other than an attempt to right the wrong which he felt had been done to Hudson's reputation.[37] If that was the case, it backfired as the critical consensus eventually swung in Epstein's favour by the beginning of 1926. However, the whole event raises questions about the consciousness of the primitive in the inter-war period.

Had Harvey's work been painted shortly after the book was published, it would have been a perfectly acceptable rendering of the subject. By 1926, the world had moved on and the knowledge of Cubist fascination with tribal art was universally recognised.[38] Harvey's naturalistic *Rima*, kneeling improbably in front of the spectator like one of Gerald Kelly's Javanese dancers, was outmoded. His imagination was strained to breaking point. He had been compelled to move beyond the confines of the world he knew, and wander into realms beyond his power to control. Where the Procters adapted modernist neo-classicism to their own ends, Harvey became more and more uneasy the further he strayed from Newlyn harbour, a point which was made when his solo exhibition at the Leicester Galleries in February 1927 was reviewed by *The Morning Post*.[39]

35. In works like *The Balloon Seller* (1921) (Richard Green Galleries, 1995, no. 26).
36. For a full discussion of Epstein's project, see Terry Friedman, *The Hyde Park Atrocity, Epstein's 'Rima', creation and controversy* (The Henry Moore Centre for the Study of Sculpture, Leeds City Art Galleries, 1988).
37. Harvey's views on the Epstein debacle are unknown.
38. Although Ozenfant's *Foundations of Modern Art*, which makes the links between ethnographic sources and contemporary painting, was not published until 1928 (English trans., 1931; Dover reprint, 1952), the concept of the primitive had, by the mid-1920s, been overhauled in numerous articles in the art magazines. Artists like Charles Sims and Glyn Philpot, for instance, contemporaries of Harvey, had completely overhauled their style in the light of this.
39. *The Morning Post*, 8 February 1927.

Rima was accompanied at the Academy by a painting of the Holy Family, *The Flight* (1925; see p. 86), and by a more conventional *Interior*. This latter work represents a woman wearing a Flemish style head-dress, washing a child in a tin bath. One of a long series of mother and child pictures produced throughout the inter-war period, it carries much of the devotional feeling with which Harvey wished to invest his work.[40] In such subjects the many influences which had played themselves out in his painting were reconciled, according to the critic of *The Morning Post*. The writer observed influences from Millet, the Pre-Raphaelites and the 'Clausen-Forbes' convention, all three of which merged 'to form the beauty of *The Mother*,' the first painting in the 1927 show. Mothers, on occasions, become madonnas and with these a more complex set of cross-references, going back to the Renaissance, led to his decorative and religious works – to *A May Procession* (1935; see p. 89) and *Ancilla Domini* (1938).

Throughout the late thirties there is a constant desire on Harvey's part to fill his canvases with local reference. A standard set of backdrops established in the 1920s return with renewed insistence. In works like *Daffodils* (1927; see p. 8) for instance, a female figure is projected upon an expanse of coastline stretching into the distance. In pictures like *The Blue Door, Newlyn* (1934) and *The Little Maiden* (1934; see p. 109), figures are projected against the backdrop of Newlyn harbour, while in *Allotments* (1938) a local family is seen against a claustrophobic landscape of rolling hills. The laboured stereoscopy of these gives the concept of 'envelopment' a wholly new meaning. The settings reinforce a sense of locatedness. The emblematic John-like figures in plain dresses pose in front of motifs which seem like picture postcards. They are not rooted in the setting, so much as hovering above it, as though to emphasise its identity as much as their own and the viewer is brought back consistently to the artifices of the painter. This becomes clear in the comparison of Harvey's *Daffodils* with Norman Garstin's *The Tryst* (c.1895). Garstin's rustic lovers are about to meet on a hilltop path overlooking the sea. They are viewed from afar. The man could be identified, but the observer will have to wait in hiding behind the foreground flowers to see who is to join him. Both figures occupy a tiny part of the landscape. Its scale is to some extent portrayed by the distance which separates them. Atmosphere and evening light do the rest. The viewer has before him or her, a convincing illusion. By contrast, in *Daffodils*, the foreground flowers have been picked by a consciously designed young woman who, as much as the setting, is the subject of the picture. Her spring beauty is synonymous with its. Her head almost touches the upper edge of the canvas and her feet, the bottom edge. She envelopes the landscape.

In his last year Harvey revisited one of the themes of his youth. *August 1939* (see p. 106), shown at the Royal Academy in 1940 is as much a punctuation point as Forbes' *22nd January 1901*. It shows holiday-makers in Cornwall sunning themselves within a few weeks of the outbreak of war. They all innocently sport themselves on the

40. This work was illustrated in *The Studio*, vol. 92, 1926, p. 41.

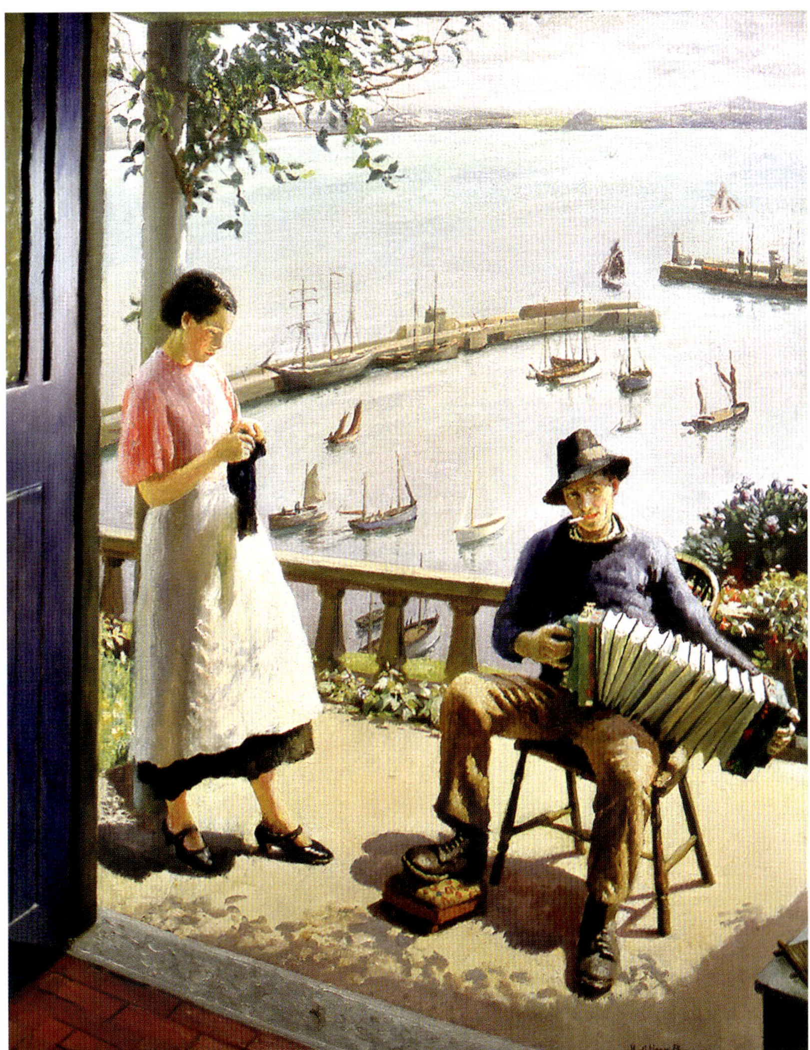

The Blue Door, Newlyn
1934 | oil on canvas | 76 x 63.5 cm
PRIVATE COLLECTION; IMAGE COURTESY THE NINE BRITISH ART

sand, under the stone wall of the promenade. Overhead, a balmy breeze agitates the tropical trees. It was an ambitious work, 70 x 60 inches, probably intended to call to mind the peace which had now been lost. Yet it appears at first confused and inconsequential. Like the fisher families in the early Mousehole harbour scenes, there is a tension in the seeming randomness of the lower middle-class invaders who crowd the shore. In place of the hearts of oak and rustic charities of Harvey's youth, there is vulgarity and fatuity. Courting couples converse; a woman is engrossed in her knitting; another leans back and shuts her eyes; children play in the sand; sunbathing; nakedness; a solitary dog sniffs the pavement. In this image, vast distances have been traversed. Yet, as in Forbes' interior nearly forty years before, this is the day that everything changes and a painter is brought to the ugly end of the world and feels bound to tell.

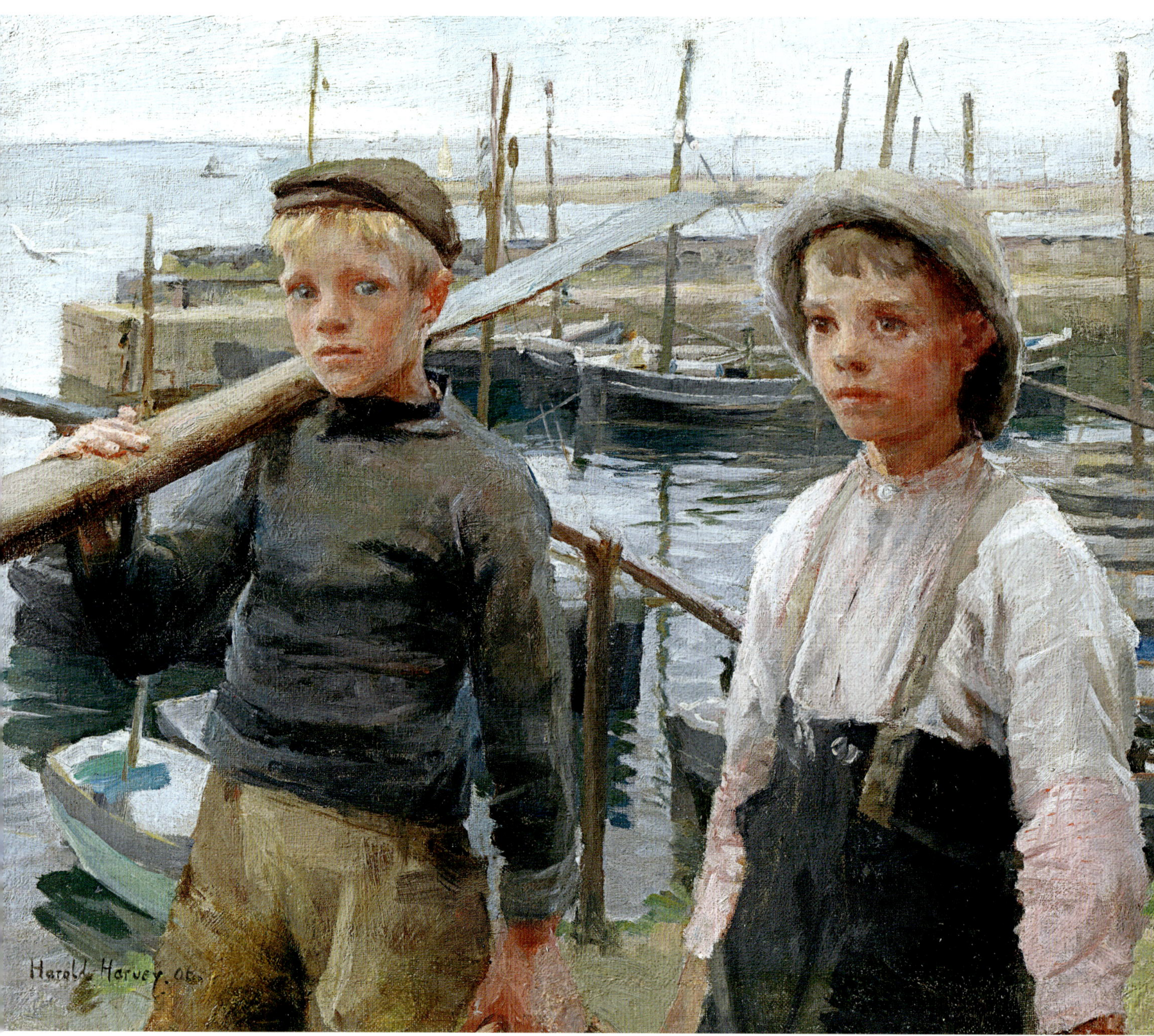

Carrying the Oars
1906 | oil on canvas | 34 x 40.5 cm
RICHARD GREEN GALLERY, LONDON

One   A Cornish boy

In Cornwall, where local tradition is probably more alive than in other counties, a man crosses a road or a stream which divides his parish from the next village and he is in a strange country, among people with a different tradition from his own.

Bernard Walke, *Twenty Years at St Hilary*

To plant one's easel down in full view of all and work away in the midst of a large congregation needs a good deal of courage.

Stanhope Forbes

Harold Charles Francis Harvey was born on 20th May 1874 at 20 North Parade, Penzance, less than a decade before the neighbouring village of Newlyn turned into one of the most important artistic colonies in the history of British art. Growing up in Penzance in the 1880s, the young Harold Harvey must have been aware of the colony of artists in Newlyn and, like most of his contemporaries, he would have had childhood memories of watching artists from a distance, as they practised the very public art of painting 'en plein air' – literally 'in the open air'. Indeed, ten years old at the time, he might well have been amongst 'the congregation' over the many weeks it took Stanhope Forbes to complete his most famous painting *Fish Sale on a Cornish Beach*, painted in situ on the Newlyn sands in 1885.

If Harold was one of the watchers, then perhaps he heard the local gossip: 'He give her ninepence for three skate an' all he did was paint 'em. Well, next time he called she told him … "That turbot'll cost you twelve shillin', mind, you only want it for a hour, you can have it for four" … caught on see.' The artists must have seemed eccentric in the extreme, willing as they were to pay money for the hire of a fish, merely to paint it.

As a native of west Cornwall, the young Harold Harvey was a member of the same community that fed the artistic movement which became the 'Newlyn School', yet his family belonged to another class from the models used by the artists. North Parade, where he was born, is an attractive Regency terrace in the centre of Penzance, a far cry from the one up, one down cob cottages of Newlyn. Clearly, the family were comfortably off, as were many of the painters who colonised Newlyn, not living the hand-to-mouth existence of fishermen and their families. Nevertheless, as a local child he would have been aware of the realities of life in that community in a way in which most 'foreigners' could never be.

The census for 3rd April 1881 records the Harvey family at North Parade as Francis McFarland Harvey, bank cashier, with his wife Mary (née Bellringer) and their four children: Harold (aged 6), Percival George (4), Frank (2), Arthur William Hext (3 months), together the family's two servants, Susan M. Pascoe (19) and Janie Johns (18). Harold's father, Francis, was born in 1843 at Penzance and died in 1915. Harold's mother, Mary, was born at Penzance in 1847 and married Francis in 1872, when he was twenty-nine and she was twenty-five; she died in 1912. Harold was the first of eight children, the last arriving in 1890. One of a family of six children himself, Francis was the only one to leave issue. His parents, Harold's grand-parents, were Arthur Harvey (born 1808 at Penzance) and Peggy (née Sherris) born 1811 on the Isles of Scilly, where two of her sisters-

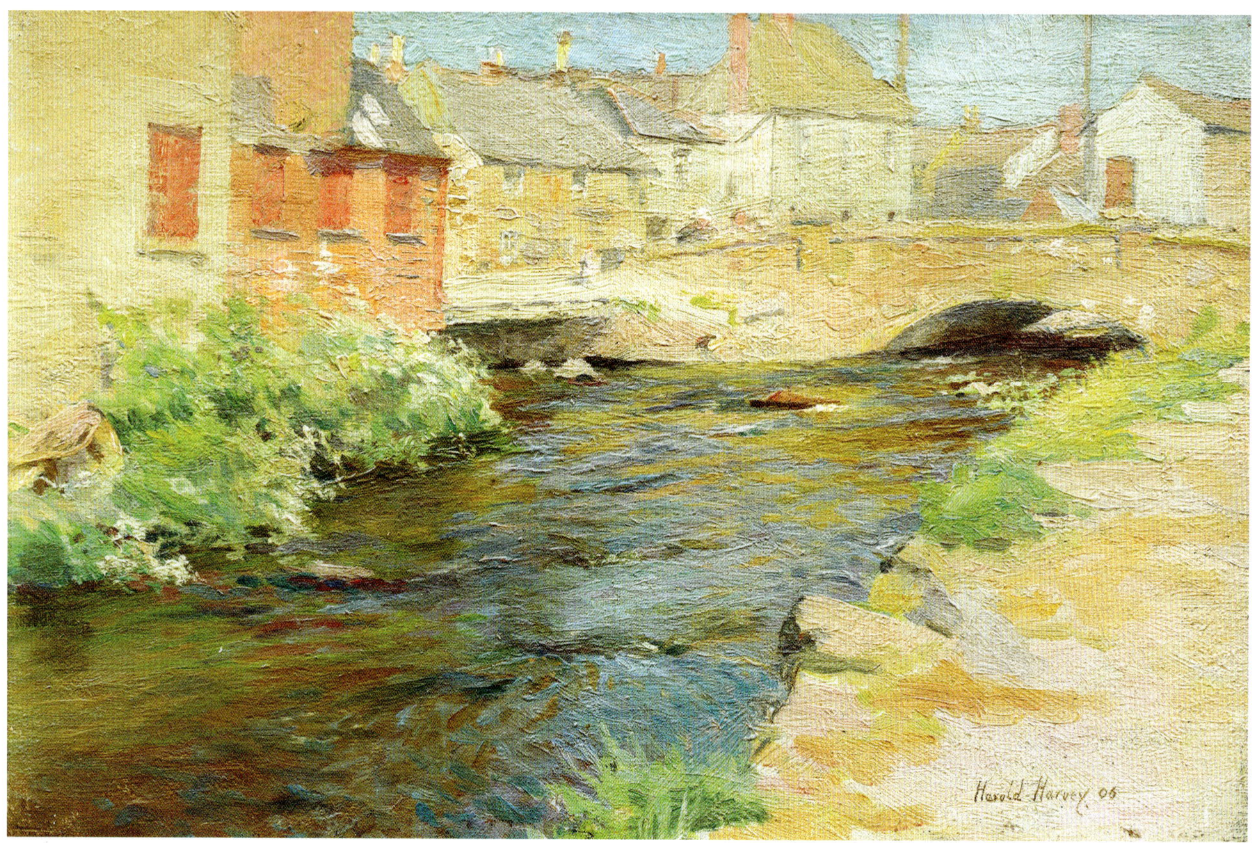

Newlyn Bridge
1906 | oil on canvas | 19.5 x 30 cm
PENLEE HOUSE GALLERY & MUSEUM

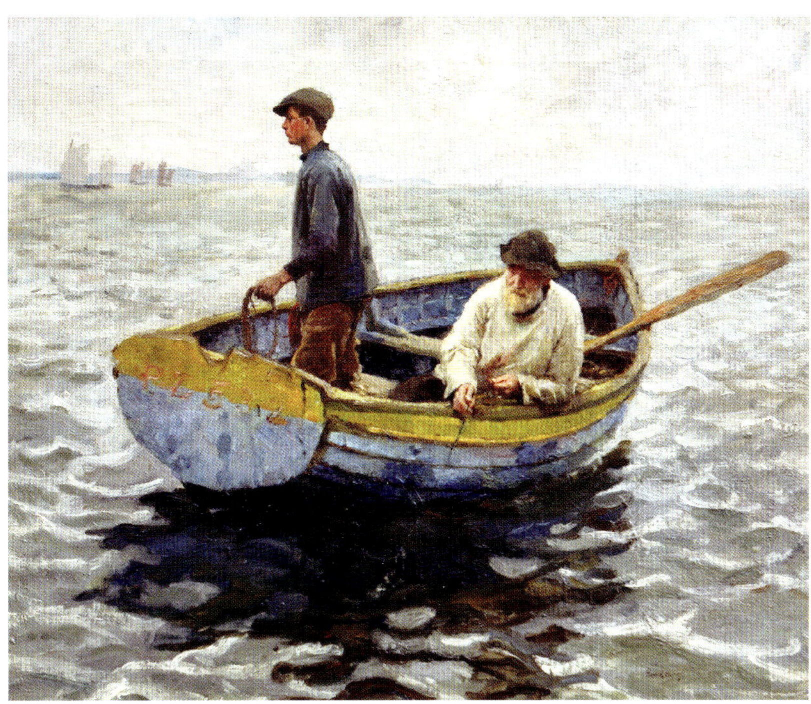

In the Whiting Grounds
*c.*1900 | oil on canvas | 61 x 76 cm
PENLEE HOUSE GALLERY & MUSEUM

in-law were also born. Arthur was the tenth of eleven children, and his parents were William (1757–1819) and Thomasina Ford (died 1839), his second wife whom he married in 1791.

A 'family tree' traces the lineage back to John Hervey [sic], senior, of Tharley, Buckinghamshire, who died some time after 1475. The first family member in Cornwall appears to have been Francis Hervey (1562–1606) who was ordained Deacon at St Breage in 1591 and was vicar there in 1593. In the eighteenth and nineteenth centuries some of the Harvey family travelled far overseas, and their deaths were recorded in Jamaica, Colombo, Calcutta, Bangkok and New Zealand, while others were born in Bermuda and British Columbia. The Harveys were typical of their class and time: there are many such stories recorded in local cemeteries, child graves and the burials of those 'come home' from foreign parts.

There are several branches of the family, mostly still settled in Cornwall and the south west. Some are the descendants of James Harvey, who came from Great Yarmouth in the 1850s for fishery business. Harveys listed in the 1881 census who can be identified as related to Harold include his aunts Thomasine and Hannah, who were then living with Harold's grandmother, Peggy, at 29 Clarence Street, Penzance, and Joseph Smith Harvey (aged 50) who had a chemist and druggist business at 11 Market Jew Street, with his wife Grace (45) and their four children, John William (15), Lucretia Davis (14), Elizabeth Isabel (13) and Marion Nunn Harvey (10), with their servant Ann Barnicoat (29).

By 1891, Harold's own family had moved to 5 Trewartha Terrace, at the north eastern end of Penzance, not far from that hub of communication, the railway station. It was a substantial residence, built after 1881 during the town's expansion, and the move to such a property was indicative of Francis Harvey's success. The Harvey family needed a large house. The census of April 1891, when Harold was 17, recorded the household as containing twelve people. Francis and Mary now had eight children, Wilfred Vignes (aged 7), Leonard (5), Gladys Maud (3), and Cyril (8 months) as well as the four older children, Harold, Percival, Frank and Arthur. The family still had two servants, Elizabeth A. Murley (29) and Elizabeth Browning (27). Francis continued to advance in his career, the 1893 edition of *Kelly's Directory for Cornwall* shows him as general manager of Batten, Carne and Carne's Banking Co. Ltd. in Market Place, Penzance.

Harold Harvey was educated at home.[1] There is no clear reason for this – whether the education was deemed better than that at the local schools, or whether he was felt to be insufficiently hardy for the rough-and-tumble of school life is a matter for conjecture. Either way, the experience perhaps encouraged a sense of being 'the loner', which is how those who knew him describe Harvey. His niece, Rhoda Littler, who remembered him well, described him as 'a man within himself', and in later life he is known to have loved walking and fly fishing, both solitary pursuits. He was clearly a keen observer of his surroundings, as is evidenced in his paintings, which suggests lone contemplation.

We know very little about this private man. Although he kept a notebook, it was little more than a list of models and payments. He kept no diaries, he did not write of the struggle of the artist (unlike his friend Laura Knight, whose autobiographies *Oil Paint and Grease Paint* and *The Magic of a Line* are a wonderful insight into the creative mind). However, he was a prolific painter who dated and signed nearly all his works,[2] thus providing a visual diary. Besides displaying his own development as an artist and the changing trends in the Newlyn movement, his subjects denote changes in his own life, such as the concentration on interior scenes after his marriage, and religious themes after his conversion to Catholicism.

Equally, little is known about how his family reacted to the news that he wished to pursue a career in art. Francis Harvey was a successful businessman and when his eldest son decided to be a painter, an occupation not known for its financial rewards, his decision was probably not greeted with enthusiasm. Yet his studies would have to have been paid for, and it must be assumed therefore that his family gave him at least some support. This Cornishman's education and background enabled him to communicate with the incomers of the art colony, while at the same time having an innate understanding of Newlyn life. However, being a colonist in your native land sets you apart – another reason for being something of a 'loner'.

1. Dolman's *Dictionary of Contemporary British Artists*; and 'at home' according to his entry in *Who's Who in Art* (1929), for which Harvey most probably contributed the information.
2. Harold usually signed his name in full as 'Harold Harvey', but there are a few instances of 'H. Harvey', and of just initials, e.g. *The Fond Farewell* (c.1900). Most often the signature was in capital letters, square style, but a few early works are in script form. The most usual position was bottom left or bottom right, but a small number are signed in a top corner. Most often the signature is in black or dark blue paint. *The Old Slip, Newlyn* (1908) has the signature set within a drawn rectangle, and *Woman Reading* (1914) sets it within a rectangular border upon a yellow-green ground. *A Summer Evening* (1923) has the signature and date within horizontal parallel lines. These distinctive devices were used rarely, possibly because they distracted from the paintings themselves. Red paint was adopted, possibly to enhance the visibility of the signature, evidenced from *Moored Fishing Boats in Newlyn Harbour* (1907) through to *The Onion Boy* (1940). There are also a few signatures in white or yellow, e.g. *Sea Pinks* (1913) or *A Summer Evening* (1926). Dates appear both in full and foreshortened, as in '09', although not all the paintings are dated.

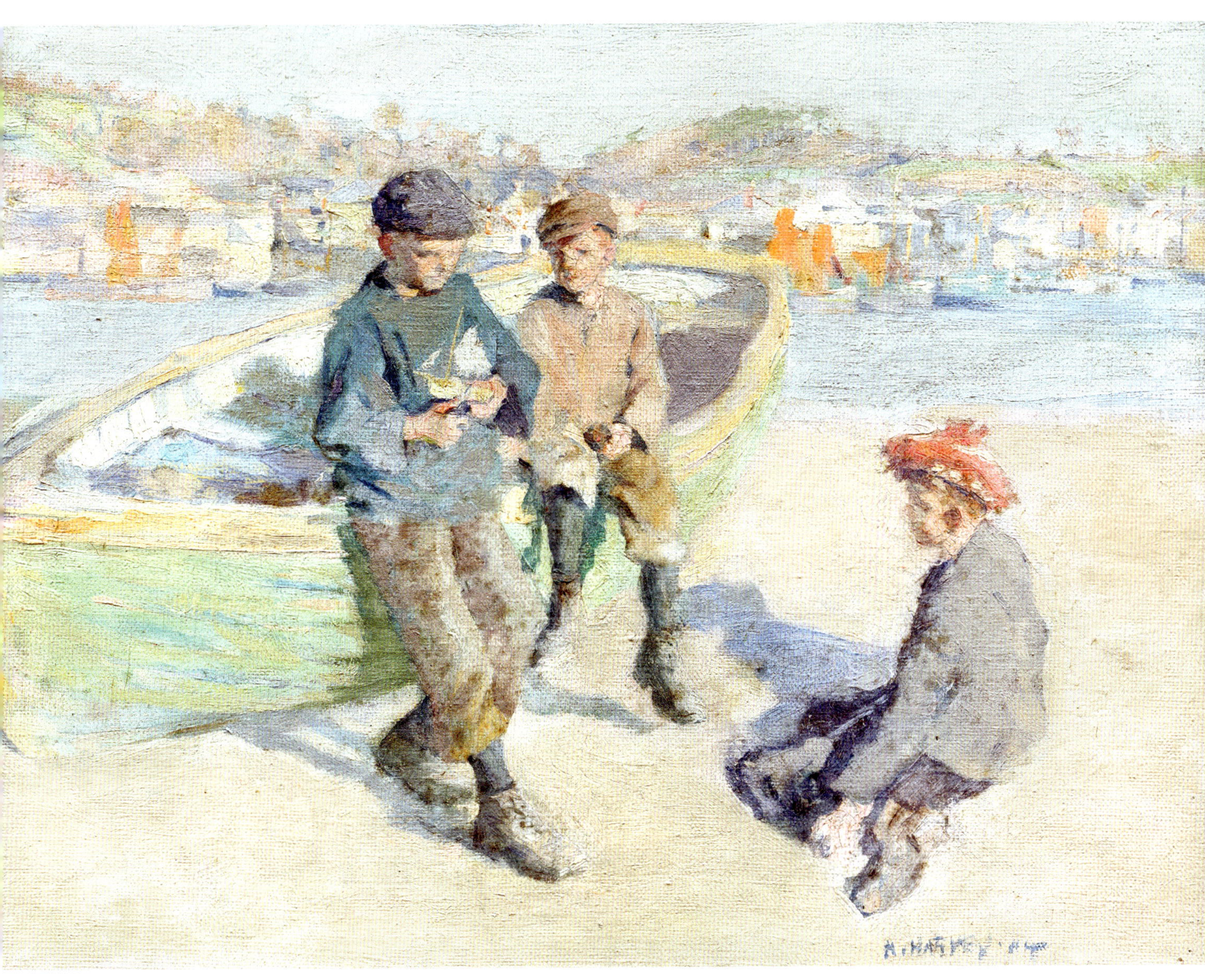

Children in Newlyn Harbour
1904 | oil on canvas | 26.5 x 37 cm
PENLEE HOUSE GALLERY & MUSEUM

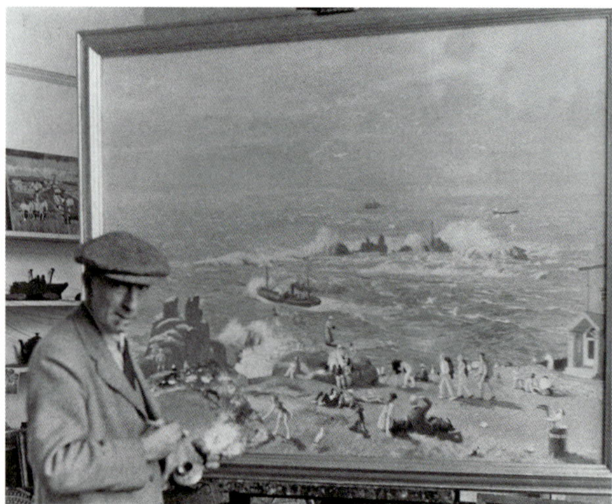

Painting the large version of *The Longships Lighthouse*, 1936
PRIVATE COLLECTION

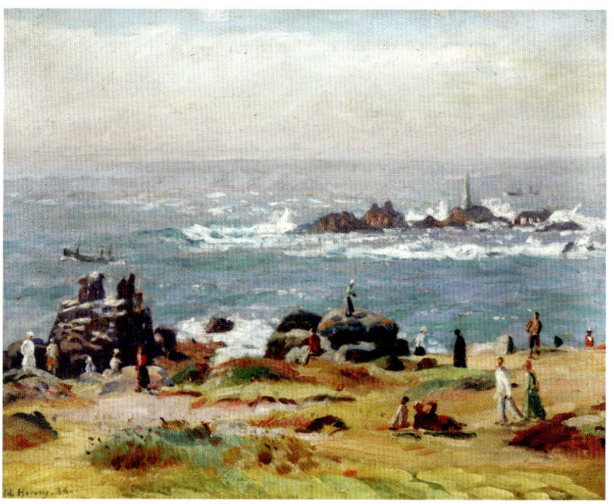

The Longships Lighthouse
1936 | oil on canvas | 34 x 44 cm
PENLEE HOUSE GALLERY & MUSEUM

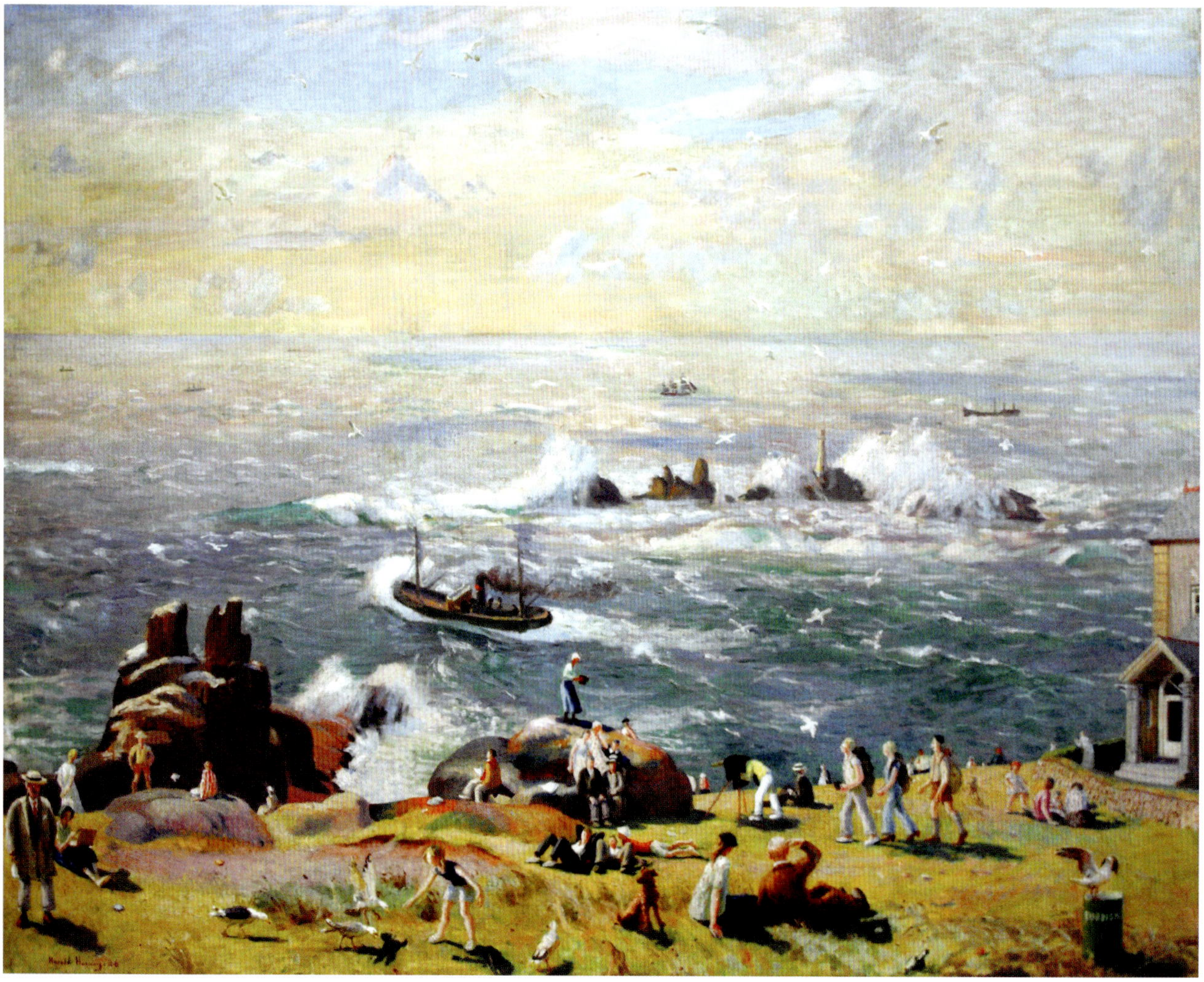

The Longships Lighthouse
1936 | oil on canvas | 120 x 150 cm
PRIVATE COLLECTION ON LOAN TO PENLEE HOUSE GALLERY & MUSEUM

A diffident man, most of those who knew him describe him as gentle and unworldly. According to Rhoda (who stayed with Harold and Gertrude when she was in her teens), Harvey didn't promote himself, having a mistrust of wordly honours. The couple were not well off, they rarely visited London and the walls of Rhoda's solicitor father's office were covered in 'payments in kind'. However she also remembered a 'delicious irony' and a warm welcome from the childless couple who loved children.

Brian Harvey, a great-nephew of Harold's, remembered his one and only meeting with great-uncle Harold. 'It was in the very early days of the War, some time during 1940, in Miss O'Connor's Tea Rooms in the Greenmarket, Penzance – part of which is Warren's Baker's shop today. I was having tea with my mother and she pointed out an elderly gentle-man in a long black overcoat. He was taking tea alone. "That's your Great Uncle Harold," she said. I went over to say hello to him; all I can recall is that he seemed extremely large, very friendly and that he drew me a picture of a lamb on his white paper napkin. Needless to say I didn't keep it, but I do remember the kind gesture.'

We have only the memory of others and Harold Harvey's own work to lead us to the man. A man who kept himself to himself, with a delightful sense of humour. There is a lovely story recounted by Morgan Hosking, whose uncle, Benjamin Ridge, was a friend of Harvey's:

> My uncle was one of the first to have a telephone in the house and a lot of people used to come round to use it. Mr Harvey used to come round, he made a lot of calls. One day the telephone bill arrived, quite a proportion of which was calls made by Harold Harvey to his London contacts and others. My uncle mentioned this to Mr Harvey, who said: 'A bill? What do you mean? Do you mean you have to pay to talk to people on that thing!'

Unworldly or a display of Cornish irony? Either way, the artist was clearly embarrassed, and he asked Benjamin Ridge to choose one of his paintings in lieu of cash to pay for his calls. The painting he chose was the small version of *The Longships Lighthouse* (1936). Whether or not he appreciated the fact at the time, this was a generous exchange for a few phone calls. When Morgan Hosking himself inherited it, the painting had accumulated in value so much that he balked at the number of security measures his insurers insisted upon, instead choosing to keep it uninsured but hidden, for safety, in a wardrobe – a secret he shared only with his family and close friends – a group encompassing half the population of Newlyn! The painting is now in the collection of Penlee House Gallery & Museum, Penzance.

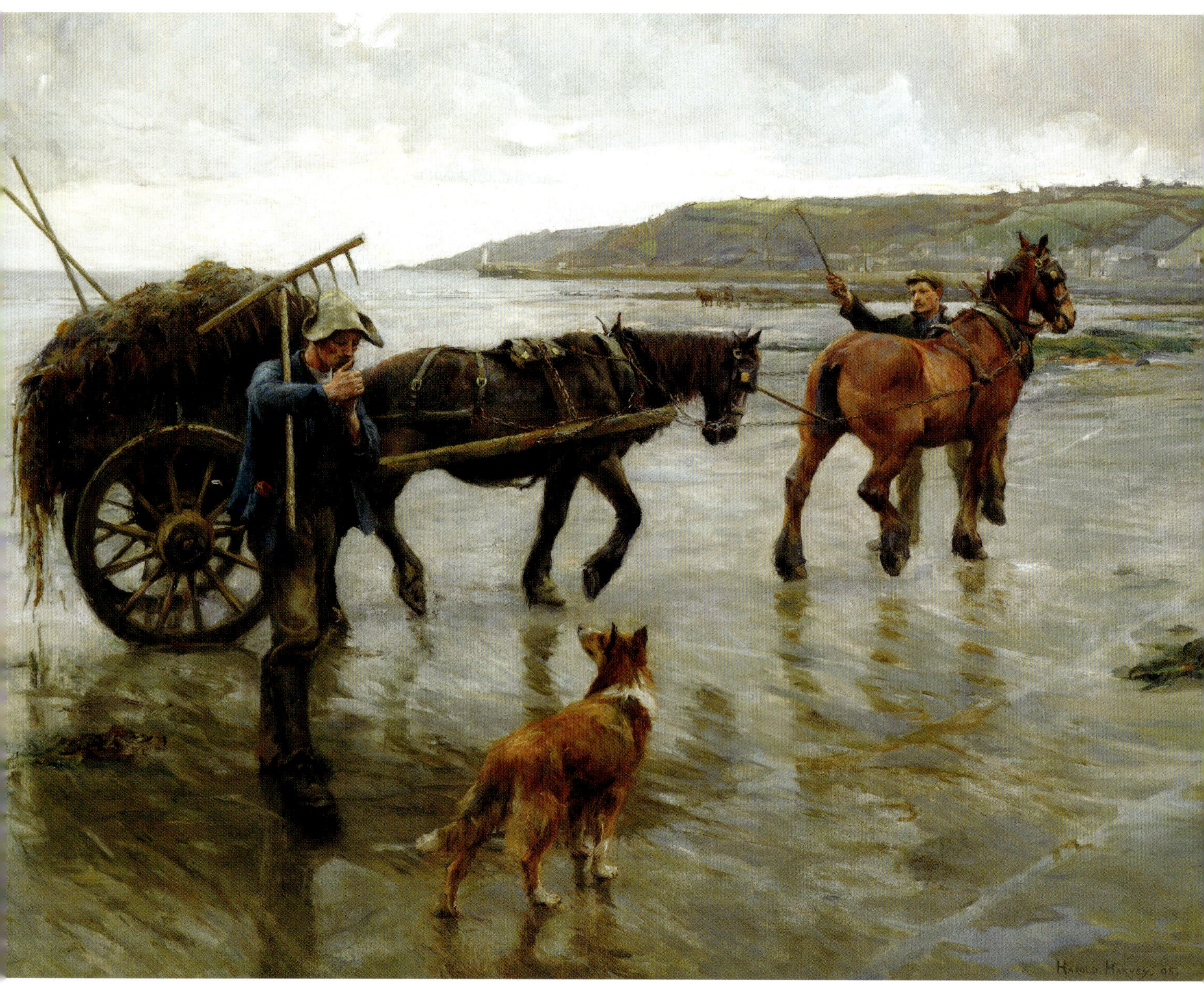

Seaweed Gatherers
1905 | oil on canvas | 91.5 x 122 cm
BOWERMAN CHARITABLE TRUST

Two

Newlyn

'Primitive and suitable for artists'

'Newlyn is near to Penzance and yet far enough for the place to be quite primitive and suitable for artistic purposes.' So wrote Stanhope Forbes in 1884.[1] The paintings of the Newlyn School are viewed today with a certain amount of wistfulness. Today's galloping technology and global climate change lend an extra romanticism to a period when the railway had only just reached Penzance, there were few cars, and a telephone was a rare and wondrous invention. However, living in the fishing village of Newlyn was no romantic idyll, and although improved communication did bring benefits, the nature of social evolution is that change occurs for better and worse.

An early *Guide to Penzance and its Neighbourhood*, published by Frederick Rodda in 1875, stated: 'There are no architectural beauties to tempt the Visitor … Penzance, as a town is wretchedly laid out and worse built.'[2] There is barely a mention of Newlyn and an 1865 *Handbook* is quite blunt: 'There is nothing worthy of particular attention in the town of Newlyn, excepting those objects of interest which are necessarily connected with its fishing operations.' Many might wish it had stayed that way, but the world was growing smaller. It was fashionable in the art world to 'capture the past', but in so doing the artists brought about change, and what was captured was the beginning of the future.

It was a time of political and social awareness amongst the literati; to the painters it was also a reaction to Classicism and the Pre-Raphaelites. The fashion for 'plein-air' painting grew in France, where there was a tradition of artists going to live in the country to paint nature at first hand. In the early days, painting out of doors took a degree of determination. The artist not only had to carry easel, stool and canvas, but also all the pots and solvents with which to mix the colours – tubes were a convenience introduced in 1830.

Works by French Realists were exhibited in England from the 1860s, and some English artists went to work in France, but it was the influence of the painter Jules Bastien-Lepage which was to transform

1. In the Stanhope Forbes letters, Tate Archive, London.
2. 'JHH' *Tourist's Guide to Penzance* (Frederick Rodda, 1875).

British art. In 1848, the year Karl Marx published his *Communist Manifesto*, Bastien-Lepage was born in Damvillers in the Meuse region of France. The artist Norman Garstin summed up the feeling of his fellow artists by describing Bastien-Lepage as '… the greatest of our day – almost all his contemporaries have felt his power; many imitated him, no one surpassed him … his men and women breathe air, not linseed oil.'[3] Bastien-Lepage became a figurehead for a whole generation of British artists. He showed a devotion to realism and believed it was important to live among his subjects. He painted many pictures of beggars, in particular children, although he was often more concerned with the appealing expression of the child than the harsher realities of poverty (*Going To School*, 1882), as were some of those who imitated him.

Painting 'en plein air', painting the action where it happens, meant that it was essential to live amongst the people whose lives were the painters' subject matter, and so the artists came to live in Newlyn. Although artists had visited the west Cornwall peninsula since the early nineteenth century (including, notably, J.M.W. Turner), it was the realist painters seeking to live as a colony in the late eighteen hundreds, now identified as the 'Newlyn School', who came, stayed and began to document what was, in reality, a changing society. These artists, intent on recording the frugal reality of life in this fishing community, were partly drawn to Newlyn by the existence of the railway (the link between Penzance and Truro was completed in 1852 and Brunel's bridge at Saltash in 1859 meant that at last Cornwall was linked to the national rail system). They used the trains to transport work to the Royal Academy and elsewhere. Meanwhile, the railway link between Cornwall and England was subtly changing the countryside, as the balance of the commercial economy altered. The railway allowed fresh primary produce to be delivered overnight to distant markets such as Bristol, the Midlands and London. Although this helped the fishing industry, it also marked the beginning of diversification, encouraging the growth of cut flowers, and a change from arable to dairy farming as Cornish milk, butter, cheese and cream could be transported quickly to markets throughout England.

In the 1850s, the fishing season was almost year-round, with pilchards in late summer and autumn, mackerel in winter and spring, and herring between late spring and late summer. The chief method of fishing in Newlyn was by drift-net and seine-net, while other fishing villages in the south-west were more likely to use trawling or lines. In 1865, Mount's Bay had 250 boats of between 12 and 22 tons for drift nets alone, and gave employment to over 4,000 people.[4] In his *Cornish Journal*,[5] Charles Lee wrote that, on 22nd November 1892, one catch alone brought in 3,500 herring, but that herring were only fetching a shilling a hundred that day, rather than the 2s.6d. or 3s. a hundred they could fetch, 'owing to a big catch by a couple of boats who let down a seine outside Penzance'. The price of the catch would be divided into shares, the boat's owner carrying one share, the owners of the nets one, the captain one and the men who give their labour

3. Caroline Fox, *Stanhope Forbes and the Newlyn School* (David & Charles, 1993), p. 19.
4. *The Handbook of Western Cornwall, Penzance & Neighbourhood*, 1865 edition.
5. K.C. Phillipps (ed.), *The Cornish Journal of Charles Lee* (Tabb House, 1995).

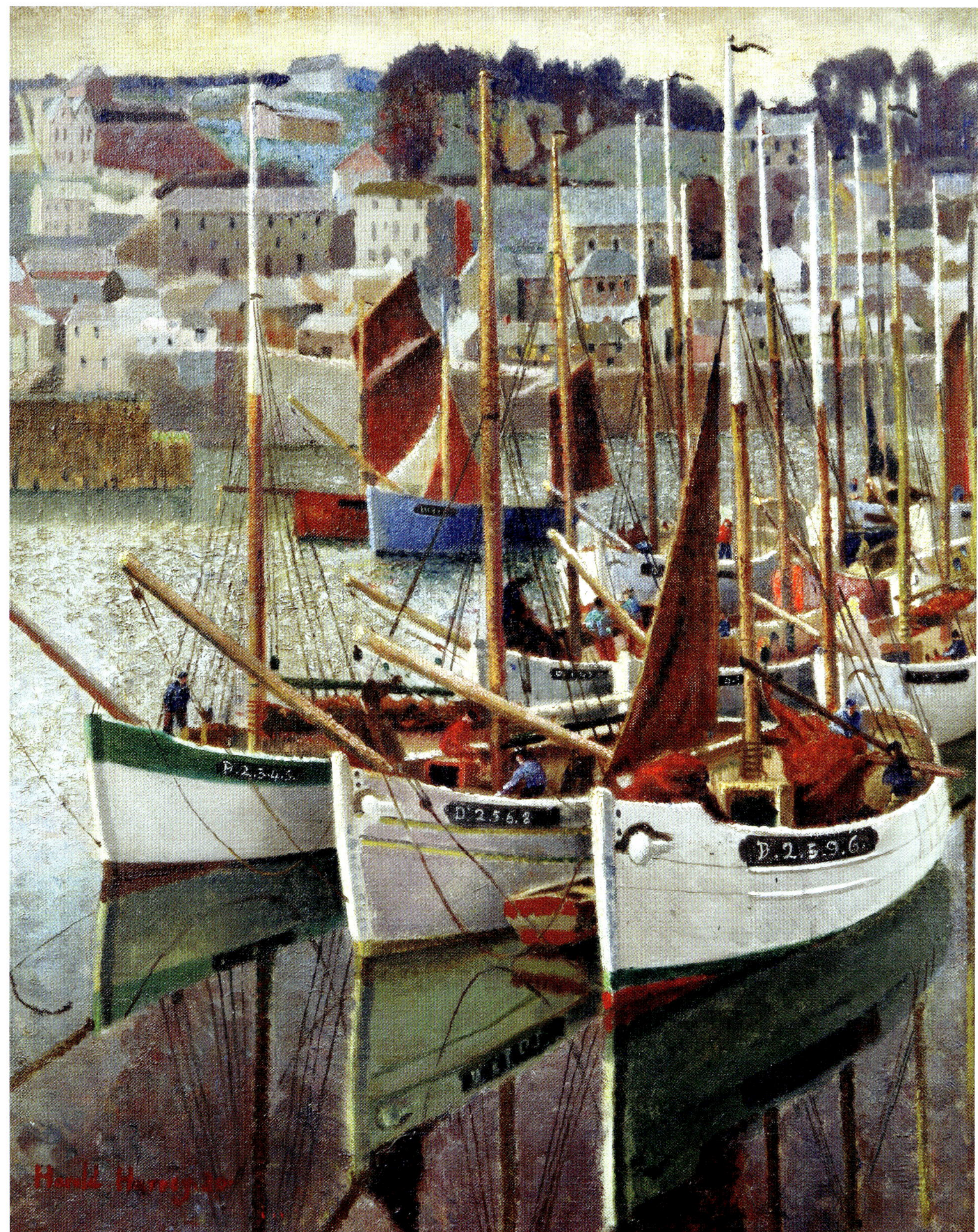

French Crabbers
1930 │ oil on canvas │ 54 x 44.5 cm
PRIVATE COLLECTION, ON LOAN TO PENLEE HOUSE GALLERY & MUSEUM

only half a share. Netting pilchards, herrings and mackerel close to shore was one of the two ways the Newlyn fishermen made their living from the sea. The other was to travel far out into the North Sea and sometimes beyond. One captain, according to Lee, declared that 'he would rather go whaling or to the workhouse than belong to the North Sea fleet'. The problem was that the men were not their own masters, and were made to sign up to work on boats remaining out at sea for six weeks at a time, in all weathers. If the boats ran back to the harbour, the crews were dismissed.

Harold Harvey would have been eighteen at the time Charles Lee was writing in Newlyn. Change was afoot, market forces were affecting the local economy, and pilchard fishing was already in decline. Neighbouring Penzance was at the height of its prosperity in the 1880s, with a large harbour, a market and good public buildings.[6] The town had expanded rapidly in the 1800s and developed a cultural and intellectual presence, evidenced by the founding of several important institutions: The Royal Geological Society of Cornwall (1814); The Public Library (1818); The Natural History and Antiquarian Society (1839); The Penzance Institution (1848); The Penzance School of Art (1853) and The Choral Society (1858). Gas lighting, piped drinking water and sewerage had all been installed by 1865. Conditions for the 'bucketarses'[7] of Newlyn were basic by comparison, and this was part of the village's charm for the artists.

> … The street scenes in Newlyn lack nothing of subject for the painter; paved with cobblestone, some of the narrow streets are occasionally strewn over with fishheads and entrails, so that one's progress in going 'up' or 'down'-a-long is sometimes considerably facilitated by an alarmingly quick slide to an unexpected destination …

This was Frank Richards' description of the fishing village in 'Newlyn as a Sketching Ground', published in *The Studio* in 1895. He also said:

> … Newlyn itself is bright, the colour of everything is decidedly fresh, pure and brilliant, according to the day: the sea and sky effects are charming, especially in summer, when we get a good deal of Italian blue …

The artists were, for the most part, from the advantaged classes and their arrival and the arrival of visitors generally, had an impact upon the native community. In their late twenties and early thirties, the first generation of artists would have been colourful characters to an impressionable ten-year old, such as Harvey. Walter Langley (1852–1922) was the first artist to settle in Newlyn when he was given a commission for a year's work there by a Birmingham art dealer. He had already visited the fishing village in 1880, after which he sold five views of Newlyn at auction. Of working class origin, Langley's sympathy for the people of Newlyn is powerfully evident in his depictions of village life: *But Men Must Work and Women Must Weep* (1882) and *Among The Missing* (1884).

6. Major building works were completed in the 1800s, changing the appearance of the town significantly: St Mary's Church (1835), The Market House (1837), St Paul's Church (1843), the Promenade (1844), The New Pier, opened by Prince Albert (1846), and extended again in the 1860s with jetty and lighthouse; The Queen's Hotel (1862), The Public Buildings (1867, including hall, library, museums, Town Hall, police station and council chamber), and a statue of Sir Humphry Davy (1872).

7. 'Bucketarse' – a colloquial term coined in Penzance for Newlyners, probably because of the lack of mains sewerage in the village; derived from 'buccas', the name by which Newlyn boys were known, which itself is derived from 'Buccaboo', the name for a storm devil.

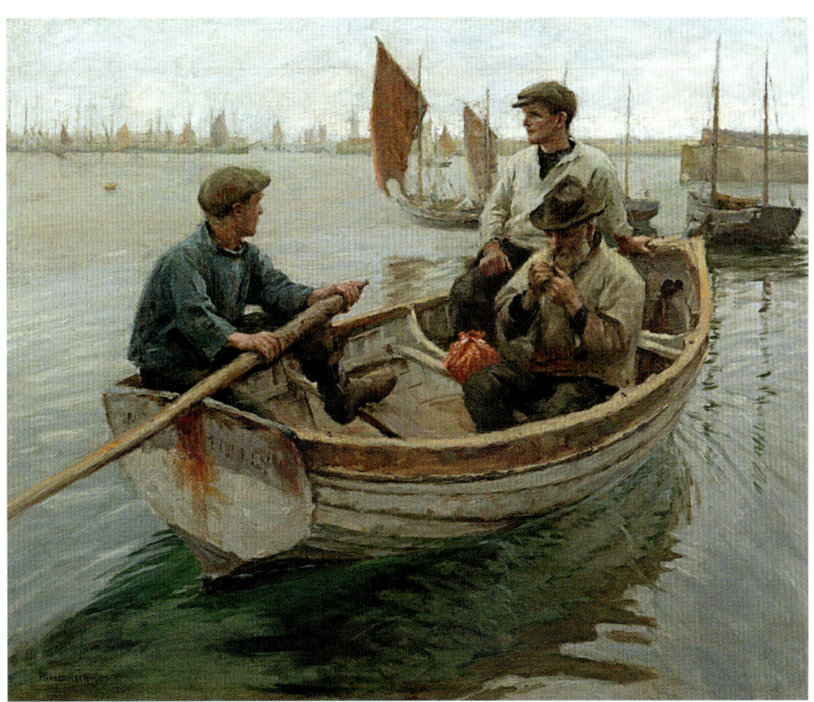

Whiffing, Newlyn
1907 | oil on canvas | 63.5 x 76 cm
RICHARD GREEN GALLERY, LONDON

Langley was soon joined by many others including Edwin Harris and his wife who settled there in 1883, Ralph Todd (also 1883), Henry Scott Tuke (arrived 1883, moved to Falmouth 1885), Frank Bramley (1884), Stanhope Forbes (1885), Norman Garstin and his wife (1886), and Thomas Cooper Gotch with his wife Caroline (1887). By 1884 *The Cornishman* reported that there were 'twenty-seven artists residing in Newlyn.'[8] Public recognition came when Frank Bramley's *A Hopeless Dawn* (1888) was bought by the Chantrey Bequest, and the coherence of the painters as a group became recognised as 'The Newlyn School'. Their paintings were regularly exhibited at the Royal Academy and were well received by critics. The artists gave the name 'Rue des Beaux Arts' to an alley off Trewarveneth Street and Bramley had his home and studio on the corner (although the present alley by that name, between Boase Street and Trewarveneth Street, is not the original).

Forbes and Garstin created iconic images which have become recognisable symbols of the Newlyn School. Forbes' *Fish Sale on a Cornish Beach* (1885), already mentioned, depicts the sale of fish freshly landed on the open beach at Newlyn before the present piers were built. Garstin's *The Rain It Raineth Every Day* (1889) shows the shimmering wet pavement of the promenade at Penzance. Both are painted on the large scale; Forbes' viewpoint no longer exists since the building of a new pier, but Garstin's can still be identified.

In 1899, as the core of the Newlyn colony began to dwindle, Stanhope and Elizabeth Forbes opened their school of painting in Newlyn 'for

8. *The Cornishman* is still the local newspaper at time of going to press.

the student who wishes to learn how seriously to study painting and
drawing according to the recent developments in English art.' Stanhope
and Elizabeth stressed the need for absolute fidelity to nature, simplicity
and the avoidance of 'tricks' of all kinds. However they also believed
that having grasped the basics, pupils should experiment and develop
their own idiosyncrasies.

> In summer the students are often seen dotted about the big sunshining
> garden which surrounds the classroom, making studies of the masses
> of blooms as they grow under the open sky; and on the fine afternoons
> a ring of easels surrounds the model, posed out of doors.[9]

The School of Painting became the focal point for a new generation of
artists. Lamorna Birch, Harold and Laura Knight, Ernest Procter and
Doris Shaw (who became Mrs Dod Procter) and Alfred Munnings were
among those attracted to the area, Procter and Shaw being amongst those
to attend the School, while the other artists were drawn by the continued
existence of a community of artists. With the new generation came
more colour, more innovative composition and less moralistic subject
matter. The colonists did not always understand the natives, and vice
versa. Frank Richards, again in the 1895 article for *The Studio*, wrote:

> The monotony of Newlyn becomes insufferable oftentimes in the
> winter months … little amusement of an intellectual nature to be
> had. Perhaps the greatest inconvenience we suffer is the impossibility
> of obtaining nude models, at least from among the natives; and I
> honestly believe that if a painter commenced a nude subject and had
> a native model, he would suffer some insult from the folk – in all
> probability they would 'chuck'n over clift'.[10]

The following year brought excitement enough in the form of a riot
in Newlyn. More than three hundred fully-armed troops of the
Royal Berkshire Regiment were stationed on the streets and along
the quayside of Newlyn, three navy gunboats patrolled in Mount's
Bay and police reinforcements were drafted from other districts after
pitched battles were fought along Penzance promenade. All this may
have seemed an unnecessary show of force against the monotony of
Newlyn – especially as the riot arose from a few hundred God-fearing
fishermen who refused to go to sea on Sundays, but whose livelihoods
were threatened by Sabbath-breaking crews from the East Coast.[11]
The community was a close one and as the riot of 1896 illustrates,
the villagers were capable of making their feelings known. The
'bohemian' lifestyle of the flamboyant artists did not always sit
comfortably, but was tolerated. In this Methodist village, the nude
models were professionals from London, often Italians, and young
female students from the Forbes' School who lodged at 'The Myrtage'
(Myrtle Cottage) had to be chaperoned.

The artists brought their own social life. Musical evenings were held
at the Forbes' house at Higher Faugan; there were amateur dramatic

9. Mrs Lionel Birch, *Stanhope A. Forbes,
A.R.A. and Elizabeth Stanhope Forbes,
A.R.W.S.* (London, Paris, New York and
Melbourne: Cassell and Co., 1906),
p. 115.
10. Frank Richards writing in *The Studio*
(1895).
11. Simon Parker, *A Star on the Mizzen:
The story of the 1896 Newlyn fishing
riots* (Liskeard: Giss'on Books, 1996).
Interestingly none of the painters
documented this event.

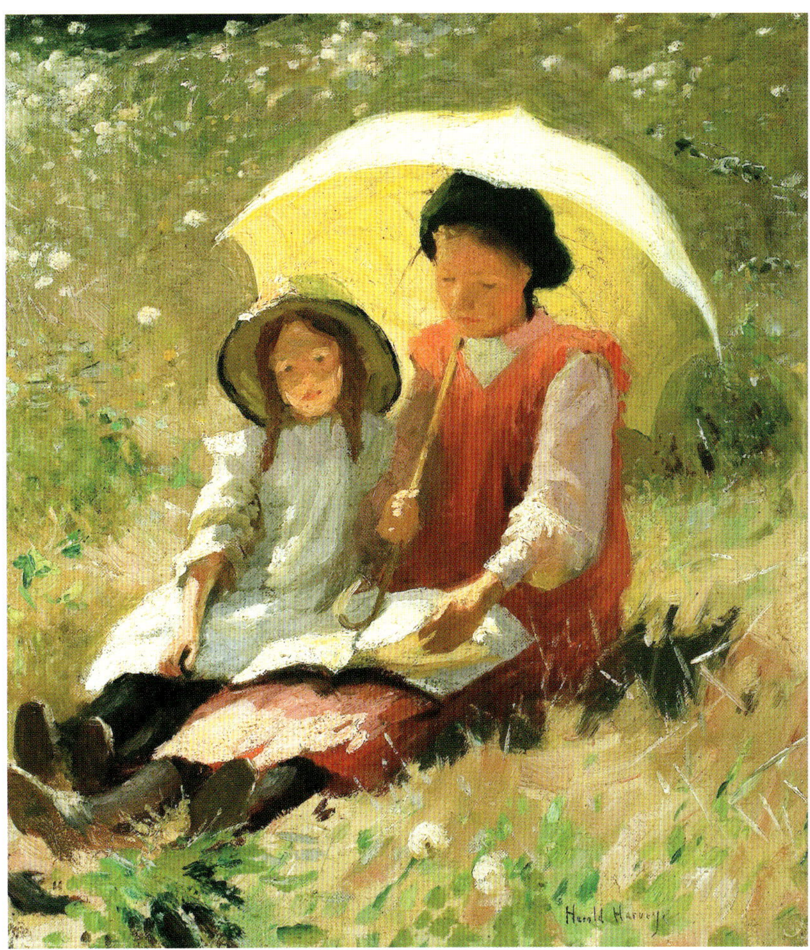

Holiday
*c.*1912 | oil on canvas | 41 x 36 cm
NATIONAL MUSEUMS AND GALLERIES OF WALES

shows at St John's Hall in Penzance, and the Newlyn artists versus St Ives artists cricket matches. In 1894 questions were asked in the council chamber about 'the fly posting of large posters, gorgeous in hue and grotesque in design'[12] which advertised 'a presentation by that unique little lot of inartistic incapable aboriginal amateurs known to the police as Lubly Lobengula's Impecunious Impi.' This was possibly the one and only time Walter Langley took part in the colony's annual theatre show: however on another memorable occasion he led a solemn procession of artists through the village streets at two o'clock in the morning, playing his banjo and singing 'As we went home by the light of the moon'. The villagers looked on with curiosity, some suspicion and a strong belief – still held to this day – that artists are 'weird as fish'. As Penzance Town Council considered the problem of the 'gorgeous and grotesque posters' for Lubly Lobengula, the eldest son of the general manager of Batten, Carne and Carne's Bank, twenty-year old Harold Harvey, went to study art in France.

12. Roger Langley, *Walter Langley: Pioneer of the Newlyn Art Colony* (Bristol: Sansom & Co., 1997), p. 100.

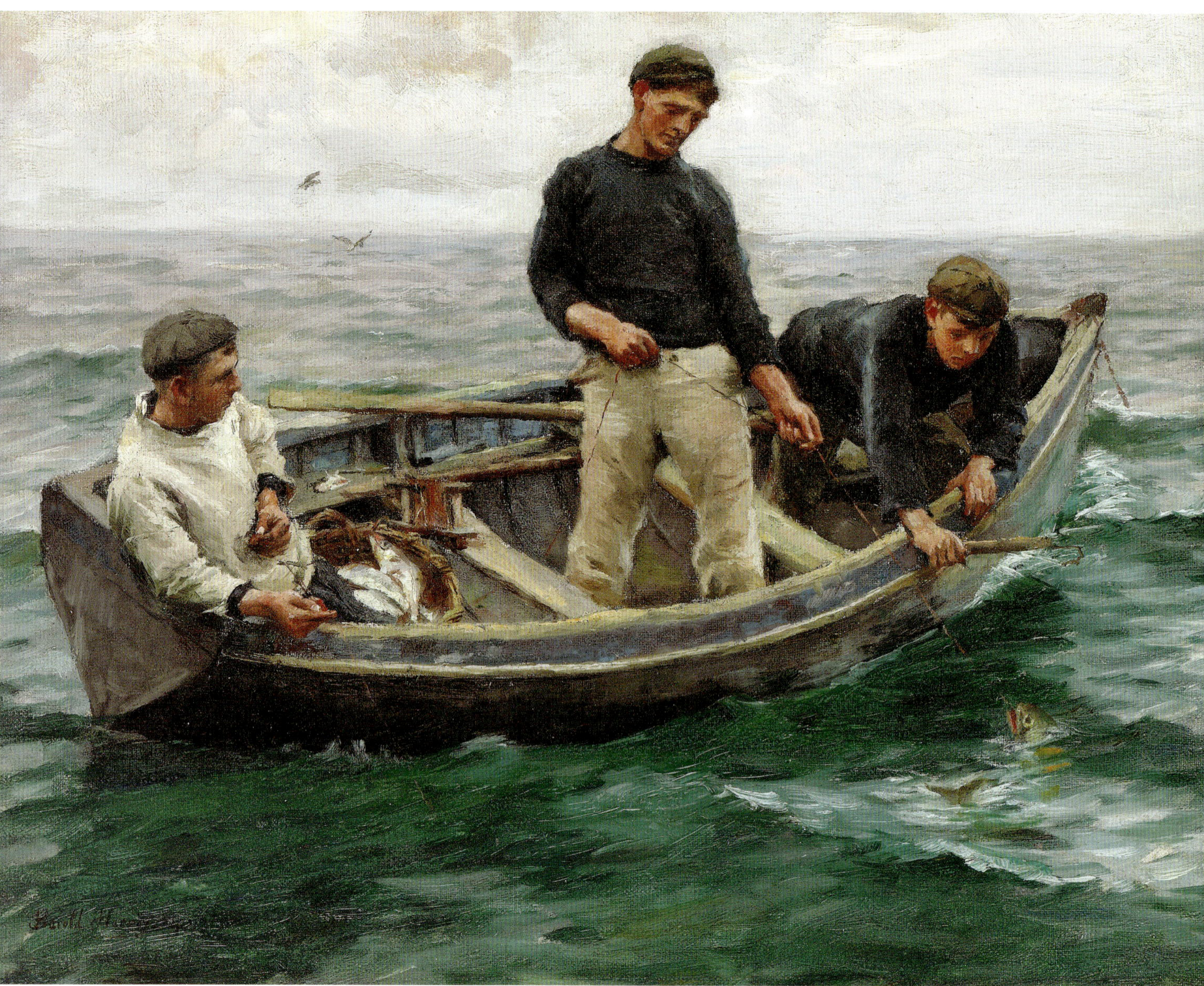

Whiffing in Mount's Bay
1904 | oil on canvas | 30.5 x 40.5 cm
PRIVATE COLLECTION; IMAGE COURTESY CHRISTIE'S

Three

Learning to paint
Paris and back to Cornwall

Harvey first studied painting at Penzance School of Art.[1] His tutor was Norman Garstin (1847–1926), who had himself studied at the atelier of Carolus-Duran in Paris, where the teaching was inspired by the study of artists such as Velasquez. Carolus-Duran taught that colour should be secondary to tonal relationships, that painting should contain only essential elements, and that everything unnecessary should be left out. Garstin's most famous work, *The Rain It Raineth Every Day*, is evidence of his adoption of these principles.

The Garstin family had been victims of the Irish potato famine of 1846/7 and although he was never politically active, Norman Garstin was a profound believer in the Socialist cause. What the Harvey family thought of Harold being taught by 'an impoverished half-blind Anglo-Irish gentleman who had been by turns a diamond prospector, journalist, as well as an accomplished painter and teacher'[2] is unknown. According to the David Messum catalogue for the 'A Breath of Fresh Air' exhibition (1990), Harold Harvey's family strongly disapproved of his ambition to be a painter, but the family must have supported him through his studies, particularly in Paris. Garstin's approach to art is given in an interview with Elizabeth Forbes for the magazine *The Paper Chase*[3] in 1909, when he explained his theory on painting:

> My chief theory on painting is not to have a theory, painting is purely a personal matter; I don't know how different people see nature, but certainly in passing through their consciousness it is bound to be transmitted absolutely different. What one is chiefly interested in is less the thing depicted than the personality of the painter who did it. Very modern painting [appeals to me most] because of the freshness of it; and I am always fond of those experiments that young men make.

Norman Garstin's verbal talents, in addition to those of painting, enabled him to become director of the Newlyn Art Students' Society which supplemented his income from picture sales. His teaching clearly

1. As recorded in Harvey's obituary published in *The Cornishman* in 1941.
2. Nic Hale, *Norman and Alethea Garstin: A brief biography of two painters* (Helston: An Lyverji Kernewek, 1999).
3. *The Paper Chase* was printed by Reginald Dick and Jim Mackenzie, Newlyn Press, Gwavas Studio.

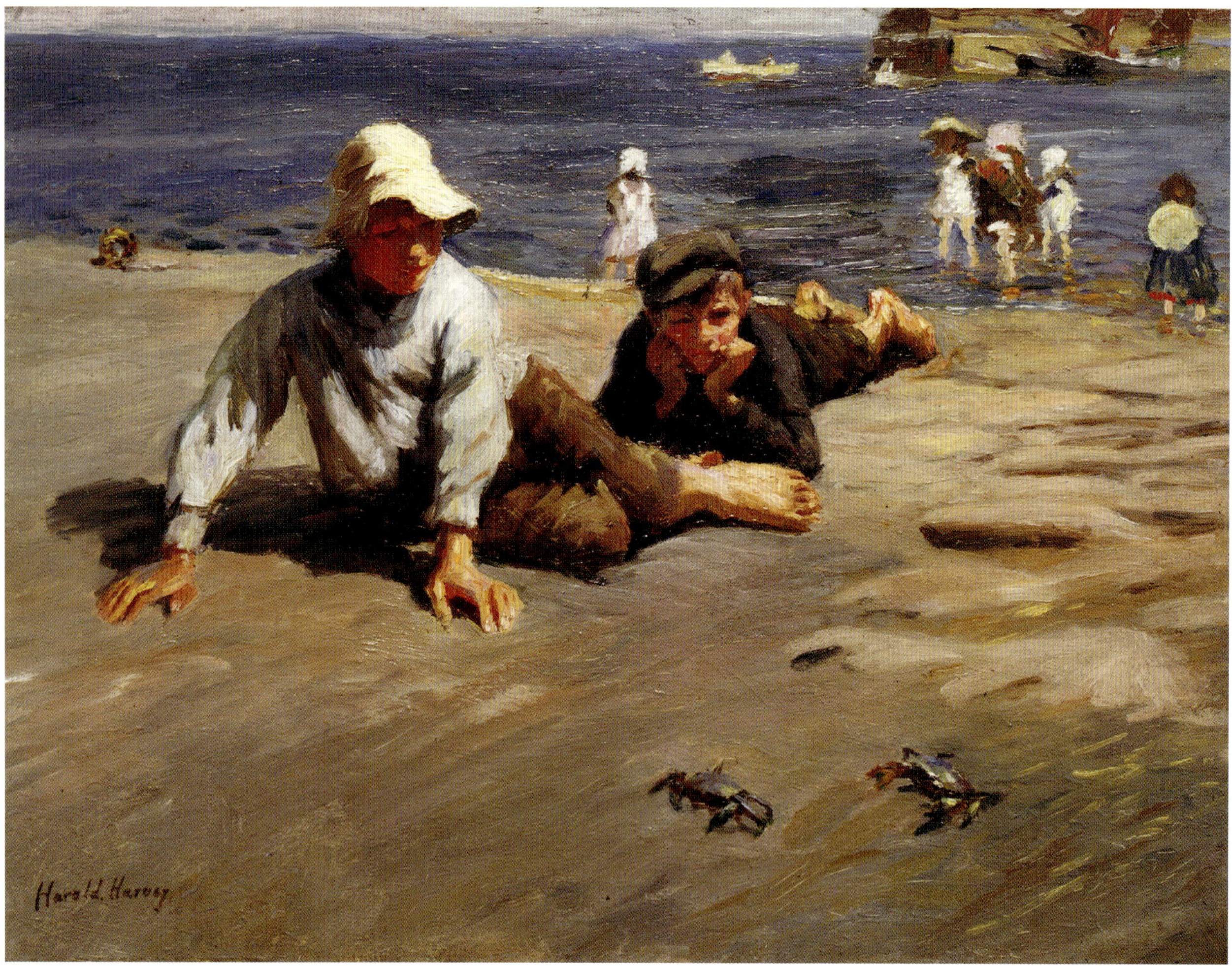

Sport on the Shore, A Crab Race
*c.*1890 | oil on canvas | 30.5 x 40.5 cm
THE BOX, PLYMOUTH

encouraged the young Harvey, who became determined to follow
an artistic career. Harvey's first studio is thought to have been close
to Penzance harbour. The earliest known work to have survived[4] dates
from about 1890 (when Harold was 16), and is called *Sport on the Shore,
A Crab Race*. The painting is 12 x 16 inches, painted in oils, and shows
two boys watching two crabs.

Having decided to become an artist, and no doubt advised by
Garstin and other artists of the colony, in 1894 Harvey travelled to
Paris, living at 20 Avenue Victoria. For the next two years, he studied
at the Academie Julian as a pupil of Benjamin Constant and Jean-Paul
Laurens (as had both Gotch and Tuke). Jean-Joseph Benjamin Constant
(1845–1902) painted many portraits during the 1880s, including Queen
Victoria and other members of the British royal family. Jean-Paul
Laurens (1838–1921) was a noted history painter, whose work decorated
the Paris Hotel de Ville and the Pantheon. The Academie Julian was
opened by Rodolphe Julian in 1868 and accommodated many foreign
students not accepted by the Ecole des Beaux Arts because of the

4. Tom Cross, *The Shining Sands:
Artists in Newlyn and St Ives 1880–1930*
(Devon: Westcountry Books, 1994).

language entrance examination. Several branches of Julian's opened in Paris between 1878 and 1892, and the Academie still exists at 31 Rue du Dragon, near St Germain des Pres (it merged with ESAG Penninghen in 1968). In Harvey's time there, four of the best-known professors from the Ecole, including Laurens, visited the ateliers weekly.

The guiding principle of Julian's was similar to the Ecole's – drawing was the cornerstone of art, and work from the model was the focus of study. The Academie Julian also offered lithography and printmaking; students were allowed to pursue their work with little interference and could choose and pose their own models. Study was intensive, from eight a.m. to four or five p.m., six days a week. The air was thick with cigarette smoke and the fumes of paint scraped onto the walls, there was severe overcrowding and constant noise. A New Zealand student is reported to have said in 1901 that 'a little of Julian's goes a long way, and a year spent in his studio will probably teach all that can be learnt with profit there.' Harvey also studied at the Academie Colarossi and at the atelier of Auguste-Joseph Declusse (1855–1928), himself a student of Carolus-Duran who taught Garstin. Many British artists studied in Paris at this time, but in view of their later friendship it is worth noting that Harold Knight was also at the Academie Julian for nine months in 1894 and it is likely that he and Harold Harvey met each other at this time. *The Dinner Hour*, one of Harvey's earliest works (1897), was painted shortly after his return from France. The size of the picture (37 x 48 inches) suggests that he intended to submit it to the Royal Academy Summer Exhibition, but it was not until 1901 that it was exhibited at the Walker Art Gallery, Liverpool.

While Harvey was studying in France, a new gallery was opened in Newlyn, financed by John Passmore Edwards. This renowned Cornish benefactor's motives in funding this particular gallery were later explained by J.J. Macdonald in *Passmore Edwards Institutions*, London 1900:

> Art and colonisation did not always accompany each other, but they were, all the same, two distinguishing elements of human activity; and so it happened that whilst artists were forming a colony of their own in Cornwall, Cornishmen, in greater proportion to the inhabitants of any English county, were peopling the new colonies of the world. One of the motives of J. Passmore Edwards in complying with the request made to him to build an Art Gallery in Newlyn was to assist to root these artistic colonists in that locality. Being there he should like to keep them there. He was, naturally, interested in anything appertaining to the good of Cornwall; and as the mines of Cornwall were drying up, under the soil, he was desirous that the world at large should know more of the scenic wealth of Cornwall on the soil, and which was scattered in rich abundance around their rugged rock-bound coasts. The Newlyn School and Colony of Artists were illustrating and interpreting wealth in line and colour on canvas and thereby benefiting themselves, Cornwall and the world.

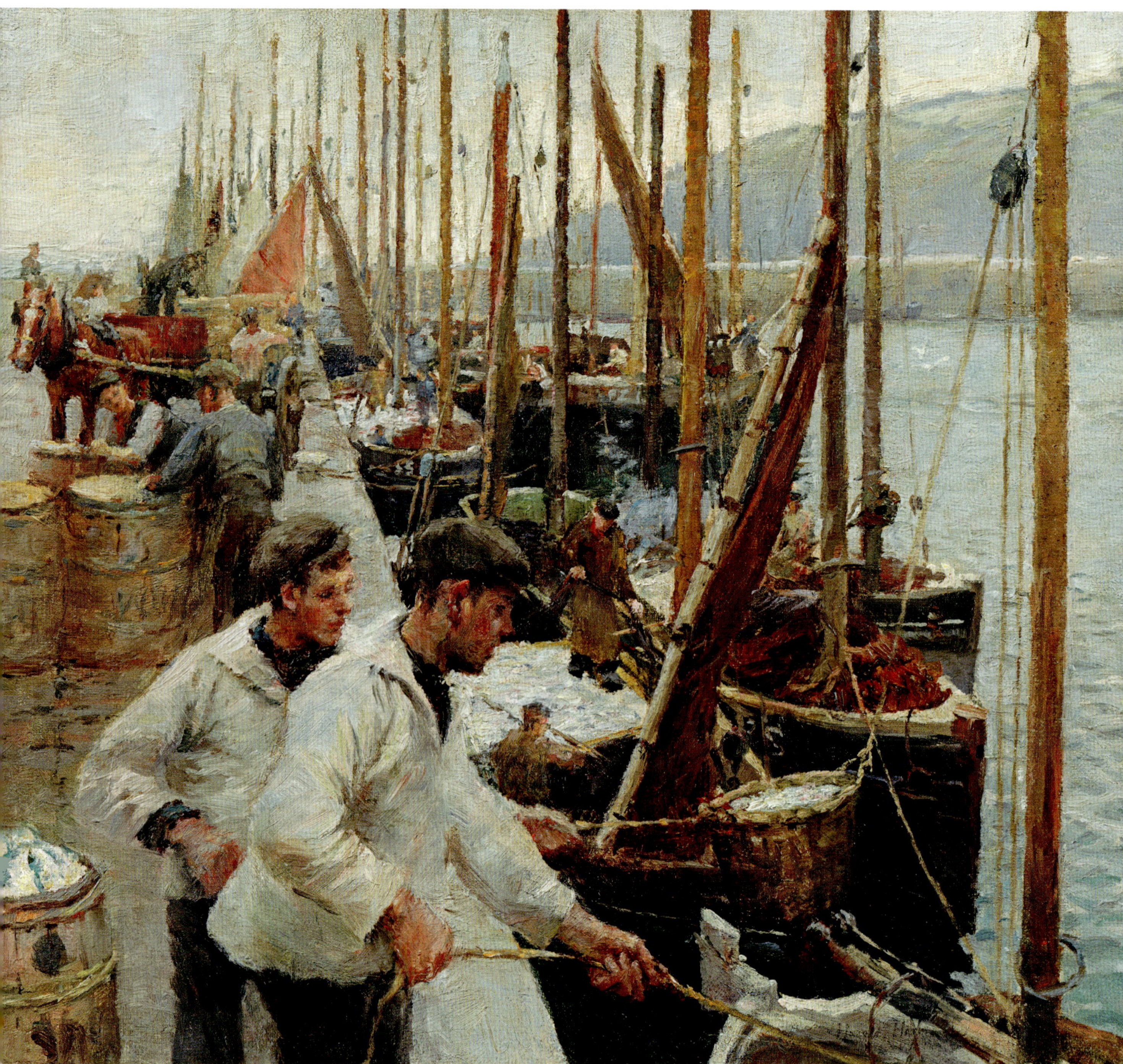

Unloading the Catch, Newlyn
*c.*1905 | oil on canvas | 30.5 x 35.5 cm
RICHARD GREEN GALLERY, LONDON

Arthur Quiller-Couch was one of the speakers at the inaugural lunch-eon of the Passmore Edwards Art Gallery in Newlyn on Tuesday 22nd October 1895. He called upon those present to 'witness a testimony in solid stone and mortar to a brief experiment in the history of Art …' by which he meant that the gallery should be a monument to living art '… for in art finality means death. Art lives by experiment and in pursuit of an idea.' He praised the artists for their personification of Cornwall and Cornish people. 'There are carpet-baggers in Art as well as politics. I have known people quite capable of coming to Newlyn shore and painting there a highland lassie with a pet lamb in a snow-storm. But these gentlemen of Newlyn have studied Cornwall patiently and given us much which is why this memorial now stands at Newlyn.[5]

The inaugural exhibition ran from 22nd October to 14th November 1895. Harold Harvey's work was exhibited along with Walter Langley, Stanhope Forbes, Norman Garstin, the Gotches and many others. The title of Harvey's picture is not recorded and he made no sale. In 1896 Harvey returned permanently to west Cornwall, to the family home at Trewartha Terrace, and he did not venture abroad again. Two years after his return from Paris, his career as a painter passed its first major milestone when he had his first work exhibited at the Royal Academy. The painting *In A Cornish Cottage* went on to be shown in the same year at the Walker Art Gallery, Liverpool. Also in 1898, Harvey's painting *Convalescence* was exhibited at the Society of Oil Painters, London, a venue which was to show *In A Cornish Cottage* in 1899 and other works in 1901 and 1902.

Between 1898 and 1910 Harvey had work accepted for exhibiting most years: at Liverpool from 1898 to 1903; at the Royal Society of Art, Birmingham in 1900, when four works were exhibited; at the Royal Glasgow Institute in 1902; at the Royal Academy 1907, 1908 and 1910; at Leeds in 1908 and at the Royal Cambrian Academy in 1909 (three works) and 1910 (two works). His unidentified painting exhibited with the South Wales Art Society in Cardiff, 1910, was mentioned by *Art News* on 7th July as being 'good work'. Meanwhile he was a regular exhibitor at home in the new Passmore Edwards Art Gallery. His first sale was on 18th September 1900: two sketches were sold to John Simes of Highgate, London, for £2.10s each. The sales book at the Passmore Edwards Art Gallery records 56 of his works sold between September 1900 and August 1912 for a total of £346.8s, and on 3rd March 1910 *Art News* carried a notice regarding an exhib-ition of his works at the gallery called 'Some Cornish Pictures'.

Having become an active painter in the 1890s, Harvey straddled both the first and the second generations of Newlyn artists, so it is natural that he should have taken inspiration from members of both. His early work is very much of the style of the founders of the Newlyn School. *The Pedlar* (1902) reflects both the style and subject of Forbes' *The Letter* (1898) and during much of the first decade of the 1900s, Harvey con-tinued to paint in the Forbes tradition. *The Watering Place* (1908) and

5. Reproduced in Melissa Hardie (ed.), *100 Years In Newlyn: Diary of a Gallery* (Patten Press, 1995), p. 24.

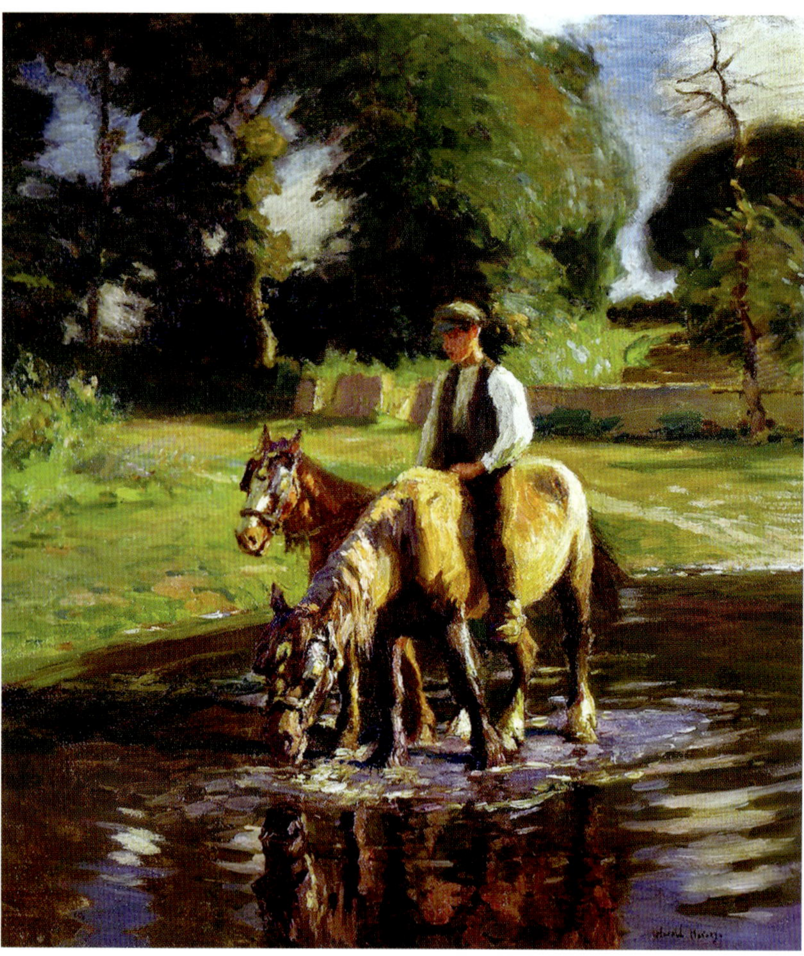

The Watering Place
oil on canvas | 75.5 x 91 cm
GRANT FORD LIMITED

Close of a Summer's Day (1909) are similar to Forbes' *The Drinking Place* (1900) while *Sailing in Newlyn Harbour* (1906) parallels Forbes' *Newlyn* (1906). Harvey was not alone in being influenced by Forbes and sticking to the principles of 'plein air' naturalism. Painters from the Newlyn School had been among the founding members of the New English Art Club, set up in 1886 as a response to dissatisfaction with the Royal Academy. In 1886/7 Stanhope Forbes, Thomas Cooper Gotch, Henry Scott Tuke, Frank Bramley, Norman Garstin, Leghe Suthers and Elizabeth Armstrong all exhibited with the NEAC. Over subsequent years, their work was persistently criticised by fellow members of the Club, such as Walter Sickert, for adhering to outdated principles, and the Newlyn members left the NEAC 'en masse' in 1890. Harvey did not become a member, and like the colonists of Newlyn, remained true to the French realist style.

In 1909, Harvey became an Associate Member of the Royal Cambrian Academy at Conwy in North Wales. During his membership he exhibited only six works at the RCA. He was also recorded as being a member of the South Wales Art Society in 1910, but the period of

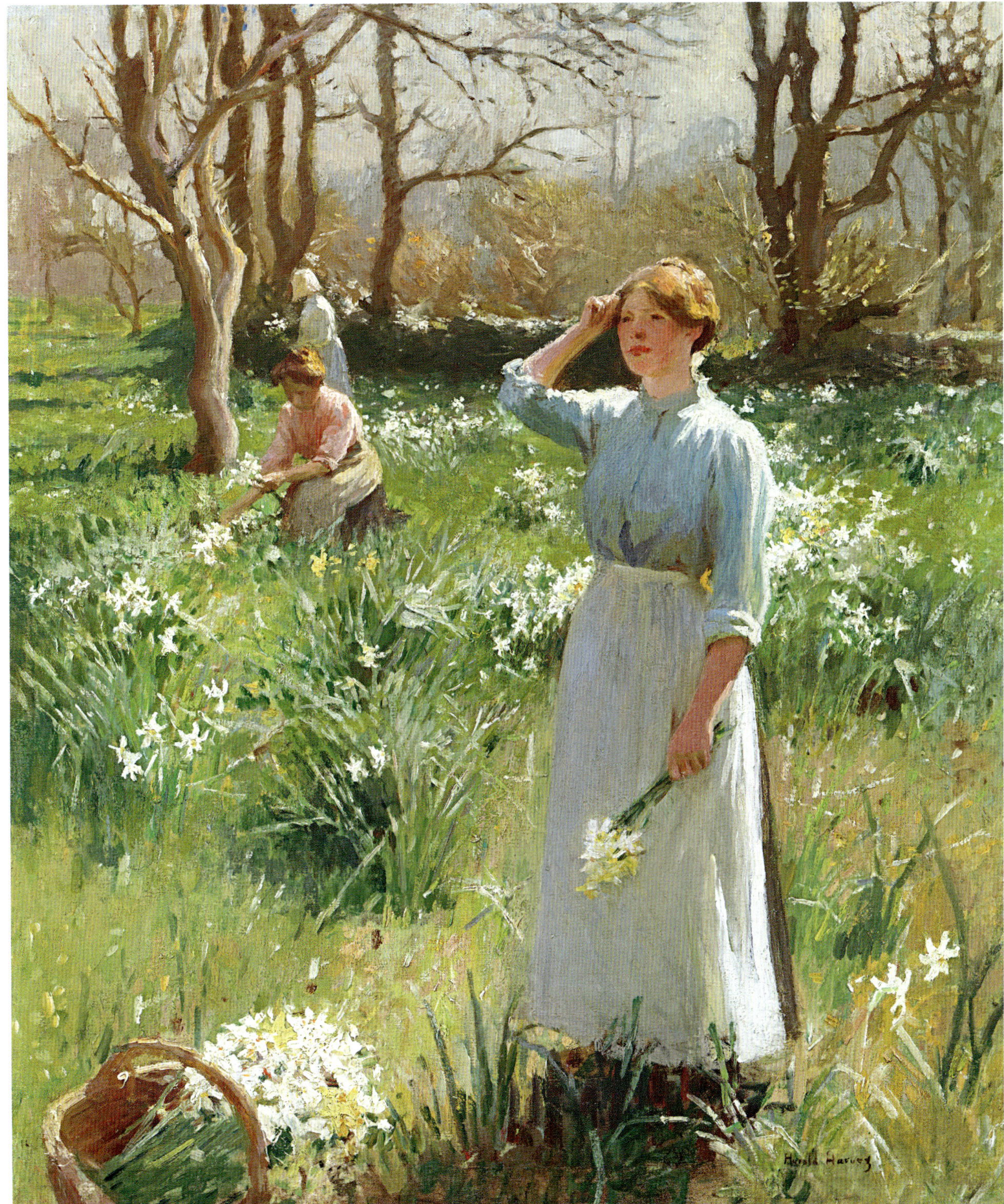

Daffodils
oil on canvas | 81 x 66 cm

PRIVATE COLLECTION; IMAGE COURTESY RICHARD GREEN GALLERY, LONDON

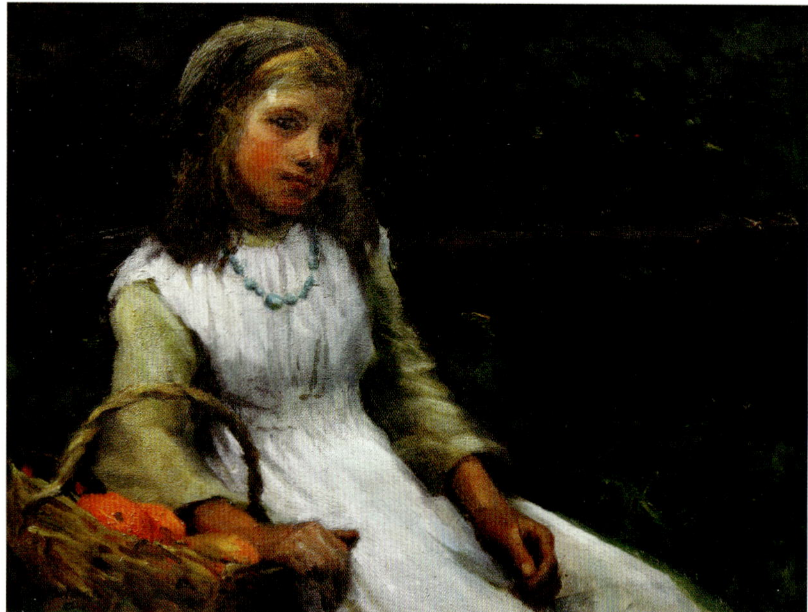

The Orange Girl
1905 | oil on canvas | 31 x 40 cm
ROYAL INSTITUTION OF CORNWALL, ROYAL CORNWALL MUSEUM, TRURO

his membership is not known. Harold's brother, Percival, went to live in Wales in 1906, and Harvey visited him there, which is probably how the membership of this Welsh art society came about. Also in 1909 Norman Garstin selected two of Harvey's paintings to illustrate his article 'West Cornwall as a Sketching Ground', published in *The Studio* magazine. The paintings reproduced were *A Boat's Crew, Newlyn Harbour* and *Seaweed Gatherers, Mount's Bay*, and this was, as far as is known, the first time that Harvey's work appeared in print. Garstin's article describes the dramatic changes that had taken place in Newlyn since the arrival of the artists, but also the picturesque lifestyle of the locals which had first attracted them. 'The Newlyn of today' he wrote 'and that of the first artist settlers twenty-five years ago are two quite different places.' As he points out, when Forbes painted his *Fish Sale on a Cornish Beach* there was no harbour, but by 1909 there was a new and spacious one which, large as it was, was crowded with fishing boats, steamers, sailing vessels and craft of all descriptions:

> All this has brought a life and animation that no one could have dreamt of a quarter of a century ago. These men in sabots and berets are French crabbers, Bretons who supply 'les petites soupers parisiens' with delicate langouste caught outside our three mile limit. These large men with blue eyes and fair beards are Norwegians, come down from the North with ice to pack the fish in. Yonder black-hulled steamer just leaving the harbour is bound for Genoa with pickled pilchards to help devout Italians through Lent. Here is a circle round a man with a hand-bell and high wading boots; he is selling a 'lot' of fish. Carts are being loaded up to catch the 'perishable' train. All is activity and bustle; but here and there are little knots of imperturbable fishermen, hands in

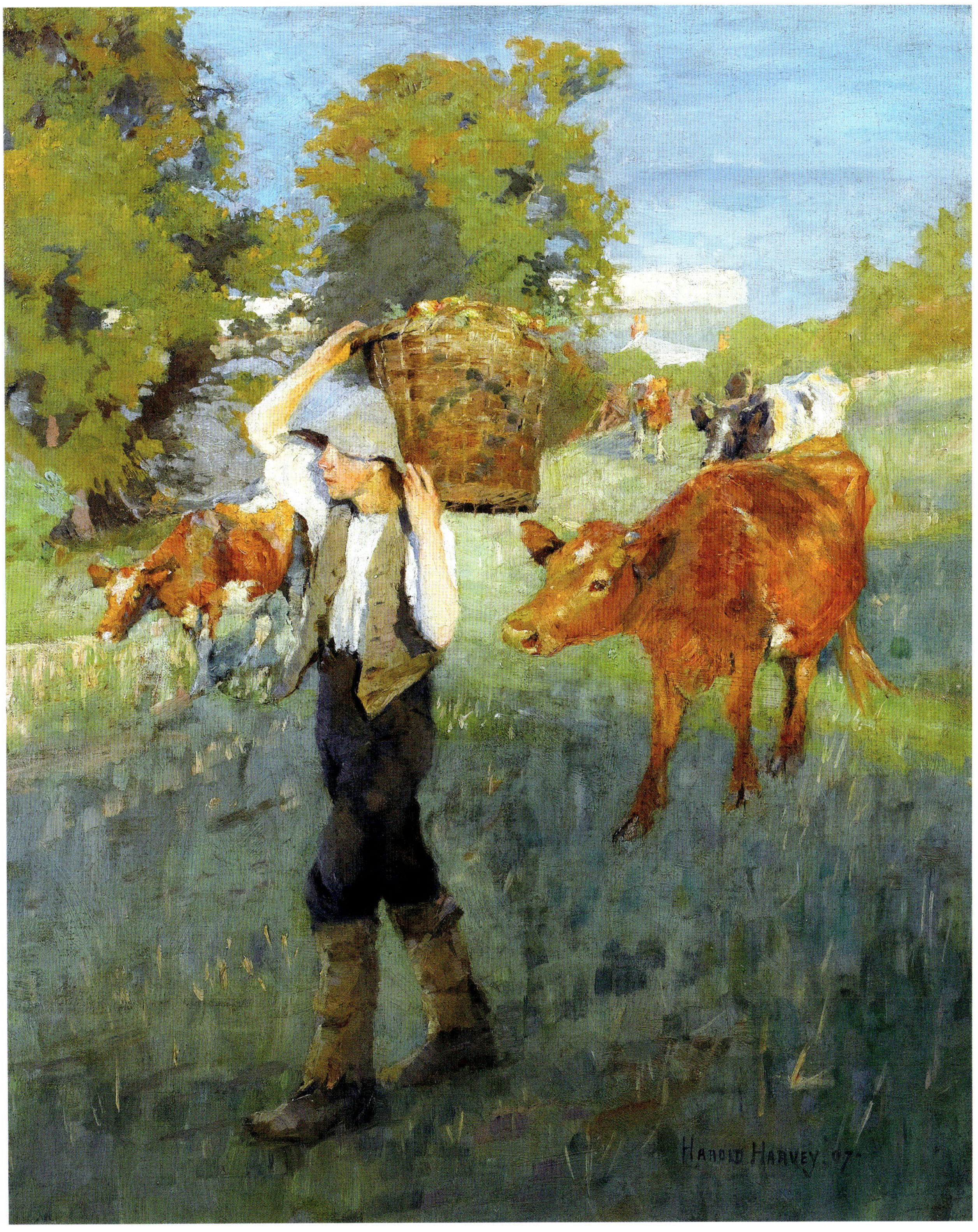

Returning from the Orchard
1907 │ oil on canvas │ 91 x 51 cm
PRIVATE COLLECTION; IMAGE COURTESY BONHAMS

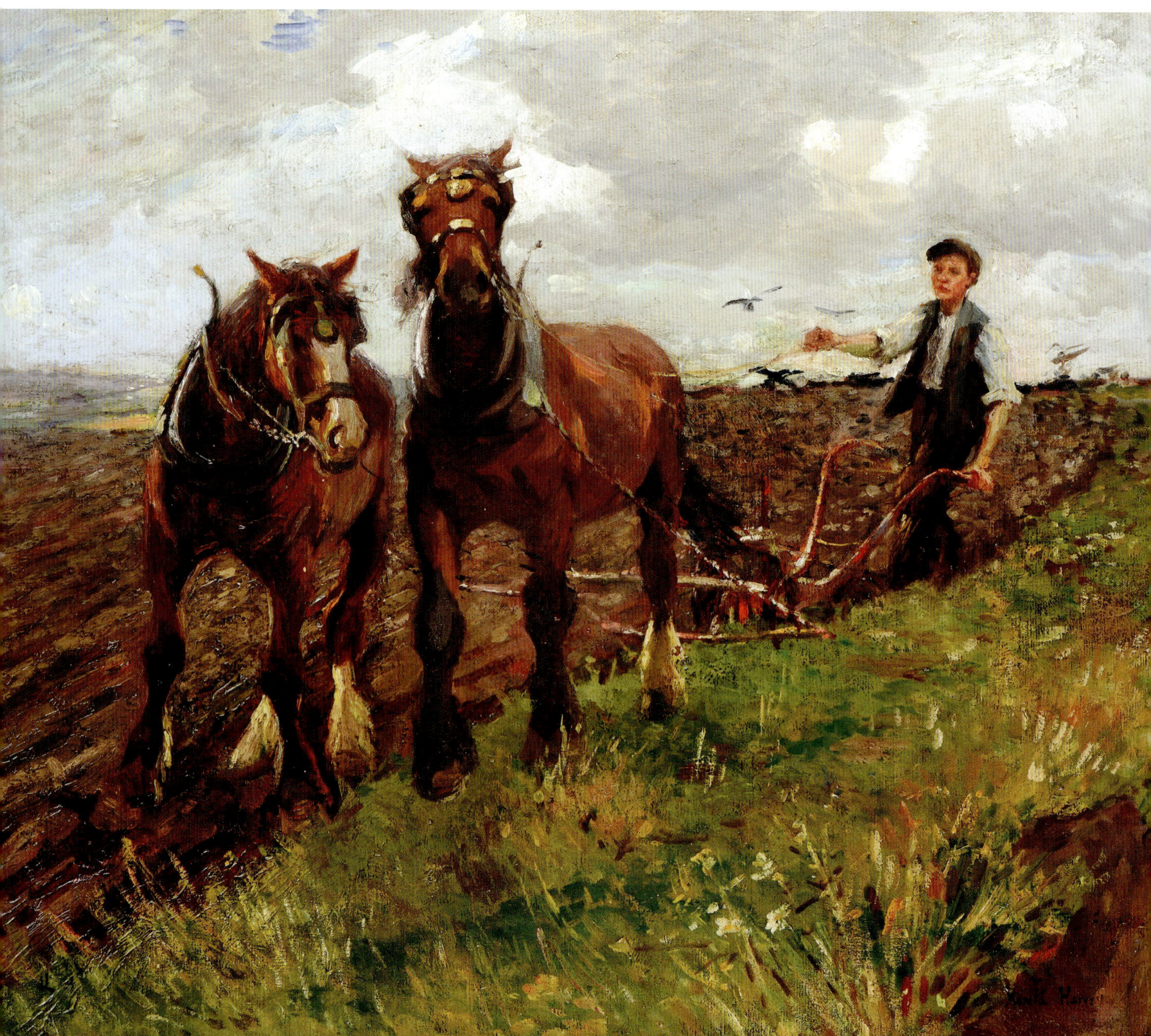

The Young Ploughman
*c.*1905 | oil on canvas | 64 x 76.5 cm
BOWERMAN CHARITABLE TRUST

trouser-pockets, pipes in mouths, who make brief quarter-deck turns. Slow of speech are these men, grave, and with eyes that seek the horizon.

Above all this life and movement rises the village, grey and for the most part of a respectable age; solid granite cottages that climb the hill in irregular streets, or lanes cobbled and resounding to the footsteps of the heavy-booted fishermen who lurch up and down to their luggers that lie in marshalled lines, each mast having a gull standing like an heraldic emblem on the summit. Women group themselves at doorsteps gossiping, holding babies or chiding children with shrill vehemence and pelting them with equally strange epithets. In amongst these simple primordial folk who get their living by catching sea creatures, there lurks that ultra-sophisticated being, the artist, who gets his by catching the catcher, immeshing his character in lines more or less cunningly set.

Meanwhile, the school set up by Stanhope and Elizabeth Forbes was attracting a great many artists of varying abilities. The school consisted of three wooden studios in the heart of Newlyn known as 'The Meadow'. The smallest hut was for beginners and the largest was for the more proficient artists, who painted and drew from clothed models. The models were mainly Newlyn people eager to earn a little extra money, and this class would have taken place outdoors in summer. The third hut was the 'life' room, where nude models (professionals brought in from London) were posed for the most experienced artists. Every Saturday during term the 'Crit' was held in one of the studios; this was a review of the work of the students, which were unsigned in order to ensure impartiality and 'the professor', Stanhope Forbes, would pronounce on the work.

The existence of the school caused the Newlyn colony to expand. Charles Simpson arrived around 1905; Laura and Harold Knight in 1907 and Ernest Procter and his later wife Doris (Dod) Shaw in the same year. Not far away, at Lamorna, worked Lamorna Birch, Robert and Eleanor Hughes, Frank and Jessica Heath, and Charles and Ella Naper. The new wave of painters were Harvey's generation. There was less than three years age difference between Harvey and the ebullient Laura Knight, both in their early thirties at the time she moved to Newlyn. This new generation came to study, inspired by plein-air virtues and influenced by Impressionist colour. Like them, Harvey would have seen the shining colours of Impressionism while studying in France. 'It was a revelation to London of a new world of colour …' wrote Frank Rutter in response to the Grafton Galleries' exhibition early in 1905 of work by Monet, Manet, Renoir, Pissarro, Degas and Cézanne; '… never before had we seen nature painted in all the prismatic radiance of summer sunshine'.

In October the same year, the Third Salon d'Automne, held at Grand Palais in Paris, showed the first large-scale display of 'Fauve' painting. The term 'fauve' (wild beasts) was used to describe the powerful colour and 'virulent imagery' of painters such as Derain, Matisse, Manguin,

Marquet, and Vlaminck. Although there had been many smaller exhibitions of their work, at this Salon they dominated the show and achieved critical recognition which was favourable despite the pejorative use of the word 'fauve'. There was a general trend towards a greater use of colour, and soon Harvey's own work began to reflect the changing styles. He had already broken with the tradition of muted colours with *The Dinner Hour*. His colours brightened generally from about 1905, as in *Newlyn Harbour* (1905); and from about 1905/1910 there is a simplification of composition. *Three Fishermen* (see p. 14), painted in 1909, illustrates both tendencies.

In 1908, Elizabeth Forbes began to edit and publish *The Paper Chase*, the journal to which the Newlyn artists contributed. Elizabeth Forbes' illness and death meant that only two editions were produced, neither of which contain works by Harvey. However, one edition contains two woodblocks by Charles Simpson – one showing a horse drinking in a pool, the other a wagon gathering seaweed – both of which have a strong sense of Harvey's composition. He might well have inspired the young Simpson who, ten years Harvey's junior, was a friend and a witness at Harvey's wedding two years later. Despite these stylistic changes, Harvey remained deeply committed to the 'plein-air' methods and his work depicts ordinary Cornish people in their environment. His truth to his subject demonstrates his understanding of that which he paints. Harvey knew well that the villagers of Newlyn were a strong lot, capable of facing the might of the English military for the right to keep their tradition; capable of sailing a 36-foot lugger to Australia (the *Mystery*, 1854), or of sailing a fishing boat up the Thames to confront the government (the *Rosebud*, 1937). Newlyn also gave birth to the famous Chartist, William Lovett.

The remoteness of the far west of Cornwall, described by some as 'Cornwall's Cornwall', fostered a close-knit community, where Cornish language, *kernewek*, had been spoken for longer than elsewhere. Harvey's background gave him an innate knowledge of what it is to be Cornish; he is not merely looking on, he has a native feeling for his subjects, a hereditary knowledge of what lies behind the eyes of his people. The emotions are not heightened for the sake of social commentary. But he wasn't a Newlyner, he was a Penzance boy, and as with all neighbouring villages, a degree of suspicion exists between the two: 'Penzance boys up in a tree, looking as wisht as wisht can be; Newlyn boys, as strong as oak, knocking them down with every stroke.'[6]

Although Harvey did not train at the Forbes' School, the social life which flourished around it encompassed the whole artistic community and he would almost certainly have been part of it. Musical evenings were held at the Forbes' home at Higher Faugan where 'the professor' would entertain his audience with his cello. Concerts were also held elsewhere; in particular by Charles Simpson who formed a Beethoven Society. There were also the 'drencies', fancy-dress dances organised by the students in the school studios. Phyllis Gotch, daughter of

6. Simon Parker, *A Star on the Mizzen: The story of the 1896 Newlyn fishing riots* (Liskeard: Giss'on Books).

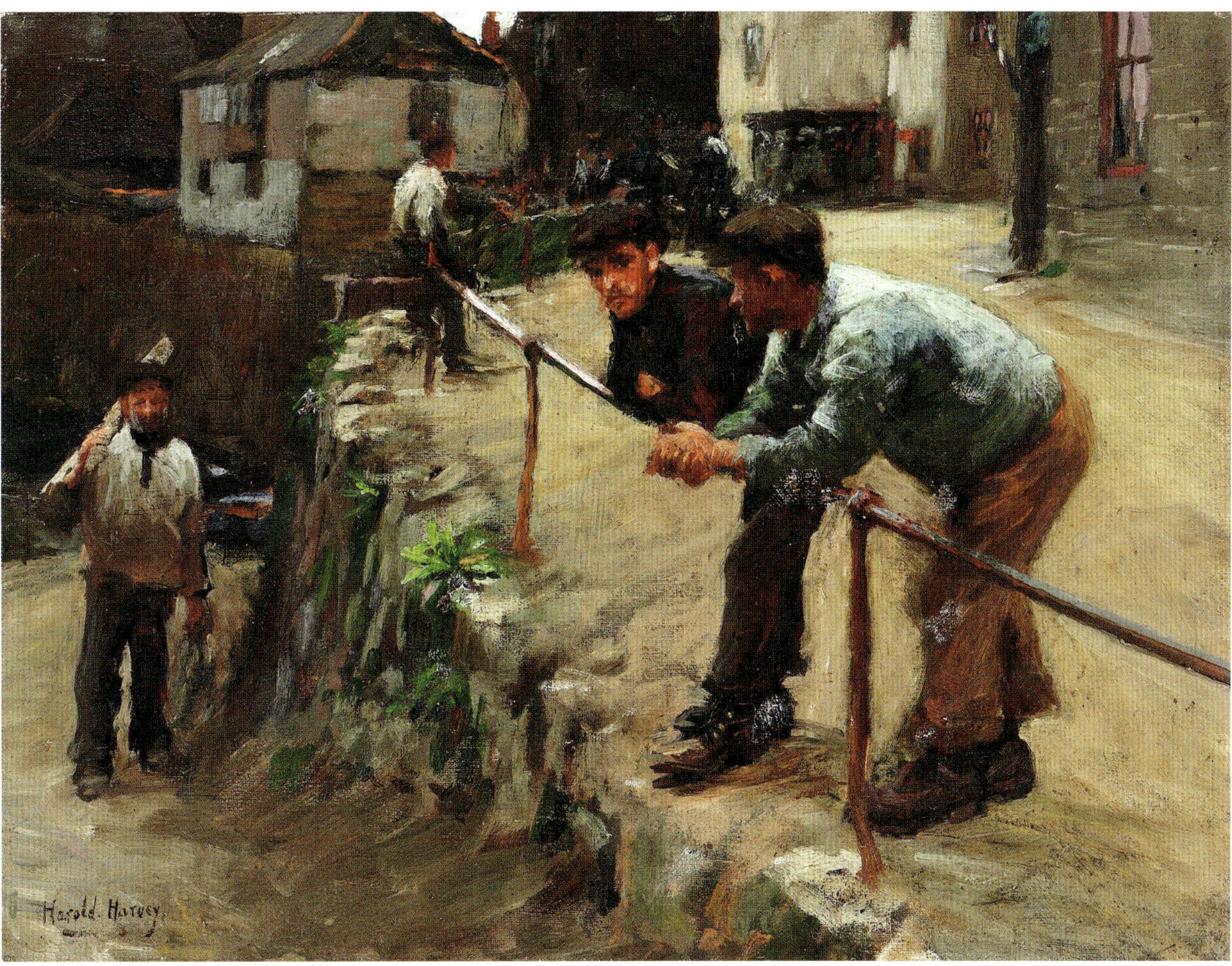

Figures on The Cliff
oil on canvas | 30.5 x 40.5 cm
CHRISTIE'S

Caroline and Thomas Cooper Gotch had a passion for parties and dances, which were frequently held at 'Wheal Betsy', the home of her parents. One such 'beano' was described by 'Fryniwed' Tennyson Jesse as 'a sort of Baccanalian orgy' at the end of which the Knights had quite a fling, 'Little Mrs Knight had been the wildest of the wild, dancing with hair streaming and ragged skirts a-whirling – even Harold [Knight] had been seen dancing and kicking with a broomstick in one hand and the other round Boto's waist …'[7] There were also picnics at Lamorna. It is not surprising that countless romances blossomed amongst the students, many of whom met their future spouses. Being a Cornishman from an area which still had a strong Methodist tradition, Harold would have felt something of an outsider at these gatherings. No wonder that one gets the impression of one who watched the 'gypsy beanos' from the wings.

7. Fryniwed Tennyson Jesse, in her intermittent diary (private collection).

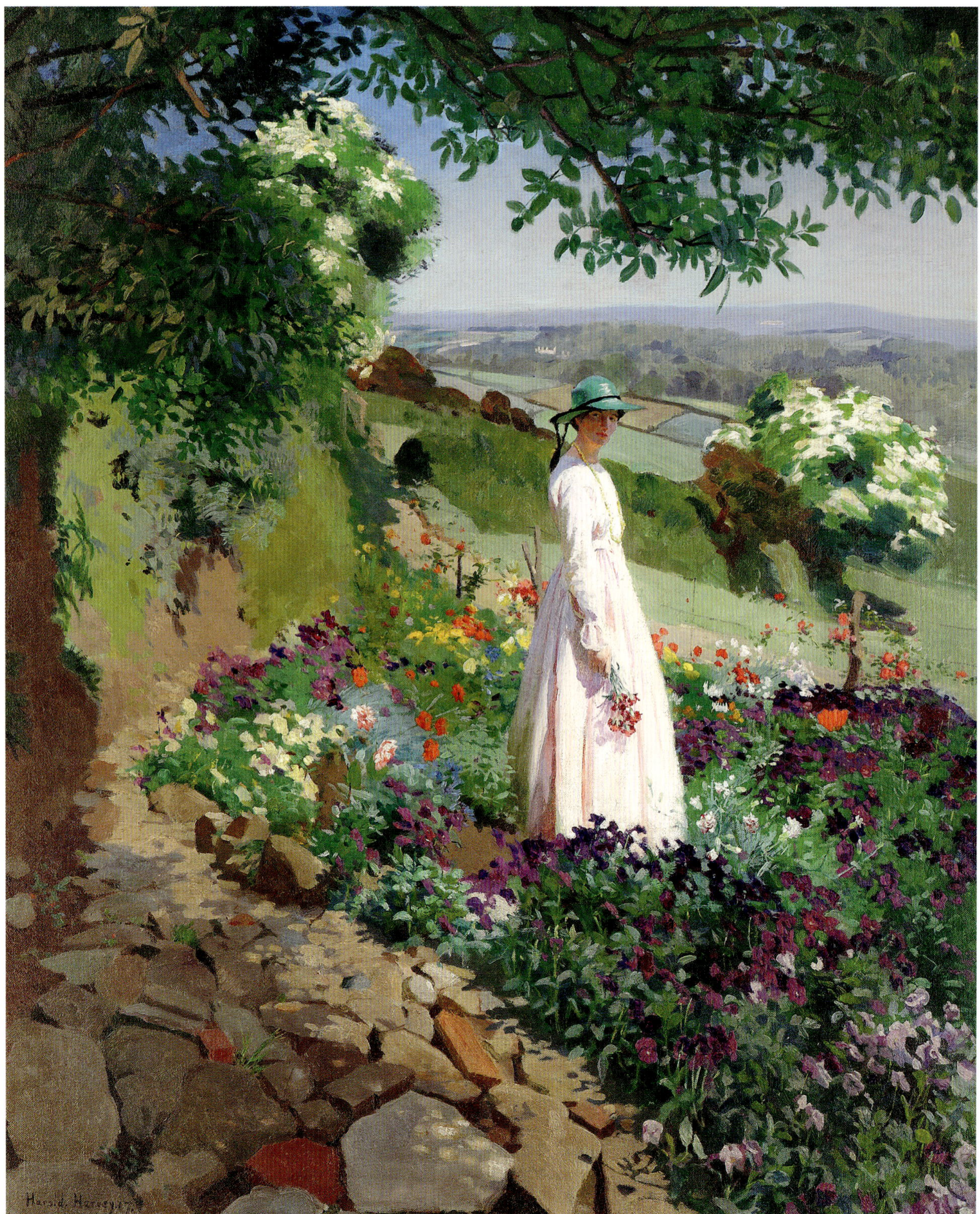

Summer
1917 | oil on canvas | 92 x 77 cm
CHRISTIE'S

Four

Life with Gertrude

Among the crowds at social gatherings, possibly at one
of Charles Simpson's evenings of fine violin playing,[1] was
a young Cornishwoman by the name of Gertrude Bodinnar,
who also occasionally modelled for the artists. How and when she and
Harold met is not recorded, but the two were to marry in 1911, main-
taining a close and loving marriage for thirty years until Harold's death.

Gertrude was born on 27th November 1879 at Pembroke Lodge in
the parish of Newlyn. Her father was John Mathews Bodinnar, a
cooper born in 1838 in the parish of Paul, and her mother Ann was
also born in Paul. She was the eighth of ten children[2] and the family
lived in the heart of Newlyn at 49 Trewarveneth Street. One of those
who almost certainly used Gertrude as a model was Laura Knight,
although only one undated pencil sketch is positively identified to
date. Harold Harvey is also thought to have used her as a model on
a number of occasions before their marriage, the earliest recorded work
being *Portrait of Gertrude Bodinnar*, painted shortly before the couple
married. The wedding was held at St Peter's Church, Newlyn on 19th
April 1911; Harvey was thirty-six and Gertrude thirty-one. The wit-
nesses were Gertrude's sister Sophie and Harold's friend, the Newlyn
artist Charles Walter Simpson (1885–1971). A year after the wedding,
in 1912, Harold's mother died, at the age of 65.

Gertrude and Harold Harvey set up home at Maen Cottage, Newlyn.
The cottage (actually a right-hand semi-detached two-storey house)
stands above Elms Close Terrace, approached from a turning halfway up Chywoone Hill. The house is high above the rest of the
village, bordering then on open countryside, and has a magnificent
view of Newlyn Harbour, Mount's Bay and Penzance. A narrow porch
leads to an entrance hall, from which open on the left the front sitting-
room, the dining-room behind it, and the kitchen at the back. On the
right, stairs lead up to the front and back bedrooms, a box room and
a bathroom. Many features remain as they are shown in Harvey's
paintings – the brass door plates, mantelpieces, cupboards beside

the fireplace, skirting boards, the kitchen dresser. The chair rail which appears in some paintings has gone, as have the doors to the pantry.

The gardens slope away to the front and rear of the house, stone steps lead up to a path to Tredavoe at the rear. Gertrude was proud of her house and garden, and Harold's own love for his home is evident in his paintings. Members of the family remember a warm welcome for visitors at Maen Cottage. Harold's niece, Rhoda, frequently stayed with the couple as a young girl and she remembered Gertrude spending long hours in her beloved garden while Harold was ensconced in his studio. Gertrude's love of plants may well have come from her grandfather William Curnow. Born 1809 in Madron, a few miles outside Penzance, he had had a market garden of eleven acres and employed two labourers.[3] He had considerable status as a botanist, writing papers on hepaticas and mosses, and was elected an honorary member of the Penzance Natural History and Antiquarian Society.[4] Some of his letters and plants are in the Natural History Museum in London. As well as painting from the house, Harvey obtained a studio at 'Rosevean' in Tredavoe Lane. The couple were not particularly well off, and there is nothing to indicate that he had any income other than that earned by painting.

In 1910 Harvey had been entrusted, with Norman Garstin and Henry Rheam, to hang the Autumn exhibition at the Newlyn Gallery and he was elected to the committee on 7th April 1911. Harvey, Langley and Simpson hung the Autumn 1911 show, and Gotch, Laura Knight and Harvey hung the 1912 show of work going to the Royal Academy. He retired from the committee on 6th June 1914 (as did Garstin), but remained a member of the Newlyn Society of Artists for some years. In the 1911 Passmore Edwards Art Gallery Annual Exhibition of Works for the Royal Academy, he attracted a mention in the *Art News* of 15th April which said: 'Harold Harvey exhibited an excellent study of *Morning Sunshine*'. Colwyn Edward Vulliamy (1886–1971), whose autobiography *Calico Pie* depicts his life while studying at the Forbes' school, counted the Harveys, Procters and Charles Simpson as his particular friends during his three year stay in Newlyn. The lithographer Geoffrey Sneyd Garnier and his wife Jill were also friends of the Harveys. They would work, walk and meet at The Wink in Lamorna for a smoke and a game of euchre.

For all the artists, life changed dramatically during the First World War, not least because it became unpatriotic to paint the landscape.[5] In 1915 restrictions were put on painting any part of the coastline; even to draw the straight line of the horizon could be interpreted as a sinister act. Everyone was suspected as a spy and outdoor sketching was forbidden. In his autobiography, *Twenty Years at St Hilary*, Rev. Bernard Walke wrote that at the time '… nothing was too impossible to be believed: the ringing of bells from the church tower was held by some to be a method of signalling to the Germans; to be seen often on

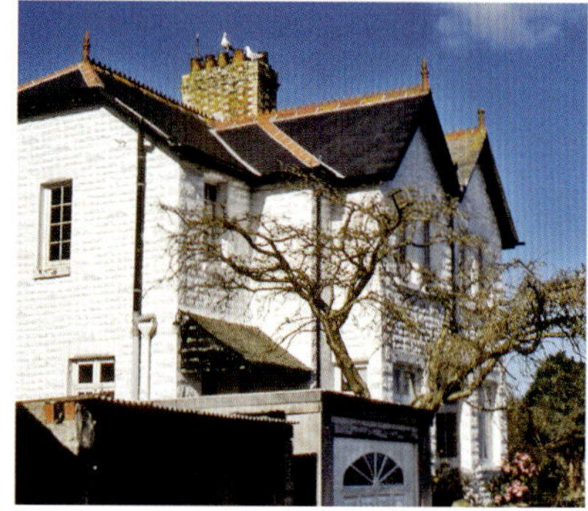

Maen Cottage and (below) the view from there to St Michael's Mount, the setting for *The Blue Door* (see p. 21)

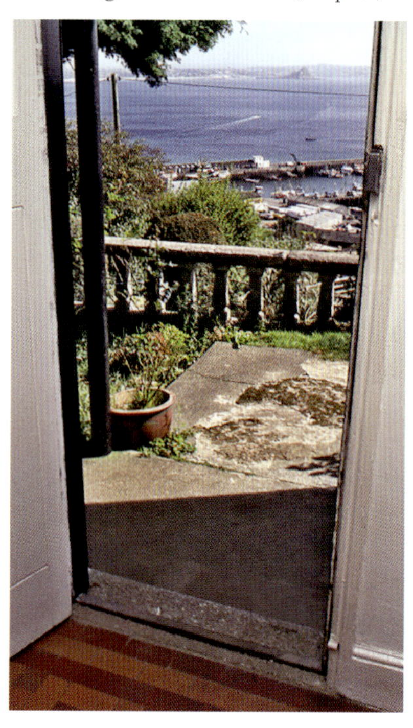

3. Recorded in the 1881 census.
4. An entry is devoted to him in *Dictionary of British and Irish Botanists and Horticulturalists* (1994) by Ray Desmond, and F.H. Davey's *The Flora of Cornwall* (1909) has another.
5. Penzance became an auxiliary naval base in August 1914 and 'Defence of the Realm Regulations' prohibited sketching or painting within sight of the coast.

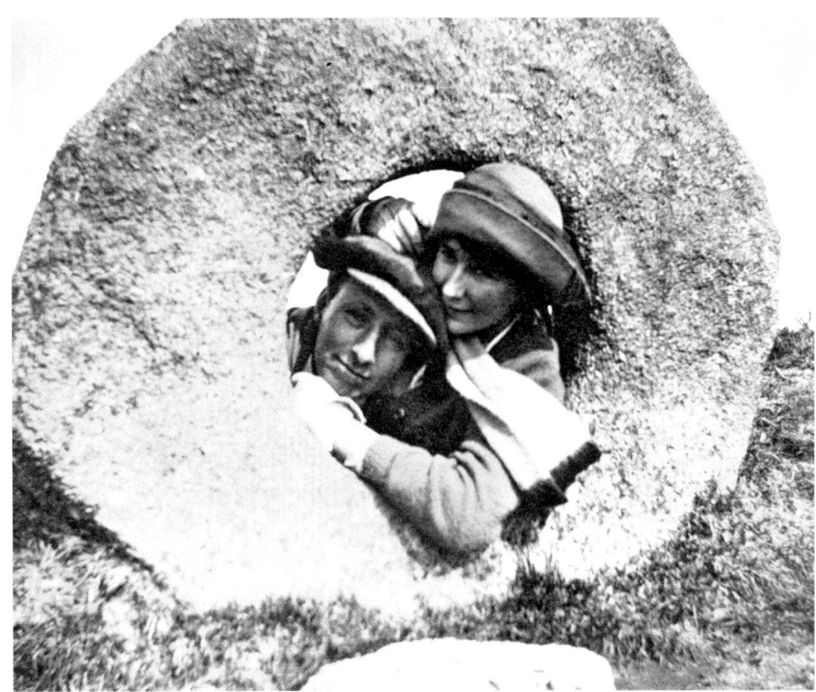

Harold and Gertrude at Men-an-Tol
PRIVATE COLLECTION

the cliffs was taken as proof of being engaged in supplying petrol to enemy submarines.'[6] He also recounts his visit to Corpus Christi Fair in Penzance with Laura Knight, where 'I kept a lookout for the police while Laura made sketches in a note-book.' The vicar and the artist flagrantly broke the law. Despite prohibition, Laura Knight crouched among the brambles and gorse behind her Lamorna studio to make quick sketches – had she been seen by a coast-watcher she could have been imprisoned.[7]

The less flamboyant Harvey turned indoors and concentrated on a new phase of work, regarded by many as his best. *Winding Wool* (1914) is the first picture in which we see signs of a style and subject to which Harvey returned frequently. It is an interior scene from Maen Cottage; the room is distinguished by a chair rail which runs right across the composition. It features two girls, one sitting rolling a ball of wool from a skein held by a standing girl. The standing girl, who has very long plaits, may be Mornie, daughter of the artist S.J. 'Lamorna' Birch, who was a popular model with many artists (including Laura Knight and Augustus John). Harvey also produced *Woman Reading* in the same year, which features Gertrude seated in the front room in a large armchair.

Harvey's friend Harold Knight had studied the Vermeers in the Rijksmuseum in Amsterdam and had been painting interiors since *A Cup Of Tea* in 1905. Both artists produced a work entitled *In The Studio* – Harvey in 1918, and Knight in 1920/21 and it is clear that the two friends were in tune with each other's ideas. Another influence

6. Bernard Walke, *Twenty Years at St Hilary* (London: Methuen, 1935; repub. London: Anthony Mott, 1982) p. 83.
7. Tom Cross, *The Shining Sands: Artists in Newlyn and St Ives 1880–1930* (Devon: Westcountry Books, 1994).

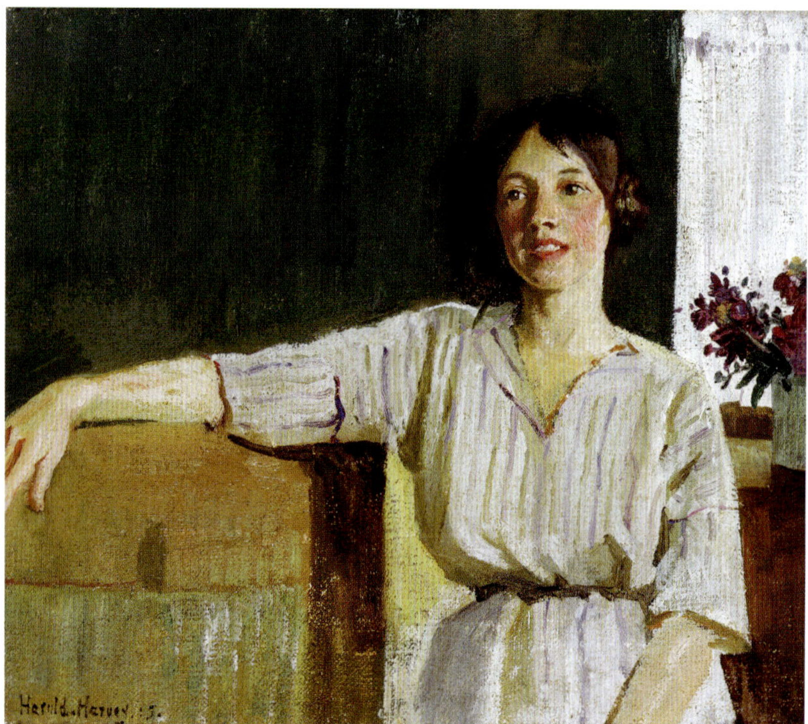

The Artist's Model, Newlyn
1915 | oil on canvas | 31 x 36 cm
NATIONAL MUSEUMS AND GALLERIES OF WALES

at this time was Ernest Procter. In any community of artists it is
inevitable that there will be a degree of cross-reference and shared
inspiration. The Harveys and Knights had become close friends. In
the summers leading up to the First World War, the Harveys joined
the Knights and Charles and Ella Naper on month-long painting trips
to Dozmary Pool on Bodmin Moor. Harold and Laura Knight would
heap their car with all the necessary equipment for camping out at
a hut the Napers owned there, and which Charles had built.

In *Oil Paint and Grease Paint*, Laura Knight describes one such
expedition, in 1914: 'Our "Belsize" was drawn up at our gate. On
the running boards, mattresses and bedding were rolled and roped,
kettles, saucepans and frying-pans hung all round; in the dickey-seat
sat Charles Naper, wrapped round with an old red eiderdown.' On
the way, they stopped at Truro to buy groceries, where Ella Naper
impressed the flighty Laura Knight by 'miraculously' managing to
calculate precisely how much tea, rice, flour and sugar was required
for the duration of their stay, and ensuring that essentials such as
matches were not overlooked. Laura, meanwhile, shopped for less
essential items, trying to distract herself from the horrors of the
previous weeks, during which the inquest had been held into the
suicide of Florence Munnings, wife of the artist Alfred Munnings.
'In a shop I found a blazer striped like the rainbow, which Gert
Harvey christened my suit of mourning, for although I bought
the gay thing, I could not stop weeping.'

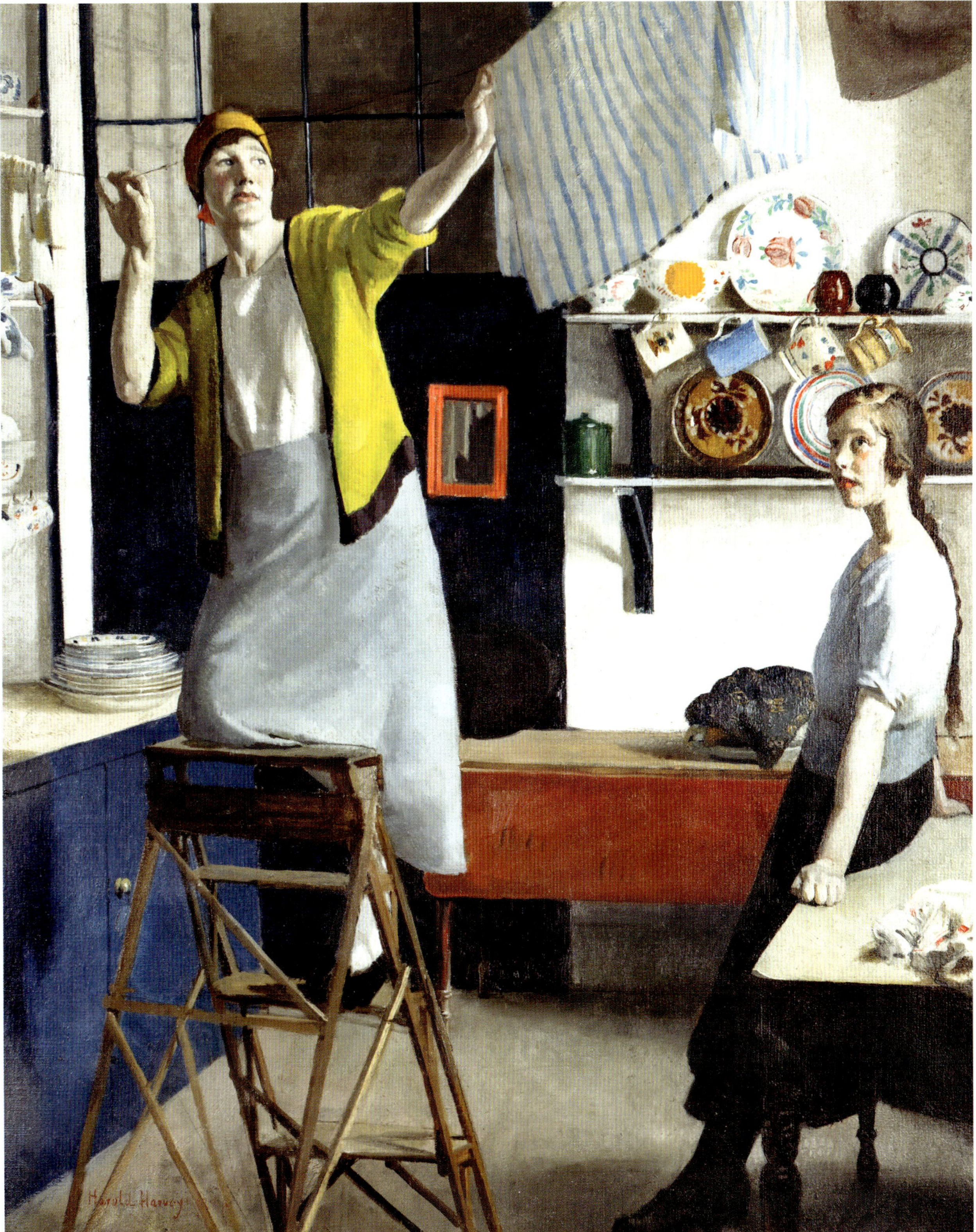

On the Line
1922 | oil on canvas | 69 x 57 cm
BRIGHTON & HOVE MUSEUMS

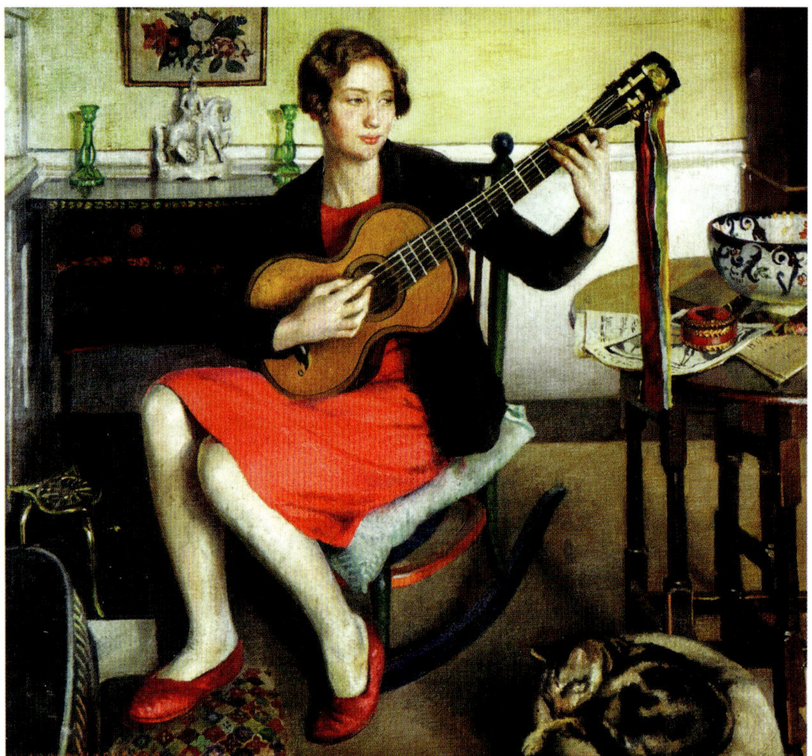

The Spanish Guitar
1928 | oil on canvas | 52 x 62 cm
PRIVATE COLLECTION

Once at Dozmary Pool, the Napers created an 'open house' for the group at their hut, although only they slept in the hut itself, in a bed stretched across the whole of one end. Harold and Laura slept in a low tent outside, until it was blown away in a gale one night. Gertrude and Harold Harvey slept at the farm close by, where they burnt nothing but peat in the open fire, that Laura noted 'flavoured deliciously our home-made bread and scalded cream'. The whole group would crowd into the small hut for meals, filling every inch of space, and they used a nearby stream for washing. The three women clearly enjoyed the freedom away from the prying eyes of Newlyn society. Laura wrote: 'The moor was glorious up at Dozmary … We worked and tramped miles over the moorland. One hot afternoon, Gert, Ella and I found ourselves in a wood where Pan might have lived and nymphs danced … a thick carpet of emerald moss, bright red pine needles – the sumptuously marked grass snake slithering through – the River Fowey, peat-stained water – we stripped and went into the pool naked. I shall never forget seeing my two companions in such a setting; one black, pearly of skin, the other dusky with straight black hair …' For the several weeks they stayed at Dozmary, they were a complete community, away from all outside contact. The news of the day did not reach them and it was only while the Harveys, Knights and Napers motored back into the world that the imminence of war came to their notice. At Plymouth, while crossing on the ferry, Laura Knight recalled hearing the statement: 'If Russia chips in, France chips in; if France chips in,

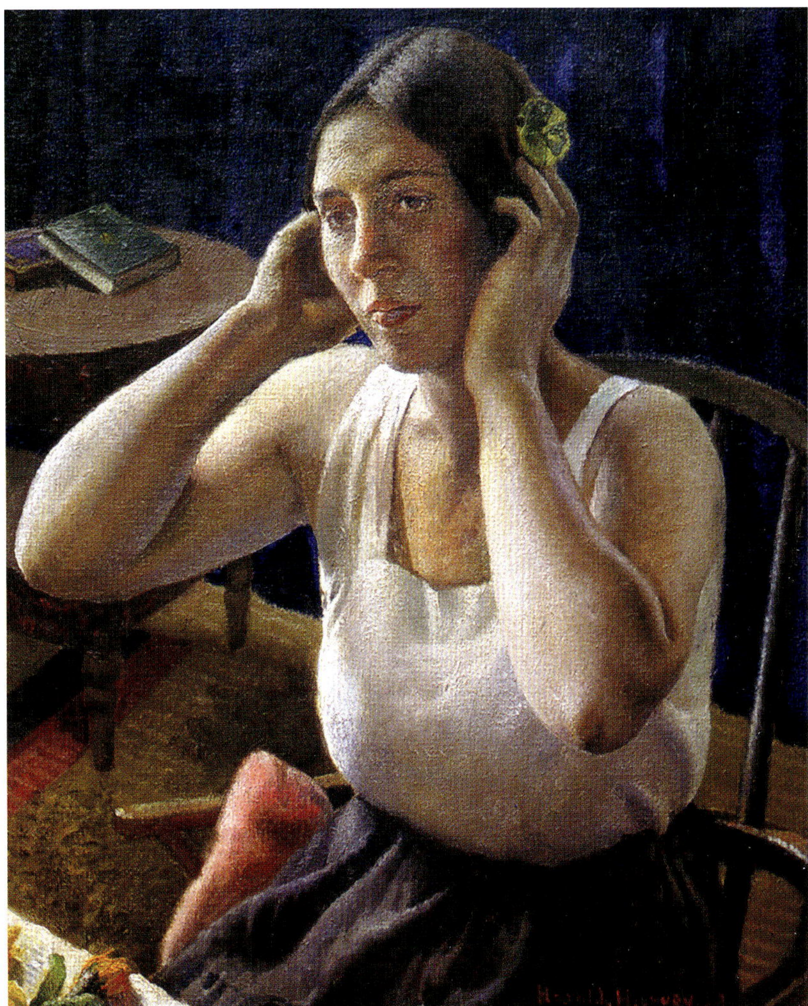

The Dressing Table
1929 | oil on canvas | 65 x 56 cm
PRIVATE COLLECTION

we chip in …'. Having first heard about the outbreak of war together, the Harveys and the Knights also spent Armistice Day 1918 together. Laura wrote: 'We went to Newlyn and stayed the night at Harold Harvey's to join in the celebrations and see the fireworks from the vessels in Mount's Bay.'

The war inevitably fractured the old patterns of life. Vulliamy joined the army at the fifth attempt and served in France, Greece and Turkey. Frank Heath joined the Royal Fusiliers 2nd Sportsmen's Battalion, and Munnings – after being rejected three times because of a blind eye – found work at a horse's remount depot and then as a war artist with the Canadian Cavalry Brigade. Ernest Procter, a conscientious objector, served with the Friends' Ambulance Unit from mid–1916 until early 1919. He was made a war artist in November 1918. Geoffrey Garnier entered the army, was discharged for medical reasons, and joined the Royal Navy. Harold Knight was conscripted in 1916, declared himself a conscientious objector and was put to work on the land. It is not

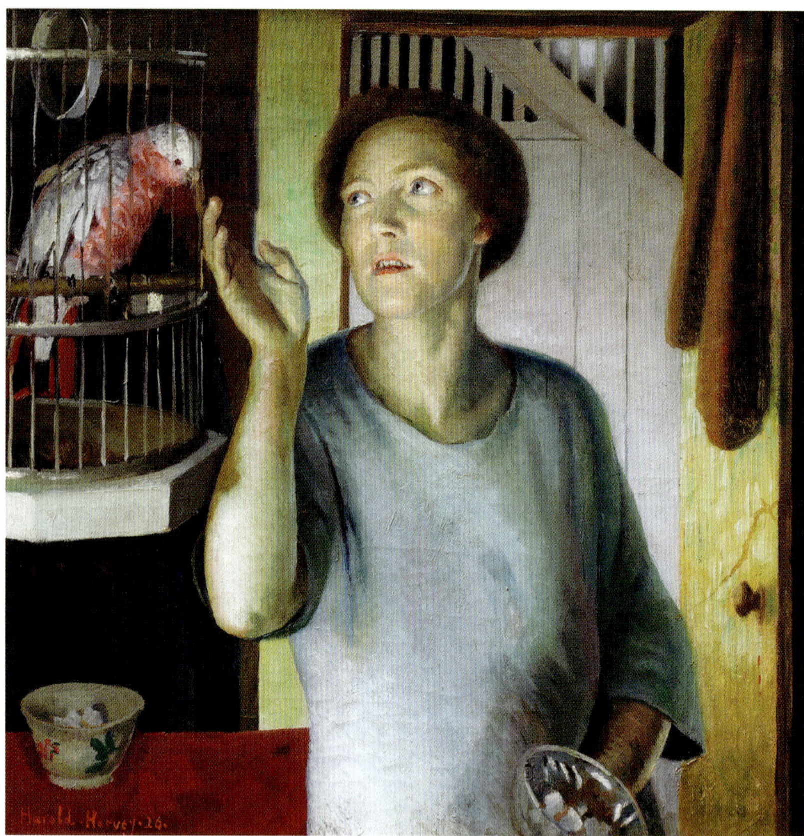

Gertrude Harvey with a Parrot
1916 | oil on canvas | 46 x 46 cm
BONHAMS

known whether Harvey was exempted from service, as he was 40 in
1914; he does not seem to have joined the forces, but neither does he
seem to have been a conscientious objector. The war had little direct
impact on his work. Although Cornwall had many hospitals and
convalescent homes, these are not among his subjects. In *Laura
and Paul Jewill Hill* (1916; see p. 17), Paul holds an Italian flag, said
to commemorate Italy's joining the Allies on 23rd May 1915. More
interesting is the fact that there is a self-portrait of Harvey in the
circular wall mirror. There are comparatively few paintings dated to
1915; this was the year Harvey's father died, at the age of 72. Francis
Harvey's death was sudden, occurring while out walking at Chûn
Castle; his body was carried back down the hill from the Iron Age
fort on a farm gate. After his death, the house at Trewartha Terrace
was bought by Harold's brother, Arthur William Hext Harvey.

Gertrude featured often in the interiors. *Reflections* (1916) shows
her at her bedroom dressing table examining her face with a hand-
held mirror; *Portrait of the Artist's Wife* (1916) shows her in her deck-
chair; *Gertrude Harvey with a Parrot* (1916); *Woman By The Sideboard*
(1917); *Lunch* (1918) and *Summer* (1917; see p. 52), are also Gertrude.
Sometimes she is solitary, as in *The Ribbon Skirt* (*c.*1918); sometimes
with a companion or two, *In The Kitchen* (1918).

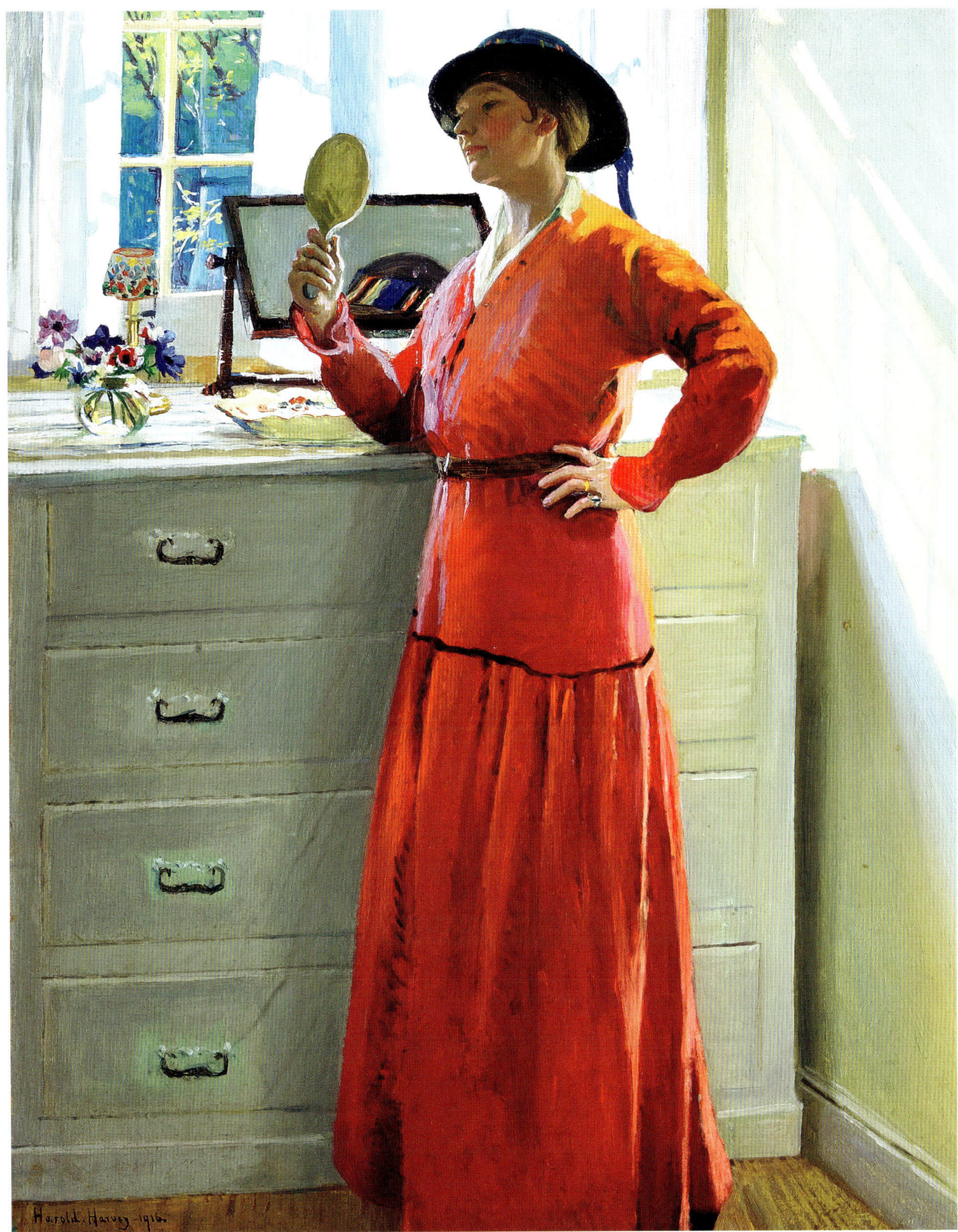

Reflections
1916 | oil on canvas | 49 x 45.5 cm
CYFARTHFA CASTLE MUSEUM AND GALLERY

He experiments with use of strong design, emphasis of verticals and horizontals in fabric patterns; and colour, use of a coloured neck scarf, orange headscarf or deep pink cardigan. *An Interior* and *Coloured Wools*, both 1919, feature a carpet which resembles those made by Roger Fry's Omega Workshop.[8] The same, or very similar carpet, appears in *The Critics* (1922; see p. 93).

1920 saw two of his most imaginative compositions to date. *At the Dressing Table* reveals a back view of Gertrude in her chemise, placed alongside a dressing table. Behind her lies a plain wall, which is strongly shadowed by the window in a diagonal pattern. The table is embellished with a cloth runner in multi-coloured stripes, which make a forceful diagonal to confront the shadows – the runner provides nearly all the colour in the painting. The geometry and colour make a remarkable image. The second work, *The Pier Glass*, contains a gilt and marble console table surmounted by a gilt-framed mirror reaching to the upper edge of the canvas. On the table stands a crystal chandelier, the mirror glass reflects the chandelier and also a female figure standing by the ornate mantelpiece, above which is a painting in a deep frame. The reflection also shows a spray of pink flowers, the tips of the real flowers just visible at the edge of the canvas; over half the canvas represents bare wall and only the central portion forms colour and incident. The subject and simplicity of treatment are similar to Dod Procter's *Venetian Mirror*, which is undated but would have been painted in the 1920s. Also in 1920, Harvey painted some urban scenes: *Market Day* in Penzance and several views of Mousehole as well as *Leswidden Pit* (1920 or '24; p. 64) one of his earliest treatments of local industry.

As well as Gertrude, Harvey used a variety of local girls as models. Gertrude must have played some part in negotiating with the mothers of these sitters, who were usually in their early teens, and it was she who smiled and greeted them on their way to her husband's studio, and who pushed half a crown into their hands on their way back.[9] Harvey worked with one model at a time, so that Kitty Batten, who posed for *The Blue Door, Newlyn* (1934; see p. 21) never met Arthur Chiffers, the model who posed for the accordion player with whom she appears, having done her sittings for Harvey in the mornings, while he posed in the afternoons.

He also frequently completed the backgrounds of his paintings in separate sessions; *Girl on a Cliff* (1926; p. 65) for example, was not painted 'on the spot' at Porthcurno, but instead the model, Cressida Wearne, was painted in her backyard sitting on an oil drum; the sea and Logan Rock were painted in afterwards. Amy Harvey's (no relation) recollection of sitting for Harvey in 1928, when she was thirteen, gives some insight into his working methods:

> There was me, and another girl, Mary Kelynack, used to model. Used to paint in the studio and outside … a big studio … everything was tidy and Mr Harvey was always polite. Nice man, but they were loners, him and his wife, kept theirselves to theirselves … He didn't say much, didn't

8. Roger Fry's Omega Workshops: a consortium of artists making fabric and furnishings in modern designs which Fry opened at Fitzroy Square, London in 1913. Harvey's friend, Gladys Hynes worked there.
9. As remembered by Amy Harvey (no relation) who sat for Harvey.

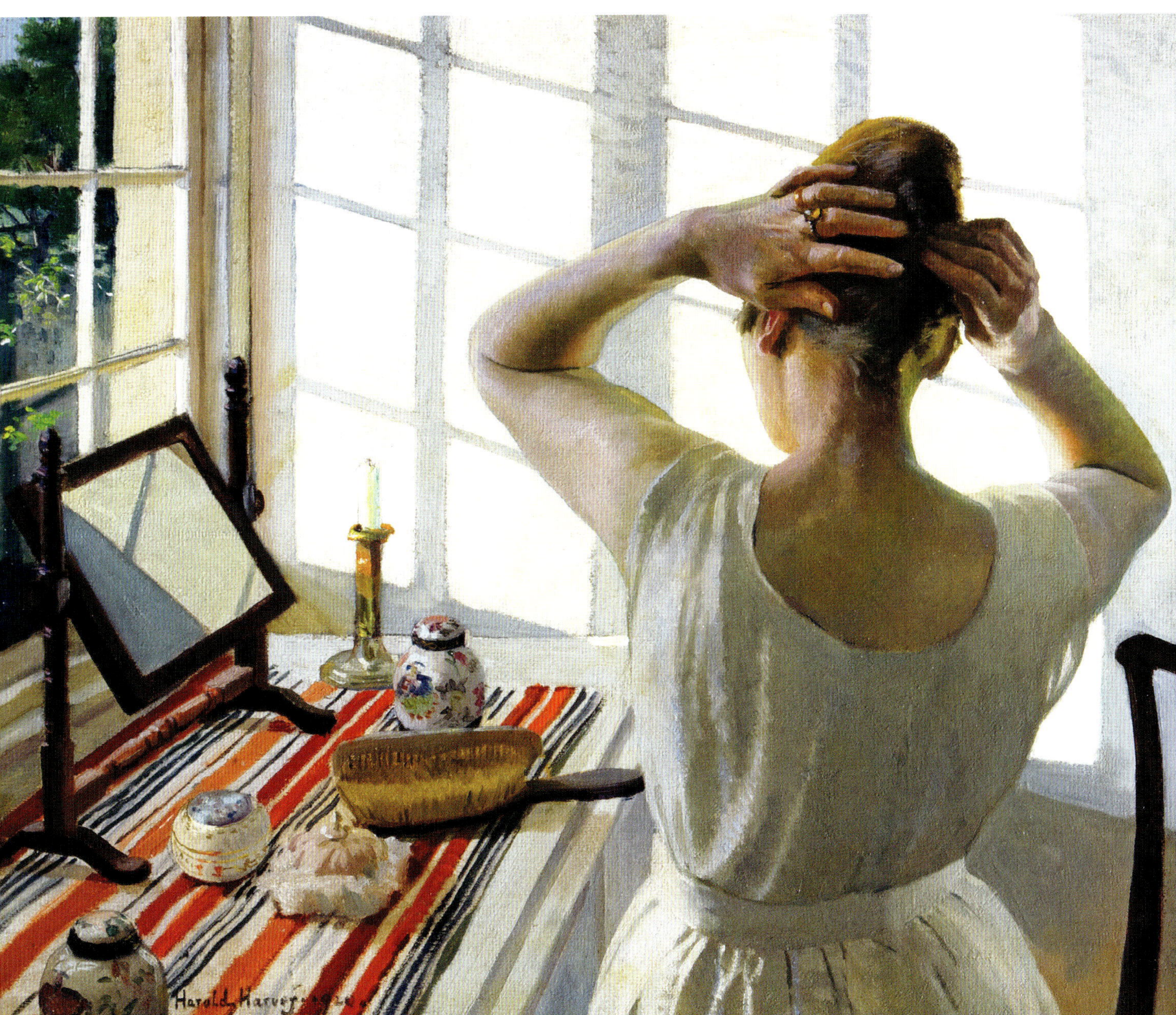

At the Dressing Table
1920 | oil on canvas | 39 x 55 cm
CYFARTHFA CASTLE MUSEUM AND GALLERY

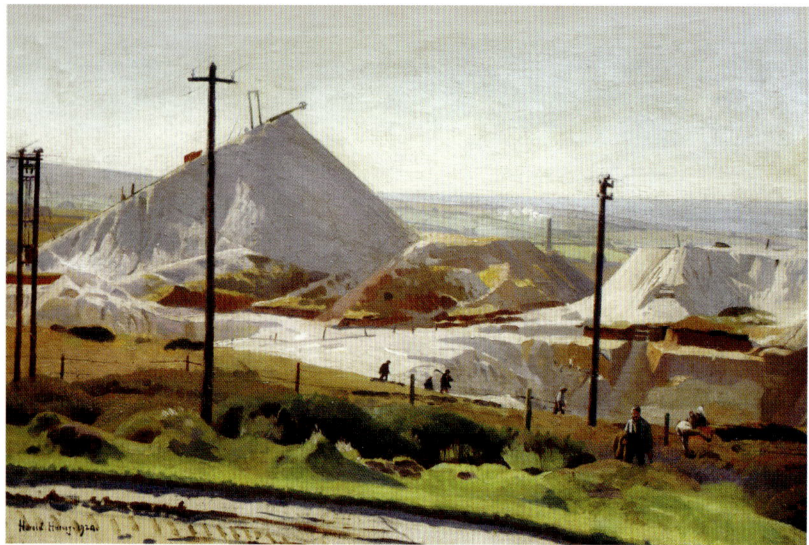

Leswidden Pit
1920 or '24 | oil on canvas | 51 x 76 cm
ROYAL INSTITUTION OF CORNWALL, ROYAL CORNWALL MUSEUM, TRURO

talk while he painted … Mrs Harvey used to say hello. Used to model
in the school holidays and Saturday mornings … give me half a crown
… Mrs Harvey used to pay … He had this motorbike and sidecar and
he used to collect me … well, Paul Hill, half way up and 'bang, bang,
bang' – frightened me to death going up that hill in that old sidecar.
Then we'd go to the studio, had to sit for hours … had a break an' that
… but it seemed like a long time, to keep still … I remember one time,
this bouquet, big bowl of flowers on a table and petals dripping off, one
fell on my hand … big round polished table, shining, and the smell of
paint an' the reflection, the reflection of the flowers all in this table …
I fainted … only thirteen … got a scar on my chin from that table …
Poor Mr Harvey, had to pick me up an' take me back home to Mother,
in that old sidecar. 'Bloody girl weighs a ton, couldn't get her off the
floor,' he said … I went up again … sitting down next time … The
painting was in the Art Gallery an' Mother an' Dad were anxious to
see it – I had long pigtails … then I think it got bought, private … don't
know what happened to it … place burned down, I think, old thatched
cottage it was, painting went up with it … but I still got that scar.[10]

Throughout this time, Gertrude herself was also painting. There are
no reproductions of her landscapes, but titles such as *Brown Willy* and
Saltash appear in the list of 25 pictures exhibited at Leicester Galleries,
London in 1918. Gertrude shared this exhibition with her husband,
who showed 27 works. Gertrude is not mentioned in a review of the
exhibition in the *Morning Post*, but Harold's work receives favourable
comment:

Going in from the unusually gloomy street one was exhilarated by the
sudden and varied brilliance of colour. Mr Harvey is to some extent a
'one man orchestra' … but [his] orchestration is so cleverly consistent,

10. 'Amy' Harvey, Mrs Emma Becket.

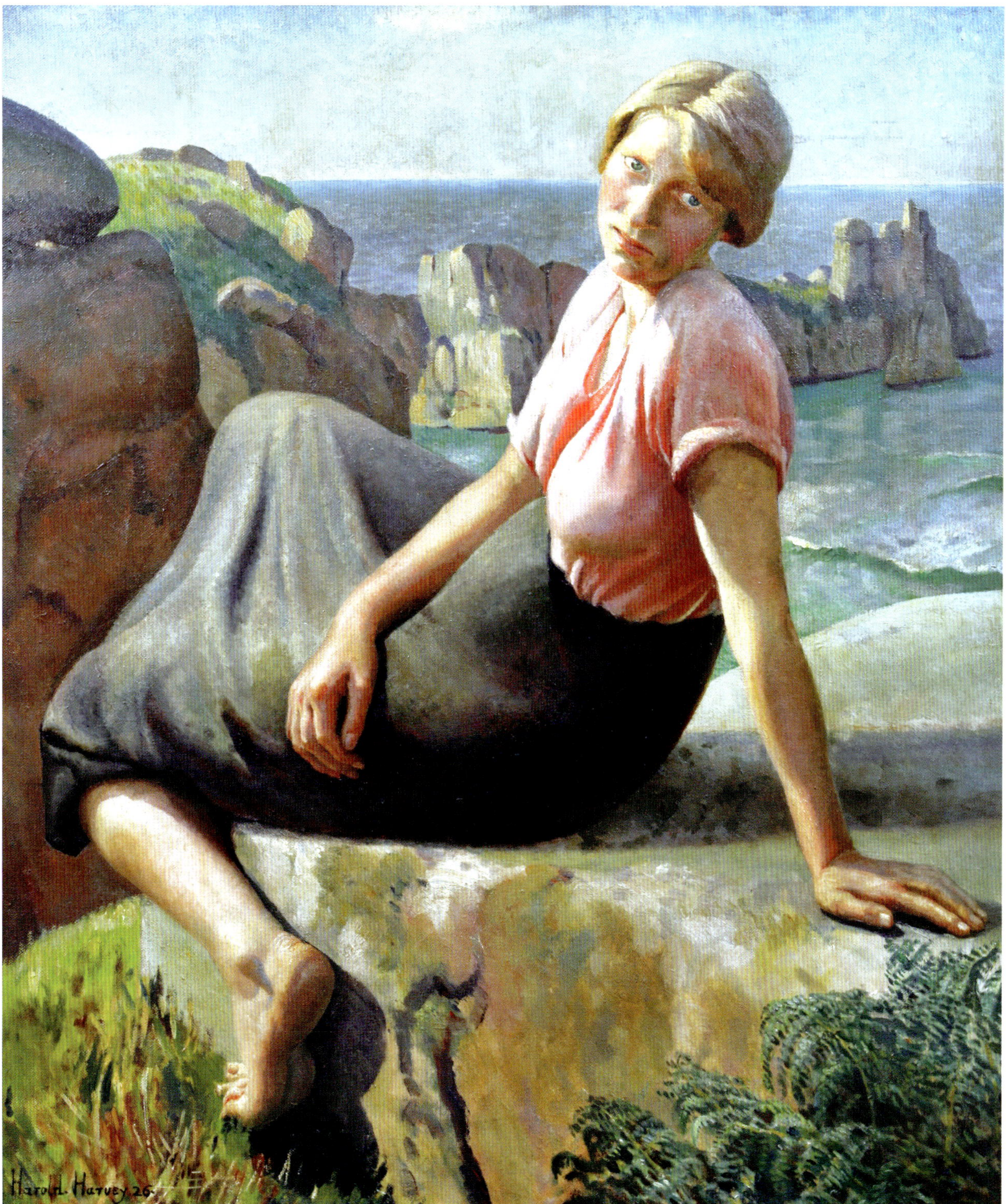

Girl on a Cliff
1926 | oil on canvas | 101.5 x 89 cm
PENLEE HOUSE GALLERY & MUSEUM

his method of expression so clean and joyous, that his performance as a whole is welcome … Greatly influenced by Mrs Laura Knight, Mr Harvey is inclined to over-emphasise the cymbal-notes, as, for example, in *Foxgloves, Lunch* and *On The Cliff*. Another fault is lack of atmospheric relation between figures and landscape. This effect is unpleasantly evident in *Early Spring*. The beautiful landscape blithely visualised and finely painted, and the women (sic) and child are pre-Raphaelite in elaboration. But there is no pictorial affinity between the figures and their setting. The landscape is harmonised by sun-warmed air, whereas the figures smack of studio artifice. The least pretentious but most perfect and charming painting is *Back Gardens, Spring*. Here vision, feeling and craft combine happily and make a picture of abiding truth …'[11]

The financial success of the exhibition for Harold was indicated by the *Morning Post*'s observation of 'numerous red stars testifying to public appreciation of his efforts'.

The Flower Painter (1930) is apparently the only depiction by Harold Harvey of Gertrude in her role as artist. Gertrude, shown so often by her husband in traditional domestic situations, and who created and cared for a wonderful garden, was a notable artist in her own right. 'She paints out of her head' was the subtitle in an undated newspaper article from the late 1930s:

> She has had no art training, unless the interest she takes in her husband's work can be accounted as training. Gertrude Harvey does not talk of technique, she has not drawn from the life; and yet from her brush there come the drenching skies, soggy moors,[12] flower pieces that hold the essence of growth, and decorative pictures that fire one's imagination. 'I remember as a child,' said Mrs Harvey, 'getting up very early one morning thinking I would paint a special mug that had buttercups on it. I don't remember if I ever did so. Sometimes I used to act as a model to the painters when I was a girl, and this fascinated me.'

Gertrude is mainly remembered for her depictions of flowers; the twenty works shown at the Royal Academy from 1930 to 1949 were all flowers or still-lifes, and it was these which formed the public perception of her as a flower painter. Only a dozen or so of over 100 paintings identified in exhibition catalogues and reviews have come into the public domain, which makes it difficult to assess her as an artist in her own right.

In her early days she showed at the Passmore Edwards Art Gallery and the sales book records the sale of 'several sketches' in September 1913 for 10 guineas. Another early exhibit, *A Cornish Landscape* (1915 at Liverpool) was priced at £10. She had a joint exhibition with Harold Harvey at the Leicester Galleries in 1918; *The Bodmin Moors, Brown Willy* and *Saltash* were listed as among the twenty five works shown. 'The landscapes of Mrs Harvey have less of this enduring quality, due

11. In 1918, Leicester Galleries had also shown Laura Knight, Paul Nash, Eric Kennington, and a memorial show for Henri Gaudier-Brzeska. The Galleries' director, Oliver Brown, took an enlightened view of modern trends, and in 1919 mounted a substantial exhibition of Matisse.
12. A reference to *Brown Willy* and *Saltash* shown at Leicester Galleries 1918.

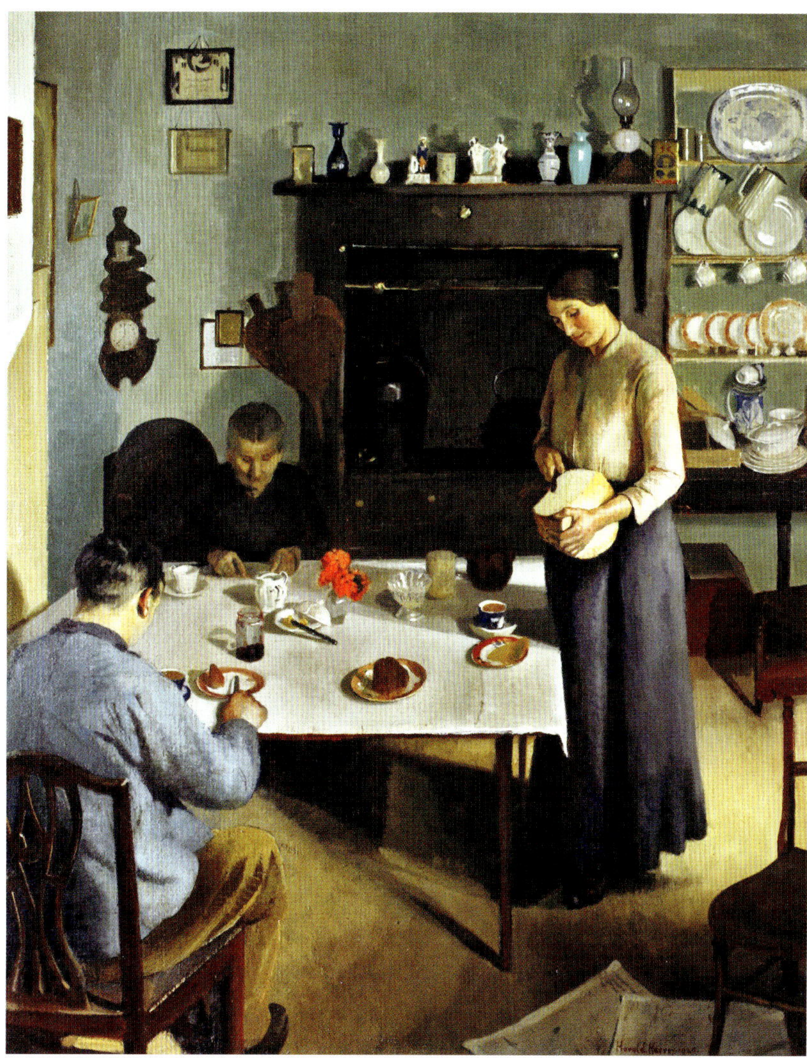

The Tea Table
1920 | oil on canvas | 75 x 59.5 cm
ROYAL INSTITUTION OF CORNWALL, ROYAL CORNWALL MUSEUM, TRURO

mainly to her uncertainty as to how far Nature can be subordinated to decorative design. Nevertheless, several of her impressions are delightful.' *The Observer*, 25th October 1918. Another joint exhibition at the Leicester Galleries in 1920, where she showed 15 works, earned merely a mention by the critics: 'a few Cornish landscapes in tempera by his wife,' *The Observer*, October, and 'some landscapes by Miss [*sic*] G. Harvey were also on view', *The Connoisseur*.

Gertrude experimented with different media: tempera, oil on board, oil on canvas, oil on card and oil/gouache on paper. Her interest in design can be seen in the use of textiles and pottery in the house (as featured in Harvey's interiors – the Omega carpet, already mentioned, and *Gertrude in the Kitchen at Maen Cottage* shows the couple's interest in craft pottery); she had an eye for the fashion of the day. Sophie Bodinnar, Gertrude's sister, was manager of the Cryséde textile factory and from 1923 managed the first Cryséde retail shop in New

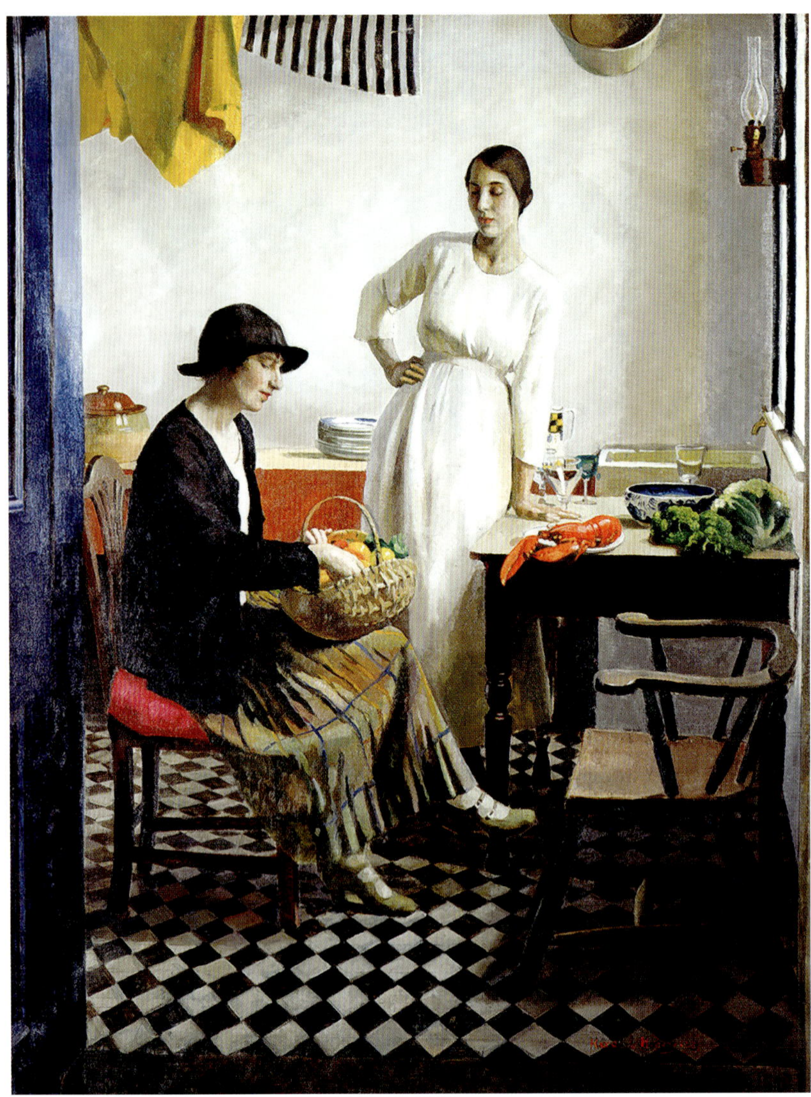

My Kitchen
1923 | oil on canvas | 100.5 x 77.5 cm
GALLERY OLDHAM

Road, Newlyn. Cryséde was founded in 1920 by Alec George Walker and his wife, Kay (née Earle) in a row of derelict cottages known as Sambo's Row on St Peter's Hill, which housed the silk printing works.[13] Walker was the youngest son of an established Yorkshire textile man-ufacturer, and came to Newlyn in 1912. Encouraged by Harvey and Ernest Procter, he began sketching to record motifs which might be used in textile designs. His work became so popular that retail shops were opened in Newlyn, Penzance, St Ives, Bournemouth, Bath, Newquay, Paignton, Falmouth and further afield.

This family contact no doubt encouraged Gertrude's interest in fabrics, which she developed by designing and making her own bags. Harold's painting, *Titbits* (1929), shows Gertrude with a brightly coloured bag over her arm – probably one of her own. She was also a dressmaker; an article of 9th February 1939 from an unidentified source, mentions

13. Sambo's Row has since been demolished. Walker's friends included Frank Dobson, Edward Wadsworth and Wyndham Lewis. Walker met Ossip Zadkine and Raoul Dufy in Paris in 1923 and was influenced by Dufy's work designing fabrics. There is an excellent account of Cryséde by Hazel Berriman.

the colourful clothes worn by figures in Harold's paintings and recorded that: 'if the garment is especially attractive, you may be sure that it has been made by Mrs Harvey herself.' Her friendship with jeweller Ella Naper[14] might also have been an influence. They exhibited together in the Newlyn Gallery show in 1924 when the committee began to admit craft works at their Christmas show: 'Gertrude Harvey's handknitted bags are delightful in design and colour', *Western Morning News*, 3rd December 1924. Jill Garnier, another Newlyn friend, was also a gifted needlewoman.

Laura Knight's autobiography makes many references to 'Gert' and they clearly enjoyed a close friendship. In 1916, when she had fallen and broken her leg, Gert was one of those she relied on to come to her rescue. 'I was nursed by Harold [Knight] and friends who came in relays – Eleanor Hughes, Ruth Simpson and Gert Harvey – the latter was a real standby; she even cleaned the cottage from top to bottom before leaving, and posed for me to draw her between whiles.' Laura

14. Ella Louise C.S. Naper (née Champion 1886–1972) wife of Charles William S. Naper (1882–1968), Ella studied at Camberwell School of Art & Crafts 1904–06 and was partly influenced by the art nouveau jewellery of Fred Partridge. While working with Partridge at Branscombe in South Devon she met Charles Naper. They married in London in 1909, came to Cornwall in 1912, had Trewoofe built as their home in 1913. That same year, Ella modelled for Laura Knight in one of her most remarkable works *Laura Knight with Model, Ella Louise Naper ('Self Portrait')* (National Portrait Gallery). Ella continued designing and making jewellery during this time and collaborated with Laura Knight on a piece in 1915. She also designed and executed the memorial in St Buryan church to the son of Benjamin Leader, killed in the war. In 1920 she turned to pottery and ran a pottery in Lamorna until 1935.

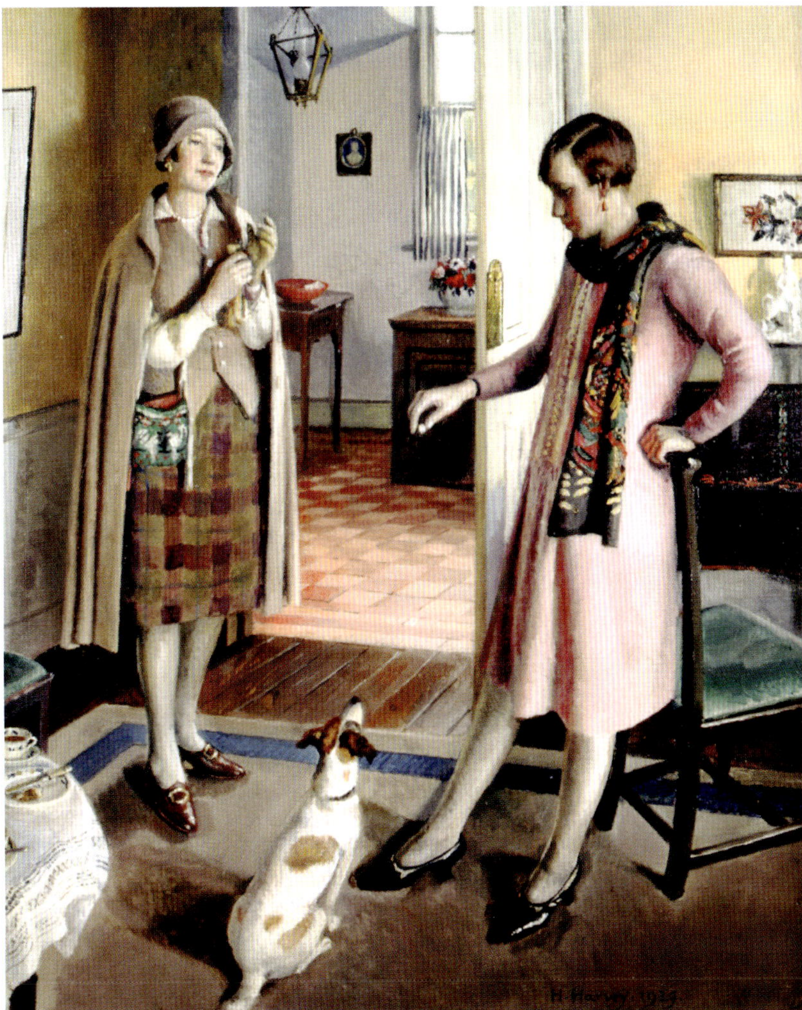

Titbits
1929 | oil on canvas | 61 x 51 cm
BOWERMAN CHARITABLE TRUST

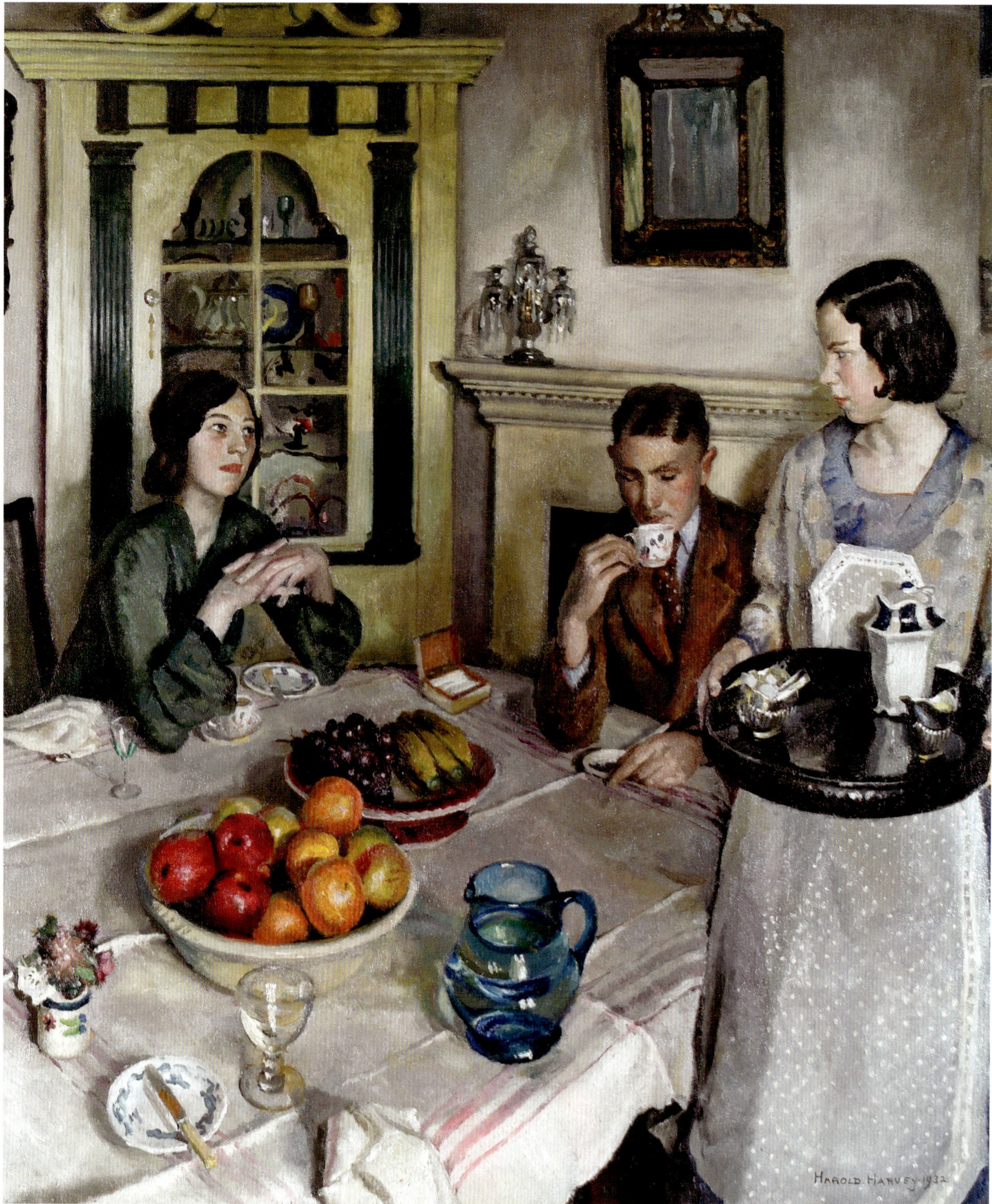

The Young Menage
1932 │ oil on canvas │ 87 x 74 cm
LEAMINGTON SPA ART GALLERY & MUSEUM (WARWICK DISTRICT COUNCIL)

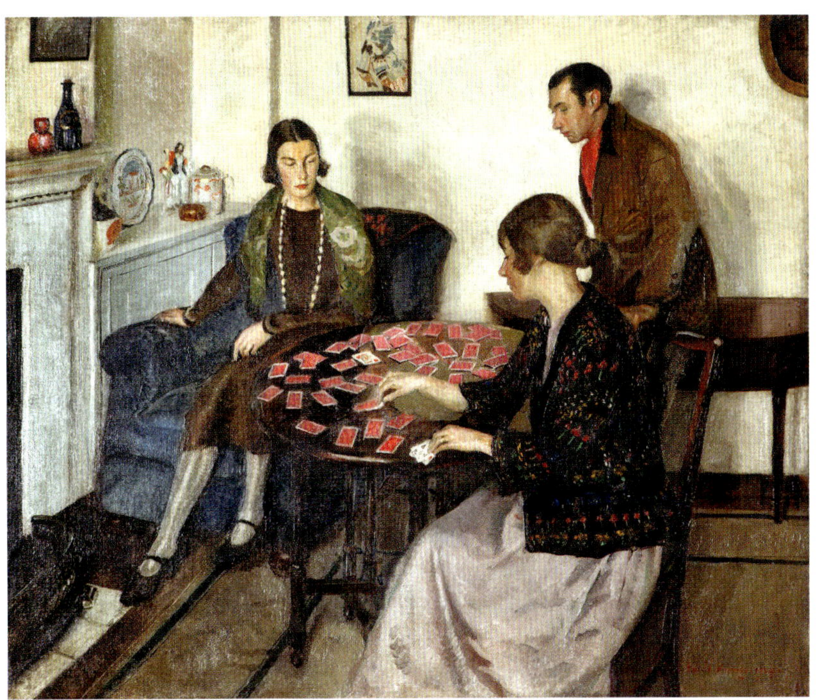

Pelman Patience
1924 | oil on canvas | 64 x 71 cm
PRIVATE COLLECTION

also loaned Gertrude her famous scarlet cardigan, which she wore when posing for one of her husband's many paintings of her. Also in 1916, Laura completed *Spring* – the painting for which she'd risked imprisonment by sketching in the open air. She wrote 'a magpie was in the foreground. When Gertrude Harvey, who is Cornish and superstitious, saw that magpie, she said, "You'll never sell that picture. It's unlucky to see one magpie; if you do you must spit on your right foot." She has said the same, nearly every time we meet, "Why don't you paint out that magpie?" However, the bird was not without compassion, for close on twenty years later (1935) the painting was bought under the terms of the Chantrey Bequest for the Tate Gallery.'[15]

Gertrude Harvey finally achieved an entry of her own in *Who's Who in Art* in the third edition, 1934. She exhibited at the Newlyn Society of Artists: in 1921 (three works); in December 1924 (*The Ruined Mine* and *Coast Near Porthleven*); in March 1925 (two works); in March 1938 one painting entitled *Fish*. She also exhibited at the Fine Arts Society (one). Like Harold she exhibited at the Goupil Galleries and had one work in each of the salons of 1924 and 1926. An unidentified newspaper reported, probably about 1939, that she was preparing an exhibition of 22 paintings to be held in Birmingham, but no record has come to light and it may have been cancelled because of the war. Three of her works were included in the exhibition 'Women Artists in Cornwall 1880–1940' shown at Falmouth and Plymouth in 1996.

15. Laura Knight, *Oil Paint and Grease Paint* (London: Nicholson & Watson, 1936).

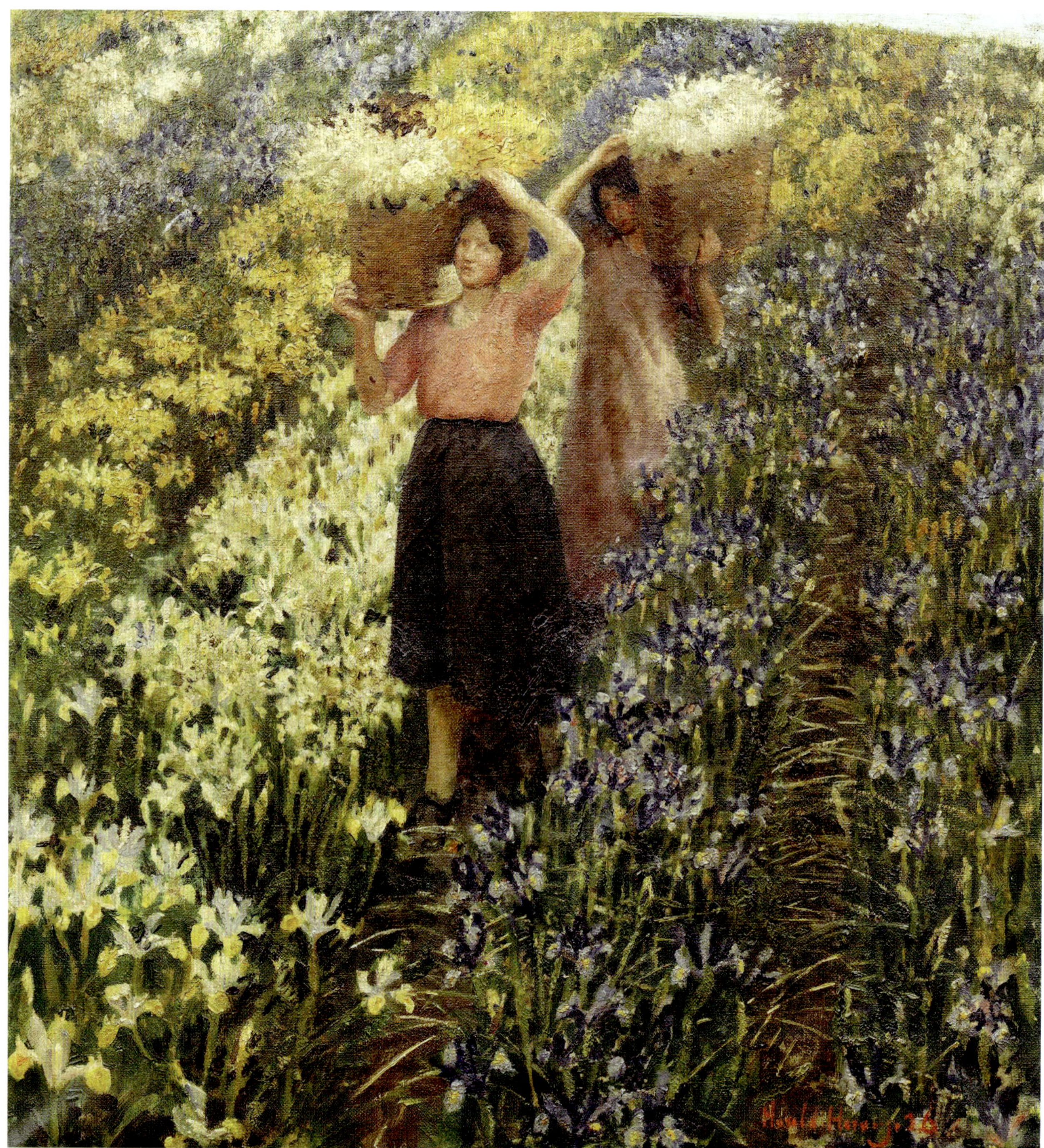

Iris Pickers
1926 | oil on canvas | 51 x 45.5 cm
PRIVATE COLLECTION; IMAGE COURTESY BONHAMS

Five

Pictures of Cornish life

I n *Stanhope Forbes and the Newlyn School*, Caroline Fox wrote 'Harold Harvey was one of the most delightful artists of the new generation. His lifelong commitment to depicting the people and countryside of west Cornwall was an important feature of his work and one that probably arose from his being a native of the area. His best work expresses a true joy in the countryside and a real understanding of the movements and gestures of the men, women and children he so often depicted.' Harvey's insistence on painting that which surrounded him led to one contemporary reviewer describing his work as 'land-scapes, interiors, portrait studies of people of no consequence',[1] and Harvey himself often entitled his London exhibitions simply 'Pictures of Cornish Life'. Some critics denounced the fact that his subject matter was normal daily life, but whether it be the gypsy family in *The Wayfarers* (1906; see p. 12); the fishermen in their three different hats in *Three Fishermen* (1909; see p. 14); the flower pickers in *The Donkey Meadow* (1924; p. 74), or one of the many paintings of Gertrude in her daily routine, one has the feeling that Harvey knew his subjects well and that, to him, these were people of great consequence.

His first major London exhibition was at the Mendoza Gallery in 1913, where fifty works were shown. The show was well received, and the *Morning Post* of 30th May 1913 praised his competent craftsman-ship, saying that his paintings were extremely attractive. *Apple Harvest*; *Monday Morning*; *Hoeing Parsley, Mount's Bay* (p. 75) and *In The Harvest Field* were all chosen for particular mention, but with the rider that his pictures are all 'wonderfully equal'. The only note of criticism in this review was that he was overly 'neat'; they suggest: 'Mr Harvey has now to "let himself go a little". If the spirit of poetry is in him to an extent he has not yet shown he ought now to make a step forward.' Another reviewer of the same exhibition felt that the paintings had 'a leaning towards sentimentality', but that they were nevertheless genuine inter-pretations of place and people, 'and since children are in most cases the characters the insistence of the tender note is perhaps not amiss.' This time *Faggot Gatherers*, *The Mother*, *Monday Morning* and *The First*

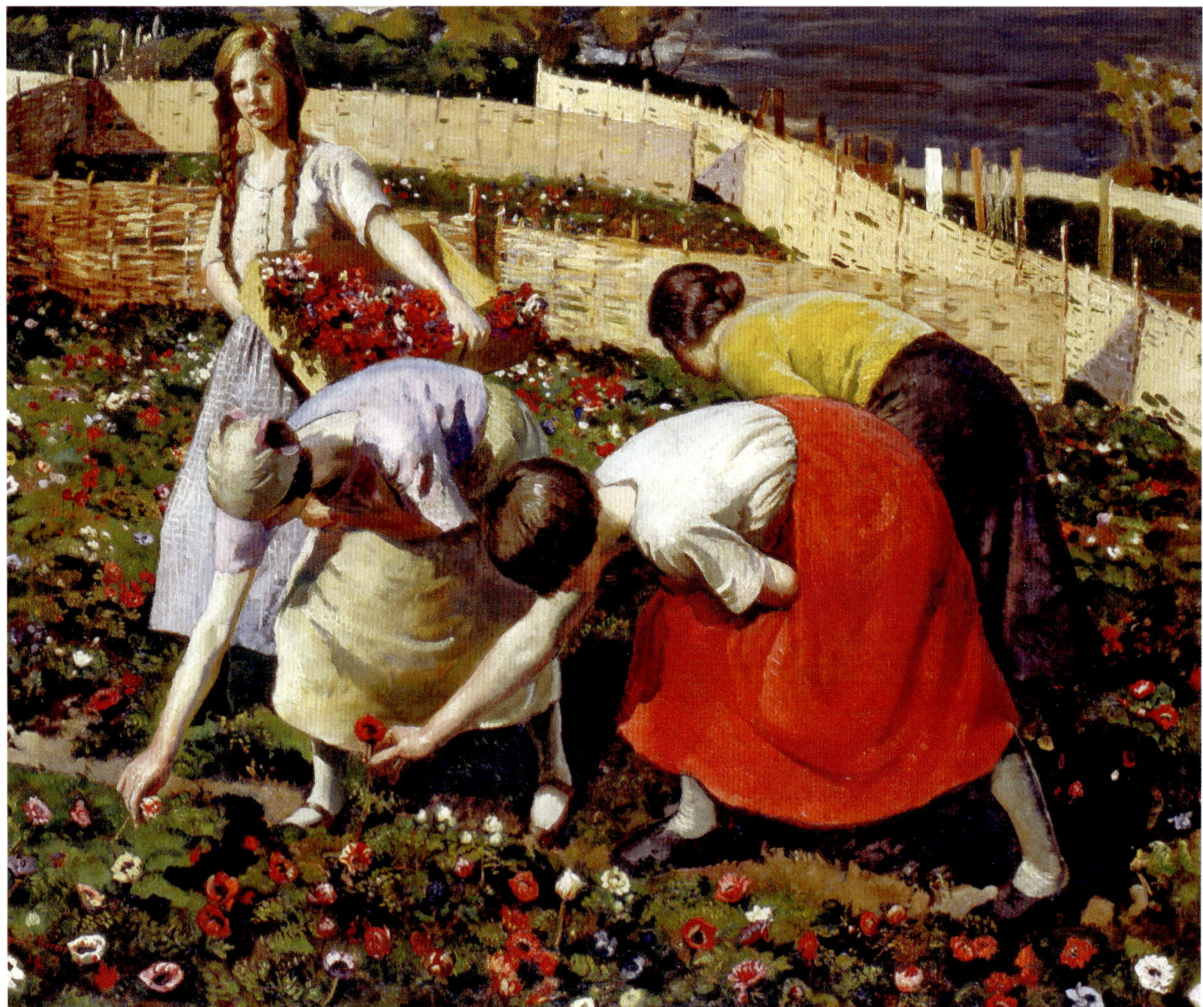

The Donkey Meadow
1924 | oil on canvas | 60 x 75 cm
PRIVATE COLLECTION

Snowdrops of the Year were picked out as the best of his pictures, and the relationship of the figures to the landscape was particularly praised. A further publication, *The Queen*, of 24th May 1913, stated that, in this exhibition, he had 'succeeded in presenting the peculiar and rather wistful geniality of this corner of England' and that his work contained 'some very charming examples of the painting of broad landscape in strong sunlight.'

The first serious assessment of Harvey's work appeared in *Colour* magazine, the cover of which showed his *Portrait of a Girl*. The article, 'About Harold Harvey'[2] emphasised Harvey's Cornish heritage:

> … in contemplating the work of Harold Harvey [you] may find satisfaction in the knowledge that he, a disciple of the 'Newlyn School', is not only a pupil of Norman Garstin, a Cornishman [Garstin was in fact born in County Limerick, Ireland, and the family originated on the north bank of the Mersey];[3] but himself

2. *Colour*, October 1920, by TIS, pp. 48–54.
3. Nic Hale, *Norman and Alethea Garstin: A brief biography of two painters* (Helston: An Lyverji Kernewek, 1999).

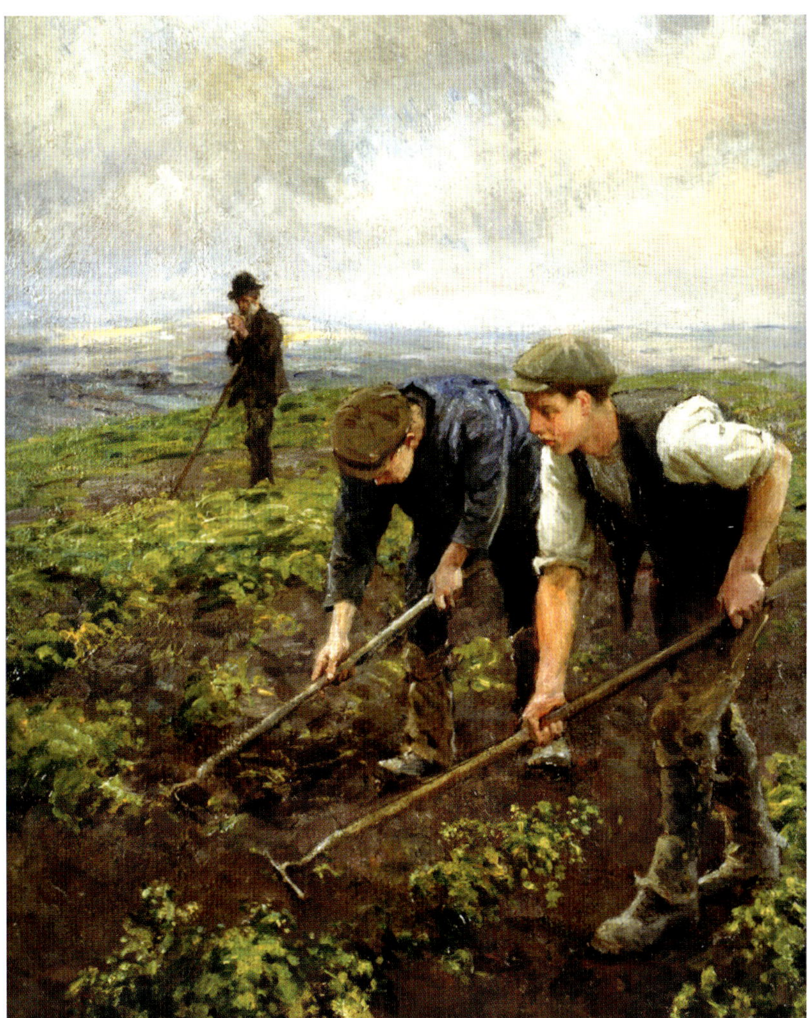

Hoeing Parsley, Mount's Bay
1913 | oil on canvas | 76 x 61 cm
BOWERMAN CHARITABLE TRUST

a Cornishman, bred and born. The Cornish language was spoken within living memory, and I see no reason why, given a Cornish Yeats or Cornish League, we may not experience another Celtic revival, and an enthusiastic claim to the Newlyn School as an expression of its national genius.

But although, as the article says 'It would be surprising indeed if the soil and the climate had no influence upon an artist's work, whatever his racial origin, and so a 'Cornish' feeling is clearly discernible in the Newlyn School, and therefore also in Harold Harvey's art', his training is acknowledged as being at least as much of an influence. Giving details of Harvey's training at the Academie Julian, the writer asserts that the influence of Paris has given Harvey his love not only for clear, disciplined draughtsmanship, but also for atmospheric truth and careful objective realism. In response, surely, to earlier criticism of the Newlyn works as being 'too French', the writer also asserts that the influence of Paris is not 'French' but universal, Paris having been central to international art for more than three hundred years. From his early beginnings in the 1890s, Harold Harvey's art constantly evolved through, as the writer puts it

> … certain successive phases in which different influences are traceable in turn. Starting out with a purely naturalistic realism, of which Bastien-Lepage was, via Stanhope Forbes, the inspirer, he in common with the other members of the younger Newlyn Generation, passes through a stage of pre-Raphaelite and then primitive Italian realism, which is 'natural' only by a stretching of the term, to rest awhile at present on the borders of 'expressionism', in which he, whilst preserving naturalism and realism in subject-matter, simplifies beyond optical, i.e. photographic accuracy.

While others too had followed these phases, the writer felt that Harvey's work was fundamentally different in that the development of his work seemed organic; the change from one style to another occurred within the flow of his work, with no distinct break with the past in each new phase. The continuity of his evolving style was enhanced by the constancy of his subjects. 'In every picture the clear bright Cornish light is present, the same pleasure in definition, the same happiness in the use of clean colour, is visible. He is obviously interested in the thing itself, i.e. in the concrete and ordinary significance of objects. He is a worshipper of light and colour, not as revealing abstract form but concrete forms.'

At a time when abstraction when sweeping into British Art, *Colour* magazine's writer seemed relieved that Harvey's subjects 'have more than purely aesthetic significance.' The three-dimensionality of the people and objects in his pictures, together with the sense of perspective and distance in the landscapes is celebrated. The writer goes so far as to warn against the abandonment of this style of painting. 'I mention this because I seem to discern in Harvey's latest work a drift towards abstraction, which I personally would regret. I ask for nothing better than the beautiful realisation of distance such as he shows in his picture – now on exhibition at the Leicester Galleries – called *The Road*, nor for more deference to abstract rhythmic qualities than in his *Planting Potatoes* (1912). Out of all his work speaks a delightful personality, one willing and anxious to please without sacrifice of principles.'

The *Colour* article coincided with the second exhibition at Leicester Galleries where Harold showed twenty-two works and Gertrude fifteen. The exhibition received several other reviews, which, although positive, were not wholly complimentary. One such appeared in *The Connoisseur* in November 1920:

> … his colour-sense has stood him in good stead on many a stricken canvas. The grey simplicity of his *Newlyn Boats*, unhampered by the intrusion of 'modern' figures, was restful in effect, but some other compositions would have been improved by an omission of the

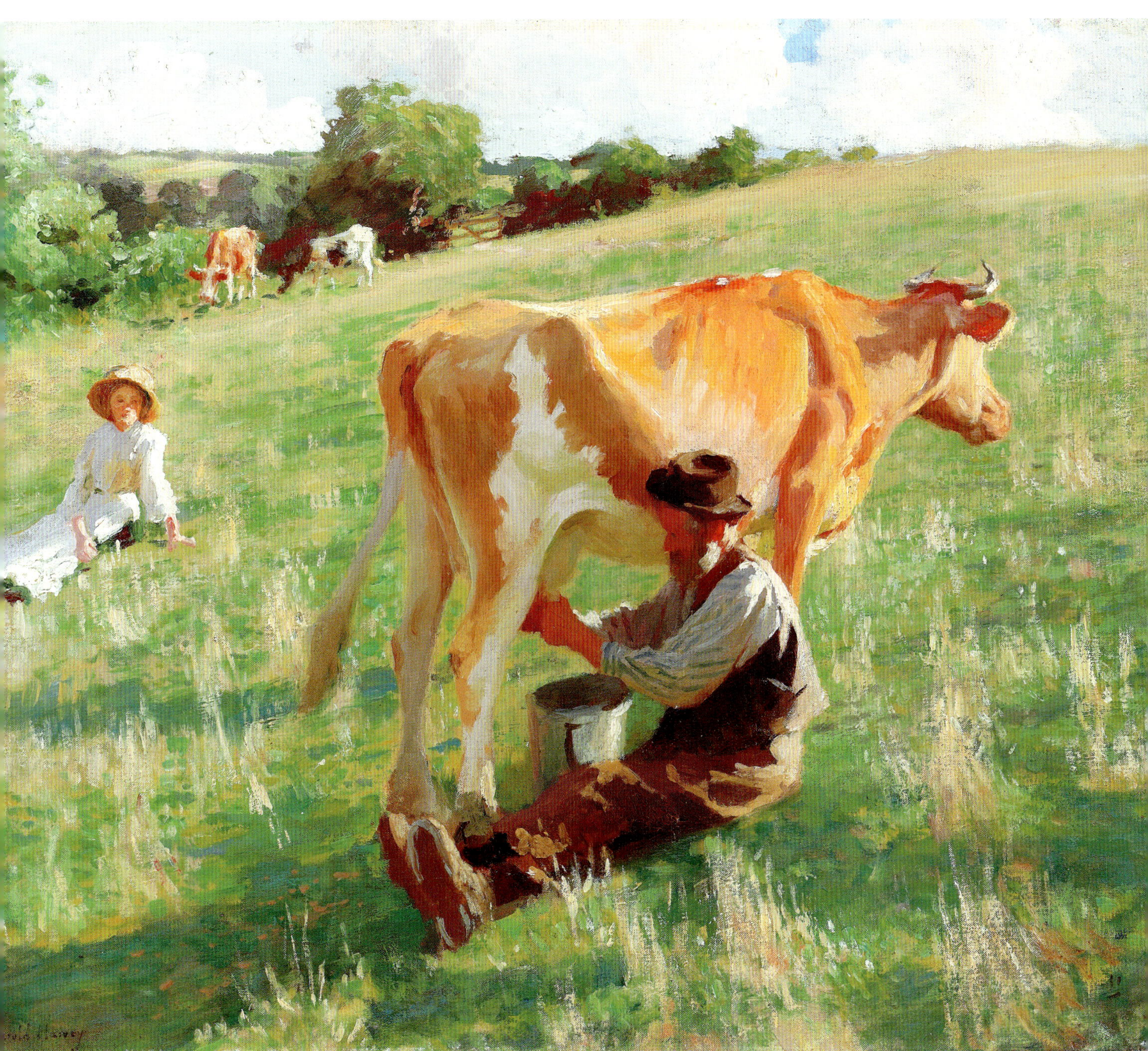

Summer Milking
1916 | oil on canvas | 63 x 76 cm
CHRISTIE'S

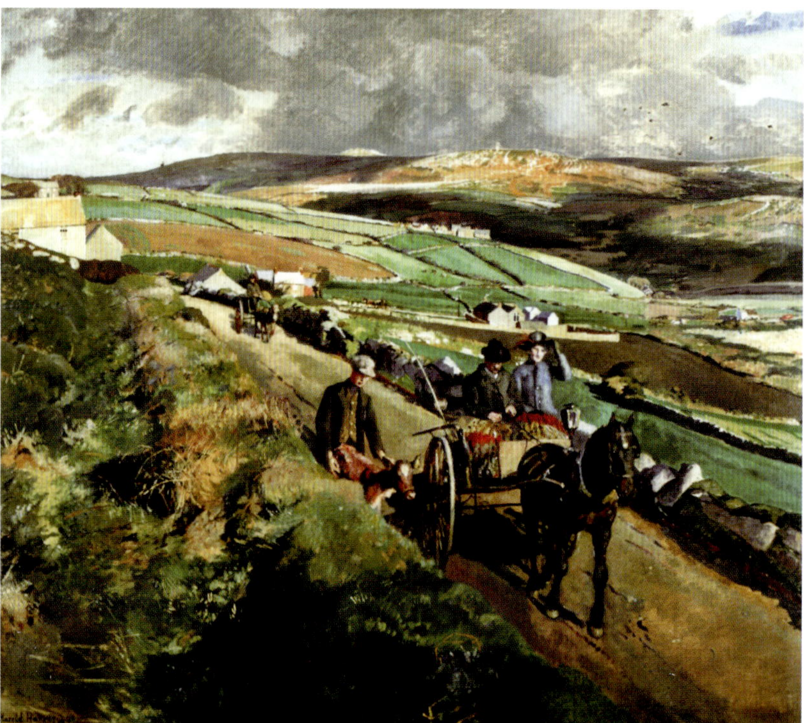

The Road to Market
1924 | oil on canvas | 109 x 127 cm
BOWERMAN CHARITABLE TRUST

up-to-date element. The curious part about it is that Mr Harvey can draw the figure if he likes – witness either *The Sunlit Room* or *Cornish Children* … but in more than one instance he has permitted his judgement to be swayed with unhappy results.

Similarly, *The Observer* wrote:

> In the majority of his paintings, it is true, he still endeavours to hold a faithful mirror up to Nature, with just the heightening of tone and brightening of colour to his transcripts. But in a few instances, especially in his Cornish peasant *Madonna*, he departs from this objective attitude and rises to real-life self-expression – to a deliberate pictorial conception in which the lines and forms of the landscape background do not depend on the accidents of Nature, but are logically adapted to the massive, simplified forms of the central group. Rare energy and concentration will be found again in the synthetic rendering of action in *Planting Potatoes*. These pictures are painted from within, and not from without, like his domestic interiors.[4]

Following on from the relative success of his exhibition, and from the publicity generated by the lengthy *Colour* article, in 1920, Harvey and Ernest Procter started their own painting school in a large studio near the harbour. Their first advertisement in the November 1920 issue of *Colour* offered 'A New School, Harold Harvey & Ernest Procter, Newlyn; Figure, Still Life, Landscape; Open all the year; Oil & Water

4. The article appeared on 3 October 1920, written by P.G. Konody.

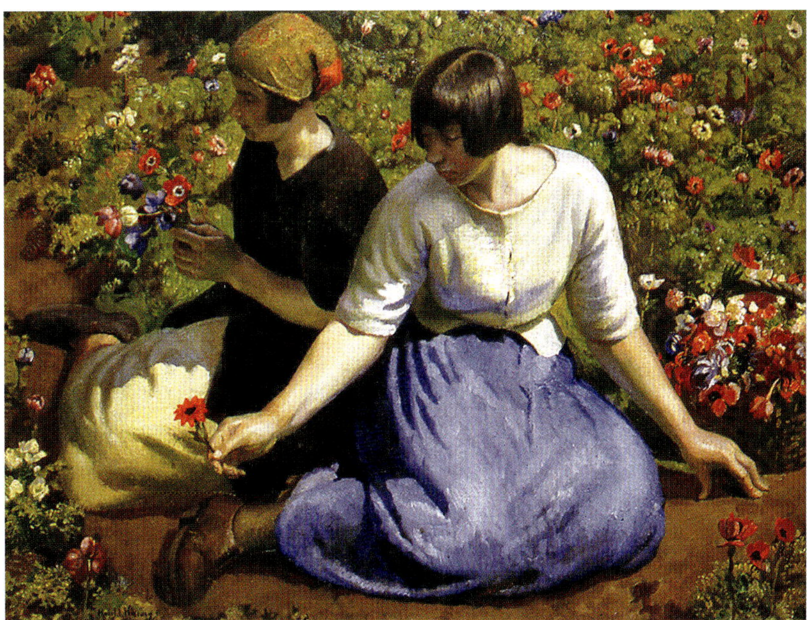

Anemones
1926 | oil on canvas | 70 x 90 cm
PRIVATE COLLECTION

colour; Particulars from either Principal, Newlyn, Penzance.' In June 1922 the advertisement remained as before, but added: 'Nude Model Out of Doors during July, August and September', while in November of that year, the advertisement omitted the nude model but instead offered: 'Life, Still Life, Landscape, Decorations.' Harvey himself never developed the nude figure as a subject, even though both Ernest and Dod Procter made frequent use of nudes in their work. Harvey was more interested in decoration and surface pattern, perhaps arising from his involvement (through Gertrude and her sister) with the Cryséde company, which specialised in making decorative silk fabrics. Use of strong pattern was becoming a Harvey hallmark. Several of his paintings show unusually patterned clothes or fabrics, such as *Lunch* (1918); *In the Kitchen* (1918); *The Ribbon Skirt* (1918); *At The Dressing Table* (1920); *Portrait of the Artist's Wife, Gertrude* (1922); *In The Bedroom* (*c.*1922); *Titbits* (1929); *Gertrude in an Interior* (1929) and *Zena* (1933).

Adverts for the Harvey-Procter School appeared in *Colour* until at least January 1927. It would seem that Harvey had the responsibility for keeping the accounts, and his notebook records attendances from April 1922 to June 1928. Among their pupils were Dorcie Sykes, 'Billie' Waters and Midge Bruford – all three exhibited with Harvey at the Walker Art Gallery, Liverpool in 1930. Dorcie Sykes (probably Doris, 1908–1998) was a water-colourist, specialising in flowers and figures. She exhibited with the Newlyn Society of Artists in 1921, 1925 and 1926; and at the Royal Scottish Academy, Edinburgh between 1934 and 1938.[5] Billie Waters (Charlotte Ethel M. Waters, 1896–1979) had studied at Heatherley's, the Chelsea School of Art and the Grosvenor School before coming to the Harvey-Procter School in 1923. She had

5. Her father John Gutteridge Sykes (1866–1941) became a member of NSA in 1928 and was elected to the committee in 1932 after T.C. Gotch died.

her first Royal Academy exhibition in 1928 and showed there every year thereafter until 1944. She showed at the Leicester Galleries in 1932, 1933 and 1935, as well as at the Royal Institute of Painters in Watercolour, Newlyn Society, New English Art Club, Society of Women Artists and Society of Wood Engravers. She specialised in flowers and animals, often including exotic creatures, such as monkeys, lemur and sifaka. Frost & Reed reproduced prints of her paintings *Crested Grebe* and *Water Lilies*. Billie modelled for Ernest Procter's *The Day's End* (1927) and for Laura Knight's *Susie and the Wash Basin* (1927). Her woodcut of Procter's *Zodiac* was reproduced in *The Studio*, volume 91, and her design for a book jacket in *Drawing & Design*, July 1922.[6] Marjorie Frances Bruford (1902–1958), 'Midge', exhibited at the Royal Academy from 1924 to 1955. She was a close friend of Mornie Birch and was painted by Dod Procter as *Indolence*. Harvey painted *Midge Bruford and Fiancé, Coombe Hill, Newlyn* (c.1920s).

That this school was an environment which encouraged the expression of talent is particularly exemplified by Joan Manning-Sanders (1913–

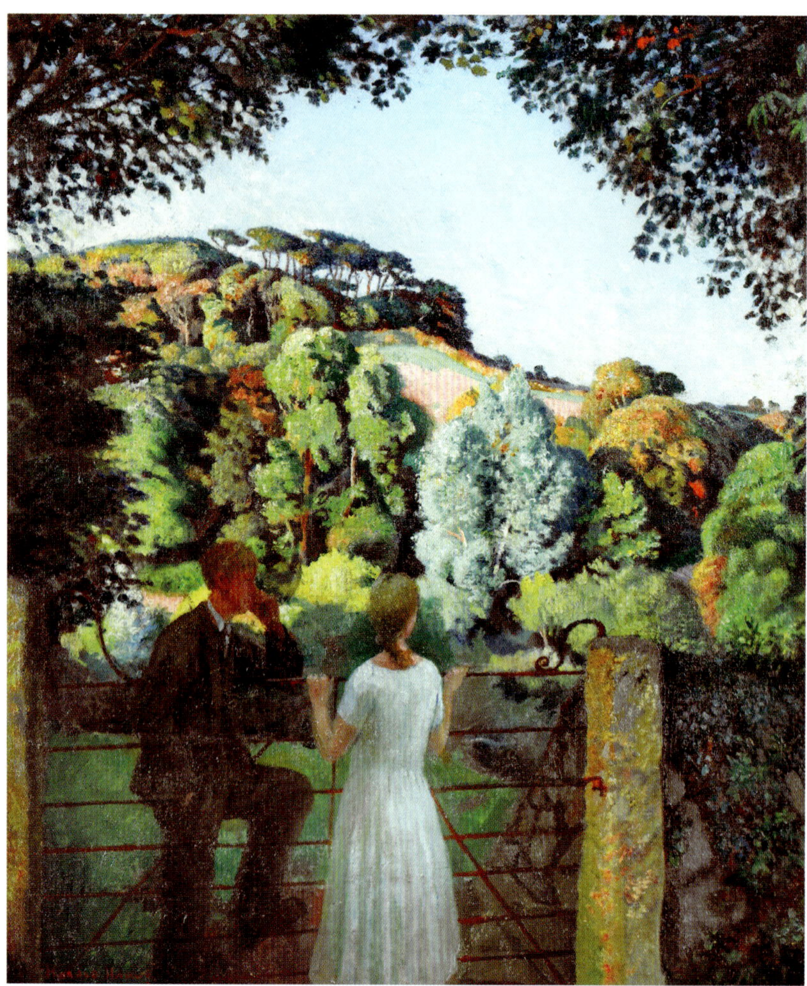

Midge Bruford and Fiancé, Coombe Hill, Newlyn
c.1920–25 | oil on canvas | 71 x 61 cm
private collection

6. Billie Waters work was included in 'Women Artists in Cornwall 1880–1940', Falmouth Art Gallery, 1996.

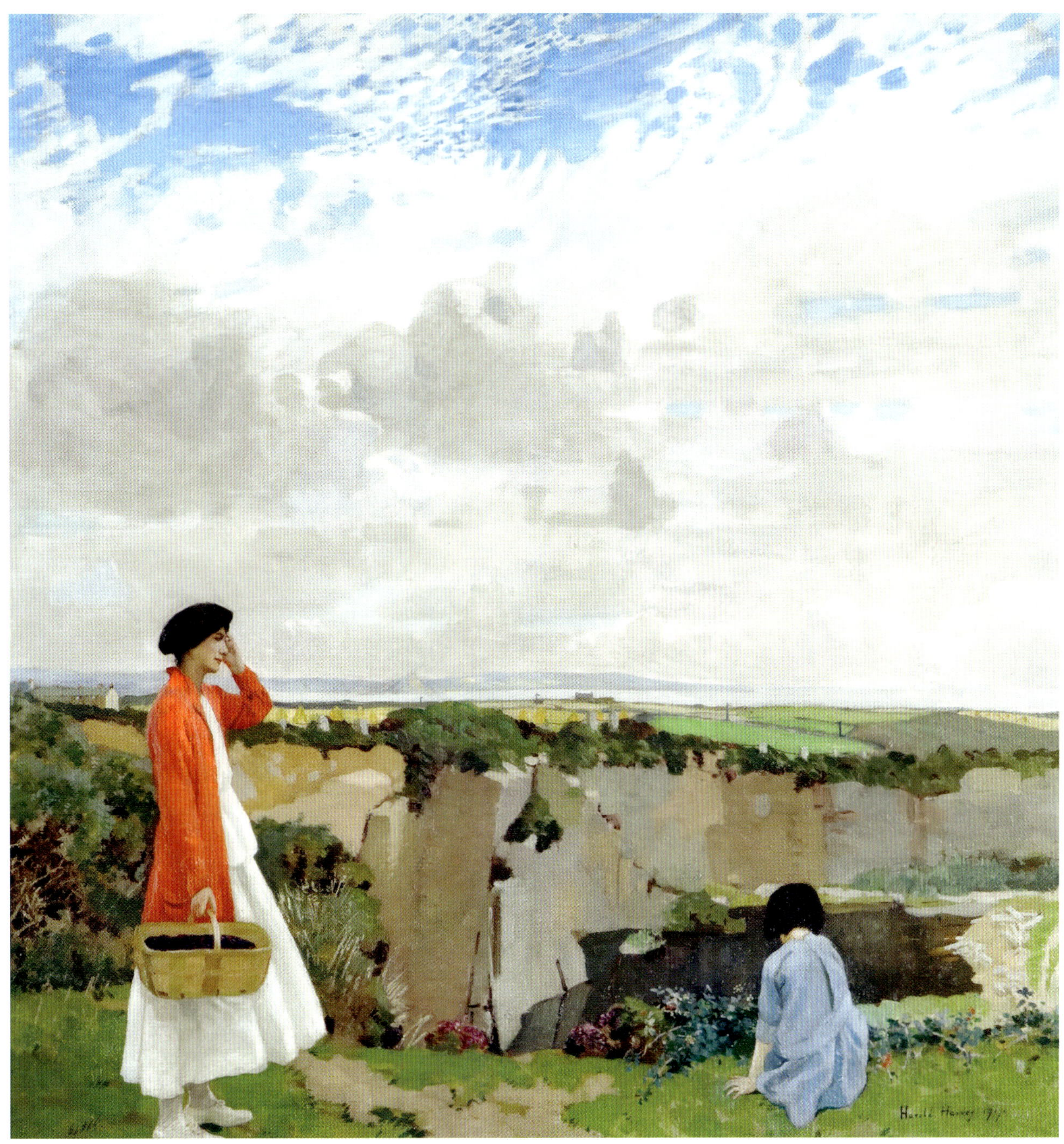

Blackberrying
1917 | oil on canvas | 72 x 71.5 cm
SOUTH SHIELDS MUSEUM & ART GALLERY, TYNE & WEAR ARCHIVES & MUSEUMS

2002) (the daughter of George and Ruth). At the age of thirteen, Joan achieved public recognition at the *Daily Express* Young Artist Exhibition with her portraits *The Pedlar* and *David and the Globe*, a portrait of her younger brother. She showed at the Royal Academy from 1928 to 1935 and she was elected to the Newlyn Society of Arts in 1929 at the age of fifteen (proposed by Forbes). In the same year, *David and the Globe* was reproduced in *Colour* and Faber & Faber published a collection of thirty-two of her paintings and drawings, with an introduction by R.H. Wilenski. At the age of seventeen, she became a member of the Royal Institute of Oil Painters and *Ann Hatch*, another portrait, was published in *Colour*. Wilenski commented on a connection between the work of Joan and Harvey; he wrote of Joan's *The Baby*: 'it shows that Joan has enjoyed the tender drawing in the Mother and Child pictures which give Harold Harvey his place in the history of English art.'

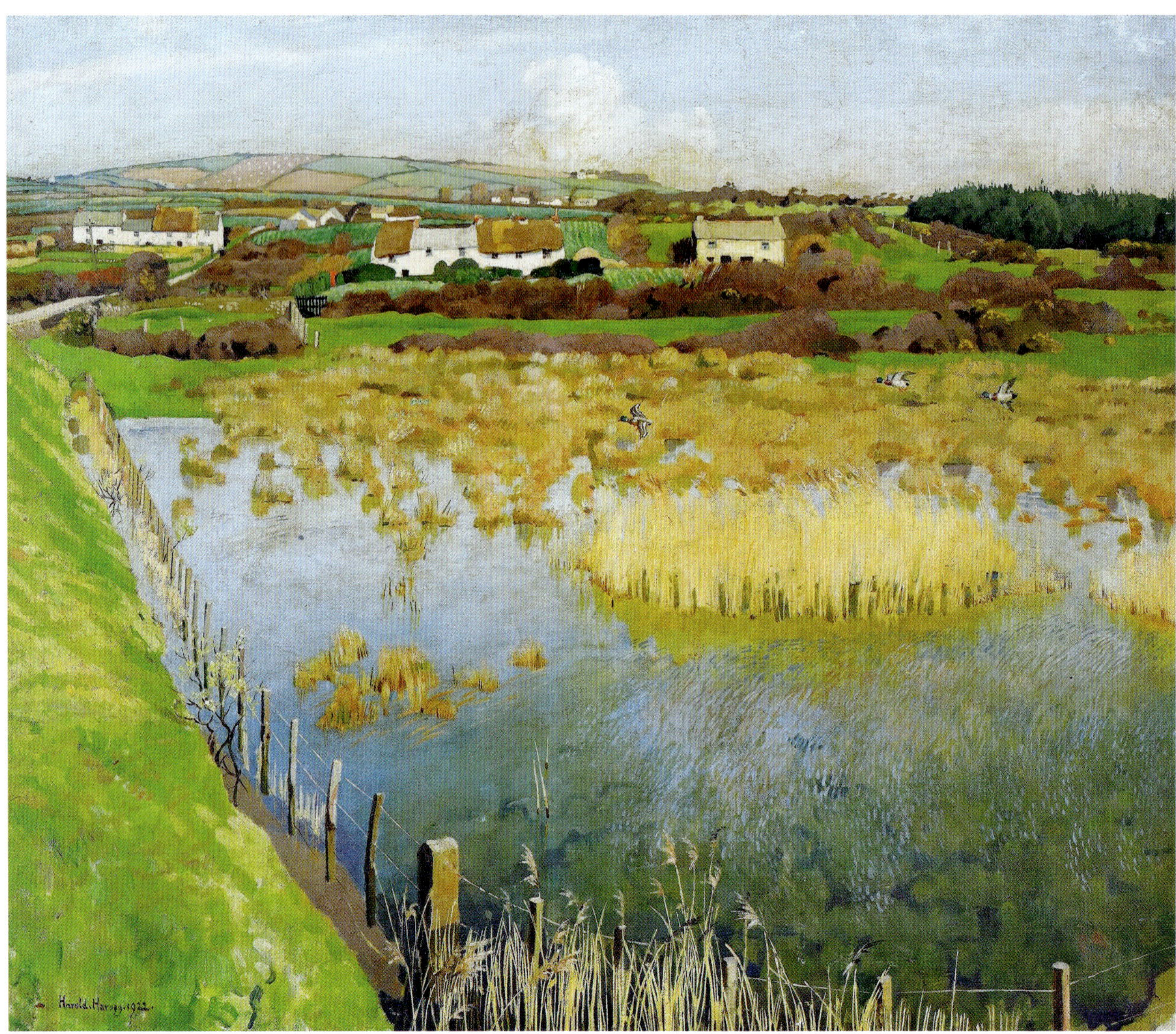

Marsh Landscape
1922 | oil on canvas | 75.5 x 91 cm
GRANT FORD LTD

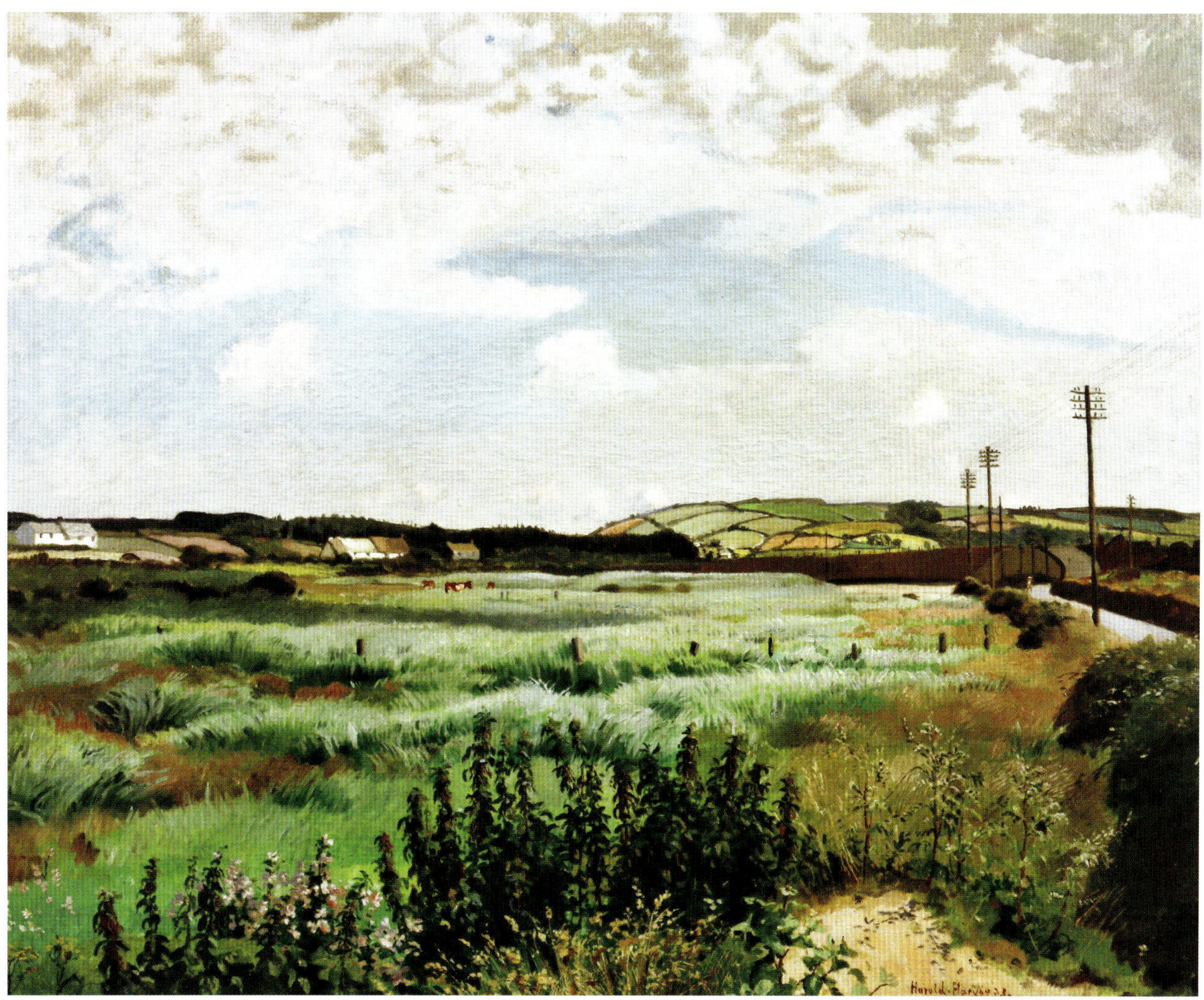

Marazion Marsh
1923 | oil on canvas | 60.5 x 76.5 cm
PENLEE HOUSE GALLERY & MUSEUM

Harvey's own teaching career was well established when, on 22nd June 1926, his old mentor, Norman Garstin, died at the age of 71. Although the Harveys were not among those named as attending the funeral, the obituary published in *The Cornishman* on 30th June mentions a floral tribute from 'some of his old students'; no doubt Harold was included. Norman Garstin had said of the younger set: 'The Newlyn group has always had the reputation of seeing through the grey fog that legend attributes to Cornwall. Whether this is so or not, the effect upon the Knights has been the exact opposite for with their advent, there came over their work an utter change in both their outlook and method: they at once plunged into a riot of brilliant sunshine, of opulent colour and of sensuous gaiety.'

The Harveys' close friendship with the Knights resulted in a mutual inspiration between the work of Laura Knight and Harold Harvey. Laura's *Boys Bathing, Newlyn Quay* (1910) is very similar to Harvey's *Children on the Quay, Newlyn* (undated but circa 1905–10). They both tackled kite-flying: Laura's *Flying a Kite* (1910) is on a large scale

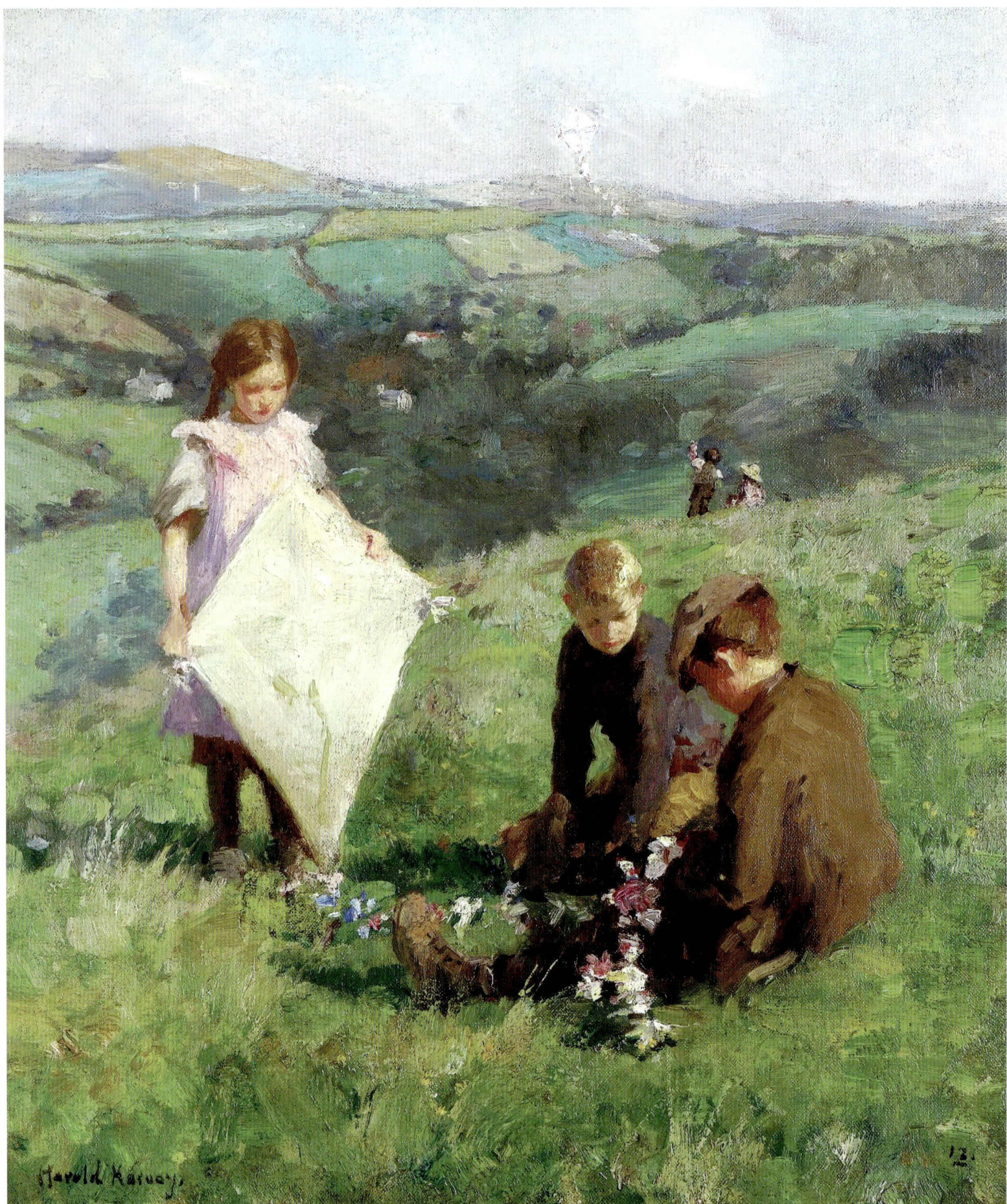

Pioneers of Aerial Navigation
1913 | oil on canvas | 46 x 33 cm
MACCONNAL-MASON GALLERY, LONDON

(59 x 70 inches) and shows two groups of children high on a hill over-looking Newlyn, the kite soaring. Harvey's 1913 work *Pioneers of Aerial Navigation* is a wry look at the seriousness with which children take their play. He returned to the subject in 1916 with *The Kite*. His work also undoubtedly shows the influence of friends such as Ernest and Dod Procter. This is particularly evident in *Anemones* (p. 79) and *Picking Tulips* (both 1926), where the figures are solid and monumental against a telescoped background.

Although the compositions are often neatly contrived, Harvey's paintings appear direct and untheatrical. He was prolific and paintings were frequently completed within the day; most of the works are small, generally less than 24 x 20 inches, a size easy to mount on a sitting-room wall. He needed to make his living by his art and producing a greater quantity of domestic-sized works, not too expensive either to do or to buy, was the surest way to produce a stable income. His work sold well, but Benjamin Ridge's telephone bill was not the only example of payment in kind, and the paintings which adorned Harvey's brother's office were almost certainly in return for financial support at times of slack sales.

Harold's notebook records annual profits of £71–17s–11d for 1923; £125-5s–1d for 1924/25 and £200-7s–1d for 1926/27. Despite increasing recognition, the Harveys' lifestyle in Maen Cottage remained frugal when sales were sparse. The couple seldom visited London and never left the British Isles. They loved their native county, enjoying the visits to Bodmin, walks to Lamorna and elsewhere, fishing, gardening. They did not possess a car, but for a time Harold had a motor-bike, complete with bullet-shaped side-car. He was prolific, often painting commissions for money, yet even as his style evolved with the new colour and simplicity of the second generation, there was always an element of honesty to his work.

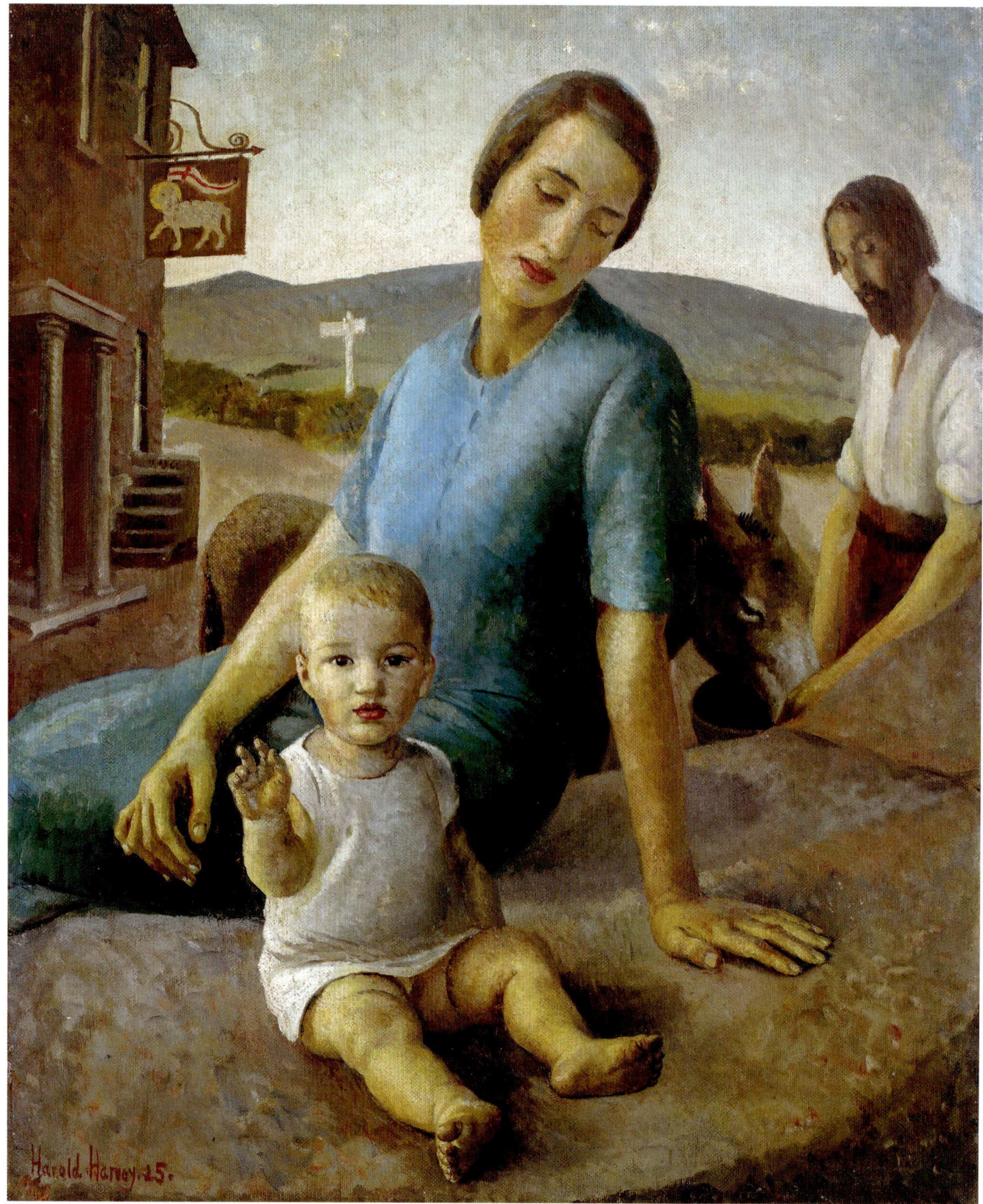

The Flight aka ***Rest on the Flight***
1925 | oil on canvas | 76.5 x 64 cm
PRIVATE COLLECTION

Six

Conversion to Catholicism

1. The church of St Hilary, north-east of Marazion, is dedicated to a fourth-century Bishop of Poitiers of that name. The tower and spire are of the fourteenth century. Spires are rare in Cornwall and this one is visible from both north and south coasts, and was formerly whitewashed as a landmark for sailors. The nave was destroyed by fire in 1853 but rebuilt and consecrated in 1857.
2. Colwyn Edward Vulliamy, *Calico Pie: An Autobiography* (London: Michael Joseph, 1940).
3. Anne Westray Fearon (1888–1965) trained at the Chelsea and London Schools of Art. Her triptych altarpiece for Truro Cathedral is in the Jesus Chapel.
4. Bernard Walke, *Twenty Years at St Hilary* (London: Methuen, 1935; repub. London: Anthony Mott, 1982, and Truro: Truran Books, 2002).
5. William Arnold Snell (1890–1971) who made the altars for St Levan and St Hilary, and a pulpit for St Pol de Leon. In addition he made the war memorials for Newlyn, Penzance, Mousehole and Sancreed, as well as the Macgrigor monument at Newlyn. In the cemetery at Sancreed are Snell's memorials to Geoffrey and Jill Garnier, Stanhope and Maud Forbes, and to T.C. Gotch and his daughter the Marquise de Verdieres.
6. Walke, *Twenty Years at St Hilary*.
7. One does not normally associate the Newlyn artists with those of Bloomsbury, but there are tangible links between the two groups – Roger Fry's reredos to an altar for St Francis, and Gladys Hynes' panel for St Morwena. Gladys was one of the administrative workers at the Omega Workshops and her sister Eileen was married to C.E. Vulliamy.

In 1926, at the age of 52, Harold Harvey converted to Catholicism. He might well have been influenced by Bernard Walke, a close friend who was the parish priest at St Hilary Church,[1] a few miles outside Penzance. Nicolo Bernard Walke, known as 'Ber' to friends, was a vigorous Anglo-Catholic, described by the writer C.E. Vulliamy as 'the least orthodox of all the queer clergymen in Cornwall. He wore a black sombrero and a cloak fastened with a silver brooch big as a saucer.'[2] Bernard Walke published his own account of life in Cornwall, *Twenty Years at St Hilary*, in 1935, and he achieved fame for the village and church by his radio broadcasts of the parish Nativity Play. Bernard's wife Anne[3] was a painter: '…parson's wife ain't no better than she ought to be … they've scat the stable to pieces … made a great window in the roof an' calls it a studio. I'd like to know what do go on in there.'[4]

Bernard Walke called upon his wife and their artist friends to help him restore the church: '… the six altars were built by the local stone-mason [William Arnold Snell][5] the painting and decoration are the work of artists who happened to be living in the neighbourhood at the time, some of whom have become famous.'[6] Harvey painted three of the ten 'saints' panels in the choir stalls. Starting from the south-west position, Harvey's paintings depict St Hilary (1916); St Fingar (1924); and St Paul (1922), then come depictions by other artists of St Petroc and St Buriana. Starting at the north-west position there are paintings of Dedication, St Endellienta (by Dod Procter), St Morwena (by Gladys Hynes), St Piran and St Senen. The works of Ernest Procter, Anne Walke, Phyllis Yglesias and Roger Fry are also featured in the church,[7] as is that of Harvey's pupil Joan Manning-Sanders, who made a series of five watercolours for the north side of the chancel screen in 1926.

Ernest Procter (who was a Quaker), John Mackenzie and Geoffrey Garnier, all friends of Harold Harvey, held strong Christian beliefs, particularly Garnier, whose early works contained many religious subjects. Garnier abandoned his beliefs after the death of his one-

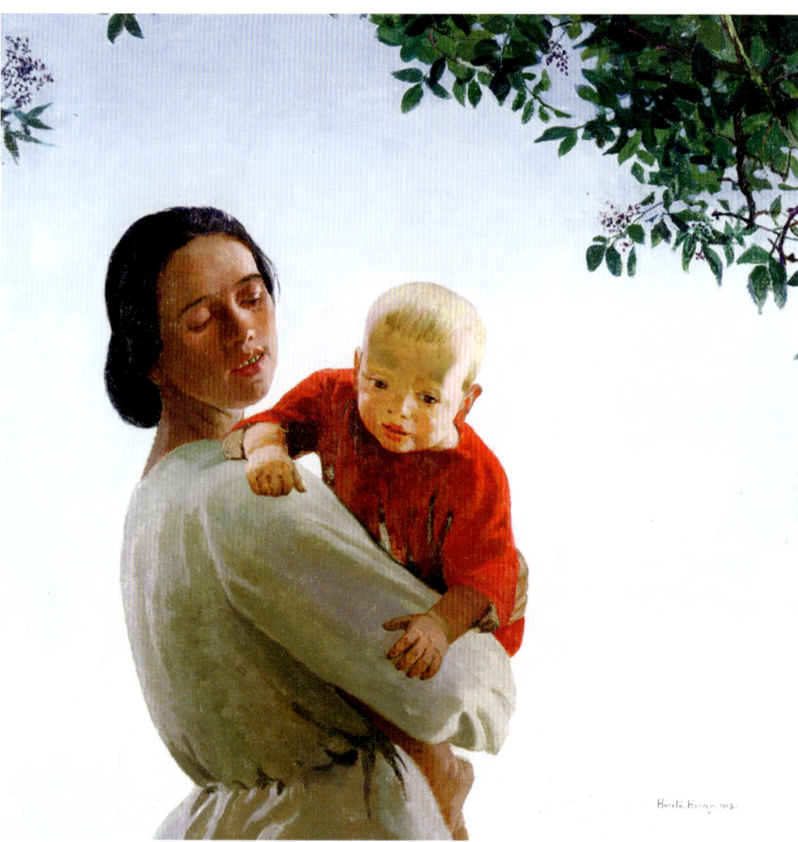

Mother and Child
1918 | oil on canvas | 61.5 x 61.5 cm
NATIONAL MUSEUMS AND GALLERIES OF WALES

year old son in 1925. It is quite possible that this tragic event helped
Harvey move in a contrary direction, towards Catholicism. He and
Gertrude loved children but did not have any of their own. It is felt
by some that paintings such as *Early Spring* (date unknown), *Mother
and Son* (1917), *Mother and Child* (1918) and *Madonna* (*c.*1920), besides
carrying religious feeling, might also express this lack in his life.

Harvey produced a number of paintings of specifically religious rel-
evance, including *The Flight* (1925; p. 86) *Madonna of the Bridges* (1930),
A May Procession (1935), and *Ancilla Domini* (1938). A newspaper article
of 9th February 1939 shows Harvey painting a large canvas (possibly
Resurrection), which his notebook records as being 50 x 60 inches.
A review in the *Daily Graphic* (1st May 1926) said of *The Flight*: 'A
Picture for a Church … if this picture is eventually placed in a church,
as it ought to be, it will inspire devotion and reverence.' Interestingly,
his two largest known works have spiritual subjects: *Mother and Child*
(1929) measures 70 x 60 inches, and *A May Procession* measures 72 x 40
inches. Both are monumental not only in size but also in scale of conception, and would not be out of place in a church. Harvey became a
member of two religious bodies, the Penzance Catholic Men's Guild
and the Confraternity of the Blessed Sacrament, and retained his faith
to the end of his life. Gertrude, however, did not adopt Catholicism.

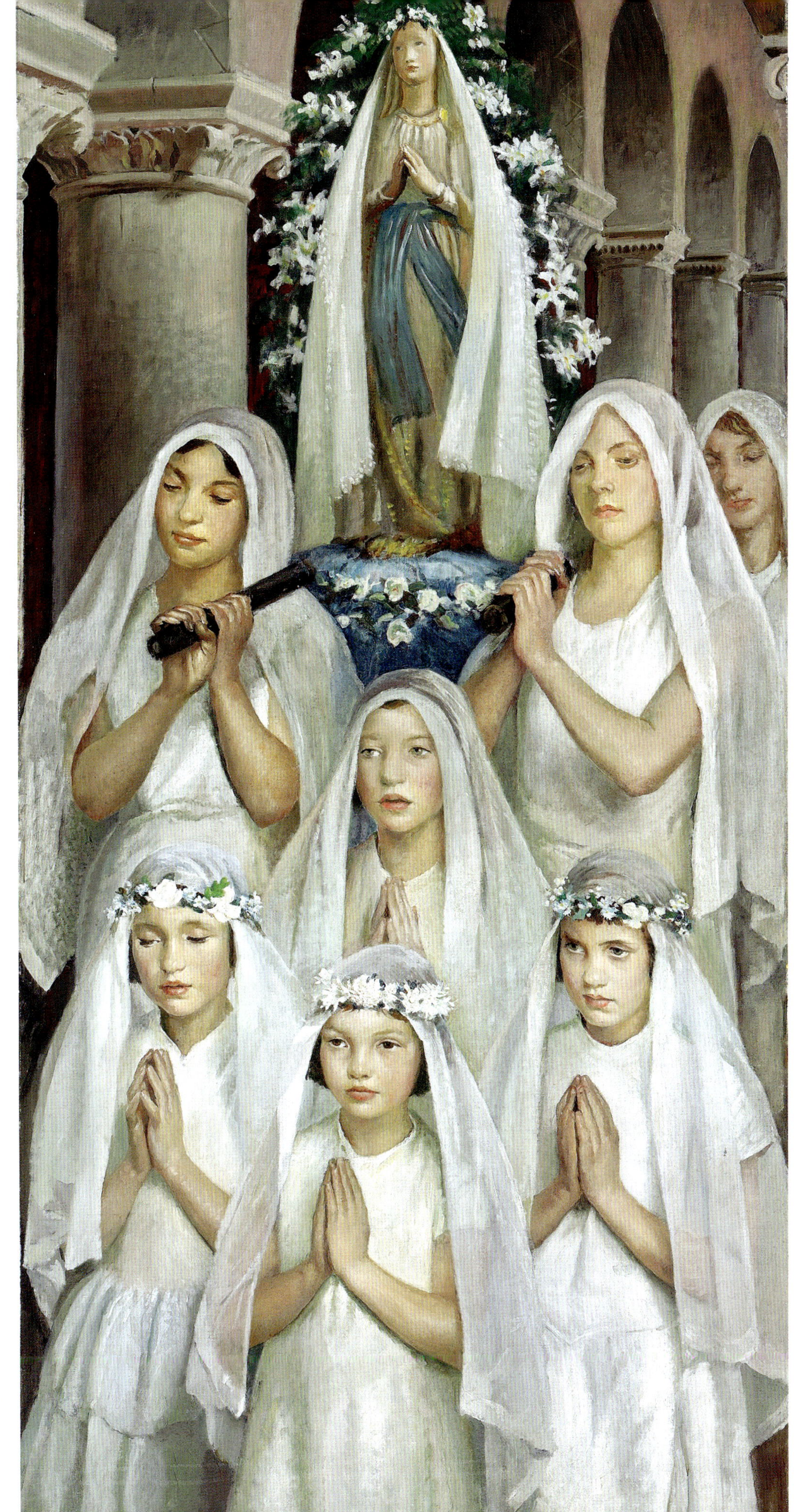

A May Procession
1935 | oil on canvas
185 x 91.5 cm
CHRISTIE'S

In 1927 he exhibited yet again at Leicester Galleries,[8] this time without Gertrude. *The Christian Science Monitor* noted:

> He has a personality, he has a real command over the technical process of painting; and he has a clear conviction of the manner in which he ought to express himself. As a result, his exhibition is more than ordinarily attractive and has an unusual degree of significance – a marked power of arresting attention. The chief characteristic of it is a sort of vivid actuality, a decisive assertion of the facts of the subjects chosen which implies a rather exceptional intimacy of observation on his part and the possession of a well-developed analytical sense. He leaves little to the imagination in his pictures; he insists upon detail with pre-Raphaelite conscientiousness and elaborates his material with almost exaggerated sincerity, but yet he does not give the idea of labour for labour's sake. His colour, too, is, as a rule, vehement to the verge of crudity, but it is so judiciously harmonised and so decoratively related that it never becomes unpleasant … a man like Mr Harvey, who has a personal creed and asserts it in what he honestly believes to be the right way, is very well worth studying.

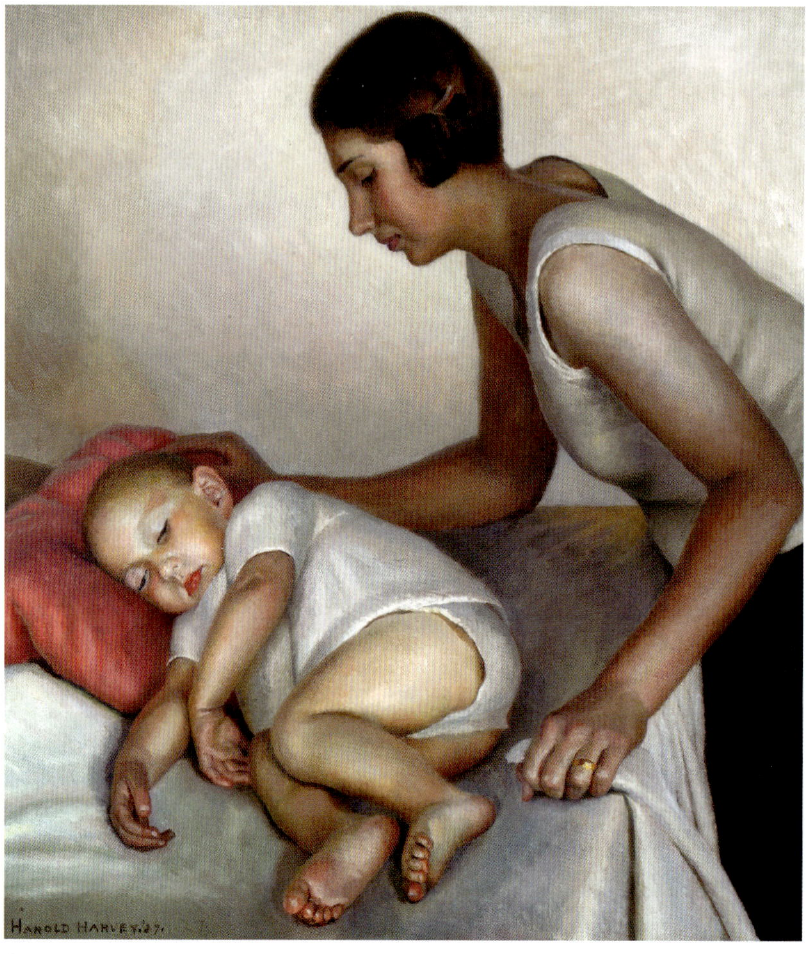

Siesta
1927 | oil on canvas | 65 x 60 cm
Leamington Spa Art Gallery & Museum (Warwick District Council)

8. Forty paintings including nine named portraits.

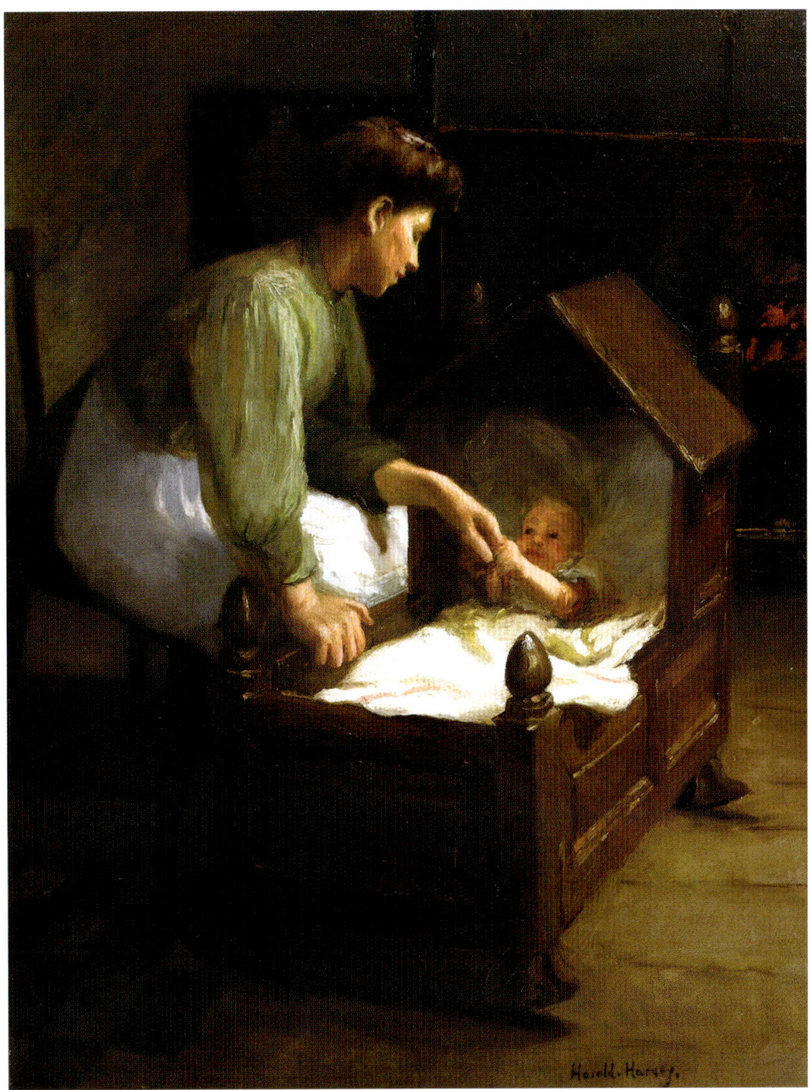

Mother and Child
oil on canvas | 68 x 51 cm
BONHAMS

In the early twenties, Harvey explored several new approaches to painting. The stylisation of his figures, as in *Anemones* (1926; see p. 79), *Picking Tulips* (1926) and *Girls Outside the Gaiety Cinema, Newlyn* (1925; see p. 6), reflects the work of Dod Procter. *Portrait of a Girl at Newlyn Harbour* (1921) has been likened to fabric design because of its concern with two-dimensional pattern, while his *Balloon Seller* of the same year is strongly coloured and reminiscent of Laura Knight. He also experimented with tight, draughtsman-like drawing in works such as *A View of Mousehole* (1922), *Mousehole Harbour* and *Time for Idle Gossip* (both 1923). At the same time he continued to paint Gertrude in domestic settings, including *Portrait of the Artist's Wife, Gertrude* (1922), *In the Bedroom* (1923), *My Kitchen* (1923, see p. 68) and *On The Line* (1922). *The Critics* (1922; p. 93) is recognised as one of his best interiors. Gertrude sits at a large shining table, Ella Naper stands looking over her shoulder and there is a third figure. It was shown at the Royal Academy in 1922 and bought by Sir Barry Vincent Jackson, a friend of Harvey's, who presented it to the Birmingham Museum and Art Gallery at the suggestion of the keeper, Sir Whitworth Wallis.[9]

Harvey went his own way: critics who wished to label him as 'old' or 'new' generation were frustrated by his excitement with different styles. 'Mr Harold Harvey is neither a veteran nor a novice, but has found his feet and proved the maturity of his powers, yet his changing choice of subject and manner indicate that he regards Art as elastic and expansive … Mr Harvey has experimented and meandered along pleasant and alluring ways where those to whom his earlier Newlyn street scenes and countryside pictures appealed, may follow him with uncertain steps and questing eyes – one has the feeling that Mr Harvey stands with one foot in the new ateliers and the other in the old Newlyn where he studied with Mr Stanhope Forbes.' [Harvey did not, of course, formally study with Forbes] *The Cornishman*, 31st March 1926.

An instance of his independence of spirit is his depiction of *Rima* (*c*.1925; see p.19). Jacob Epstein's notorious bas-relief in Hyde Park, set up as a memorial to naturalist and author William H. Hudson had been defaced with paint and attacked by the press as that 'Hyde Park Atrocity', 'Hideous', 'A Travesty of Nature', 'Sheer Bolshevism'. Epstein said of Rima (the female spirit in Hudson's novel *Green Mansions : A Romance of the Tropical Forest*) 'Rima is powerful and Rima is tragic. She was never meant to be pretty-pretty.' Harvey's Rima is very different, not so avant-garde; the plants and animals are portrayed naturalistically, the female figure is more gentle, although the composition is strong. Hudson lived in Penzance after the death of his wife, and Harvey's *Rima* is very possibly his personal tribute to the writer as a friend. The work was exhibited at the Royal Academy in 1926 but achieved little comment other than the observation in the *Daily Sketch*, 23rd March 1926 that 'it is a very different conception from Epstein's sculptured figure.'

Harvey exhibited widely throughout the 1920s,[10] including his only appearance in Venice at the 14th Biennale in 1924, showing *Estate*, which was probably his *Summer* (1917). Others of his circle who exhibited there in that year included Harold and Laura Knight, Gladys Hynes, Anne Walke (Dod and Ernest Procter were represented at the following Biennale in 1926). In both 1925 and 1926 the *Daily Graphic* critic, S.P.B. Mais, gave prominence to works by Dod Procter and Harold Harvey in the Royal Academy exhibition. On 1st May 1926 he declared, 'the two outstanding pictures from the point of view of sheer power are *The Back Bedroom* by Dod Procter and *The Flight* by Harold Harvey … Mrs Procter and Mr Harvey are to be congratulated on ploughing their more or less lonely furrows in avoiding prettiness on the one side and eccentricity on the other.' Harold Harvey's own description of himself, given in his entry in the first edition of *Who's Who in Art*, 1927, was as 'A painter in oil of portraits etc.'

9. Letter from Wallis to Harvey, 27 October 1922.

10. In addition to the Leicester Galleries, he also showed at the Royal Academy (1921–8 and 1930), the Grosvenor Gallery, London (1921–2), the British Empire Exhibition at Wembley (1925), the Royal West of England Academy at Bristol (1922–5), the Walker Art Gallery, Liverpool (1924–6), the Carnegie Institute at Pittsburgh (1922 and 1925), the Royal Glasgow Institute (1924–6), Oldham (1924), the Mappin Gallery at Sheffield (1925, 'Principal Artists of Devon and Cornwall'), Leeds, Manchester and Hull (1927, 'Living British Artists'), Bradford (1928), Southport (1934, 'Spring exhibition of Modern Art'), the Royal Hibernian Academy (1928–9) and the Royal Scottish Academy (1930). He showed five works at the Goupil Galleries, where the salon exhibitions held in the winter attracted over 300 works from well over 100 artists. He participated in their exhibition of Modern British Art in summer 1924 (*Clara*), the Salon of 1924 (*Mother and Child*), the Salon of 1925 (*Woolwork*), the Salon of 1927 (*Ethel*), and the Salon of 1928 (*Silver Sands*). On some occasions he showed there together with some of his pupils. At the 1924 Salon, Alison Rose showed *The Gossips*. In the 1925 Salon Midge Bruford showed *Sussex Landscape* and Billie Waters showed *Highland Farm and Muccomar Bridge*. Goupil's acceptance of work by Harvey's pupils shows both their talent and the effectiveness of the Harvey-Procter school. Harvey also showed a total of seven works at the Grosvenor Gallery in New Bond Street, London – two at the winter 1921 show, two in winter 1922, one at the exhibition of Modern art in March–April 1922, and one in summer 1923. At the summer show in 1922 he exhibited *Marazion Marshes* and the press rated Harvey as among the 'coming' men like Nevinson and Gilbert Spencer. He showed alongside Sargent, Lavery, Gerald Kelly and Nevinson. Among his close colleagues, Anne Walke, Ernest Procter and Harold Knight were also represented.

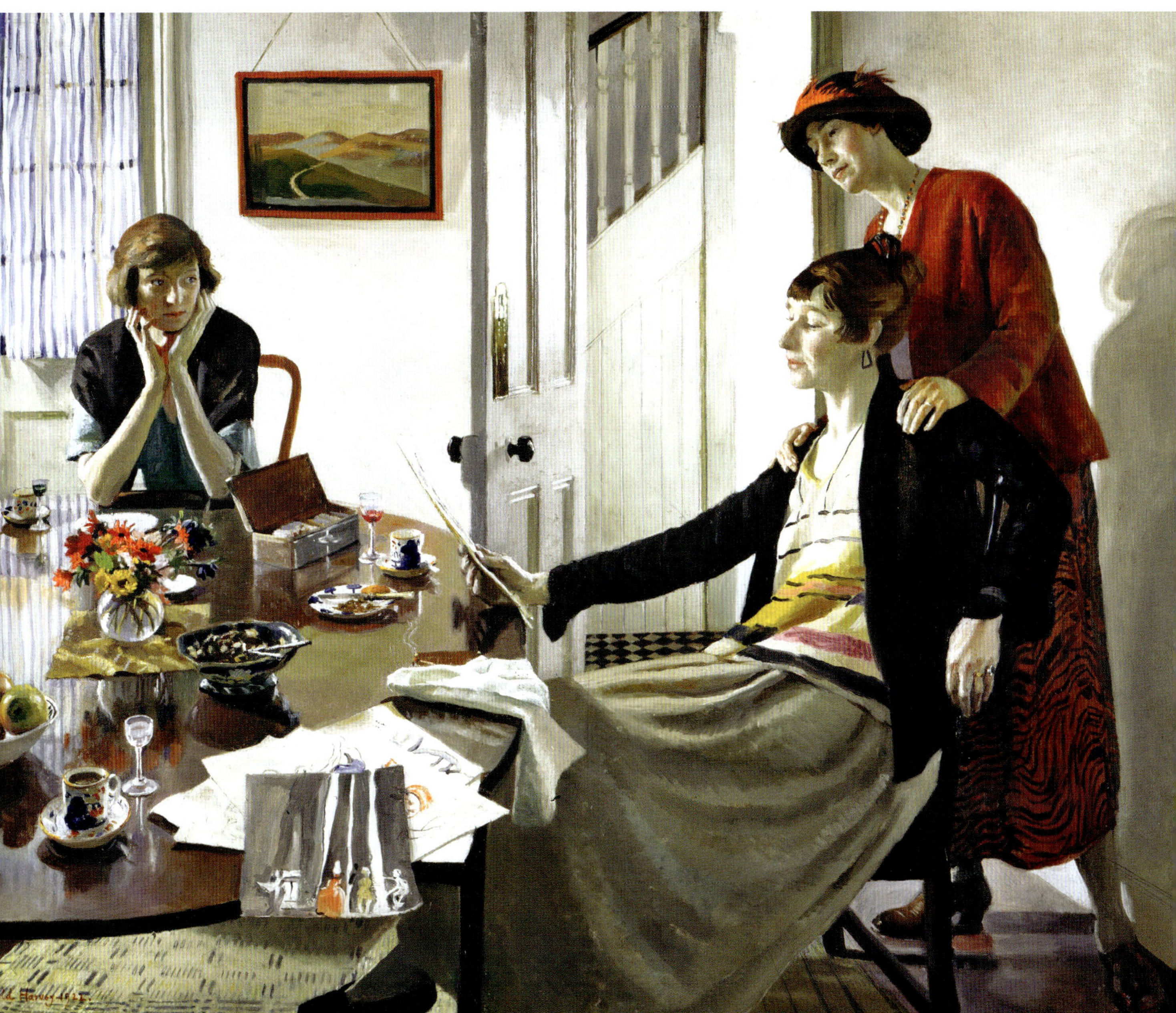

The Critics
1922 | oil on canvas | 60 x 75.5 cm
BIRMINGHAM MUSEUMS TRUST

In February that year he again exhibited at the Leicester Galleries[11] this time without Gertrude; he showed forty works, a number of which were portraits. *A Young Girl*, also known as *Girl on a Cliff* was praised by *Apollo* for its good design while *The Times* said: 'It lolls out of the canvas in a most precarious manner.' The show was generally well received. *Apollo* magazine wrote:

> Mr Harold Harvey, like his colleague Ernest Procter in Newlyn, is one of England's most typical and most excellent painters … to a sense of design and frank delight in colour, Harvey has added solidity and an appreciation of tone … Harvey, who is perhaps not advanced enough to satisfy the devotees of more abstract art, is nevertheless one of the English painters who will be remembered when others are forgotten.

The Times described his work as 'at his best in a sort of halfway house between realism and decoration', while *The Connoisseur* wrote that 'Mr Harvey's is a domesticity that is perhaps a little "arty" in the self-conscious brightness of its colours … it was again the drawing rather than the colour that pleased in Mr Harvey's landscapes … Mr Harvey can at times transcend his material and his technique and achieve something that is, though unpretentious, genuinely related to the art of painting.' A further review in *The Morning Post* (8th February 1927) adds that:

> Mr Harvey seldom goes beyond the delectable Duchy for his subjects, nor does he find it necessary to break with the mode of expression made popular about forty years ago by the Newlyn School … he tries to modernise the Newlyn outlook and mode of handling by introducing the more deliberately studied style of pre-Raphaelite realism and a touch of Jean-François Millet's nonconformist poetry … The influence of the Brotherhood is obvious in *A Corner of My Garden* and *Iris*, while the Clausen-Forbes convention is found in the *Lilian* and the charming glimpse seen *Through The Mirror*. But all three contributory influences meet and merge to form the beauty of *The Mother*. In sentiment, design and colour this picture is most attractive and painted with rare skill and charm.

The interiors show Harold and Gertrude's interest in craft and design, and in the background to *Lunch* (1918) we can see a well-filled bookcase, testimony to Harvey's enjoyment of reading. Indeed he had several close literary associates. His friendship with Vulliamy went back to the days when the latter was writing for *Socialist Review* and *Fabian News*. Another close friend was H.M. Bateman (1887–1970), the New South Wales cartoonist. Thirteen years Harvey's junior, Bateman was another shy man; his interest in art and his sense of humour appealed to Harvey. Bateman had his own exhibitions at the Leicester Galleries in 1921 and 1936, and it is likely that this is where the two met. A letter from Bateman to Harvey, dated March 1940, just after his return from a journey around the world, contains a glimpse of his struggle with painting: 'I spend most of my time these days painting – or rather

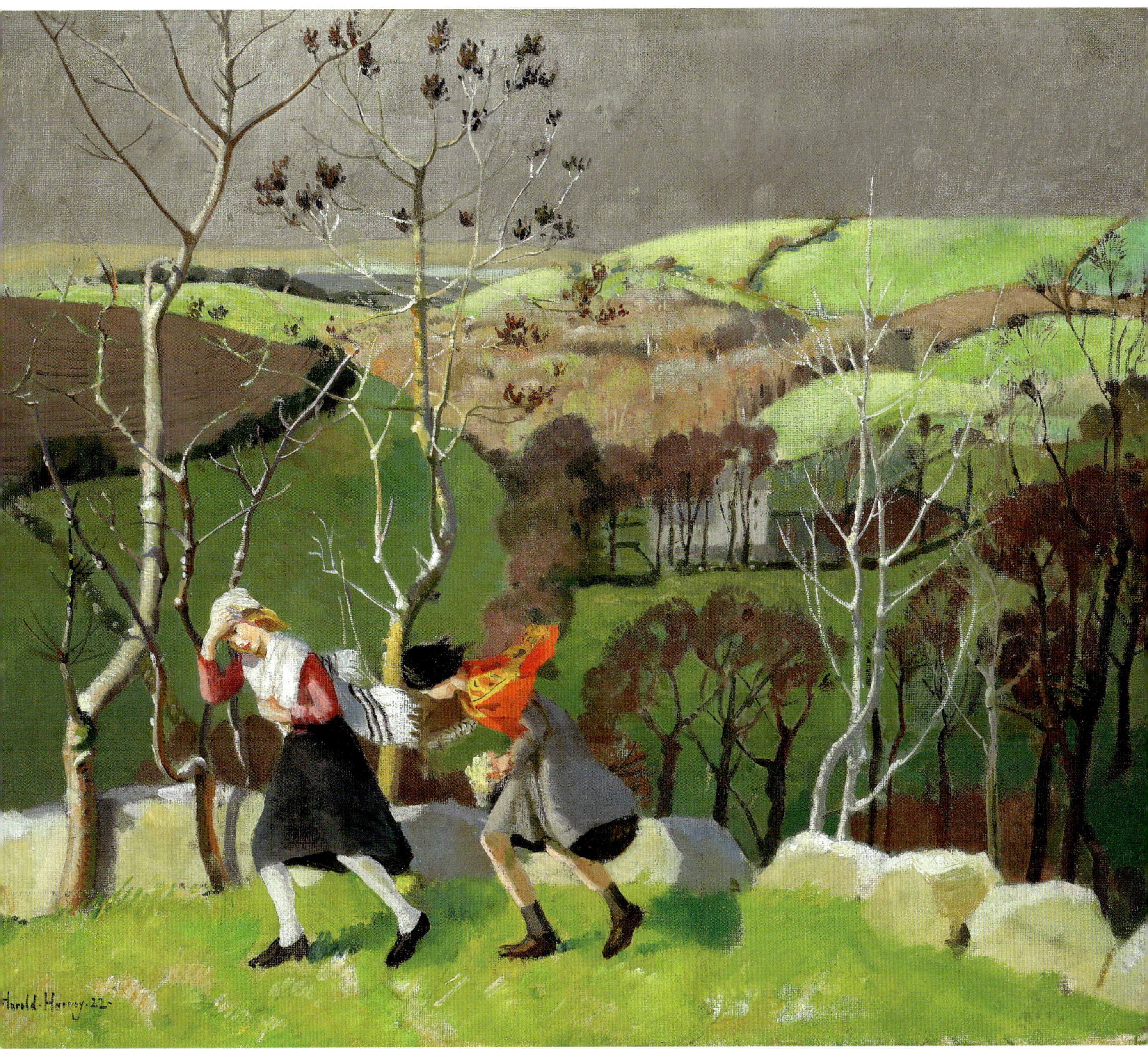

A Windy Day
1922 │ oil on canvas │ 43.5 x 52 cm
CHRISTIE'S

trying to – I'm still obsessed with the problems of technique and
how to do a thing – the result of never just mastering it and settling
a method years ago. I sometimes wonder how I still keep on the
damn thing and don't break up the outfit; but, keep hoping to
strike a vein one of these days!'

He also had acquaintances from the world of acting; his niece
remembers a visit by Charles Laughton who stayed at The Queen's
Hotel. A letter signed 'Gwen' appears to be an apology from the actress
Gwen Ffrancon-Davies in reply to an invitation to Harvey's show at
Barbizon House, explaining that she was 'so busy with rehearsals that
I haven't a second to spare.'[12] At that time she was playing Etain in
Rutland Boughton's *The Immortal Hour* at the Queen's Theatre, London.
Harvey probably met her through Harold Knight, who painted *Miss
Gwen Ffrancon-Davies as Etain in The Immortal Hour*. The dramatist
and poet Gordon Bottomley wrote to Harvey on 6th November 1929
and referred to one of his paintings (unnamed) as 'a real beauty'. Two
letters also survive from a correspondence with Walter de la Mare:
one, dated 9th June 1931, thanks Harvey for the loan of a book;
the second, 27th January 1932 (at the time of the Barbizon House
exhibition) invites Harold and Gertrude to stay at de la Mare's
home, Hill House at Taplow in Buckinghamshire.

On one of their rare departures from Cornwall, Gertrude and
Harold visited the Knights in their new home at 10 Abbey Road,
London. Laura recalled: 'Gert, in her generous way, insisted on
helping with all the painting and white-washing that Harold and
I were doing – a nice way of spending her London holiday, but she
wanted to make "all fitty" as the Cornish would say.'[13]

The minutes of the Newlyn Society of Artists show Harvey as again
being a member in 1923, despite having resigned his membership
nine years earlier. Some years later he was found to have breached
a regulation, and the minutes for 7th April 1930 record: 'The next
matter under discussion was the fact of Mr Harold Harvey having
removed one of his pictures from the gallery, after it had been
accepted and hung by the Committee for Show Days, and thereby
breaking regulation number six, agreed to by him in the Form.
A letter was drafted on the subject and agreed to by those present,
which it was decided should be sent to Mr Harvey by the Honorary
Secretary.' Harvey had resigned again by 1935.

12. The letter is dated 17th February
1932; *The Immortal Hour* ran at the
Queen's Theatre from 9th February
to 19th March 1932.
13. Laura Knight, *Oil Paint and Grease
Paint* (London: Nicholson & Watson,
1936).

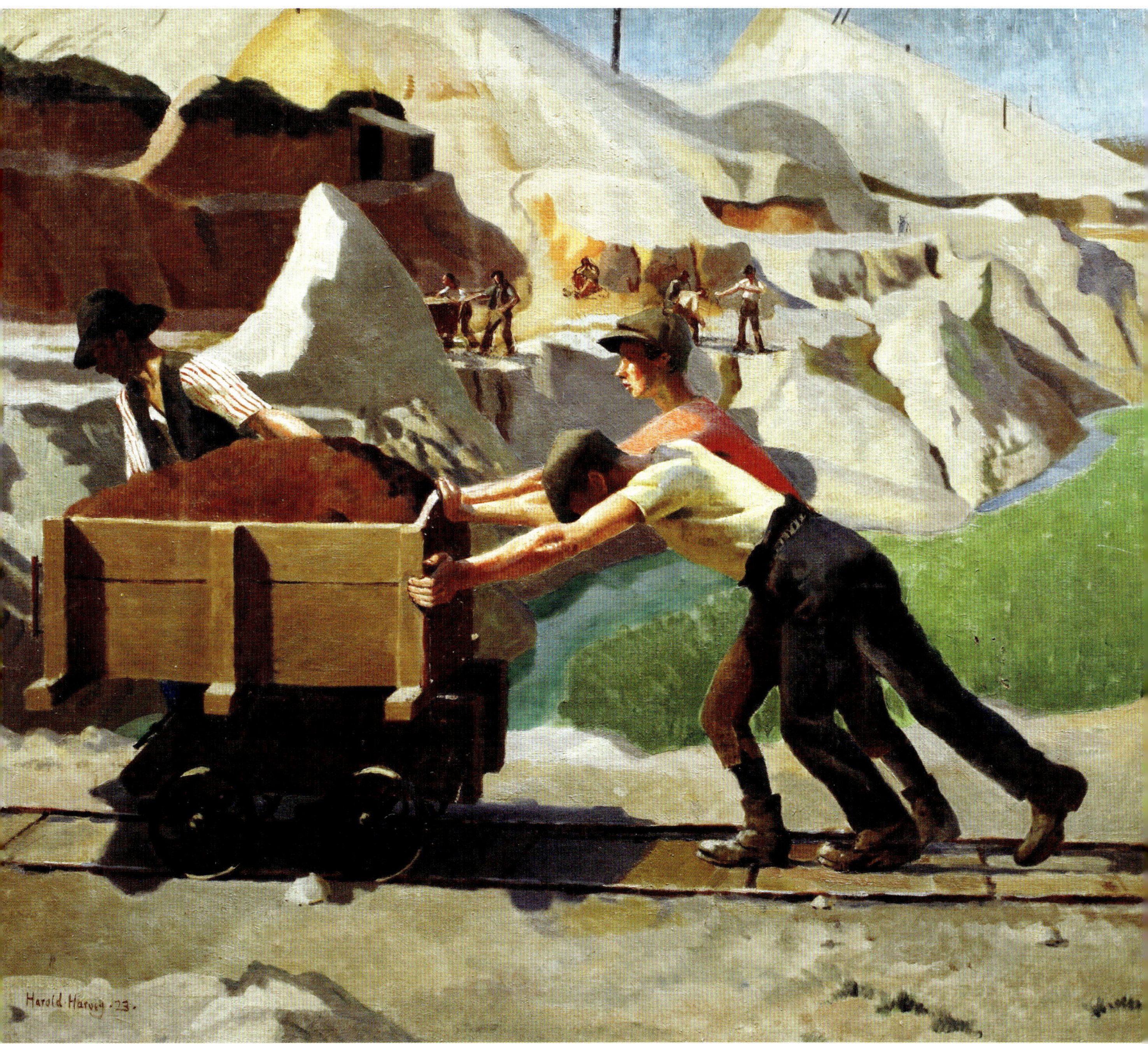

The Clay Pit
1923 | oil on canvas | 67 x 80 cm
ROYAL INSTITUTION OF CORNWALL, ROYAL CORNWALL MUSEUM, TRURO

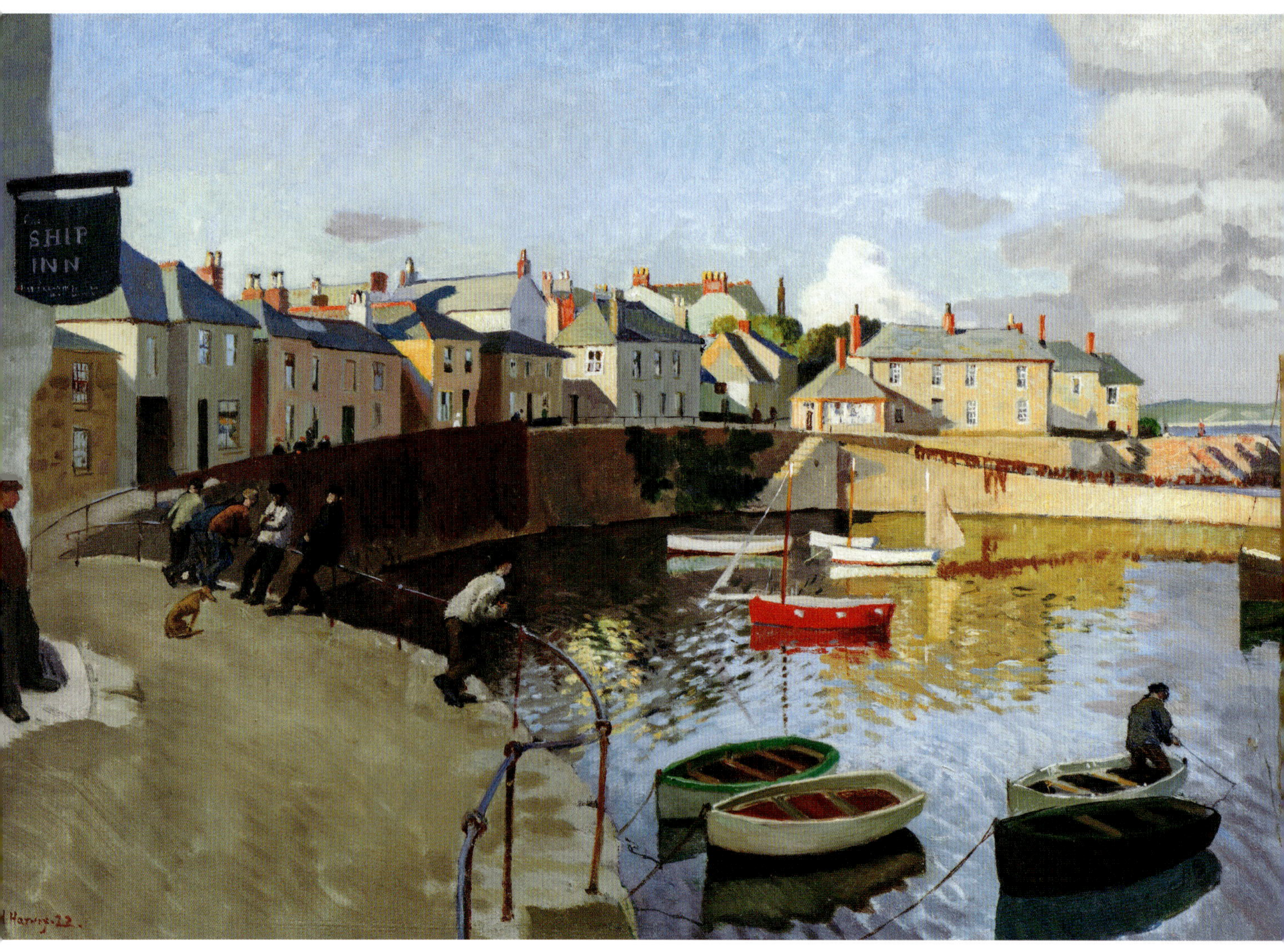

Mousehole
1922 | oil on canvas | 40.5 x 60 cm
PRIVATE COLLECTION; IMAGE COURTESY DAVID MESSUM FINE ART

Seven

The Cornish artist

The *Barbizon House Record*[1] for 1932 states: 'In February of this year recent works of Harold Harvey, the Cornish Artist, were shown and many interested people visited the exhibition.' It was a solo show. Harvey was now 58 and he still confounded any critic keen to put his work into a neat pigeon hole. The *Times* reviewer commented that 'Mr Harvey appears to be a perfectly logical development from the Newlyn School of Mr Stanhope Forbes, RA, with the brighter and more decoratively considered colour and the more deliberately plastic ambitions which belong to the present day.'[2] The *Observer*, however, took a different view, stating that '… with all his conscientiousness of representation, he entirely subordinates portraiture to pictorial organisation, and scenes of cottage or kitchen life treated more or less in the manner of the eighteenth century conversation piece. It is in this latter genre that Mr Harvey scores his most striking successes, among which must be counted: *The Shawl*, *The Dresser*, *The Mirror Picture* and *The Doorstep Picture*.'

This reviewer goes on to comment on the similarity of Harvey's work to that of Harold Knight and Dod Procter, which he rightly observes is a natural consequence of their belonging to the same artist's colony. Although some of his works are observed to approach 'the solidity and firm plastic modelling of Mr Harold Knight', he nevertheless shows his own style: 'Mr Harvey's aim is decorative throughout, and to achieve this end he resorts to an emphasis of bright, cheerful colour patterning that is the antithesis of the Impressionist method. His is an art of deliberate intention, which, though closely tied to observation of Nature and honest rendering of facts, leaves nothing to chance.'[3] Friends were also forthcoming in their praise. A letter from artist George Clausen, dated 13th February 1932, says simply: 'We saw your show this morning and were quite disarmed with it! … The clean fresh colour and honest outlook are so refreshing …'

In October 1935, Ernest Procter died, aged only 49, depriving Harold of his 'best friend'. Stanhope Forbes records in his diaries that he went

1. Barbizon House was founded in 1918 at 8 Henrietta Street, London and ran until 1938 when the address was renamed Henrietta Place.
2. *The Times*, 5 February 1932.
3. *The Observer*, 7 February 1932.

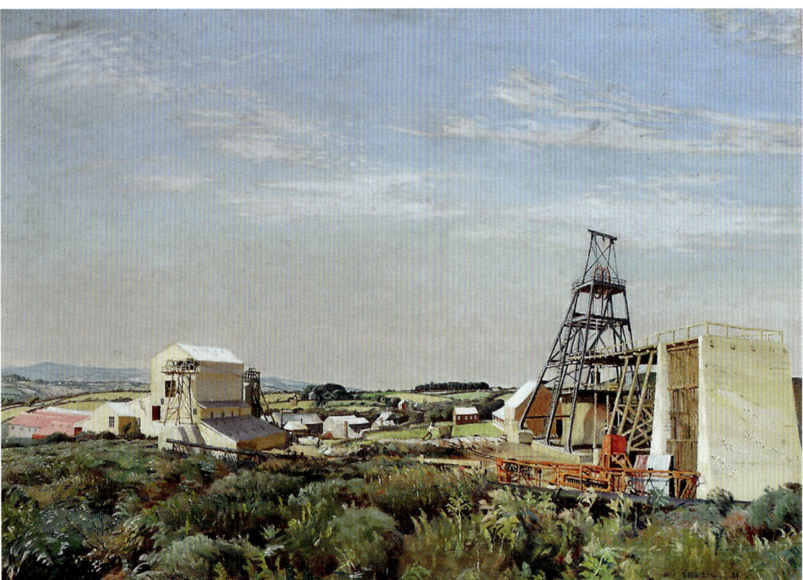

Wheal Reeth
1934 | oil on canvas | 86 x 127 cm
CHRISTIE'S

to Maen Cottage to take the sad news to the Harveys but he spoke
only to Gertrude; whether Harvey already knew, or whether Gertrude
deemed it better to relay such sad news to her husband herself is not
known. Procter was in Newcastle at the time of his death and was
cremated at South Shields, but his remains were brought back to
St Hilary on 29th October. Harold and Gertrude attended the
funeral, together with many others.[4]

Ever prolific, Harvey habitually threw himself into his work, except
for a few months after the sudden death of his father, when grief must
be presumed to have halted his output.[5] Throughout his career he continued to paint domestic interiors, portraits, landscapes and genre com-
binations. *Fête Champêtre* (1934) commemorates the gala held in Newlyn
every Whit Monday. In it, Harvey captures a procession of villagers,
children and visitors as they parade beneath a banner[6] designed by
Frank Bramley and John Mackenzie; the parade is accompanied
by two brass bands to nearby manor house, Trereife. A new theme
appeared in 1934 (*Wheal Reeth*), and which he had explored earlier
with *Leswidden Pit* (1920) and *The Clay Pit* (1923). A new flat treatment
marks both these paintings with an almost poster-like quality, but
with the familiar detailed portraiture in the foremost faces. Models
were, as usual, authentic local characters; Sidney Angove (left) and
Nicholas Grenfell (right) feature in *Cornish Miners*, for example.

From 1930 to 1941, he exhibited every year at the Royal Academy and
most years also at the Royal Hibernian Academy, Dublin.[7] He also
showed at the Royal Scottish Academy (1930); the Royal Glasgow
Institute (1933, 1941); Southport (1938); and in four successive years at
the Pittsburgh Carnegie Institute (1933–6). As well as painting Gertrude

4. *The Cornishman* reported the event
on 31 October saying: 'There were
many beautiful floral tributes and the
grave was lined with evergreens and
anemones.' The Leicester Galleries
held a memorial exhibition for Procter
in 1935.
5. Francis McFarland Harvey died
in 1915.
6. The banner now hangs in the
Centenary Methodist Chapel.
7. Harvey exhibited here in 1931–2,
1934, 1936–9.

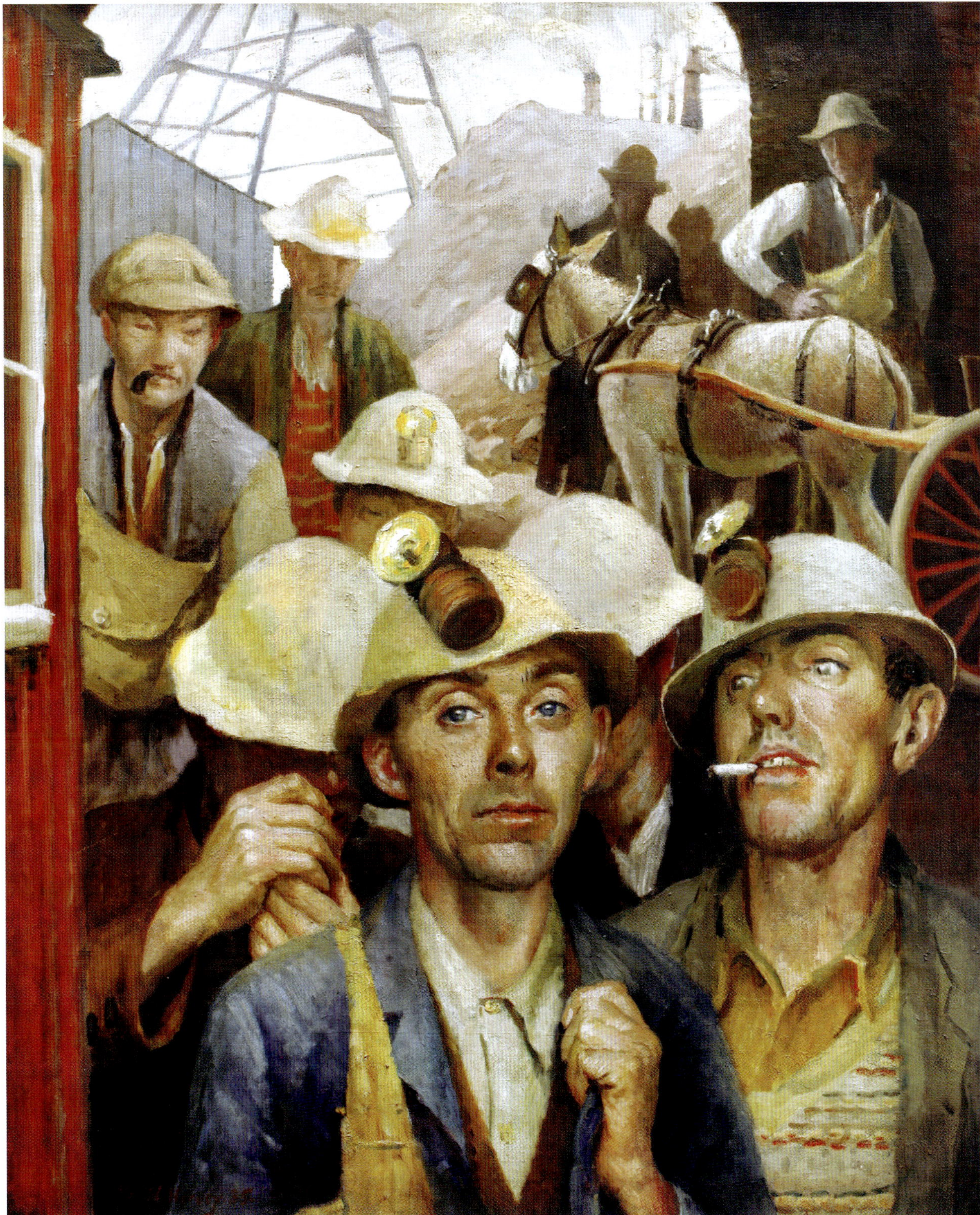

Cornish Miners aka ***St Just Tin Miners***
1935 | oil on canvas | 75 x 62 cm
ROYAL INSTITUTION OF CORNWALL, ROYAL CORNWALL MUSEUM, TRURO

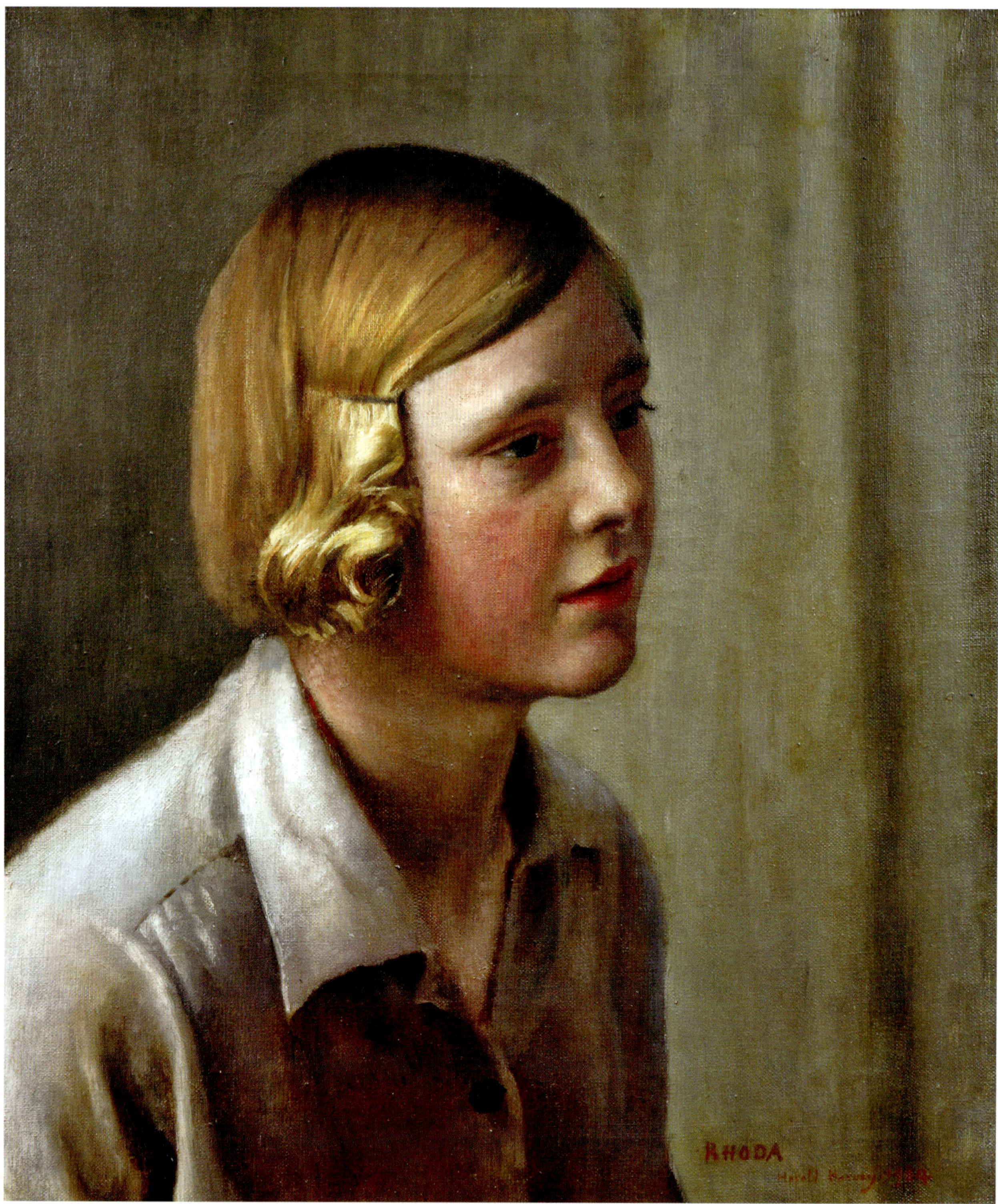

Rhoda
*c.*1934 | oil on canvas | 56 x 51 cm
PENLEE HOUSE GALLERY & MUSEUM

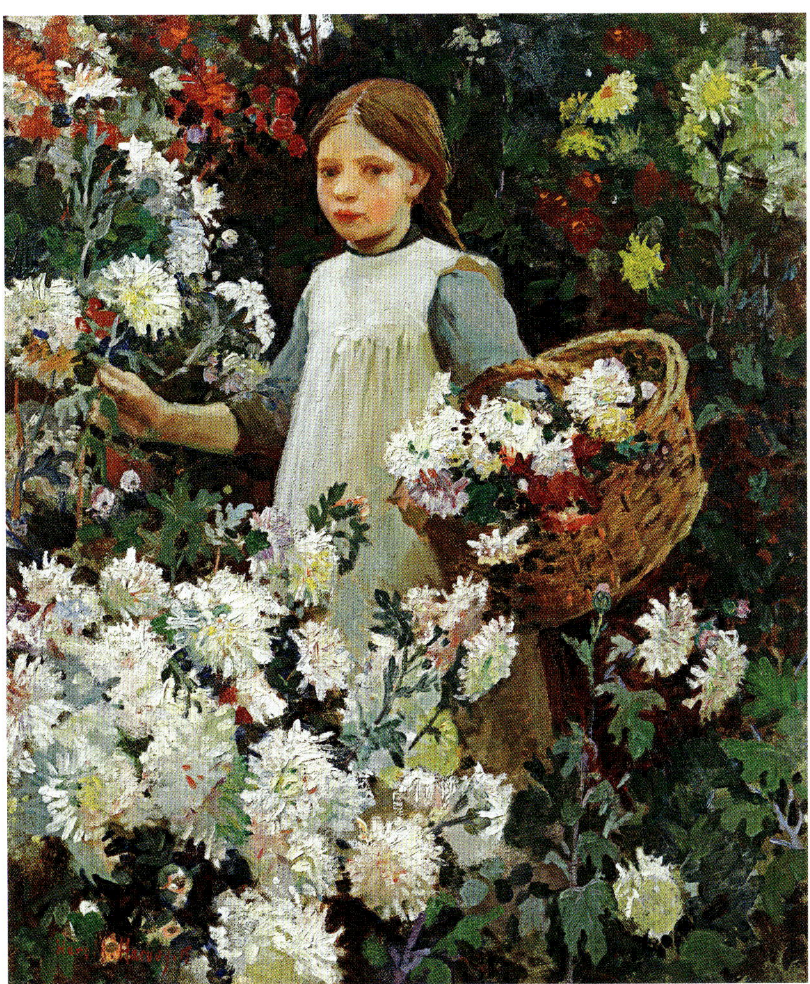

Picking Chrysanthemums
1915 | oil on canvas | 54 x 46.5 cm
RICHARD GREEN GALLERY, LONDON

and local models, he also painted a series of family portraits. He had shown *Josephine* at the 1927 Royal Academy, depicting Gertrude's niece. He painted *Rhoda*, his niece by his brother Arthur, in 1934, a stunning portrait of her as a fresh-faced young girl, but which Rhoda's family described as wearing her 'soppy look'; he also painted her sister Kathleen Alice (known as Kitty). Rhoda is one of Harvey's few relatives to be known to have inherited the artistic gene, as she exhibited in Newlyn in 1939, receiving enthusiastic reviews; she was a close friend of artist Ben Nicholson in the 1950s. Another portrait was *Ailsa* (*c*.1940), the wife of Harold's nephew Raymond.

Harvey always liked to have people in his paintings. In the years leading up to the war, Helen Kitchin[8] was working on a farm belonging to her cousin Joyce Howell and her partner Marjorie Clarry who commissioned Harold Harvey to paint their house, *The White House*. Helen remembers that he agreed to the commission on the condition that she and her fellow workers pose in the foreground 'to make it more interesting'. Helen also remembers being told 'to wear something

bright. I managed to find a green skirt and a terracotta sweater,
I didn't normally work in these clothes but I had the skirt to travel
in. There were four of us, picking daffodils, Marjorie and Joyce, and
Grahame – he lived in the village – he had a basket of flowers on his
shoulder … you can only see the back of me … picking daffodils for
the flower train.' She remembers that the picture was painted in a
day and remembers very little of the artist, other than that he was
quiet. 'You know, I can't even remember what he looked like.'

Before the war *Picture Post* ran a series of articles on 'Great British
Artists'; the third issue, 15th October 1938, featured the Newlyn
'Colony'. It included photographs of Harold and Gertrude, Dod
Procter, Stanhope Forbes, Leonard Fuller and Borlase Smart, as well
as some Newlyn fishermen posing for a 'life class at Newlyn'; and a
view of an exhibition of the Cornwall Group at St Ives. Harold can be
seen, cigarette holder in his mouth, standing before his easel working

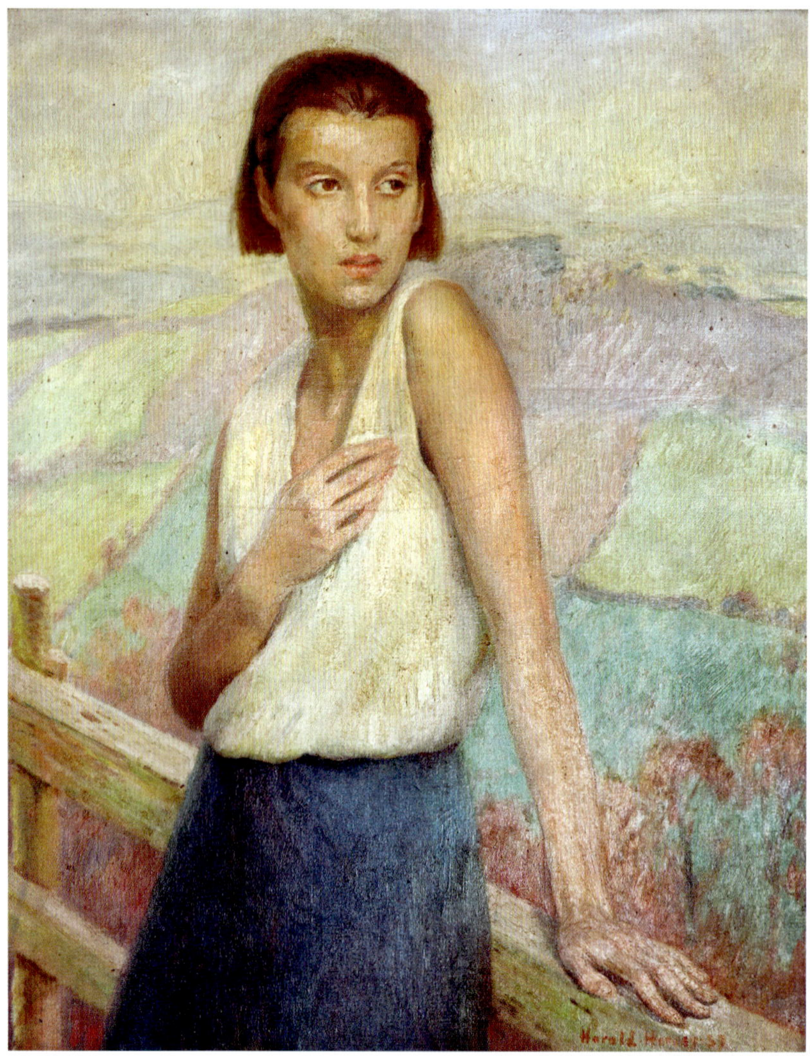

Joan James
1937 | oil on canvas | 90.5 x 76.5 cm
PRIVATE COLLECTION

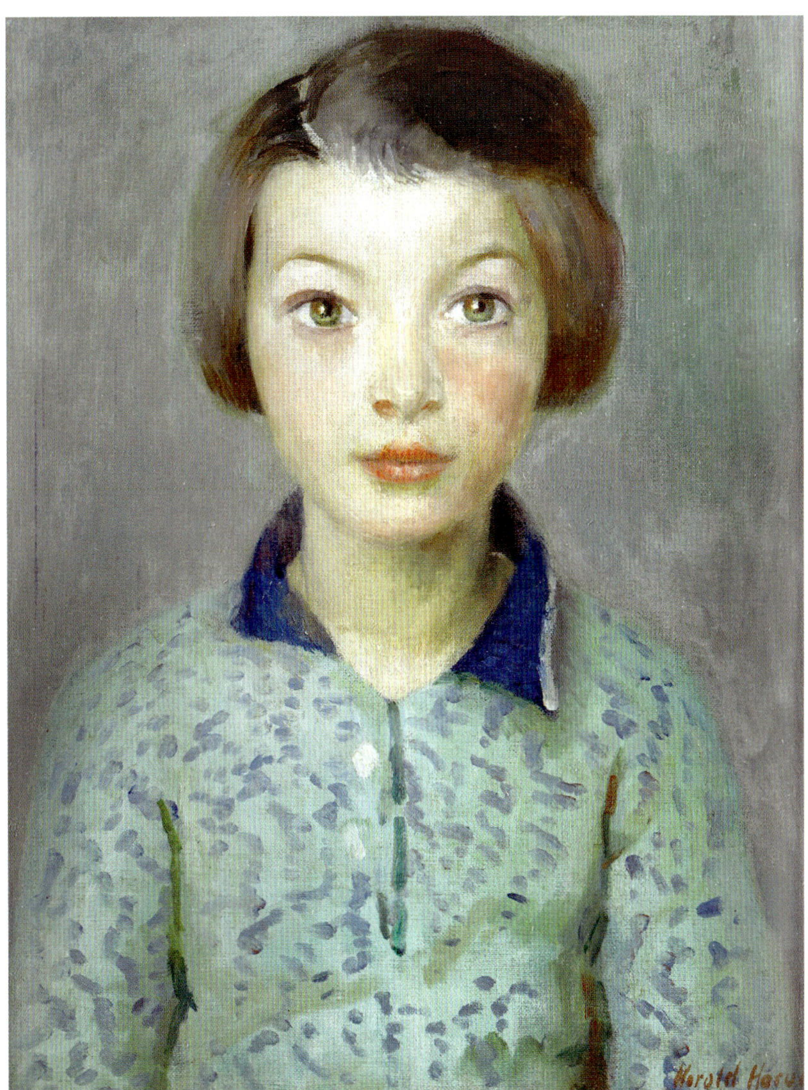

A Daughter of Newlyn
*c.*1936 | oil on canvas | 44.5 x 39.5 cm
PRIVATE COLLECTION; IMAGE COURTESY BONHAMS

on *Allotments* (shown at the Royal Academy in 1939). The caption reads: 'One of the few Cornishmen in the Cornish group. He makes a speciality of character studies. Harold and Gertrude are husband and wife.' In the Second World War, Gertrude and Harold Harvey took in an evacuee, Sam Kemp. He appears as *The Onion Boy* in 1940. The impact of the war is gently alluded to in *Allotments*, where a young couple and their daughter tend plants in a sunny landscape which extends far off into the distance, and prefigures the 'Dig For Victory' campaign to produce food. *August 1939* (1940; overleaf) recalls the last summer of peace with a beach scene.

In 1937 Frost & Reed held an exhibition of Harvey's paintings at their gallery at Clare Street, Bristol. The local critic refers to *The Poplars, Monmouth* painted while Harvey visited his brother, Percival, in Wales. It is a rare example of his depicting a scene outside Cornwall, another

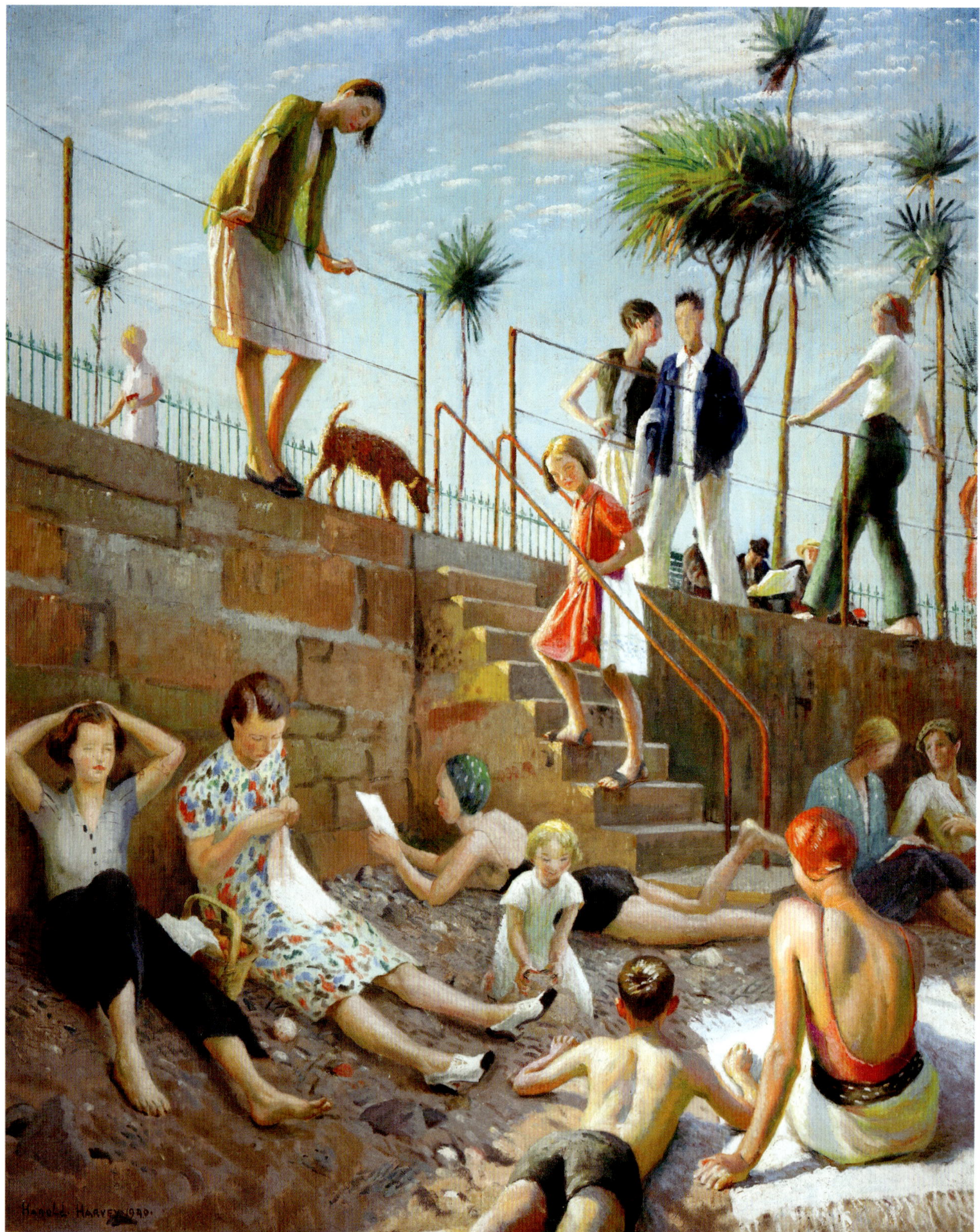

August, 1939
1940 | oil on canvas | 142 x 112 cm
PRIVATE COLLECTION

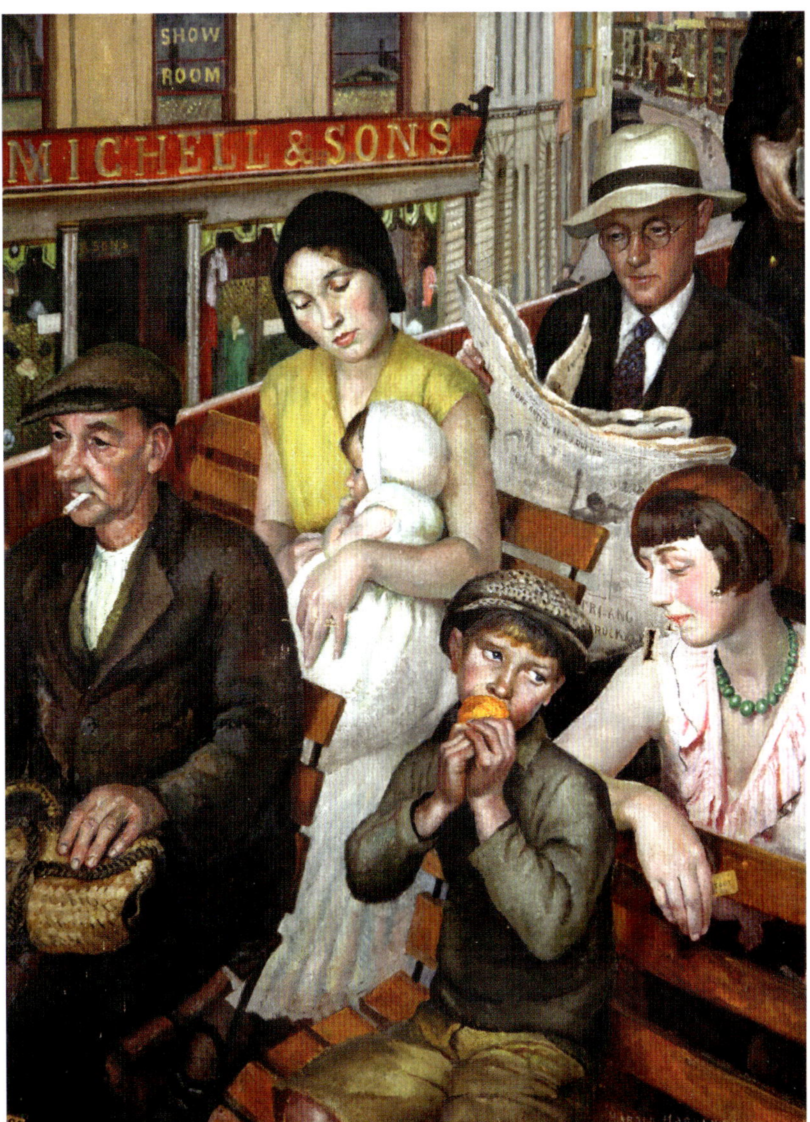

The Top of the Bus
1932 | oil on canvas | 102 x 76 cm
PRIVATE COLLECTION

being *Monnow Hill*, which was presumably painted at the same time. Two years later Frost and Reed held another exhibition of about thirty of Harvey's works. This review, from an unidentified newspaper, appears to be the final significant assessment of Harvey's work during his lifetime:

> They deal entirely with Cornish life and landscapes, as viewed by a man with a keen eye for colour and a fondness for what is bright and harmonious. He seems to take his subjects as they come, without elaborate prearrangement, relying entirely for their effect upon the way he handles them. This is particularly noticeable in *April* and *A Shower*. In one of these rain is seen in the distant fields, and in the other children are seen sheltering beneath a hedge. In both there is an unmistakable open-air atmosphere. The same influence pervades *Cutting Broccoli*

and *Over the Hills*. His studies of interiors are equally realistic. They are not overladen with detail, but the detail is clearly painted in a way which strengthens the central idea. Every one of his pictures contains figures, and several of them animals. All bear evidence of the directness of his methods, and this directness is balanced with simplicity. His colours are strong, at times almost daring, and the manner in which they are applied gives evidence of distinct individuality.[9]

Early in 1940, during a blackout, Harvey must have had an accident which incapacitated him. A letter from Bateman (8th March 1940) says: 'Sorry to hear you have been laid up for such a spell and hope you have got quite well again. I had an idea that, apart from the sea, Cornwall was about the safest place to be during war time, but the Blackout is a danger anywhere.' Around this time Harvey listed the contents of his studio in his notebook, by subject and size, under the headings: Portraits and Heads (26 works); Figure Pictures & Studies (42 works); Landscapes (51 works) – a total of 119 pictures. Several of these can be related to works already identified, but a good many remain unknown.

Harold Harvey died on Monday 19th May 1941 at his home Maen Cottage, the day before his 67th birthday.[9] The causes of death were recorded as oedema of the lungs and Mitral disease, and the Registrar was informed by his brother, Arthur William Hext Harvey. A requiem mass was held at the Church of the Immaculate Conception of Our Lady on Rosevean Road. There was an appropriate coincidence of the name Rosevean, in that his studio had been in the grounds of the house by that name. He was buried at Penzance Cemetery on Friday 23rd May; a simple stone cross was erected over his grave with the inscription: 'In loving Memory of Harold Charles Francis Harvey, Artist of Newlyn. Born 1874, Died 1941.' In remembrance of him, the Newlyn Art Society and his friends presented one of his late paintings *The Gate* (1940) to the Royal Institution of Cornwall in Truro. A lengthy and appreciative obituary was published in *The Cornishman* and *Cornish Telegraph* on 22nd May. Stanhope Forbes published his own tribute in the same issue. He and Lamorna Birch were among those at the funeral. The *Cornishman* obituary ran as follows:

> ***Death of Mr Harold Harvey – well known local artist***
> We regret to announce the death of Mr Harold Harvey, which occurred suddenly at his residence, Maen Cottage, Newlyn, at the age of 67 on Monday. Mr Harold Harvey was one of the best-known artists of the Newlyn School, and for many years had been a regular exhibitor not only at the local exhibitions but at the Royal Academy. Mr Harvey's pictures were noted for their daintiness, their careful craftsmanship, and their rare beauty. He often specialised in figure studies where the dresses of the women portrayed were magnificently done. Many local scenes were also the subject of his brush. One of his paintings in oil – a portrait of the late Alderman W.H. Julyan in his robes as Mayor of Penzance – hangs in the Mayor's Parlour at Penzance.

9. When Harold died, all his brothers and sisters survived him except Leonard who died in 1935 in Nairobi. Harold did not live to learn of the death of his youngest brother, Cyril, in 1942 at Benghazi, nor of the destruction by Luftwaffe bombing in September 1943 of his brother Arthur's solicitor's office at 6 North Parade.

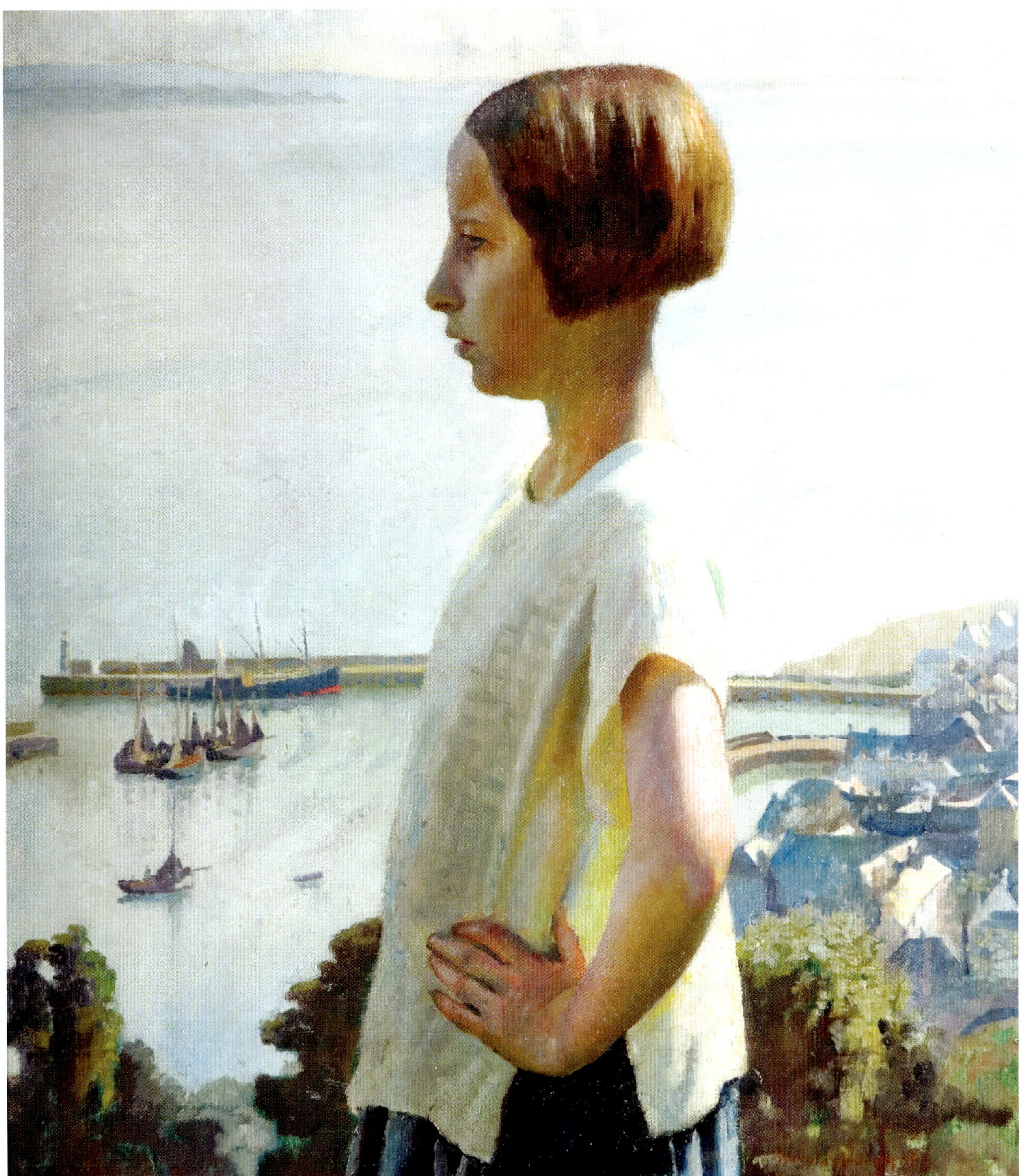

The Little Maiden
1934 | oil on canvas | 51 x 46 cm
WOLVERHAMPTON ART GALLERY

Mr Harold Charles Francis Harvey was born in 1874, and was the eldest son of the late Mr Francis McFarland Harvey, who as a banker was well-known to an earlier generation. He received his early training at the Penzance Art School under the late Mr Norman Garstin. He completed his studies at the Julian School in Paris. He was of a rather retiring nature and never mixed in public affairs and neither did he ever seek publicity. He was content to live for his art, and may often have been seen depicting on canvas some beautiful little glimpse. He was a familiar figure in Newlyn, where he was greatly liked and respected by all.

Mr Harvey leaves a widow (Mrs Gertrude Harvey), who is known for her beautiful paintings of flowers and still life, and much sympathy is felt for her in her sudden bereavement. Mr Harold Harvey is survived by his brothers Dr P.G. Harvey (Monmouth), Dr Frank Harvey (Harley Street), Mr A.W.H. Harvey (solicitor, Penzance), Mr W.V. Harvey (retired inspector of Lloyds Bank), Captain Cyril Harvey (Seaforth Highlanders, also a solicitor) and Miss Gladys Harvey (nurse, of Barnsley).

Mr Harold Harvey had for some time complained of heart trouble, but had been painting up to within a few days of the fatal ending of his illness, which he did not expect. He did not look his 67 years of age, and had been most helpful to the present curator and secretary of the Passmore Edwards Art Gallery.

Mr Harvey was an enterprising colourist and good draughtsman. His pictures were usually notable for the freshness of his varied palette, the excellence of the composition, and the realistic portrayal of his models and the Cornish environment. He was one of those whose work had been accepted by the Royal Academy for this year's exhibition.

The deceased artist was keenly interested in world problems and had no use for Totalitarian Governments or their outlook on social life. Mr Harvey deplored the death of Mr Ernest Procter, who was his 'best friend'. He also missed Mr Frank Heath and quite recently Mr Reginald Dick, who had been the designer of the works in copper and other metals, and who at one time had painted many interesting pictures. Mr Dick had almost completely lost his sight before he passed away; and Mr Heath had had hospital treatment, but Mr Procter's early demise was unexpected and came as a great shock to Mr Harvey and other artists.

Mrs Gertrude Harvey is recognised as one of the most talented and artistic flower painters in England. If a foreign signature had been affixed to her canvases many admirers think she would have had a Continental as well as English reputation …

Despite his heart trouble, as the obituary states, Harvey had painted right up until the time of his death. Among his last paintings there are three dated 1941, *Bridge over a river in a Cornish village*, *Mine Workings*, and *The Mantelpiece*. Two other works were exhibited at the Royal Academy that year and might have been painted in 1941; they are *Joan* and *A Window in Newlyn*. Fox and Greenacre say his last work showed daffodil picking at a farm near his home, where anemones and tulips were also grown.[10]

10. Caroline Fox & Francis Greenacre *Painting in Newlyn 1880–1930* (London: Barbican Art Gallery, 1985).

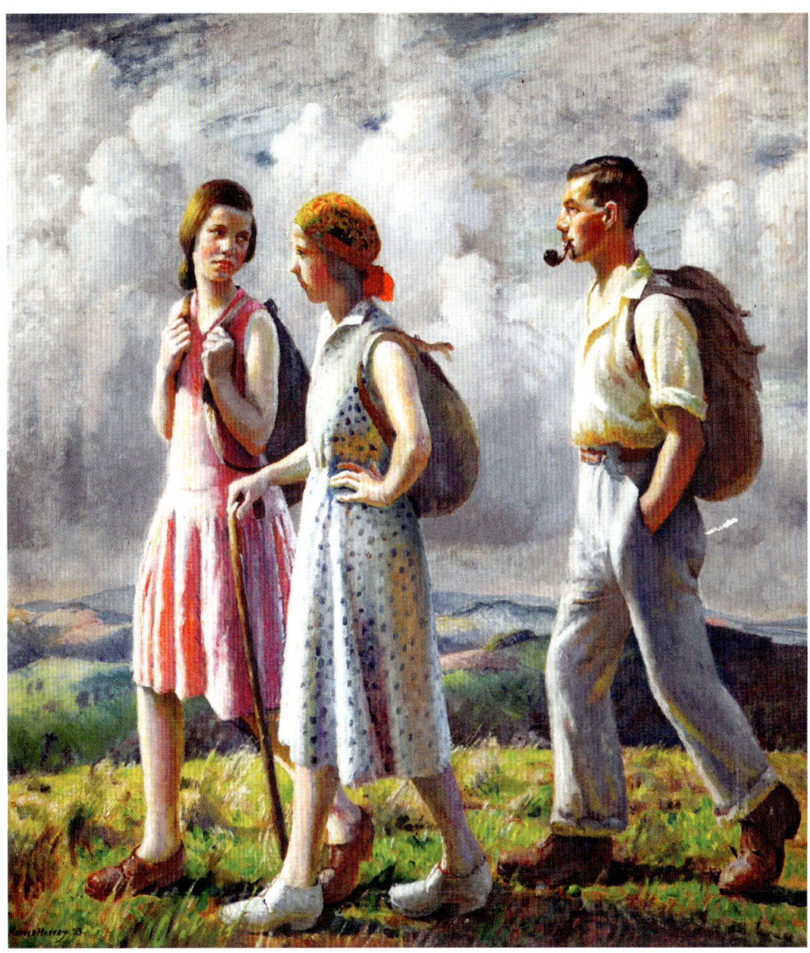

Walkers
1933 | oil on canvas | 102 x 92 cm
PRIVATE COLLECTION

The national papers were reporting the arrival in Scotland of Hitler's deputy, Rudolf Hess; the sinking of first HMS *Hood* and then the *Bismarck*; the German invasion of Crete, and the pro-Axis revolt in Iraq. In these desperate times, little attention was paid to the passing of this most prolific and notable British artist. *The Studio* published a review of his achievement a year after Harvey's death, in 1942, illustrated with four of his works: *The Young Artist* (1933), *In the Bedroom* (c.1922), *Fête Champêtre* (1934), and *Bog Farm* (1938). Wallace Nichols wrote: 'His portrait and figure work possess the simplicity of a landscape in which the non-essentials have been pared away … he was particularly skilled in rendering the effects of light against light, so definite a feature of Cornish landscapes.'

Little may be known about the personal life of this private man, but his work stands in testament to, in Nichols' phrase, 'one of the truest and sincerest of British painters'.[11]

11. *The Studio*, March 1942.

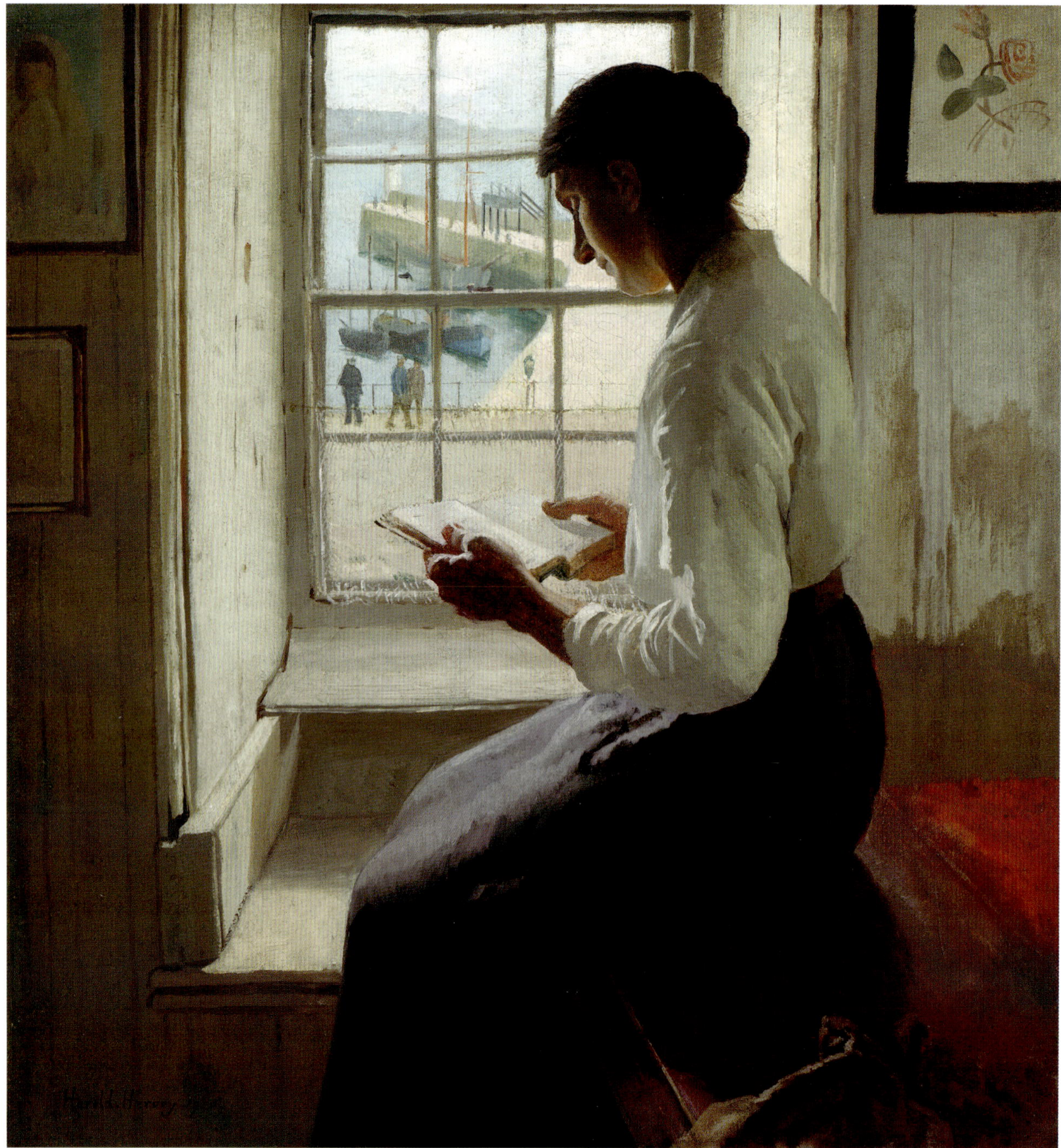

The New Book
1920 │ oil on canvas │ 50 x 47 cm
PRIVATE COLLECTION; IMAGE COURTESY RICHARD GREEN GALLERY, LONDON

Postscript

After Harold died, Gertrude remained at Maen Cottage for some years and her sister Sophie moved in with her. Eventually, deteriorating health led her to the Benoni Nursing Home at St Just, where she was supported by the Artists' General Benevolent Institution. Tragically, 'The Flower Painter' (as Harold had labelled her) suffered from increasingly bad eyesight which eventually failed altogether. She died on 18th March 1966 at the age of 86. She was buried with Harold at Penzance cemetery on Tuesday 22nd March, but there is no inscription to mark her presence.

Harvey's earliest recorded paintings are thought to date from around 1890 when he would have been sixteen, and go through to 1941, the year he died. There are about 800 paintings catalogued to date and works are still coming to light. At least two of his models are uncertain as to the whereabouts of the paintings for which they sat, which implies that more may yet be found. It is known that as a working artist Harvey undertook commissions, and some families may not appreciate the value of the painting in the attic that 'come in payment' to Grandad.

The preliminary drawings and sketches have all but vanished; relatively few are known. Some of those which still exist are preparatory sketches, others are developed works in their own right, such as a painting of the man playing an accordion featured in *The Blue Door, Newlyn* (1934; see p. 21). Another sketch is captioned *My Bedpost* and shows a carved image not dissimilar to Oceanic art.

The majority of his works are oil on canvas, although a few watercolours exist, some with black chalk. There are also some oils on board, a common medium, sometimes used as an experiment in painting on surfaces other than canvas, or because canvas was unavailable or too costly. In some instances the finished work is canvas on board, but no analysis has yet been done as to whether he painted on the combined support, or only on the canvas which was subsequently mounted on board. Works on or with board range in date from 1907 to 1937.

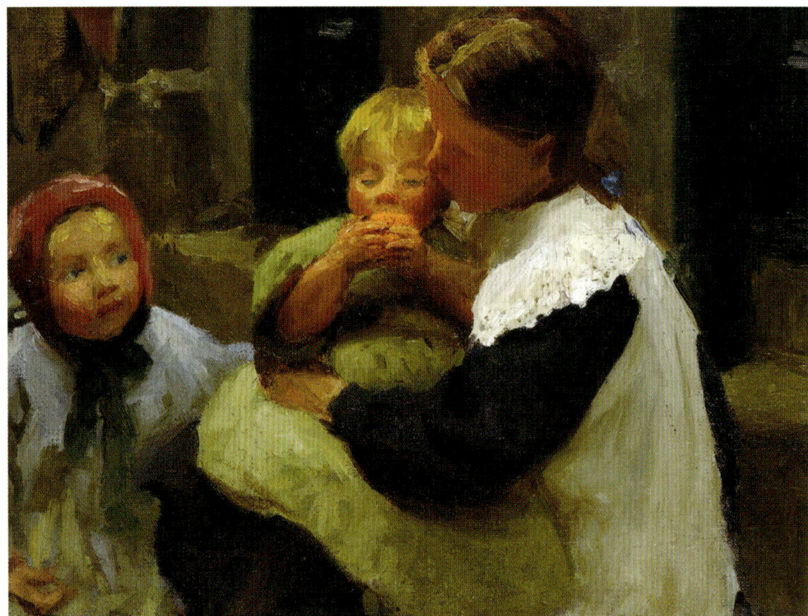

Three Children (Little Brother)
c. 1909 | oil on canvas | 35.5 x 45.5 cm
BOWERMAN CHARITABLE TRUST

Harvey was not an innovator, he did not pioneer new styles or push out the boundaries of existing styles. He was, however, single-minded, and painting was how he earned his living. From the outset it must have taken strength to break with the somewhat conservative and secure banking family in order to become an artist. His prolific output and reliance on sales or 'gifts' to support himself is another sign of his strength. When most of the Newlyn School joined the breakaway New English Art Club, he remained outside the new group. He did not seek advancement through organisations or contacts. He did not join the Allied Artists Association founded by Frank Rutter in 1908, an organisation which had several hundred members and held un-juried exhibitions in the Albert Hall; such an organisation might well have increased his reputation.

For many artists Cornwall was just a visit, an interlude; for Harold Harvey it was his life and the truth of a Harold Harvey painting is perhaps best denoted by a comparison between *Pioneers of Aerial Navigation* and the work of his close friend Laura Knight, *Flying a Kite*. While Laura Knight's painting expresses the freedom, joy and exuberance of the kite – a symbol of childhood – Harold Harvey's picture shares the emotional experience of play.

Stanhope Forbes wrote in *The Cornishman*, 22nd May, 1941, '…Cornwall may indeed be proud to have produced so fine and sincere an artist.' Judging by the warmth of affection with which his work is held in his native Penzance, Cornwall is still justly proud.

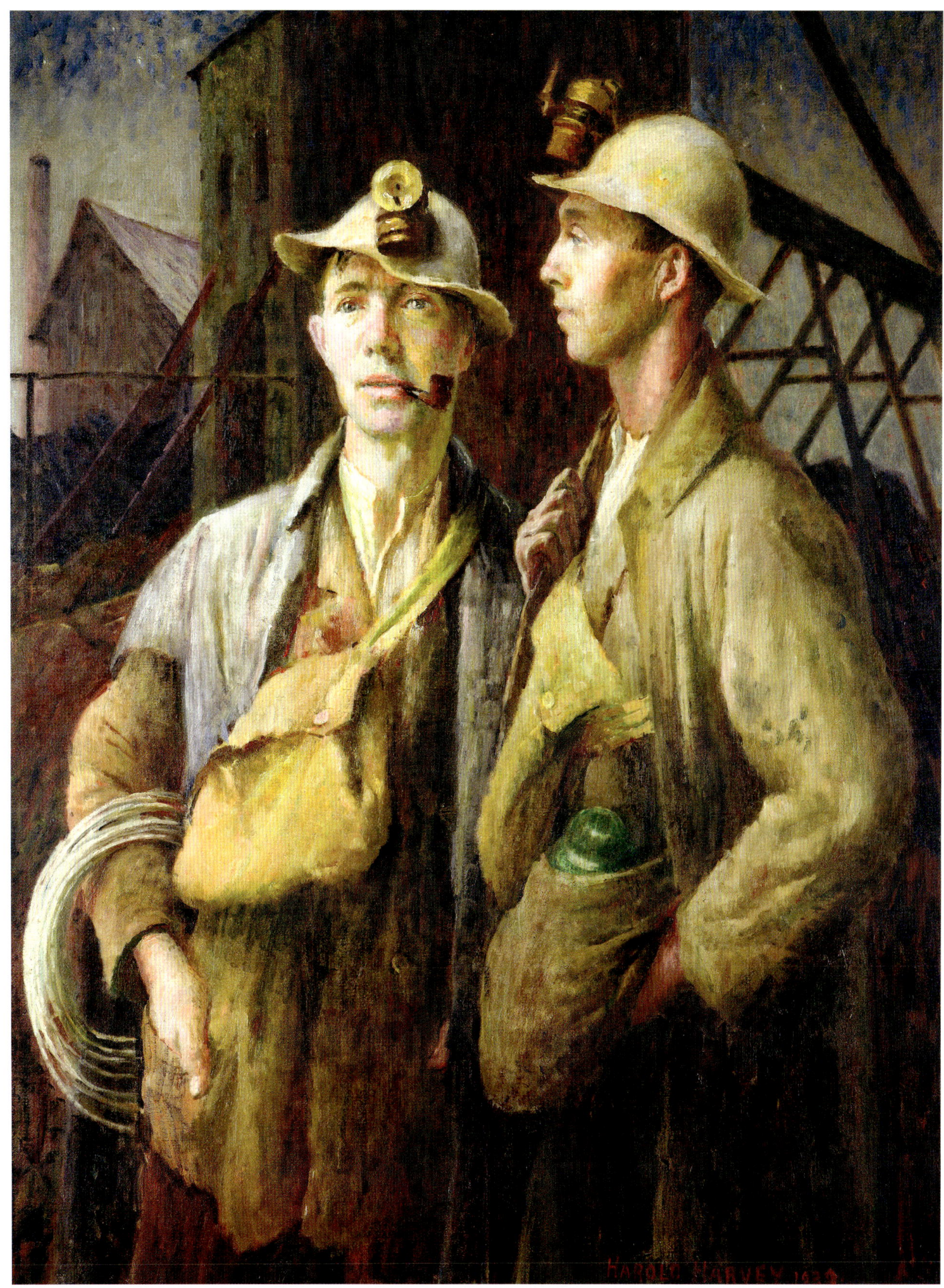

Tin Miners
1939 | oil on canvas | 101.5 x 76 cm
BOWERMAN CHARITABLE TRUST

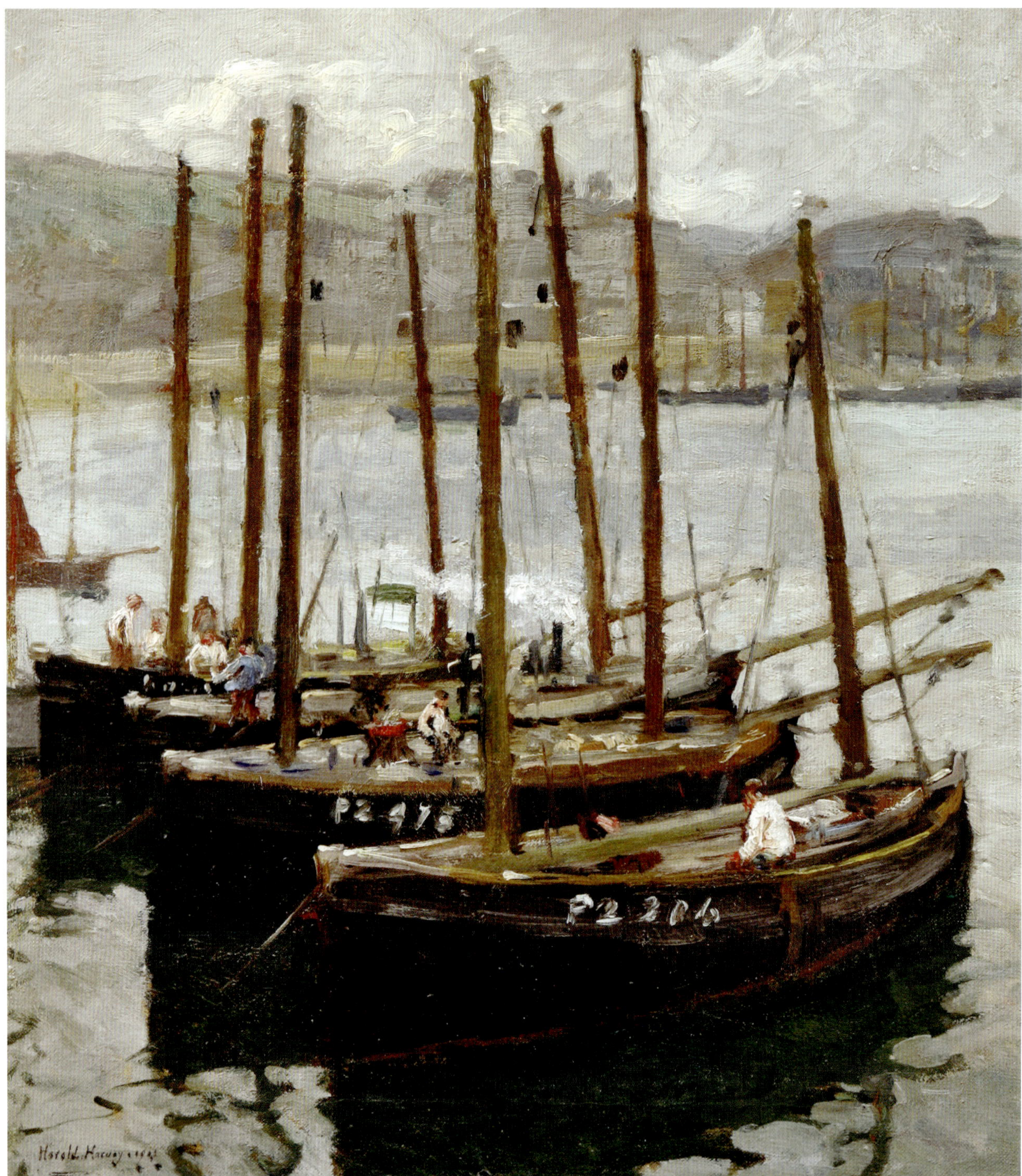

Waiting for the Tide, Newlyn Harbour
1903 | oil on canvas | 47 x 42 cm
PRIVATE COLLECTION

Catalogue raisonné

Peter Risdon

The following pages list paintings by Harold Harvey the author has identified from published and other sources, up to the end of 2023. Paintings are presented in chronological order by year, derived from the date inscribed on them or the date of first known exhibition, or from other information. Where the date is determined by an exhibition, these works are placed after the dated works of the same year. Undated works whose place in the chronological sequence cannot be reliably estimated, are listed in a second sequence in alphabetical order by title (p. 141), but starting with works for which a date can be suggested on the basis of style. Works attributed to Harvey, but not confirmed, are in a penultimate listing, in alphabetical order of title (p. 146). Because it has not been possible to see every painting listed (even as an illustration), it is possible some separate entries refer to the same painting; where this is particularly suspected a note is made of the other title. Each entry consists of the following elements (where available):

- A sequential reference number
- The title (as given in a published source)
- The medium, eg. oil on canvas, oil on panel etc
- Dimensions in inches (height x width); where no dimensions are given they are unknown
- Signature
- Date (as observed or recorded)
- Description of the image
- Quotations from press reviews
- Details of exhibitions where the work was shown
- Publications which feature the work
- Details of sales catalogues which feature the work
- Alternative titles where known or suspected
- The location of a work in a public collection.

ABBREVIATIONS

bl – bottom left
br – bottom right
indis – indistinctly
inscr – inscribed
ni – not illustrated
o/b – oil on board
o/c – oil on canvas
o/cb – oil on canvas-board
o/p – oil on panel
prov – provenance
pub – publication
tl – top left
tr – top right
wc – watercolour

Institutions

BAL – Bridgeman Art Library
BG – Belgrave Gallery, London
BH – Barbizon House, London
BL – Bonham's London
B&W – Bearnes & Waycotts, Torquay
CI – Carnegie Institute, Pittsburgh
CL – Christies London
CSK – Christies South Kensington
DL – David Lay, Penzance (auctioneers)
DMG – David Messum Gallery, London
FAG – Ferens Art Gallery, Hull
FAS – Fine Art Society, London
F&R – Frost & Reed, Bristol
HSG – Harris & Sons Gallery, Plymouth
ISSPG – International Society of Sculptors, Painters and Gravers
LG – Leicester Galleries, London
LWG – Louise Whitford Gallery, London
MG – Mendoza Gallery, London
NACF – National Art Collections Fund
NEAC – New English Art Club
NMAG – Newport Museum and Art Gallery, South Wales
NSA – Newlyn Society of Artists
PAEE – Palace of Arts, Empire Exhibition, Glasgow
PEAG – Passmore Edwards Art Gallery, Newlyn
PH – Penlee House Gallery & Museum, Penzance. Note: the touring exhibition of 2001/2 (Penzance, Newport, Wolverhampton) which showed more than 100 paintings by Harvey is listed as Penzance (PH, 2001).
PL – Phillips London
QH – Queen's Hotel, Penzance
RA – Royal Academy, London
RBSA – Royal Birmingham Society of Art
RCA – Royal Cambrian Academy, Conwy
RGG – Richard Green Gallery, London
RGI – Royal Glasgow Institute of Fine Art
RHA – Royal Hibernian Academy, Dublin
RSA – Royal Scottish Academy, Edinburgh
SC – Sotheby's Chester
SL – Sotheby's London
SOP – Society of Oil Painters, London
SWS – Sotheby's West Sussex
WAGB – Williamson Art Gallery, Birkenhead
WAGL – Walker Art Gallery, Liverpool
WG – Whitechapel Gallery, London
W&H – Whitford & Hughes, London
WHL – W.H. Lane, Penzance (auctioneers)
WL – Witt Library, London (where an illustration of a work can be foiund)
WP – Woolland, Son & Manico, Plymouth

Publications

Bénézit – Emmanuel Bénézit, *Dictionnaire critique et documentaire des peintres, sculpteurs, dessinateurs et graveurs* (Librarie Gründ, Paris, 1976)
Berriman – Hazel Berriman, *Cryséde: The Unique Textile Designs of Alec Walker* (The Royal Institution of Cornwall, 1993)
Cross – Tom Cross, *The Shining Sands: Artists in Newlyn and St Ives 1880–1930* (West Country Books, 1994)
Fox – Caroline Fox, *Stanhope Forbes and the Newlyn School* (David & Charles, 1993)
Fox/Greenacre – Caroline Fox and Francis Greenacre, *Painting in Newlyn 1880–1930*, (Barbican Art Gallery, 1985)
Hardie – Melissa Hardie (ed.), *Artists in Newlyn and West Cornwall 1880–1940* (Art Dictionaries, 2009)
McConkey – Kenneth McConkey, *Edwardian Portraits: Images of an Age of Opulence* (Antique Collectors' Club, 1988)
Messum – David Messum, *British Impressions: The Progress of Impressionism 1880–1940* (Messum's, London, 1988)
PCF – *Public Catalogue Foundation*
PCF: C&SI – *Public Catalogue Foundation: Cornwall & the Scilly Isles*
RAI – *Royal Academy Illustrated*
WMN – *Western Morning News*, Plymouth
Wallace – Catherine Wallace, *Under the Open Sky: Newlyn and Lamorna Artists 1880–1940* (Truran Books, 2002)
Wortley – Laura Wortley, *British Impressionism: A Garden of Bright Images* (Studio Fine Art Publications, 1988)

WORKS BY DATE

1 | ***Apple blossom*** | o/c 23 x 19; signed bl, in black, dated 92. In an orchard are several apple trees with pink and white blossom, and yellow daffodils beneath them. Given by Harvey to his friends Geoffrey and Jill Garnier, artists who lived in Newlyn. PH 2001 (52); SL, 14 Dec 2006 (182 illus, as 25 x 21); SL, 11 Dec 2007 (64 illus).

2 | ***A Cornish fisherman*** | o/c 14 x 18; signed br, dated 93. In the foreground at left sits a young man facing the viewer, wearing a cap and pale jersey; before him is a bundle tied in a red spotted handkerchief; at right several fishing boats are moored in the harbour. BL, 30 Jan 1980 (57); LWG, Mar 1982 (35 illus, as *The young seafarer*, dated 1890); BAL, 48620 (as *The young seafarer*)

3 | ***William Harvey Julyan JP*** | o/c 42 x 32; signed br, dated 95 or 96. The figure faces half-left and is seated, probably in the mayoral chair, wearing a black robe with red trimming at the shoulders; his right hand rests on the chair arm; he has a pointed beard. Plaque on front reading: 'W Harvey Julyan Esq, JP, Alderman 1892, Mayor 1893–5, Presented by his fellow townsmen'. *PCF: C&SI*, p.112 (illus); WL. Penlee House Gallery & Museum (1989.36).

4 | ***Girl with plaits*** | o/p 14 x 10; signed, dated 97. PL, 23 Apr 1985 (26).

5 | ***Mousehole*** | o/c 17 x 23; signed bl, dated 97. In the foreground are boats and lobster pots; at left is a house with washing drying; behind are the harbour quays with figures on them. PH, 2001 (31).

6 | ***The dinner hour*** | o/c 37 x 48; signed bl, dated 97; inscr with title and Penzance on a label on the frame. The setting appears to be Tredavoe. In a sunny field being ploughed in front of a blue Mount's Bay with distant land; at right a woman stands behind two men seated with their lunch; at left a boy feeds a white horse from a pail, a brown horse behind it. The title *Dinner hour* was probably aimed at a wider audience, as the Cornish term for a meal break is 'croust time'. WAGL, 1901; Leeds City Art Gallery 1908; SL, 8 Nov 1989 (16 illus); DMG, 1990 (9 illus); DMG, 1994 (8 illus); PH, 2001 (10); WL.

7 | ***In a Cornish cottage*** | oil. In an article published on 9 Feb 1939 (unidentified source), Harvey told the interviewer that "The subject was a group of fishermen doing nothing in particular and talking to other fishermen doing nothing in particular". RA, 1898 (44); WAGL, 1898 (1083, price £52-10s); SOP, 1899 (42, price £42); RBSA, 1899 (782, price £42); WG, 1902 (16).

8 | ***Convalescence*** | oil. SOP, 1898 (156, price £31-10s); WAGL, 1899 (356, price £15-15s); RBSA, 1899 (567, price £21).

9 | ***The land of flowers*** | oil. WAGL, 1899 (208, price £15-15s); RBSA, 1899 (725, price £12-12s); SOP, 1901 (171, price £26-5s).

10 | ***Summer hours*** | oil. WAGL, 1899 (286, price £15-15s); RBSA, 1899 (566, price £10-10s).

11 | ***The lost princess*** | oil. *The Cornishman* of 30 March 1899 said "… a carefully executed work. The idea is good and the workmanship well done, though one might consider the figure of the half-reclining princess somewhat too stiff to be natural". *The Cornish Telegraph* of 23 Mar 1899 said "the princess [as *The lone princess*] … is not altogether natural". WAGL, 1899 (328, price £52-10s); RA, 1899.

12 | ***The plough team*** | o/c 8 x 16; signed, dated 1900. Probably painted at Tredavoe. In a sunny field, at left a dark brown horse and a white horse move left pulling a plough followed by a man at right wearing a cap and waistcoat over white shirt; beyond are trees and the blue sea. SL, 5 July 1983 (ni); PL, 6 Mar 1990 (74).

13 | ***Turning the plough*** | o/c 11½ x 15½; signed br. At right a man walks left behind a plough led by two large brown horses at left changing direction towards us; behind are misty trees on the horizon. BAL, SCG56694 as *Man ploughing a field*; DMG, Aug 2015 (as 1900).

14 | ***Two shire horses and ploughman heading homeward at dusk on a country lane*** | o/c 7½ x 16; signed bl, indis dated 1900. In the centre a brown and a white horse walk left on a path beside a stream; a man sits on the brown horse in hat, red scarf and dark clothes; a few trees at far left and right show autumnal leaves; the sky is clear blue above yellow. WHL, 16 Oct 1986 (527 ni); DL, 27 July 2017 (171 illus, as indis dated) as *Walking the stream*.

15 | ***The knitters*** | oil. WAGL, 1900 (361, price £25).

16 | ***Newlyn bridge*** | oil. WAGL, 1900 (944, price £33); WG, 1902 (103).

17 | ***The witch*** | PEAG sales book, 28 July 1901 (price £6-6s).

18 | ***A winter evening*** | WAGL, 1901 (226, price £84); RGI, 1902 (312).

19 | ***Young fisherboy*** | o/c 12 x 8; signed br in white, dated 01. In the foreground sits a young boy wearing a cap, black jacket buttoned at the top and brown shorts; he has a smoking cigarette at the left of his mouth; behind him is blue sea and a fishing boat; two white seagulls fly adjacent to his head. CSK, 12 July 2006 (68 illus).

20 | *The pedlar* | o/c 48½ x 36; signed br, dated 1902. An interior showing a bearded old man in dark hat and clothes peddling ribbons etc at the doorway to a room in which stand a mother holding a child, and a young girl wearing a white apron over a brown dress. WAGL, 1902 (262, price £50); Fox/Greenacre, p.83 (ni) and p.128 (illus no.64); PL, 13 Nov 1984 (72, prov QH). WL.

21 | *Portrait of a little girl in pink* | o/c 12 x 10; signed br, dated 02. Head and shoulder view of a girl in a broad-brimmed straw hat, pink blouse, two blue necklaces and one brown; she looks at the viewer; the background is plain dark green. SL, 19 July 1989 (41 illus).

22 | *Above Mounts Bay* | o/c 15 x 18; signed, dated 1902 indis. DL, 12 Oct 2004 (605 illus).

23 | *Building the hayrick* | o/c 15 x 20; signed br in pale brown, dated 1902. In the centre foreground stands a horse facing right, harnessed to a cart loaded with hay, among which stands a man; behind them is a tall rick extending to the right edge of the canvas, on top of which stands a man with a sunlit hat wielding an implement; in the distance at far left are fields below a dull sky with a rising moon. PL, 11 Nov 1986 (50 illus); BL, 23 June 2015 (106 illus).

24 | *Resting* | SOP, 1902 (94, price £20).

25 | *Guinea[?] gold* | title is indistinctly recorded. PEAG sales book, 30 Apr 1902, price £4-4s.

26 | *Lighting up* | o/c 12 x 10; signed bl in red, dated 1902. An old man with a white beard, black hat, red scarf, white pullover and dark trousers, faces half-left; he sits in the stern of a dinghy, holding a pipe in his left hand and lighting it with a flaring match in his right hand; the glow illuminates his face; beyond is calm water reflecting evening light, and a sea wall with houses above; there is no sky. Probably PEAG sales book, 6 Sep 1902, price £3-3s, as *The pipe*; BL, 10 June 2014 (152, as *Lighting up*); BL, 20 Mar 2018 (86, as *Lighting up*).

27 | *Mousehole and the Coombes* | PEAG sales book, Oct 1902, price £8-8s.

28 | *The turn of the tide* | oil. WAGL, 1902 (825, price £30).

29 | *Penzance harbour* | WG 1902 (20).

30 | *Collecting wrack* | o/c 8 x 12; signed bl, dated 03. In the foreground on a wet beach, a horse pulls a cart laden with seaweed, moving left; at right a man walks alongside; in the distance at left is another horse and cart. Marazion was the main centre for wrack or seaweed. SL, 25 May 1983 (53 illus); PH, 2001 (3, as *Collecting seaweed*); WL.

31 | *Carting Seaweed* | o/c 7 x 12; signed, dated 03. PEAG sales book, 16 June 1903. Anderson & Garland, Newcastle, 25 Jan 1983 (422, as *Collecting Seaweed*).

32 | *Fishing boats* | o/c 17 x 15; signed bl, dated 1903. In the foreground are four boats with black hulls, facing left, their masts bare; the two foremost boats have PZ (Penzance) numbers in white; men work in the boats; behind is a sketchy view of Newlyn. Beaumont, Tours, 18 May 1988 (349); WHL, 26 Oct 2000 (100 illus, as *Waiting for the tide, Newlyn harbour*, as 18½ x 16½); Falmouth, 'A Century of Art in Cornwall 1889–1989', 1989 (22); PH,

2001 (5, as *Waiting for the tide, Newlyn harbour*); *PCF: C&SI*, p.112 (illus); WHL, 14 Mar 2013 (70 illus); WHL, 13 June 2013 (100 illus, as *Waiting for the tide*). Penlee House Gallery & Museum (2001.L12P).

33 | *Homewards* | o/c 9 x 11; signed bl, dated 03. A man walks right on a wet track leading a horse and cart; he holds something in his hands, with a stick over his right wrist; painted sketchily. CL, 24 Mar 1982 (40); DMG, spring 1982 (9 illus).

34 | *The Coombe* | PEAG sales book, 16 June 1903, price £14 for nos. 27, 30, 31.

35 | *Gorse* | PEAG sales book, 16 June 1903.

36 | *A summer's morning* | PEAG sales book, 18 July 1903, price £5-5s.

37 | *Boys fishing* | PEAG sales book, 17 Aug 1903, price £4.

38 | *The cup that cheers* | PEAG sales book, 24 Aug 1903, price £5.

39 | *Newlyn* | PEAG sales book, 15 Sep 1903, price £5-5s.

40 | *Girl's head* | PEAG sales book, 22 Sep 1903, price £4-4s.

41 | *Harbour* | PEAG sales book, 25 Sep 1903, price £4-4s.

42 | *Euchre* | oil. Euchre is an American card game, and was regularly played at The Wink Inn, Lamorna. Mentioned in *The Cornish Telegraph* of 25 March 1903 as showing "every promise". WAGL, 1903 (181, price £100).

43 | *The milkmaid* | oil. RA, 1903 (733); WAGL, 1903 (1036, price £80).

44 | *Fisher boy* | o/c 12 x 10; signed bl, dated 04. A close-up portrait of a boy in a bright red hat and dark brown jersey, seen against boats in Newlyn harbour; the lighthouse is at tl. CL, 25 Sep 1992 (161 illus).

45 | *Penzance harbour* | o/c 5 x 16; signed, dated 1904. P. Bath, 8 Dec 1986 (95).

46 | *The seaweed gatherers.* | o/c 7½ x 11½; signed br, dated 04. Two brown horses in file pull a laden cart moving left; in front a young man holds the bridle of the first horse; behind, another man carries a large rake. RGG, SP178.

47 | *A view of Newlyn old harbour* | o/c 12 x 16; signed br in green, dated 1904. On the quayside at right stand two boys looking at several moored fishing boats; the nearest boat has a raised red sail; behind are the town and hillside; the sky is cloudy grey. PH, 2001 (6).

48 | *Ploughing* | o/c 12 x 16; signed br, dated 1904. At right a man in a cap, white shirt and open waistcoat walks to the left behind a plough pulled by a white and a dark brown horse; in the foreground is uncut green meadow; behind are trees, with a cloudy blue sky. This work looks identical to *The plough team* (1900), on a larger scale. PL, 13 Nov 1984 (25 ni, prov QH); CL, 2 Nov 1989 (91 illus); WHL, 5 Dec 1989 (400 illus, as *Ploughing the fallow*); WHL, 12 July 1990 (399 illus); WHL, 27 Sep 1990 (216 ni); WHL, 10 Oct 1991 (95 illus); DL, 12 June 1997 (276 illus); DL, 13 June 2002 (537 illus); DL, 1 Nov 2012 (562 illus).

49 | *Children in Newlyn harbour* | o/c 10 x 14; signed br, dated indis 04. In the foreground is a beached dinghy; two boys lean against the port side each holding something in their hands; the left boy wears a blue jersey and cap and holds a toy boat, the centre boy wears a red-brown smock; at left another boy sits on the ground looking at them, wearing a red tam o'shanter cap. PH, 2001 (33).

50 | *Newlyn fisherlads* | o/c 14 x 16; signed br,

dated indis 1904. In the foreground is a dinghy; in it are a boy facing left seated centre by a basket of fish, and a boy standing with line in hand, his cap touching the upper edge; the sea is loosely sketched. DMG, spring 1982 (8 illus).

51 | *Whiffing in Mount's Bay* | o/c 11½ x 15½; signed bl, in black, indis dated 04. In a small dinghy, a young man in a white jersey sits at the stern facing right; at centre a man in a dark blue jersey stands with both hands holding a line which has caught a fish; at right another man in a dark blue jersey leans over the starboard bow; a pile of fish lies between the left and centre men. PH, 2001 (4, as *Whiffing in Mount's Bay*, as 1906); NMAG, 2001 (70, as 1904); WHL, 30 May 2002 (220, as c.1889); CL, 23 Nov 2017 (107 illus, as 1904).

52 | *The mangolds* | o/c 9½ x 11½; signed br, dated indis 04. At left two boys load mangolds into a cart; behind are trees. PH, 2001 (21). Exeter University, as *Boys loading mangolds onto a cart*; bequeathed in the 1950s.

53 | *Three boys* | o/c 15¾ x 11½; signed bl, dated indis 1904. Three boys sitting on a grassy bank, the nearest one with bare feet, the right boy with a red cap. Fox/Greenacre, p.129 (illus no.70); PH, 2001 (11); WL. University of Exeter (FAC00207).

54 | *The Vegetable cart* | o/c 12 x 16; signed bl, in a cursive script, dated indis 1904. In a street in Newlyn a donkey cart carrying vegetables is stopped, with a mature man in brown clothes; he attends to a female customer in a red shawl; at right are houses with figures in the doorways; at left are more buildings with perhaps the Macgrigor Monument; the ground is wet with rain; the sky is cloudy and grey. BL, 31 Mar 2021 (79 illus).

55 | *Mousehole harbour* | PEAG sales book, 1904, price £4-4s.

56 | *Landing fish* | PEAG sales book, 1904, price £10.

57 | *The barge* | indis title. PEAG sales book, 1904, price £7.

58 | *Market day* | PEAG sales book, 20 Oct 1904, price £4-10s.

59 | *Newlyn harbour* | o/c 10 x 12; signed br in blue-black, dated 05. Fishing boats tied up to a jetty at left, and at right a sailing boat with red sails, a headland behind it. DMG, pub XVII (15 illus); WHL, 28 Feb 1989 (410 illus, as *Penzance fishing boats moored in Newlyn harbour with sails furled*); PL, 17 Nov 1992 (20, as *Fishing boats in Newlyn harbour*); PL, 2 Nov 1999 (17 illus, as *Penzance fishing boats in Newlyn harbour*); PL 6 June 2000 (115 illus, as *Penzance fishing boats in Newlyn harbour*); PH, 2001 (7, as *Fishing boats in Newlyn harbour*).

60 | *On the quay at Newlyn* | o/c 12 x 16; signed bl, dated 05. Three men rest against a rail overlooking the jetty; the man at left has his right leg bent, wears a red scarf and smokes a cigarette; the central man wears a bowler hat. Wortley, p.211 (illus); Messum's (39 illus); DMG, pub V (39 illus); PL, 12 Nov 1985 (43 illus).

61 | *Preparing bait* | o/c 12 x 16; signed bl, dated 1905. A dinghy in the foreground; seated in it at right facing left is an older bearded man in a brimmed hat and dark blue jersey, with a fish in his left hand; at left is a boy in a cap and grey jersey holding the steering oar; behind are moored fishing boats and Newlyn harbour buildings. SL, 6 Oct 1993 (2 illus); WL.

62 | *Seaweed gatherers* | o/c 36 x 48; signed br, dated 05. Two brown horses in file move right

over a wet beach, pulling a small cart laden with seaweed, led by a man raising a stick in his right hand; in the foreground a man in a hat and blue jacket speaks to a brown dog looking at him; behind are coastal hills under a grey cloudy sky. CL, 3 Mar 1988 (26 illus, as *Seaweed gatherers, Cornwall*); SL, 8 Nov 1989 (5 illus); SL, 17 May 2011 (67 illus); 'Amongst heroes', London, 2013; WL.

63 | *The orange girl* | o/c 13 x 16; signed bl, dated 05. A girl in a white smock and blue necklace sits looking at the viewer; her right arm holds a basket of oranges, her left hand is in her lap; behind is foliage and a wooden railing. PEAG sales book records *Girl and Oranges*, sold on 14 May 1906 for £4-10s. *PCF: C&SI*, p.191 (illus); WL. Royal Cornwall Museum, Truro (1960.4.60).

64 | *End of the day* | o/c 12 x 18; signed, dated 05. On a rural lane at left a young woman tends to a large brown horse; behind a man sits on a black horse; at far left is a thatched cottage. RGG, SP3817.

65 | *Moment for reflection* | o/c 11 x 9; signed, dated 05. Bonhams, Bath, 22 July 2002 (77).

66 | *Cottages at Newlyn* | PEAG sales book, 13 May 1905, price £7-7s.

67 | *Cattle* | PEAG sales book, 22 July 1905, price £26-5s.

68 | *Newlyn Boy* | PEAG sales book, 22 July 1905, price £26-5s.

69 | *Milking Time* | PEAG sales book, 22 July 1905, price £26-5s.

70 | *Fishing* | PEAG sales book, 22 July 1905, price £26-5s.

71 | *Boys bathing* | PEAG sales book, 15 Sep 1905, price £5-5s.

72 | *Carrying the oars* | o/c 13½ x 16; signed bl, dated 06. At left a boy in a blue cap and jersey looks at the viewer, carrying an oar over his right shoulder; at right another boy in a white shirt and dark blue trousers and whitish cap looks left; behind them is Newlyn harbour with boats and quays. Penzance Arts & Crafts exhibition, 1906; PL, 11 Nov 1986 (48 illus, prov acquired by the owner's grandfather directly from the artist); RGG.

73 | *Sailing in Newlyn harbour* | o/c 12 x 16; signed br, dated 1906. Three boys in a small sailing dinghy moving right, away from us; the left boy holds the steering oar and the other boys guide the sail with strings; in the distance are many boats and the lighthouse is at tr. Fox/Greenacre, p.128 (illus no.66); BAL, 21218; WL.

74 | *Laying the nets* | o/c 12 x 16; signed bl, in black, dated 06. A dinghy occupies the foreground, in which an old bearded man in hat and blue-grey clothes lights a pipe, facing the viewer; at right a man in a cap and pale clothes sits on the dinghy side, holding up an oar; behind at left are two boats with three men facing right, and a pile of orange nets; in the distance at left is the harbour wall with a sailing boat with orange sails moored alongside; at top right a fishing boat approaches the harbour. PL, 5 Nov 1991 (2 illus); PH, 2001 (9); WL.

75 | *Whiffing* | o/c 12 x 16; signed bl, dated 06. A dinghy moves away to the right, its stern nearest us; in the stern sits a boy in blue clothes working the rudder oar; on the starboard bow sits an old man lighting his pipe; on the port bow is a boy in a white jacket; a package wrapped in red cloth lies on a cross-beam; in the background are many sailing ships, and at tr the end of a pier. CL, 23 Nov 2001 (35 illus).

76 | *Unloading the boats, Newlyn harbour* o/c 12 x 18; signed bl, in black, dated 06. At far right a man carries a large box on his back; behind him a man in a dinghy wields a long oar; in the centre a horse draws a cart laden with boxes, moving left through shallow water; at far left an empty cart moves right; in the distance are sailing boats at right and the quay at left; the sky is grey; the colours are muted blues, greys and browns. BL, 21 June 2007 (101 illus); RGG, May 2008.

77 | *Harbour scene with three men in rowing boat* | o/c 12 x 16; signed, dated 06. Crafoord, Goteborg, Sweden, 22 May 2001 (204).

78 | *After the swim* | o/c 11 x 16; signed br in brown, dated indis 06. At left sits a boy half facing us in white hat and whitish shirt, pulling a blue sock onto his left foot, the right foot bare; at right a boy with bare torso lies on his back with left arm outstretched, wearing white hat and brown trousers; behind them is the sea. SL, 4 June 2003 (6 illus); SL, 25 Nov 2004 (417 illus).

79 | *Boys on the harbour wall* | o/c 11 x 15; signed br in black, dated 06. On the mole at Newlyn sit numerous boys; three fishing boats on a blue sea are tied up alongside each other beside the far end of the mole; a dinghy approaches the mole; beyond rise the hills behind Newlyn; the sky is cloudy. CL, 23 Nov 2017 (102 illus).

80 | *Swinging on the gate* | o/c 12 x 16; signed bl, dated 06. A five-bar gate occupies most of the picture space; in the foreground a boy in a cap and braces pushes the gate; two girls hang on the gate, the left one wearing a hat. SL, 11 Nov 1981 (156); BG, 1985 (12, as *Children on a farm gate*); Bonhams New York, 4 May 2016 (90 illus, as *Swinging on a gate*); WL.

81 | *Off to market* | o/c 12 x 18; signed br, dated 06. In the centre a white horse pulls a two-wheeled cart, moving right; sitting in it are an elderly couple, the man at left holding the reins, the woman at right with a basket; in the left foreground a boy in a hat and dark blue jacket stands behind a brown cow with calf at left; further left, a man on horseback talks to two children; at right are a church tower and indistinct buildings. PL, 14 June 1988 (11 illus).

82 | *Two Ayrshires* | o/c 12 x 16; signed bl, dated 06. In a sunlit meadow, a cow in the foreground faces left towards another; behind a young girl in a white blouse approaches them with food in her apron. CL, 3 Mar 1988 (25 illus); SL, 8 Nov 1989 (22 illus, as *A farm girl with two Ayrshire cows*); PH, 2001 (12, as *Farm girl with Ayrshire cows*); WL.

83 | *Feeding the calves* | o/c 11¾ x 13½; signed bl, dated 06. In a meadow, two calves at left approach a girl seated in the foreground wearing a white smock; she holds out greenery to the nearest calf; at her right stands a young boy in a pale hat and dark brown clothes. CL, 23 Nov 1983 (34 illus); CL, 1 July 1993 (37 illus); WL.

84 | *The wayfarers* | o/c 12 x 18; signed bl, dated 1906. A Gypsy boy on a donkey rides in front of a boy walking with a broom over his right shoulder and a girl with a younger girl holding her hand, who walk before a horse-drawn caravan; the ground is wet.

Anderson & Garland, Newcastle 30 Apr 1991 (268, as *Gypsy family*, 11 x 17); WHL, 13 June 1991 (110 illus); PH, 2001 (48).

85 | *Springtime* | o/c 13½ x 15½; signed, dated 1906. At left in a meadow overlooking the sea, a woman in a pale dress holds with her right hand a young girl wearing a large hat holding a bunch of flowers; at right are three young girls; beyond is the sea and coast. Perhaps RCA, 1909 (230, as *Spring*); BL, 17 June 1994 (235).

86 | *The blacksmith's forge, Newlyn* | o/c 12 x 16; signed, dated 1906. At left a man shoes a brown horse outside the forge; at right are several figures; beyond, a horse and cart descend a sloping road away from tall buildings. Nesbit, Southsea 28 April 2004 (484, as *Village forge*); DL, 12 Oct 2004 (692 illus, as *The blacksmith's shop by the old bridge, Newlyn*); SL, 7 June 2005 (84, as *The blacksmith's forge, Newlyn*).

87 | *The village farrier* | o/c 16 x 12; signed bl, in black, dated 06. At right a large red-brown horse is being shod on the front right hoof by the farrier; a man stands by the horse's head; behind are white buildings; at left is a stream with trees on the far bank; it is late autumn and the setting is dusk with sunlight on the horizon; the tones are mostly dark. SL, 10 Dec 2014 (62 illus).

88 | *The young farmhand* | o/c 15 x 12; signed br in yellow, dated 06. Half-length view of a boy facing half-left, in a pale hat and dark blue jacket, a cigarette at the left side of his mouth; with both hands he holds a sheaf of corn over his right shoulder. PL, 17 Nov 1998 (3 illus).

89 | *The drinking place* | o/c 11 x 15; signed bl, dated 06; inscr on reverse. A boy sits on a white horse facing left; the horse drinks from a wooden tub at bl; at right is a brown horse and at br is a segment of another tub. PH, 2001 (25).

90 | *A cooling drink by the wayside* | o/c 12 x 16; signed br, dated 1906. A dark horse drinks at a pool, a man standing beside him; at right a man sits on the bank; beyond is shrubby landscape with cottages. Rosebery, West Norwood 16 June 2009 (668 illus).

91 | *Crowst* | o/c 12 x 16; signed br, dated 1906. In a field a man sits by a hedge at right, legs extended, his hands holding his food and drink; at left are a white and a dark horse harnessed to a harrow; a boy feeds the white horse. PH, 2001 (23).

92 | *Newlyn bridge* | o/c 8 x 12; signed br, dated 06. The stream flows diagonally in the foreground, leading to the sunlit bridge; at left are buildings with greenery at the water's edge, and at right the embankment; beyond the bridge are town buildings. PH, 2001 (32).

93 | *Fishing by a woodland stream* | o/c 24 x 20; signed br, dated 06. On a grassy bank at left a boy sits on a basket fishing in a stream at right; behind, a woman in a white blouse and a girl in a white smock stand on a wooden bridge; beyond are trees. CL, 11 July 2013 (105 illus).

94 | *The ford* | *The Cornishman* of 29 March 1906 recorded "A man with two horses is crossing Newlyn River, and the general effect is charming." PEAG, 1906.

95 | *Girl and oranges* | PEAG sales book, 14 May 1906, price £4-10s.

96 | *Cows in Short's Lane* | PEAG sales book, 2 July 1906, price £4.

97 | *Cows* | PEAG sales book, 28 Aug 1906, price £5.

98 | *In harbour* | PEAG sales book, 24 Nov 1906, price £5-5s.

99 | *Alderman A.K. Barnett* | o/c 46 x 38; signed bl, dated 07; inscr on frame 'Alderman A.K. Barnett FGS, Mayor of Penzance 1907–1911, 1913, 1914'. The tall standing figure, with a trimmed beard and centre-parted hair, looks at the viewer; he wears mayoral robes, trimmed with fur collar, and the chain of office on his chest; the background is plain and dark. *PCF: C&SI*, p.113 (illus); WL. Penlee House Gallery & Museum (1989.210).

100 | *Newlyn street scene* | o/c 11 x 12; signed br in black, dated 07. Sunlit view of South Pier with the lighthouse in left middle distance and boats tied up; in the left foreground a man sits on a railing set on a rising path; at right three figures with hats are seated against a house wall, before an external stair. BAL, 38464; PL, 16 June 1987 (11 illus, as *A sunny morning*).

101 | *Trevaylor stream, near Penzance* | o/c 8 x 11½; signed bl, dated 07. The dark stream rushes over rocks in the foreground; at bl, wild flowers grow on the bank. Trevaylor is a broadleaf wood with tall beech trees growing in a narrow valley cutting into the Penwith Moors north of Penzance. SL, 6 Feb 1985 (254 illus); PL, 12 Nov 1985 (64 ni); PL, 28 Jan 1986 (53 ni); PH, 2001 (26).

102 | *Moored fishing boats in Newlyn harbour* o/cb 11½ x 9¼; signed in dark red br, dated 07. In the foreground six or seven dinghies are moored alongside each other; the nearer boat has a red hull; a further, larger, one is marked PZ 58(?); behind lies the town with a hill at tl. CL, 12 June 1987 (124 illus); WL.

103 | *Newlyn harbour* | o/c 25 x 30; signed br, dated 07. In the foreground stands a fisherman holding a long fish in his left hand; other fish are laid out on the slipway; at left a small boat is moored with two men in it; at right the slipway rises past houses. PL, 21 Nov 1995 (60 illus, as *Mousehole harbour*); Wallace, p.62 (illus); WL. Plymouth Art Gallery (L080).

104 | *Whiffing, Newlyn* | o/c 25 x 30; signed bl, dated 07. A white dinghy carries a man in a blue jersey at the tiller oar, an old man lighting his pipe, and a man in a white jersey at the prow; a bundle in a red cloth lies beside the old man; beyond are a few boats and two piers, one with a lighthouse; in the far distance are many boats with unfurled sails.RGG, 2024.

105 | *Penzance fishing boats moored in Newlyn harbour* | o/c 12 x 10; signed, dated 1907. WHL, 30 May 1989 (550 illus).

106 | *Penzance fishing boat PZ 582 moored before Newlyn slip* | o/c 16 x 12; signed br, dated 1907. Several boats are tied up in the centre; the nearest boat, PZ 582, has red nets hung upon a spar; above are the sunlit houses of Newlyn; at right a man oars a small dinghy; in the foreground the sea reflects the boats. WHL, 28 Feb 1989 (411 ni).

107 | *Fishermen* | o/c 16 x 13; signed, dated 07. Hartley, Ilkley 7 Dec 1994 (571).

108 | *Fishing for bullcod, Larrigan Rocks* | o/c 12 x 16; signed bl, dated 07. At left a boy in a white hat, blue shirt and fishing smock sits on the rocks, facing the viewer, legs outstretched before him, feet bare, and both arms balancing on rocks; at right, behind him, another boy in a white hat lies prone with his right arm outstretched to a pool, holding a fine line; beyond are sea, gulls and coast. Larrigan Rocks are between Newlyn and Penzance, where the Larrigan River enters Mount's Bay. PL, 13 June 1989 (48 illus).

109 | *The river* | o/c; signed bl, dated 07. A small river in spate, seen from a flowery bank; the other bank forms the top of the composition. The paint is loosely applied, with much canvas left visible.

110 | *Washday* | o/c 15 x 11; signed bl, dated 07. In a garden a woman and two girls lay out clean laundry to dry; the woman at left wears a white dress; the front girl has red-blonde hair and wears a white smock over a dark dress; the right girl wears a white blouse above a dark skirt; beyond is Newlyn harbour, hills and fields; the sky is pale blue-grey. PL, 6 Nov 1990 (43 illus); CL, 13 July 2016 (203 illus, as *Washday, Newlyn beyond*); WL.

111 | *Broccoli pickers* | o/c 12 x 16; signed bl, dated 07. At left, two men fill a tall basket; at right is a horse and cart with a boy standing holding the bridle; at right foreground is a filled basket; beyond is a hazy view of Mount's Bay. Tennants, Leyburn 23 Nov 2000 (820 illus); DMG, spring 2001; probably PEAG sales book, 13 Mar 1908, price £7-10s, as *Gathering broccoli*.

112 | *Returning from the orchard* | o/c 24 x 20; signed br, dated 07. A boy in grey bonnet, waistcoat open over white shirt, and gaiters walks left across a meadow carrying a large basket of apples on his left shoulder; several calves follow him; beyond are trees, a calm sea and a white breakwater; the sky is pale blue. SL, 19 November 2008 (30 illus).

113 | *Home from the fields* | o/c 12 x 16; signed bl, dated 07. At left a white horse pulls a small cart with a boy driving it towards us along a road beside a tall hedge with little foliage; the cart is laden with produce; at right a girl in white and a boy lean on curving railings, the boy extending his right hand to a dog. Woolley & Wallis, Salisbury, 8 Dec 2010 (501); Elford Fine Art, Tavistock, March 2011.

114 | *Holly* | described by *The Cornish Telegraph* of 7 November 1907 as "a clever portrait of a lad".

115 | *Summer time* | PEAG sales book, 2 Jan 1907, price £10-10s.

116 | *Girl's head* | PEAG sales book, 28 Mar 1907, price £6.

117 | *Penzance harbour* | PEAG sales book, 5 May 1907, price £4.

118 | *Woman and child* | PEAG sales book, June 1907, price £10.

119 | *Farm yard, evening* | PEAG sales book, 11 Sep 1907, price £7-7s.

120 | *Pigs* | oil. RA, 1907 (740).

121 | *Girl with cabbage* | o/c 11 x 18; signed, dated 1908. In the foreground a girl in dark clothes and with red cheeks looks at the viewer, her hands holding cabbages; at right two young girls stand before a whitewashed farm building with barred windows; some white ducks forage in the road. PH, 2001 (19).

122 | *Portrait of a girl* | o/c 11¼ x 9¼; signed br, dated 08. Head and shoulder portrait of a girl turned left but facing the viewer, with a dark blue hat over thick plaits, and a mid-blue dress; the background is plain mid-brown. CL, 12 June 1986 (87 illus); BL, 26 Sep 2019 (86 illus, as *The blue beret*).

123 | *Washday* | o/c 15½ x 11½; signed br, dated 08. Four young women with baskets moving right across a sloping, sunny meadow. LWG, Mar 1982 (34 illus, as *Washing day*); PL,

124 | *Young washergirls* | o/c 12 x 16; signed, dated 08. Lawrence, Crewkerne, 25 Sep 1980 (377).

125 | *Milking time* | o/c 15 x 18; signed bl, dated 1908. Cows in the foreground, and at left in the distance a woman carrying a milk churn. RCA, 1910 (180, price £15-15s); RA, 1911 (555); Fox/Greenacre, p.129 (illus no.67, as *Cows*); Sotheby & Bearnes, Torquay, 19 Nov 1980 (394); PH, 2001 (50); WL.

126 | *The watering place* | o/c 12 x 16; signed br, dated 08; title inscr on label on back of frame. A white horse half faces the viewer and drinks from a pool or stream; a man sits on it facing left, wearing a flat cap; in the tl a brown horse approaches, ridden by a man with white shirt sleeves. PL, 13 Nov 1984 (57 illus); BG, 1985 (13); CL, 12 June 1986 (88 illus, as *The drinking place*, prov QH); CL, 29 July 1988 (140 illus); BAL, 63790; WL.

127 | *The meeting in the lane* | o/c 12 x 16; signed bl, dated 1908. In a lane flanked by wintry trees, a young man in dark cap and clothes rides a white horse, accompanied by a black horse at left; they move towards lower left; the man looks at a young woman standing at lower right, in hat and blue clothes; her left hand is visible. A very dark painting. PL, 21 Nov 1995 (47 illus); P. Webb, Auckland, New Zealand, 14 Dec 1998 (144); WL.

128 | *The Farm gate* | o/c 34 x 44; signed br in black, dated 1908. In the centre a cart with a red body is drawn by a black horse and a white horse in file, moving left along a wet path among trees; a boy sits on the cart with the reins; at right two figures watch. The tonality is very dark. SL, 20 May 1990 (10 illus, as *A cart by the farm gates*); CL, 21 Nov 1995 (87 illus); CL, 28 Nov 1996 (69); WL.

129 | *Feeding time* | o/c 12 x 14; signed bl, in black, dated 08. At right facing left stands a girl in blue blouse and white apron, holding two pails suspended from a hoop; she approaches a seven-barred iron gate, behind which stand a white/brown and two brown calves. WP, 8 June 1920 (120); PL, 17 Nov 1998 (34 illus); *Country Life*, 4 Mar 1999, p.34 (illus advert); DMG, autumn 1999 (8 illus) and winter 2000 (9 illus); *Homes & Antiques* Nov 2000, p.69 (illus); CL, 22 Nov 2002 (39 illus); WL.

130 | *The Gypsy encampment* | o/c 12 x 18; signed bl, in black, dated indis 08. At right a young woman with red headscarf stands facing the viewer, her left hand on hip, the right hand holding a pail; beside her is a small stream; at left stand a white and a black horse; behind is a gypsy caravan and a fire with figures seated round it; the sky is pale and cloudy. WHL, 10 Feb 1998 (240 illus); PL, 2 Nov 1999 (18 illus, as *The Gypsy camp*); PH, 2001 (46).

131 | *Girl in a Gypsy encampment* | o/c 4 x 7; signed, dated 1908. WHL, 24 Apr 2001 (235).

132 | *Boys with model boat* | o/c 11 x 13; signed, dated 08. CL, 16 Mar 1977 (15).

133 | *Boys fishing on a quay* | o/c 12 x 16; signed br, dated 1908. In the foreground, two boys wearing caps, pale tops and brown shorts sit on a quay facing the viewer; the right boy has a fish in both hands, with a red one beside him on the quay; the left boy holds a line; at left a dinghy passes with two figures; behind is the town; the sky and sea are pale blue-green. CSK, 10 May 2001 (164 illus); *The Antiques*

Magazine, 26 May 2001 (illus); DMG, spring 2009 (13 illus).

134 | ***A boy with his dog*** | o/c 12½ x 16½; signed bl, dated 1908. On the grassy bank of a ditch, a boy in a white hat sits facing right with a brown dog beside him. SL, 9 Nov 1988 (30 illus); WL.

135 | ***The girl and the frog*** | o/c 12 x 16; signed bl, dated 08. On a grassy area beside a sun-dappled pond, a young girl with very long plaited hair sits facing right; she has a blue dress and bare feet; she looks at a large frog seated at right by her feet. The girl may be Mornie Birch, who had long plaits. The picture derives from the story of the princess and the prince-frog. DMG, 1990 (10 illus); WL.

136 | ***Whiffling for mackerel*** | o/c 11 x 13; signed bl, dated 08. In the foreground is a dinghy in which an older man in cap and white jersey facing right holds a line over the right side; at left lies a basket of silvery fish; behind him a younger man in cap and a dark green jersey leans over the stern; beyond is the harbour with lighthouse; above is a very thin strip of sky. The correct term is 'whiffing'. SL, 19 May 1982 (5 illus); WL.

137 | ***The Old Slip, Newlyn*** | o/c 12 x 18; signed bl, in brown, dated 08. The Slip makes a diagonal shape from left to right, rising up to Fore Street; three men walk towards us each carrying fishing tools; the right man wears a white smock and carries an oar over his right shoulder; on the foreshore are a few boats and men about them. CL, 5 June 2008 (19 illus, damaged at centre right).

138 | ***The Old Slip, Newlyn*** | o/c 16 x 12; signed bl, within a drawn rectangular box, dated 08. At right is a narrow path beside the harbour, with metal railings, and a woman walking toward the viewer; in the middle, at the foot of a path rising steeply to the town, a woman facing left in a blue blouse speaks to two men in a dinghy alongside; above the town buildings is a cloudy sky. WHL, 27 Mar 1990 (150 illus, as *Boats and figures on the Old Newlyn Slip*); WHL, 12 July 1990 (260 illus); BL, 20 Oct 1994 (42).

139 | ***The village street, Newlyn*** | o/c 22 x 18; signed bl in red-brown, dated 08. At left are thatched houses painted in blue-grey on a street curving away to the right; by a house stands a white horse with a cart, a man tending the green vegetables on it; beside him at left stands a woman holding a child in her arms, an older girl in a white dress, and another in a green blouse with a basket over her right arm; at right are the houses of the town, with two figures and a white dog by a wall; beyond are wintry trees and a grey, cloudy sky. SL, 3 July 2002 (6 illus).

140 | ***Mousehole*** | o/c 24 x 30; signed bl, dated 1908. The north part of the harbour with the sea at left; at right is the Ship Inn; in the foreground stand a boy, a mother carrying a pitcher in her left hand, and a girl child; in the middle distance stand three sailors, the left one in a white jumper leaning against the harbour railing. The colours are very muted. Perhaps LG, 1918 (16) as *Monschole harbour*; PL, 13 Nov 1984 (71 illus, prov QH); CL, 6 Mar 1986 (79 illus); WL.

141 | ***Mousehole, Newlyn*** | o/c 10 x 12; signed bl, dated 08. An almost identical version of the larger painting *Mousehole* but without the boy standing in the foreground, a different set of boats in the harbour, and less building at far right. SL, 13 July 2010 (133, as *Mousehole, Newlyn*); Newlyn School Gallery, Penzance, 2010, as *Mousehole cliff, Newlyn*.

142 | ***The day's catch*** | o/c 12 x 18; signed bl, dated 08. Label on reverse attributing ownership to Lady Lonsborough. At left is a donkey-cart facing us; at right several fish are laid on the shore and beside them stands a fisherman with a basket in his left hand; behind are many people standing watching; behind them are fishing boats and a coastal steamer, with land rising at far right; the sky is cloudy. Waddingtons, Toronto, 2 Dec 2008 (146 as *Fishermen at Newlyn harbour*); CL, 16 Dec 2009 (75 illus); Dreweatts, Newbury, 14 Dec 2010 (1204 illus); DL, 20 Oct 2011 (319 illus, as *The dawn tally*).

143 | ***Sunshine and Shade*** | *The West Briton & Cornwall Advertiser* of 2 April 1908 recorded "… depicts a mowhay from which a pair of farm horses have just been driven". PEAG, 1908.

144 | ***Sunshine and shadow*** | oil. RA, 1908 (546); WAGL, 1908 (198, price £63).

145 | ***Back from the Drying***[?] | last word of title is not clear. PEAG sales book, 24 Mar 1908, price £8-8s.

146 | ***Portrait of a young girl*** | black chalk 19¾ x 14½; signed, dated 1909. A young girl seated in a chair facing right but looking at the viewer; the chair back is draped with a blanket(?). SL, 14 July 1982 (29 illus); WL.

147 | ***Boy whittling*** | o/c 16 x 12; signed faintly bl, dated 09. A boy in cap and waistcoat open over a white shirt, with brown trousers, approaches the viewer between trees among which grow yellow daffodils; his left hand holds a stick and he applies a knife with his right hand; he is followed at left by a dog. The painting is in pale tones. PL, 13 Nov 1984 (60 illus, prov QH); WHL, 12 Oct 1993 (100, as *Boy whittling a stick*); SL, 5 Mar 1997 (33 illus); SL, 11 Dec 2007 (63 illus, as *Boy whittling a stick*); WL.

148 | ***Collecting gulls' eggs, Mevagissey*** | o/c 24 x 30; signed br, dated 09. In a meadow with wild flowers, two boys kneel at left, the furthest holding a cap with eggs in it; at right another boy stands looking with hands on his knees; in the distance are a harbour and sea. The scene has also been identified as Newlyn. Wortley, p.271 (illus).

149 | ***Boy fishing*** | o/c 14 x 22; signed, dated 09. PL, 13 Nov 1984 (58 ni, prov QH).

150 | ***Three fishermen*** | o/c 18 x 20; signed bl in red, dated 09. Close-up of three old men facing left, wearing different hats, the middle man lighting a pipe, all seated against a stone wall, probably the Old Quay at Newlyn. The fishermen have been identified as John, Joseph and William Jeffery. Fox, p.75 (illus); PL, 13 Nov 1984 (64 illus, prov QH); CL, 21 Nov 2003 (42 illus); WL.

151 | ***Inner harbour*** | o/c 10 x 14; signed bl, dated 1909. At left are Newlyn houses, with several boats in the foreground; in one boat a man stands with an oar. DMG, autumn 1974 (32 illus).

152 | ***Wading ashore*** | o/c 16 x 14; signed bl, dated 09. In the foreground a young girl stands in the surf, wearing a white smock over a red dress; a younger child is clinging to her back, in a cream hat and green jersey; beyond are more children in the sea, with sailing boats and the coast in the distance. CL, 21 Nov 1995

(92 illus); SL, 4 Mar 1998 (25); PH, 2001 (41); WL.

153 | ***Pulling in the creels*** | o/c 12 x 16; signed bl, dated 09. Two fishermen in a small boat moving right, the left man holding the steering oar, the right man pulling in a basket. Creels are lobster pots. SL, 2 Nov 1983 (4 illus); SL, 18 July 1984 (238).

154 | ***Seaweed gatherers*** | o/c 11 x 15; signed bl, in black, dated 09. A white and a black horse pull a laden cart, moving left across wet sand; at right a man rakes seaweed. Barnes Thomas, Penzance, 5 Sep 2011 (282 illus).

155 | ***The close of a summer's day*** | o/c 50 x 40; signed bl, in brown, dated 09. Inscr with title and artist's address on a label on the stretcher. A boy on a white horse crosses a stream towards us; he looks left at a man on the bank with two brown horses; behind are tall trees. WAGL, 1909; Fox, p.76 (illus); Christoper Wood, *Paradise Lost: Paintings of English Country Life and Landscape 1850–1914* (Barrie & Jenkins, 1988), p.68 (illus, as *Watering the horse*); SL, 2 Nov 1983 (16); RGG, May 1984 (20 illus); CL, 5 Mar 1987 (45 illus); DL, 30 Mar 1989 (724 illus cover); SL, 13 Dec 2005 (69 illus); WL.

156 | ***The village pump*** | o/c 16 x 13; signed, dated 09. Mentioned in the *Western Daily Mercury* of 23 Aug 1912 as having "specially caught our eye". HSG, Aug 1912 (42); WP, 20 June 1920 (136); Bearnes, Torquay, 7 Mar 1995 (573).

157 | ***Spring in Cornwall*** | o/c 12 x 16; signed bl, dated 09. A brown and white cow stands in the foreground of a meadow, with other cows behind at right; the skyline is high. WHL, 6 Mar 1997 (101 ni, as *Springtime in Cornwall*); SL, 1 Oct 1997 (42 illus); DL, 17 Feb 2000 (544 illus); PH, 2001 (13); WL.

158 | ***Boy with a calf*** | o/c 12 x 16; signed br, dated 1909. A boy stands in a rural road with a calf walking before him on a lead; the calf is brown with a white patch on the forehead; at right is a hedge; a thin sliver of sky is visible; the boy and calf are in strong contre-jour. PH, 2001 (16).

159 | ***The lane to Paul*** | o/c 12 x 16; signed bl, dated 09. A young woman carrying a pail in her left hand walks towards us behind a calf on a country lane; behind are trees, and a full moon at left. PH, 2001 (15).

160 | ***Newlyn Coombe*** | o/c 16 x 12; signed bl, dated 09. The stream cuts diagonally across the br, and at left are houses, behind which rises a long hill with trees; snow lies on the roofs and on the ground. Given by Harvey to his nephew Raymond as a wedding present in 1937. PH, 2001 (8).

161 | ***A view of Newlyn*** | o/c 12 x 13½; signed bl, in black, dated 09. The foreground shows a harbour roadway with handrail at right and houses at left; beyond are the sunlit town and harbour with boats; the sky is cloudy. DMG, 1978; PH, 2001 (30).

162 | ***Supper time*** | o/c 22 x 20; signed bl, in black, dated 09. At left a young mother in dark blouse and pale skirt sits in a wooden chair feeding a girl on her lap; reddish firelight shines on the mother's skirt; at right is a pot plant on a sill, and dusky light comes through the window. RCA, summer 1909 (272, price £26-10s); CL, 21 Nov 2003 (43 illus); CL, 5 June 2008 (23 illus); CSK, 3 Sep 2008 (217 illus); CSK, 25 Feb 2009 (988 illus).

163 | ***A boat's crew, Newlyn harbour*** | Three men in a dinghy moving left away from the viewer; at the stern a man stands holding the steering oar; the harbour wall is in the distance. *The Studio*, 1909, p.116 (illus).

164 | ***Boats in a harbour*** | o/c 12 x 16 bl, dated indis 09. In the foreground are small fishing boats, one with a red sail, and two dinghies; behind are two stone jetties, the further with a white and red lighthouse; in the distance is faint land under a grey-blue sky; the scene is sunny. Woolley & Wallis, Salisbury, 26 Aug 2020 (202).

165 | ***Seaweed gatherers, Mount's Bay*** A young man with back to the viewer leads a white and a dark horse pulling a cart laden with seaweed, moving right on a beach; beyond is the sea. *The Studio*, 1909, p.117 (illus).

166 | ***Ploughing*** | o/c 12 x 18; signed bl, dated 09. At left a brown and a white horse move left pulling a plough worked by a man in cap, waistcoat and white shirt; the foreground is green meadow, with ploughed land beyond; in the distance are low hills; the sky is cloudy with blue patches. This work is very similar to *The plough team* (1900) and *Ploughing* (1904).

167 | ***Palms*** | PEAG sales book, 29 Mar 1909, price £9.

168 | ***Spring*** | RCA, summer 1909 (230, price £10-10s).

169 | ***A Cornish lane*** | RCA, summer 1909 (244, price £10-10s).

170 | ***Fishermen in harbour*** | o/c 16 x 13; signed, dated 1910. SL, 18 Sep 1979 (6).

171 | ***Whiffling outer harbour*** | o/c 16 x 14; signed br in black, dated 1910. In the foreground a dinghy moves towards the viewer; seated at its bow is a young man in brown cap and white shirt; at the tiller sits an older man in cap and dark blue jacket; behind at right is the harbour quay and lighthouse; at upper left is a large sailing vessel. The correct term is 'whiffing'. PL, 10 Mar 1987 (12 illus); WHL, 28 Feb 1989 (100 illus, as *Father and son in small rowing boat sculling across Newlyn harbour*).

172 | ***Hayfield*** | PEAG sales book, 1910, price £10-10s.

173 | ***Boats*** | PEAG sales book, 24 Sep 1910, price £5.

174 | ***Evening*** | RCA, summer 1910, price £10-10s.

175 | ***Ducks swimming*** | o/c 16 x 14; signed, dated 1911. BL, 22 Feb 1978 (132 ni).

176 | ***Morning sunshine*** | o/c 36 x 28; signed br, dated 1911. On a grassy hillside two young women walk towards the viewer, the right one in blue skirt and green blouse and carrying a basket in her right hand; the left woman has pale pink clothes and a green hat. RA, 1911 (307), PL, 20 June 1983 (17 illus); FAS, 1985 (17 illus, as *Bringing in the washing*); CL, 6 Mar 1986 (80 illus); WL.

177 | ***Returning from the fields*** | o/c 24 x 30; signed, dated 11. At left a young woman in a white hat moves right carrying a hoe, beside a stream bordered with wild flowers; behind, a man and woman move left on a wooden bridge over the stream. RGG, RH885.

178 | ***Pulling in the catch*** | o/c 12 x 16; signed br, dated 1911. A dinghy in the foreground, in which a boy at left stands holding the rudder; at right a man in a white jersey pulls in a net from the right; by the net are seagulls; the coast is in the distance at right; the sky is pale cream. The paint is thickly applied. PL, 10 Nov 1987 (15 illus); PL, 14 June 1988 (10 illus); WL.

179 | ***Newlyn harbour at dusk with figures*** | o/c 16 x 18; signed br, dated 1911. The Old Quay is in the foreground and houses at left, with boats moored beyond; in the distance are houses and lights. WHL, 28 Feb 1989 (370 illus); DMG, autumn 2010 (26 illus, as *The old harbour at dusk, Newlyn*); DMG, May 2012 (6 illus, as *The old harbour at dusk, Newlyn, 1911*).

180 | ***Portrait of Percival George Francis Harvey*** | o/c 12 x 10; signed br, dated 1911. P.G.F. Harvey (b.1908) was Harold's nephew. Head and shoulders view of a young boy turned left but facing the viewer, with a mop of blonde curly hair and open-mouthed smile, wearing white clothes; the background is neutral dark. NMAG, 2001 (34).

181 | ***Portrait of Gertrude Bodinnar*** | o/p 10 x 8. Painted shortly before her marriage in 1911. Gertrude faces left, her hair done up; she wears a pale green dress; the background is plain dark brown. PL, 23 Apr 1985 (32 ni); PL, 18 June 1985 (55).

182 | ***The tea party*** | o/c 24 x 30; signed bl, dated 1912. At a table with a white cloth sit three girls; the left one has a long plait down her back; the centre girl drinks from a cup; the right girl has her back to us; at left is a window. Label verso for Hull (*Autumn*) 1912. Perhaps RA, 1912 (724 as *A tea party*); PH, 2001 (37); *PCF: C&SI*, p.112 (illus); WHL, 27 Sep 2012 (100 illus). Penlee House Gallery & Museum (2004.L3P).

183 | ***Polishing day*** | o/c 18 x 16; signed, dated 1912; title inscr on the back. In a dark cottage room, two young women by a window clean a variety of copper and brass utensils; the left figure wears a red jacket; at the lower edge are a polished kettle and other items; at right is a wooden arm chair. B&W, 23 May 1984 (378); PH, 2001 (35).

184 | ***Feeding the pigeons*** | o/c 16 x 20; signed br, dated 1912. On a sunny terrace with white columns a girl in a dark blue dress over a white blouse stands holding a flat basket in her hands; before her a few pigeons eat their feed; at right is a deck chair. WP, 8 June 1920 (103).

185 | ***The wayside minstrels*** | o/c 15 x 18; signed bl, dated 1912. Inscr Wayside Minstrels on the stretcher. On a hillside overlooking the sea, among wild flowers, sit a man and a young woman; the man sits at left looking left and wears a red scarf, a cigarette in his mouth, holding an accordion; the woman sits at right looking at the man, and wears a patterned headscarf and pink blouse; on the sea are several small sailing boats. MG, 1913, of which *The Queen* wrote on 24 May 1913: "the charm of the picture lies in the placing of the two seated figures on the grass with background of sea and sky". WP, 8 June 1920 (35); William Hardie, Glasgow, 31 Aug 1994 (74 illus, as *The accordionist*, as dated 1902). CL, 22 Nov 1994 (244 illus, as dated 1922); SL, 7 June 2005 (89, as dated 1922).

186 | ***Apples*** | o/c 60 x 50; signed br, dated 1912. In a sunny orchard, at left a girl facing centre stands wearing a red smock over a white blouse and dark skirt; with both hands she holds a large pannier of apples; at right a girl in white blouse and dark skirt kneels under a tree gathering apples and puts them into a pannier beside her. RA, 1912 (362); WAGL, 1913 (88, price £100). *PCF: C&SI*, p.191 (illus); WL. Royal Cornwall Museum, Truro (1921.34), bought 1921 for £50.

187 | ***April showers*** | described in the *Western Daily Mercury* of 23 Aug 1912 as "a masterful work, strength and beauty of colouring being the principal features". HSG, Aug 1912 (2); WP, 8 June 1920 (91).

188 | ***Blackberry harvest*** | mentioned in the *Western Daily Mercury* of 23 Aug 1912 as "no one could wish for a prettier picture". HSG, Aug 1912 (29); WP, 8 June 1920 (116).

189 | ***Blackthorn over Newlyn*** | o/c 14 x 16; signed, dated 1912. White blossom bushes against a distant blue sea with coast; in the foreground a girl faces right towards two younger girls, one in a red hat. DMG, pub VIII (57 illus); SL, 28 Sep 1994.

190 | ***Maytime*** | o/c 21 x 27; signed bl, dated 1912. Among sunlit trees by a stream, a woman at left stands watching four young girls dancing around a young tree; a girl in a large brimmed hat and white dress sits by the woman. Wortley, p.221 (illus).

191 | ***Maytime*** | mentioned in the *Western Daily Mercury* of 23 Aug 1912 as "A more charming figure of gracefulness could hardly be imagined than that of the young woman reclining on the warm grass in 'Maytime' (44) but the small figure of the child in the middle distance rather jars on the nerves." This does not seem to be the painting illustrated in Wortley. HSG, Aug 1912 (44).

192 | ***A field of flowers*** | o/c 16 x 14; signed br, dated 1912. Two young girls in a green meadow; the right girl faces left and has a cream dress and bare feet; the left girl wears a large cream hat and lies on her left side, holding red flowers in her right hand. SL, 10 Mar 1982 (96 illus, as *Two children in a field*, as dated 1922; SL, 21 May 1986 (68 illus); CL, 16 June 2005 (139 illus); WL.

193 | ***In the orchard*** | o/c 15 x 18; signed bl, dated 1912, inscr on the stretcher 'In the Orchard Harold Harvey'. In an orchard with blossoming trees, women at left rake the ground; the foremost woman has a red headscarf; in the distance buildings rise above the trees. HSG, Aug 1912 (9); WP, 8 June 1920 (94); PL, 11 Nov 1986 (45 illus); CL, 11 Mar 1994 (3 illus); WL.

194 | ***The poppy field*** | described in the *Western Daily Mercury* of 23 Aug 1912 as "A more daring composition than The Poppy Field it would be hard to imagine, but Mr Harvey has made a really striking picture of it." HSG, Aug 1912 (17).

195 | ***Springtime in the orchard*** | o/c 29½ x 22; signed bl. A woman in white clothes sits in the left foreground by a narrow path on a sunlit sloping meadow with trees in pale-pink blossom; a child stands beside her in white smock, yellow brimmed hat and blue skirt, with hands behind its back; a few people stand among the trees; beyond at right is Newlyn harbour and Mounts Bay; the sky is cloudy grey with some blue patches. Described in the *Western Daily Mercury* of 23 Aug 1912 as "one of the largest pictures in the (HSG) collection … it contains many passages of wonderfully fine colour … it is a striking picture." HSG, Aug 1912 (35); Sothebys, New York, 8 Nov 2012 (68 illus).

196 | ***Cows in a lane*** | o/c 18 x 20; signed br, dated 1912. At left stands a pale brown cow turned right, facing the viewer; in front stands a white calf with darker head; at right another cow eats grass, attended by a man in a hat and black clothes. CL, 10 Nov 1988 (49 illus); PL,

23 Jan 1990 (10 illus); WL.

197 | *End of the day* | mentioned in the *Western Daily Mercury* of 23 Aug 1912. HSG, Aug 1912 (8); WP, 8 June 1920 (76).

198 | *Faggot gatherers* | o/c 20 x 22; signed bl. In a copse, a girl in the foreground faces left wearing a white blouse and a coloured head-scarf, holding a bundle of wood wrapped in a cloth; behind her, at left, another girl bends to the ground, her right arm outstretched. The woods at Higher Faughan were a source of faggots. The *Western Daily Mercury* of 23 Aug 1912 said "The large work Faggot Gatherers will repay careful inspection. The girl in the foreground is a typical Cornish girl and there is no mistake about the way in which she hugs to her breast the big bundle of faggots confined in an old brown wrapper". HSG, Aug 1912 (7); probably Mendoza Galleries 1913, reviewed as among the best of his pictures there; CL, 11 June 1982 (5 illus, as *Two girls gathering faggots*).

199 | *The rainbow* | o/c 18 x 20; signed, dated 12; title inscr on the stretcher. At lower left stand four cows beside a hedge; beyond at right is an extensive landscape view with a white farmhouse catching the sun; at right is a rainbow; the sea beyond may be Mount's Bay. PL, 12 Nov 1985 (54 illus).

200 | *A Cornish summer landscape* | o/c 18 x 20; signed bl, dated 1912. In the foreground at left a man walks behind two cows and a calf, moving right in a meadow; beyond are rolling fields; the sky is grey and cloudy. Sotheby Taunton, 26 Sep 1979 (506); PH, 2001 (14, as *A Cornish landscape*).

201 | *Planting potatoes* | o/c 18 x 16; signed br, dated 1912; title inscr on the back. In the foreground two women work with buckets of potatoes; the left figure wears a black blouse and headscarf; the right figure wears a red headscarf and grey waistcoat; at right two men work on a sloping field; beyond are trees and fields. PH, 2001 (22).

202 | *Mending the nets* | o/c 18 x 20; signed bl, dated 1912. In a grassy meadow, in the foreground a young man with his back to the viewer and in a cap and blue jacket, works on a brown net laid on the grass; at right a boy lies on the grass, with a white shirt and a cap, holding a pipe in his right hand, watching the man work; at tr is a glimpse of blue sea. HSG, Aug 1912 (41); DMG, autumn 1974 (25 illus).

203 | *Old Newlyn harbour* | oil on paper 12 x 14½; signed, dated 1912. Several small boats in the left foreground; at right is the harbour with larger boats; done in pale blues and greys. DL, 12 April 2012 (467 illus).

204 | *The baker boy on Newlyn Bridge* | o/c 24 x 20; signed br, dated 1912. A boy with a basket full of bread sits on the wall of the bridge at Newlyn; on the right is a man sat on a horse and cart, talking to a standing man; three young girls walk towards us on the bridge, and three men stand together at the centre of the bridge; behind the bridge is a tall building. WHL, 24 April 2001 (50 illus).

205 | *Girl with blue bow* | o/c 16 x 12; signed, dated 12. Head and shoulders view of a young girl facing the viewer, with a blue bow in her hair above her right ear; she wears a dark grey dress over a grey shirt; the background is plain black. PL, 11 Nov 1986 (49 illus).

206 | *April showers* | the *Western Daily Mercury* of 23 Aug 1912 noted "a masterful work, strength and beauty of colouring being the principal features"; the *Western Daily Press* on 2 April 1913 observed "two little girls shielded from the rain by an umbrella". HSG, Aug 1912; F&R, 1913; WP, 8 June 1920 (91).

207 | *Marbles* | o/c 12 x 18; signed bl, in brown. On a path beside the sea four children play marbles; at left two lean against a fence, at centre a boy in a red jumper throws a marble towards four others; at right a boy stands with hands on knees; left of the fence is a meadow and in the middle distance are tall trees and factories with chimneys; beyond is Penzance and a patch of sea. The *Western Daily Mercury* of 23 Aug 1912 said "Nothing could be finer or more true to local colouring and character than 'Marbles.'" HSG, Aug 1912 (21); RGG, May 2008 (SP4661, as *c.*1905).

208 | *Holidays* | o/c 15 x 19; signed br in red, dated 12. A sunlit view; in the foreground a young girl in a bright pink dress holds a coloured whirler; behind her is a younger girl in a green coat with a whirler; at right on a grass-topped stone wall a boy in brown clothes lies down and a girl in a bright pink dress sits; beyond are blue sea and pale grey sky. Plymouth Art Gallery, 1913; B&W, 5 Sep 1984 (247); Pyms Gallery, autumn 1984 (30 illus); SL, 9 Dec 2008 (152 illus); Lyon & Turnbull, Edinburgh, 29 Nov 2012 (65 illus).

209 | *Holiday* | o/c 16 x 14; signed br. A girl in a red dress, with a cream sunlit parasol, and a book open on her lap, sits on a grassy bank, with a small girl in a white dress sitting beside her at left. Cardiff 1914; PH, 2001 (40). National Museums & Galleries of Wales, Cardiff (A2173), bought in 1912 for £10.

210 | *On the rocks* | the *Western Daily Mercury* of 23 Aug 1912 said it "is a delightful picture of skilful drawing and bright crisp colour." HSG, Aug 1912 (3).

211 | *The meadow by the sea* | the *Western Daily Mercury* of 23 Aug 1912 said it is "another charming work." HSG, Aug 1912 (15).

212 | *In the harvest field* | described in the *Western Daily Mercury* of 23 Aug 1912 as "a mother resting with her baby during the heat of the noonday (which) reminds one of some of our best representations of the Madonna and Child. The modelling of the figure of the mother is extremely good; the face is hidden beneath a sun bonnet, but is so finely suggested that the beholder can form his own idea of beauty from it." Mentioned in the *Morning Post* 30 May 1913 for its "pleasing manner in which homely matters are rendered". HSG, Aug 1912 (24); MG, 1913 (43); WP, 8 June 1920 (73).

213 | *Tired out* | o/c 18 x 15; signed br (underlined); inscr Harold Harvey on label on reverse. A woman in yellow blouse and white skirt, facing left, holds in her arms a young girl with a white smock over a dark dress; in the background are orchard trees, with red blossom at upper left. The *Western Daily Mercury* of 23 Aug 1912 noted its "depth of elegant tone and loving carefulness in drawing"; mentioned by the *Western Daily Press* on 2 April 1913. HSG, Aug 1912 (16); F&R, 1913; LG, 1927 (27); Fox/Greenacre, p.129 (illus no.68); PH, 2001 (47); WL.

214 | *Under sixteen* | o/c 13½ x 15½; signed bl, in black; *c.*1906; title inscr on reverse. A young boy stands centre, facing the viewer, a lit cigarette in his mouth; he wears a cap and dark blue jersey, and carries a basket of green vegetables over his left arm; behind is a white house. Described in the *Western Daily Mercury* of 23 Aug 1912 as showing "a keen sense of humour in (the) delightful drawing of a boy smoking a cigarette"; noticed by the *Western Daily Press* on 2 April 1913. HSG, Aug 1912 (31); F&R, 1913; WP, 8 June 1920 (137); PH, 2001 (18).

215 | *The new calf* | RCA, summer 1912 (22, price £10-10s).

216 | *The gate* | PEAG sales book, Aug 1912, price £11.

217 | *The kite* | mentioned in the *Western Daily Mercury* of 23 Aug 1912 as "It is surprising that such an artist as Mr Harold Harvey should have introduced such a niggling passage of colour as that seen in *The Kite* (43). The land-scape, although somewhat dwarfed by the figures, is good, and the figures themselves are very finely modelled; but the tail of the kite!" HSG, Aug 1912 (43).

218 | *The shop* | PEAG sales book, Aug 1912, price £11.

219 | *Hoeing parsley, Mount's Bay* | o/c 30 x 24; signed bl, dated 1913. In the foreground two young men facing left are hoeing; behind them stands another man with a hoe; the front man wears a white shirt; the centre man has a blue jacket; the farthest man looks old and appears to be lighting a pipe or cigarette; the sky is overcast. MG, 1913 (34). Mentioned in the *Morning Post* 30 May 1913. WP, 8 June 1920 (58, sold for £11); CL, 27 Nov 1997 (156 illus, as *Hoeing above Mounts Bay*); PH, 2001 (20, as *Hoeing above Mount's Bay*); 'Amongst heroes', London, 2013; *Amongst heroes*, p.36 (illus).

220 | *Pioneers of aerial navigation* | o/c 18 x 16; signed bl, dated 13. Sunlit view of a girl with plaits standing holding a white kite; at right are two boys sitting; in the middle distance two children fly a kite. Perhaps MG, 1913 as *The kite*, of which *The Queen* said on 24 May 1913 "(it) is another which deserves mention"; WP, 8 June 1920 (104); PL, 12 Nov 1985 (97 illus); W&H, 1986 (12 illus); BAL, 48619.

221 | *Ring a ring of roses* | o/c 14 x 18; signed bl, title on overlap. Three young children in a green meadow hold hands in a ring; the right girl wears a red cap; noticed by the *Western Daily Press* on 2 April 1913. F&R, 1913; WP, 8 June 1920 (140); RGG, CA132.

222 | *The shop window* | o/c 18 x 16; signed bl, dated 1913. A shop window fills the tr corner of the picture; at left stands a girl in a white smock holding a young child in her arms, who reaches to touch the window; at right another young child in a beige hat and blue smock stands under the window reaching up to it. The shop depicted may be a popular grocery shop in Fore Street, Newlyn. PL, 11 Nov 1986 (44 illus); CL, 11 Mar 1994 (2 illus, as *The village shop*); WL.

223 | *Mother and child in a wooded landscape* | o/c 13¾ x 15¾; signed bl, dated 1913. At left a young woman in a white dress sits facing right, and on her lap is a young girl in a white smock over a blue dress; at right is a stream bisected by a sapling; the models are thought to be Mrs Lamorna Birch and her daughter Joan. SL, 10 Mar 1993 (16 illus, as *Mother and child*; bought at Morrab Studio, Penzance, 1919); Court Gallery, Nether Stowey, 1996, (as *By the stream, Lamorna*); BAL, 60248 (as *Mother and child in a wooded landscape*); PH, 2001 (28).

224 | *A quiet paddle* | o/c 20 x 18; signed

bl, dated 13. Two young girls sitting on a rocky beach, both with plaits and bare feet; the left girl wears a white dress, the right girl a pink dress. SL, 10 Mar 1993 (11 illus; bought from Morrab Studio, Penzance 1918). Exhb. Barbican Art Gallery, London 1995 'Impressionism in Britain' (96 illus) and Dublin 1995; WL.

225 | *A summer breeze* | *The Cornishman* of 20 March 1913 recorded "A trio of children are daintily treated … resting by a Cornish stile." PEAG, 1913.

226 | *The bathers* | o/c 19 x 21; signed bl, dated 1913. In the foreground a nude boy sits facing left, his back to the viewer; another boy is nude in a pool, and beyond two more boys undress; in the distance are sea and coast. W&H, autumn 1986 (13 illus); DMG, autumn 2010 (27 illus); DMG, May 2012 (7 illus); CL, 11 July 2013 (108 illus); BAL, 33519 (as *On the rocks near Newlyn*).

227 | *Sea pinks* | o/c 14 x 16; signed br in white, dated 1913; inscr verso. Three young girls sit on sand dunes by the sea, facing left; the left girl wears a white hat and takes off her left sock; the middle girl wears a pink dress and a black hair band; the right girl appears older and wears red bows on her plaits and a white smock over black clothes; their feet are bare; at lower right grow the sea pinks, *Armeria Maritima*; above is a pale blue sky. Mentioned in the *Western Daily Press* of 25 Nov 1915 as "of interest by reason of (its) strong resemblance to nature." F&R, 1915; PL, 12 June 1990 (99 illus); WL.

228 | *A Cornish beach* | wc 5½ x 9; signed, dated 13. DL, 9 Sep 1983 (825 ni).

229 | *Boats at Newlyn harbour* | o/c 20 x 18; signed bl, dated indis 13. In the foreground a fishing boat with two masts is moored, with a dinghy alongside carrying a man in a blue shirt; behind, the pier lies laterally across the canvas, with boats alongside and a yellow dinghy; the sea is calm and reflects the cloudy grey sky. BL, 10 July 2013 (131 illus).

230 | *Boy with horse and cart* | o/c 12 x 16; signed bl, dated 13. A boy smoking a cigarette and looking at the viewer drives a cart with red shafts pulled by a brown horse moving right. Fox/Greenacre, p.129 (illus no.69); PH, 2001 (17, as *Boy on a cart*); WL.

231 | *The afternoon ride* | o/c 13 x 18; signed, dated 13. A man sits side-saddle on a large brown horse moving right across a meadow overlooking blue sea and a headland; the man looks at a small black and brown dog in the foreground. LWG, Mar 1982 (36 illus).

232 | *Shoeing a horse* | o/c 10 x 14; signed br, dated 1913. In the centre a man wearing a pale shirt shoes the front right hoof of a large brown horse facing right; beyond a cart wheel rests against a wall. The style is sketchy and thickly painted. PL, 13 Nov 1984 (56 illus, prov QH); DL, 17 Oct 2002 (1448 illus, as *Outside the blacksmith's shop*); WL.

233 | *A day of rest* | o/c 18 x 16; signed bl, dated 13. A young woman with a white shawl and dark cap and gloves, holds a red book inscribed with a cross. The location is said to be Mount Misery, Newlyn. PL, 12 Nov 1985 (65 ni, as *Going to church*); PL, 28 Jan 1986 (52 ni); DL, 6 Feb 1992 (20 illus, as *Day of rest*); PH, 2001 (57, as *Sunday best*); WHL, 27 Nov 2008 (50 illus, as *Sunday best*).

234 | *Spoils of the hedgerow* | o/c 16 x 18;

signed bl, dated 1913; title inscr on the back. Three children on a grassy bank; the left figure is a girl in a white smock over a red dress; the centre figure is a boy lying with legs outstretched towards the viewer, with a cap and waistcoat; the right figure is a younger boy kneeling with his head on the other boy's left shoulder; all three look at what the centre boy is holding; behind is a ditch or stream. WP, 8 June 1920 (117); PH, 2001 (36).

235 | *Gathering seaweed* | o/c 10 x 14; signed bl, dated indis 1913. A man leading two horses pulling a cart laden with seaweed on a flat beach, all moving left. SL, 10 Mar 1993 (15 illus, bought from the Morrab Studio, Penzance, 1919).

236 | *The apple harvest* | mentioned in *The Morning Post* of 30 May 1913; MG, 1913; WP, 8 June 1920 (127).

237 | *The blackberry harvest* | noticed by the *Western Daily Press* on 2 April 1913; F&R, 1913; WP, 8 June 1920 (116).

238 | *The happy days of childhood* | the *Western Daily Press* on 2 April 1913 observed "some youngsters at a rude gate near the sea are having their fill of pleasure"; F&R, 1913; WP, 8 June 1920 (93).

239 | *Darning a sock* | o/c 17½ x 19½; signed, dated indis 13. In an interior, at right a woman in a white blouse sits darning; at left a young boy in a red pullover sits on a table, his feet bare; behind is a window with a net curtain. PH, 2001 (38); WHL, 13 Dec 2012 (260 illus); WHL, 14 Mar 2013 (180 illus); WHL, 13 June 2013 (80 illus).

240 | *A girl with her doll* | o/b 14 x 7; signed bl, dated 13; inscr labels on frame and stretcher with Harvey's name and address. A full length standing view of a girl in dark clothes facing right, holding a doll with red clothes; at right is a green stable door with the top half open; at br is a red area on the ground. CL, 16 June 2005 (23); BL, 29 Nov 2005 (4 illus, as *Girl holding a doll*); WHL, 27 Nov 2008 (523 as *Her favourite doll*); WHL, 12 June 2012 (70 illus, as *The favourite doll*).

241 | *The mother* | MG, 1913 (7).

242 | *Monday morning* | mentioned in the *Morning Post* 30 May 1913. MG, 1913 (16); WP, 8 June 1920 (59).

243 | *The first snowdrops of the year* | MG, 1913 (45); WP, 8 June 1920 (50).

244 | *Summer breezes* | oil. RA, 1913 (695); WAGL, 1913 (272, price £20).

245 | *Gathering bracken* | o/c 18 x 15; signed, dated 14. P. Bath, 18 Apr 1983 (148).

246 | *Falmouth harbour* | wc 14 x 10; signed, dated 14. DL, 25 May 1987 (186 ni); DL, 30 Mar 1989 (512 ni).

247 | *Winding wool* | o/c 25 x 30; signed bl, in black, dated 14. Two young girls in a room, the right girl with a spotted dress, with thick plaits down to her waist, standing facing left holding a skein of red wool in her outstretched hands; the left girl has a dark blue dress, and sits in a chair facing away, winding the wool into a ball; at right is a dark round table bearing green and red wool. The right girl resembles Mornie Birch (1904-1990), daughter of S.J. Lamorna Birch and who was much painted by others (John, the Knights). Mentioned in the *Western Daily Press* of 25 Nov 1915. RA, 1914 (843); WAGL, 1914 (120, price £42); F&R, 1915; SL, 21 May 1986 (85 illus); DMG, 1990 (23 illus); DMG, 1994 (52 illus); SL, 14 Dec 2006 (186 illus);

CL, 20 Nov 2018 (23 illus); MacConnal-Mason, March 2022; WL.

248 | *Woman reading* | o/c 20 x 18½; signed br, dated 1914 within a rectangular green-yellow field. A young woman in a pink blouse and black skirt sits in an armchair facing left and reads a book; behind her is a white painted cupboard with china bowls on it. SL, 21 May 1986 (86 illus); WL.

249 | *The tea time letter* | o/c 20 x 17; signed bl, dated 1914 (or perhaps 1904). At a kitchen table set with tea-time items sit a woman at right and a girl at left. The woman wears a pink blouse and white apron and pours tea into a cup; the girl holds a letter in her right hand. Behind is a dresser with several pieces of china; at left is the glow of a fire; at right is an empty wooden arm chair like the one the woman sits in.

250 | *Thatching the rick* | o/c 18 x 16; signed bl, dated 14. A man with a trilby stands on a ladder facing right, adjusting a yellow hay rick. SL, 10 Mar 1993 (12 illus, bought from the Morrab Studio, Penzance, 1918); DL, 2 June 1994 (299 illus); CL, 23 Mar 1995 (21 illus); WL.

251 | *The drinking pool* | o/c 20 x 18; inscr on the stretcher; signed bl in red, dated 14. In the foreground a young man in a hat, waistcoat and white shirt sits on a dark brown horse facing right, away from the viewer; the horse drinks from a stream; at left is a bank with foliage; at right are fields, trees and a haystack. PL, 14 June 1988 (12 illus); DL, 6 Oct 1994 (273 illus); DL, 27 July 2017 (466 illus).

252 | *The flowered counterpane* | *The Cornishman* of 26 March 1914 said "the figures are strongly drawn and the light filters through the fabric on the line with telling effect. The figures are attractive, the counterpane becomes a thing of beauty and the sunlight makes it a delightful composition". PEAG, 1914.

253 | *The ford* | o/c 15 x 18; signed bl, dated 14; indis inscr on the stretcher. In a stream, a girl in a white blouse sits on a donkey standing facing right; at right a young man with a cap pulls on the harness in an attempt to get the donkey moving. SWS, 23 Feb 1984 (1744); RGG, 1984 (22 illus); SL, 19 November 2008 (31 illus); Barnes Thomas, Truro, 17 Dec 2008 (23 illus); Nicholsons, Haslemere, 16 Dec 2010 (1653 illus, as *The obstinate donkey*); Sheppards, Durrow, Eire, 1 Dec 2016 (1535 illus, as *Taking the donkey through the water*); WL.

254 | *The ford* | oil on copper 5 x 6½; signed br, dated 1914. As the o/c version of *The ford* (1914). East Bristol Auctions, 20 Aug 2021 (555).

255 | *The shire horse* | o/c 20 x 24; signed bl, in black, dated 1914. A large red-brown horse facing left in a rural landscape, bearing a man facing the viewer, wearing a hat, resting his left hand on the horse's haunch. CL, 21 Apr 1961 (60); CSK, 3 June 1999 (37 illus); DMG, autumn 1999 (11 illus, as *Doing his rounds*).

256 | *Two boys fishing* | o/c 18 x 16; signed bl, dated 14. Two young boys sitting on rocks, the left boy in a green jersey, the right boy a white shirt. SL, 10 Mar 1993 (13 illus, bought from the Morrab Studio, Penzance).

257 | *The young fishermen* | o/c; signed, dated 1914. In a dinghy a boy in dark clothes leans over a basket of silver fish; behind him a boy stands with a line in his hands; the blue sea is painted with large strokes.

258 | ***Dozmary Pool*** | o/c 11½ x 14; signed br in black, dated 1914. A moorland scene with the blue Pool in the middle distance and houses on the further shore; at right a boat sails on the water; the cloudy sky occupies half the canvas. PH, 2001 (42).

259 | ***Street scene*** | *The Cornishman* of 26 March 1914 recorded "… a vendor of coloured paper-windmills, with a cluster of children – mostly clad in white pinafores – eagerly bartering glass jars for these frail but gaudy 'buzzabouts' which the pedlar, with the aid of a pin, makes a thing of beauty and a joy for a day. Even the older girl with the long pigtail and earthenware pitcher, stops to view the multi-coloured pile of windmill heads … in the background we see the sun striking the cottages on the steep hill and the clothes-line with its freight of sheets from the wash."; noticed by *The Cornishman* of 23 March 1916. PEAG, 1914; Opie Memorial, 1916.

260 | ***A Cornwall farmhouse*** | o/c 12 x 14; signed bl, dated 1915. A large farmhouse stands amid grass; in front are trees and a low stone wall beside a country lane, with a person walking at left; the large sky is blue. SL, 17 Dec 2015 (69 illus).

261 | ***The hillside farm*** | o/c 20 x 18; signed br in red, dated 1915. In the foreground is a stream and beyond is a bank with lean trees and green meadows; on the crest are several stone buildings; it is winter and nests are visible in the tree tops; the sky is pale grey. SWS, 9 June 1982 (1226 illus, as *A Cornish view across a river*); CL, 12 Nov 1982 (40 ni); CL, 5 Nov 1999 (192 illus).

262 | ***Newlyn harbour*** | o/c 14 x 12; signed bl, dated 15. A pier projects diagonally from the left and several small fishing boats are moored alongside; behind them are two larger sailing ships; at br a dinghy is beached. The scene is sunlit and tonality is bright.

263 | ***In the garden*** | o/c 20 x 18; signed bl, dated 15. A sunlit garden with the house behind; on a path at left a young girl pushes a toy pram containing a doll; in a lawn are two shrubs with bright red flowers. RA, 1916 (919). Mentioned in *The Times* of 30 April 1916 as among "several other pleasant examples of modest merit". SWS, 28 July 1983 (2802, as *Camellias*); SL, 2 Nov 1983 (7 illus, as *Bodinar*); B&W, 31 Oct 1984 (296, as *Girl with toy pram*); CL, 12 June 1986 (89 illus, as *In a summer garden*); CL, 9 Nov 1989 (18 illus, as *In a summer's garden*); WHL, 27 July 2000 (50 illus, as 20 x 18, as *Taking dolly for a walk*); PH, 2001 (78, as *Taking dolly for a walk*).

264 | ***Picking chrysanthemums*** | o/c 21 x 18½; signed bl in red, dated 15. A young girl with plaited hair stands centre facing half-left, in a white smock over a pale blue dress, holding over her left arm a large basket containing white, red and yellow chrysanthemums; her right hand is stretched out to a tall white bloom; she is surrounded by flowers and there is no other background. BL, 25 June 2014 (129 illus); RGG.

265 | ***The artist's model, Newlyn*** | o/c 12 x 14; signed bl, dated 15. Half length of a young woman standing at right facing the viewer, wearing a white striped open-neck dress, her right arm outstretched left; at far right is a pot of flowers on a window sill; the background is plain green. Perhaps LG, 1918 (18, as *The model*); Fox/Greenacre, p.129 (illus no.71); PH, 2001

(67); WL. National Museums & Galleries of Wales, Cardiff (A2078), presented on 18 March 1920 by Miss Howell and Mrs Edwards in memory of Miss Fanny Logan Williams.

266 | ***April*** | described by the *Western Daily Press* of 25 Nov 1915 as "children amidst a gay landscape eloquent of truth and nature", and by another review as "rain in the distant fields". F&R, 1915.

267 | ***A shower*** | described by the *Western Daily Press* of 25 Nov 1915 "children endeavouring to shelter themselves from the rain". F&R, 1915.

268 | ***Cutting broccoli*** | described by the *Western Daily Press* of 25 Nov 1915 as "especially strong, the rural scene presented with a fidelity which evinces that it powerfully appealed to the limner"; another mentioned its "unmistakable open-air atmosphere". F&R, 1915.

269 | ***Over the hills*** | the *Western Daily Press* of 25 Nov 1915 said "the heights represented are given with vigorous fidelity"; an unknown review mentioned its "unmistakable open-air atmosphere". F&R, 1915.

270 | ***Summer*** | described by the *Western Daily Press* of 25 Nov 1915 as "robust and of interest by reason of (its) strong resemblance to nature". F&R, 1915.

271 | ***The sun bath*** | described by the *Western Daily Press* of 25 Nov 1915 as "robust and of interest by reason of (its) strong resemblance to nature". F&R, 1915.

272 | ***The poplars, Monmouth*** | the *Western Daily Press* of 25 Nov 1915 mentioned its "trees standing out darkly". F&R, 1915.

273 | ***The reader*** | described in the *Western Daily Press* of 25 Nov 1915 as "a female form surrounded by a scheme of light colour in charming contrast." F&R, 1915.

274 | ***On the pier, Newlyn*** | o/c 7½ x 8½; signed bl, dated 15. A man lies sprawled out on the pier ledge, his right foot resting on the pavement; at right a man sits on the ledge clasping his left knee; between them stands a lean dog; behind is the town. ISSPG, 20th exhibition 1916 (138); PH, 2001 (63).

275 | ***The bonfire*** | o/b 6¼ x 7½; signed bl, dated 15. Sketch of four children on a coastal meadow; the far left girl is seated facing right wearing red dress and white hat; next to her stands an older girl facing us holding a tin pot in her right hand and with left hand raised to her long blonde hair; next is a seated boy in brown waistcoat over a white shirt, tending the small fire; at right a boy lies facing the fire, with brown cap and white shirt; beyond is a rocky coast. This may be a sketch for *On the beach at Newlyn* (1917). SL, 10 March 2005 (270 illus).

276 | ***Gathering seaweed*** | o/c 14 x 12; signed bl, dated 15 over 16. On the beach between Newlyn and Penzance, two horses pull a cart laden high with seaweed, accompanied by a man; at far right another man sits waiting for them; in the middle distance the Larrigan Rocks break through the blue choppy sea, and beyond lie Penzance and St Michael's Mount; the sky is bluish with cloud. Bought at a Red Cross sale in WWI.

277 | ***Children feeding a goat in a pen, landscape beyond*** | o/c 14 x 19; signed bl, dated 15. A broken wooden fence runs diagonally across the picture. At right a white goat facing left is being fed foliage by a girl in a dark blue dress standing on the fence; at left a young boy in a brown jacket and black beret leans over

the fence, looking at us; beyond the fence is a green meadow; there is no sky. On the verso is a sketch of a cottage garden. Bearnes, Hampton & Littlewood, Exeter, 24 Jan 2017 (FS33/428 illus).

278 | ***Fishermen playing checkers*** | o/c 15 x 17; signed bl, in black, dated 15. Two fishermen in work clothes sit on a wall looking down at a draughts board between them; behind is the blue harbour with a red-sailed boat and two dinghies; beyond is a long jetty and on the horizon is St Mary's church in Penzance. Messum's, Dec 2018.

279 | ***Portrait of the artist's wife*** | o/c; signed bl, dated 16. Gertrude is seated in a deckchair facing the viewer, head resting on a striped blue and white cushion; she wears a black hat and blue jacket, and holds a red book; at right are yellow flowers, and beyond is an undulating landscape.

280 | ***Gertrude Harvey with parrot in the artist's home*** | o/c 17 x 17; signed bl in red, dated 16. At centre, Gertrude stands facing the viewer in a simple blue-green dress with round neck, her right hand raised to a red and grey parrot in a wire cage at left; she holds a glass bowl in her left hand; at lower left is a dark red table cloth bearing a patterned bowl. Cross, p.190 (illus); DL, 5 Oct 1989 (229 illus, as *Woman with parrot in interior*); Sven Berlin, *Artists from Cornwall* (Royal West of England Academy, Bristol, 1992), (88 illus); *Artists of Newlyn 1880–1930* (White Lane Gallery, Plymouth, 1993) (27 illus); *Art & Antiques*, 16 Oct 1993, p.13 (illus); CL, 21 Mar 1996 (34 illus, as 18 x 18); CL, 27 Mar 1997 (168); Portscatho Gallery; BL, 26 Sep 2018 (114 illus, as 18 x 18).

281 | ***Reflections*** | o/c 18 x 19½; signed bl, dated 1916. Gertrude in the bedroom of Maen Cottage, with a black hat and red dress, standing at right before a chest of drawers, facing left and holding up a face mirror; her left hand is on her hip. Fox/Greenacre, p.130 (illus no.74); PH, 2001 (66); WL. Cyfarthfa Castle Museum, Merthyr Tydfil (CCM.235.990), presented by W.H. Renwick, 1916.

282 | ***Anemones*** | o/c 12 x 16; signed bl, dated 1916. Gertrude in a flowered hat and pale patterned shawl over a full, dark skirt, sits centre facing left, at a small console table; her left hand holds a sprig of flowers; her right hand touches a small glass bowl on the table, which holds a larger bunch; two candlesticks are on the table and above it is an oval mirror. BL, 6 Nov 1980 (136).

283 | ***Lady in an interior arranging flowers*** o/c 20 x 16; signed br in yellow, dated 1916. A woman (Gertrude Harvey) stands at right facing left, in a blue-black hat with green band, a long green skirt or dress with a cream blouse or inset, and a cream patterned shawl; she wears a coral necklace; her left hand, with wedding ring, holds up a posy of anemones and her right hand arranges a bunch in a plain glass bowl, which stands on a small rounded console table; the wall behind her is pale yellow, with a small coloured Japanese print and at left the edge of a black picture frame. This may be *The green gown*, shown at the RA, in 1916. CL, 14 Dec 2016 (84 illus).

284 | ***Charles F Barham MD*** | o/c 48 x 38; signed bl, dated 1916. The figure sits facing half-left at a desk; he has a black coat and tie, white shirt and dark red waistcoat; behind him at tl is a sketched landscape painting; on the desk at bl, are books, water jar, ink bottles etc. Barham (1804-1884) was Hon secretary of the Royal Institution of Cornwall 1837–59 and President 1859-61. This painting was probably done from an etching. *PCF: C&SI*, p.191 (illus). Royal Cornwall Museum, Truro (1916.23), donated by Dr R. Pearce, 1916.

285 | *Portrait of Francis Elliot Voyle in evening dress* | o/c 24 x 18; signed bl, dated 1916. Half length view of a mature man seated facing us; he wears a black formal jacket over a cream waistcoat and dress shirt with bow tie, and gloves; he has a large moustache and long side whiskers; his left hand holds a walking cane, his right hand is in his lap; beside him at right is a small table bearing his top hat; behind him is a yellow wall with a fragment of picture at top right. This may be Francis Elliot Voyle (1815–1877) who served in the Bengal Staff Corps of the Indian Army, latterly as a Major-General. DL, 26 Jan 2017 (99 illus).

286 | *Laura and Paul Jewill Hill* | o/c 19 x 17; 1916. Two children stand by a console table under a circular mirror, the girl at left leaning on the table holding a goldfish bowl; the boy at right holding an Italian flag which celebrated Italy's joining the Allies in May 1915. They were the children of James and Laura Hill of Penzance. A self-portrait of Harvey is reflected in the mirror. Laura jnr was painted again by Harvey as *Laura Jewill Hill – the unwilling sitter* (1932). Stephen Paul Jewill Hill was painted again as *Portrait of Paul Jewill Hill as a boy* (1920). Fox/Greenacre, p.130 (illus no.72, as dated 1916); PH, 2001 (54); *PCF: C&SI*, p.113 (illus); WL. Penlee House Gallery & Museum (2004.30).

287 | *The green gown* | RA, 1916 (889); WAGL, 1916 (216, price £30); Opie Memorial 1916. *The Cornishman* of 23 March 1916 said it "… is in a way a portrait of a lady attired in an elaborate green gown".

288 | *St Hilary* | o/b; signed bl, dated 1916. Inset in a choir stall at St Hilary church. At right a bishop with two black-robed priests stands facing left, blessing a group of people kneeling at left; he is no doubt St Hilary, bishop of Poitiers; at centre, between two groups, is a tall crucifix, behind which a castle rises upon a rock.

289 | *The poachers* | o/c 24 x 30; signed bl in red, dated 16. Among trees on a hillside, two men crouch at left, facing away from the viewer; the left man has a peaked cap and shows his right profile; the right man has a cap and a red and white neck scarf, and a large satchel hung over his left shoulder rests upon his right hip; the barrel of a shotgun is visible beyond his right arm; in the right foreground are birds and a rabbit or hare. PL, 17 June 1986 (23); PL, 10 Mar 1987 (15).

290 | *The kite* | o/c 30 x 24¾; signed in red bl, dated 1916. On the reverse is a sketch of figures with a horse and haywain. Full length view of a young woman standing in foreground with a red cap and a vertically-striped skirt and plain blue shirt, shielding her eyes with her left hand, her right hand on hip; behind her are three figures, one a man holding a flying red kite; behind is a sunny landscape with a young tree at left. *The Times* 10 May 1917 said "'Kite' is really a landscape, although there is a strong emphasis on the figure of the girl; but she is painted as part of the landscape and very boldly

modelled in light"; mentioned in the *Daily Mail* 7 May 1917 as among several "canvases to which the Academy walls owe much of their brightness." RA, 1917 (272); WHL, 20 July 1974 (32 illus, as *The kite flyer*); WHL, 26 July 1978 (264 illus, as *The kite flyers*, dated 1911); PL, 14 Nov 1989 (32 illus, as *The kite flyer*); S. Billingshurst, 25 Oct 1994 (348 illus); WL.

291 | *Children among blossom* | o/c 20 x 18; signed br, dated 1916. At centre stands a girl in a bright red beret, pale blouse and blue skirt, her right hand reaching up to white blossom, her left hand down to a lower flower; at left stand two younger girls, the right one facing the viewer and with an olive green dress, her left hand on hip; the left girl faces right and has a pale dress, her right hand out to the blossom. On the reverse is another painting, *Cattle in a farmyard*. PL, 13 Nov 1984 (69 illus, prov QH); WL.

292 | *Children on the surf* | o/c 20½ x 18; signed bl, dated indis 1916 (?), title inscr on reverse. A girl with fair hair and white dress lies on rocks beside the sea; she holds a closed red-bound book in her outstretched right hand, and rests her head on her left hand; at left two girls sit close to the sea; one wears a red blouse, the other holds her hands to her hair; beyond, the waves foam on the rocks and in the distance is a steeply rising landscape. WP, 8 June 1920 (118, as *Children of the surf*).

293 | *Cattle in a farmyard* | o/c, on reverse of *Children among blossom*. In the centre foreground stands a brown and white cow, facing left; behind at left are a black and a dark brown cow facing right; thickly painted. PL, 13 Nov 1984 (69 illus, verso, prov QH); WL.

294 | *Summer milking* | o/c 24½ x 29½; signed bl, in black, dated 1916. In a meadow sloping upwards right, a man sits facing left, milking a brown and white cow facing right; at far left in the distance sits a girl in white clothes and a hat; the thin strip of sky is cloudy. Fox/Greenacre, p.83 (ni) and p.130 (illus no.73); PL, 13 Nov 1984 (66 illus, prov QH); CL, 16 Dec 2009 (77 illus); CL, 23 Nov 2017 (123 illus); WL.

295 | *Monmouth mill and river* | o/c 18 x 15; signed bl, dated 1916. The river occupies the foreground; at left is the bank with trees reaching the upper frame; in the distance are buildings with a red chimney. A brother of Harvey's (Percival George Harvey) lived at Monmouth. PH, 2001 (61).

296 | *Girl in a window* | o/c 29 x 20; initials br, dated indis 1916. Full length view of a girl at left sitting on a window sill wearing a long green dress, with bare feet; the right foot is in front of the left; behind her are large windows with many small panes, through which greenery and a house can be seen. The authenticity of the initials is uncertain, but the painting itself is well within the manner of Harvey. PH, 2001 (80).

297 | *Girl with a red hat* | o/p 10 x 14; signed br, dated 16. A girl lies facing left in a deck-chair, wearing a red cap and bluish-white dress, with crochet in her raised hands; her head rests on a large striped cushion; at far left are colourful garden flowers. Sothebys New York 4 Nov 2010 (70 illus); RGG, London 2012.

298 | *A Cornish boy* | o/b 16 x 12; signed, dated 1916, tr; title inscr on reverse. A young boy turned half-left looks at us, wearing a black beret and dark brown jacket over a green shirt; his mouth is slightly open; the background is

plain off-white. Bonhams New York 5 Nov 2014 (94).

299 | *A Cornish girl* | o/p 14 x 10; signed br in red, dated 1916. A head and shoulders portrait of a teenage girl in a dark blue dress, with blue eyes and two very thick light brown plaits which descend to the lower frame; her lips are red; the background is pale yellow-green. Perhaps WHL, 15 Mar 1984 (191 ni, as *Half portrait of a young girl with plaits*, 13½ x 9½); CL, 12 Nov 1987 (166 illus, wrongly dated 1926); Gorringes Lewes, 21 Mar 2017 (856 illus); WL.

300 | *In the garden* | *The Cornishman* of 23 March 1916 said "a brilliant bit of colouring, showing a little boy amidst summer flowers". Opie Memorial 1916.

301 | *Paper windmills* | oil. RA, 1916 (129).

302 | *The fishmarket* | oil. ISSPG, 20th exhibition 1916 (134a).

303 | *Daffodils* | o/c 20 x 16; signed br in red, dated 17. A boy faces the viewer, with a brown jacket and hat with a daffodil in the brim, carrying on his right arm a basket of daffodils; behind is a plain blue sea with rocks at the left edge. SC, 7 Oct 1983 (1370); RGG, 1984 (21 illus, prov the artist's family); CL, 13 Nov 1986 (50 illus); SL, 11 Nov 1987 (22 illus); CL, 28 Nov 1996 (78, prov the artist's family); WL.

304 | *The farm girl* | o/c 17¾ x 14½; signed bl, and signed with monogram; indis dated, *c*.1917. A young woman in a pale blouse, red scarf and blue skirt walks towards the viewer carrying a pail in her right hand; on the left are farm buildings and three white chickens. PL, 17 June 1986 (26 illus, as *The milkmaid*; prov given by the artist to the owner's parents as a wedding gift in 1917); SL, 12 Nov 1986 (43 illus); WL.

305 | *The blackberry girl* | o/c 20 x 17; signed br in red, dated 1917. In the left foreground a girl stands on a path with hands on hips, a filled basket over her right arm; she wears a hat and dark clothes; at right the path leads past a mine building; beyond is the coast. DL, 28 Aug 1986 (532 illus); DMG, spring 2001 (36 illus, as *Picking blackberries*); WL.

306 | *On the beach at Newlyn* | o/c 24 x 30; signed br in red, dated 17. In the foreground at bl, sits a girl in a bright red dress and cream hat, her right arm visible; right of her stands a girl with a red cap pushed back on her head, her left hand raised to her head and her right hand carrying a metal pot; right of her sits a boy in a grey waistcoat over a white shirt tending a small fire; further right a boy lies resting on his left elbow, with a cap and white shirt, looking at the fire; in the distance is Penzance. The children are probably boiling winkles on Tolcarne beach. See also *The bonfire* (1915). PL, 12 Nov 1985 (98 illus).

307 | *Audir Lane, Paul Hill, Newlyn* | o/c 20 x 16; signed br, dated 1917; indis inscr on the stretcher. The picture is dominated by three tall trees in leaf seen against a blue sky; at bl, is a man in a hat and dark jersey, his lower legs obscured by the frame, walking towards the viewer carrying something in his left hand; a stone sunlit wall runs alongside the trees. Granite faces were sometimes added to hedgerows to stop earth falling onto the path. The title is a misnomer for Adit Lane in Newlyn. PL, 8 Mar 1988 (6 illus); PL, 9 May 1989 (10); SL, 22 June 1994 (14b illus, as *On the way to harvest*, dated 1917); CL, 20 June 1995 (280 illus, as *On the way to harvest*, dated 1919); WL.

308 | ***By the sea*** | o/c 16 x 20; signed br, dated 1917. On a grassy path overlooking the sea, three female figures walk left; the left one (the eldest) has a greyhound(?) on a lead; she is followed by two younger girls, the centre one in a large white hat and with a red bow in her plaited hair; the right girl wears a blue dress; all three have white shoes; they appear well-to-do people. LG, 1918 (11); *Colour*, Oct 1918, p.51 (illus); C. Glasgow, 12 Nov 1987 (568 illus); Benezit records 'Pres de la Mer' sold for £25-4s in Feb 1925.

309 | ***Mother and child*** | o/c 19½ x 16; signed bl, dated 1917. At left is a woman in a pink and green striped shawl over a white dress, facing right, holding a baby in a white shawl; her left hand supports the baby and has a ring with a stone; she looks at the baby and almost fills the height of the picture; behind is a calm blue sea. SC, 15 Jan 1987 (3263 illus); PL, 15 Nov 1988 (50 illus).

310 | ***Mother and son*** | o/c 27¾ x 27¾; signed br, dated 1917. On a cliff overlooking a cove or flooded quarry, a woman stands at left with a dark beret, red jacket and white dress; her left hand touches her hair and her right hand holds a basket of dark fruit (blackberries?); at right sits a boy with dark hair and blue clothes; in the distance Mount's Bay; a cloudy sky fills more than half the picture. LG, 1918 (15); *Colour*, Jan 1919, p.147 (illus); *PCF: Tyne & Wear Museums*, p.255 (illus, as *Blackberrying*). South Shields Museum & Art Gallery (TWCMS G4271), as *Blackberrying*.

311 | ***Woman in an interior sewing*** | o/c 20 x 18; signed bl, dated 17. In the front room of Maen Cottage Gertrude sits in an armchair facing left, in a long pale dress and a long necklace; she holds her sewing up with both hands; at right is a console table, on which is a bowl of flowers; at far right is an open door. Pyms Gallery, London, autumn 1981 (12 illus).

312 | ***Portrait of Gertrude reading*** | o/c 16 x 14; signed br, dated 1917. Gertrude sits in a white armchair facing half-left, holding up a book in her right hand, wearing a pale blue dress and a red necklace; at left is a cupboard with ceramics on the shelf, and part of the fire fender; at right is part of a rounded console table; the carpet is plain light brown. Woolley & Wallis, Salisbury, 24 Mar 2010 (379 illus).

313 | ***Woman by the sideboard*** | o/c 21 x 17½; signed bl in red, dated 17. Gertrude in an ankle-length deep blue dress, with a red (coral?) necklace and a cream shawl with red flowers, stands facing left beside a small sideboard, her right hand touching green and purple grapes on a stand; on the sideboard are two candelabras each with three holders. DL, 25 Feb 1988 (350 illus); SL, 9 Nov 1988 (35 illus); SL, 11 Dec 2007 (72 illus, as *Woman by the sideboard, portrait of the artist's wife Gertrude*); SL, 15 July 2008 (100 illus, as previous title); WL.

314 | ***Two girls on a settee*** | o/c 20 x 24; signed bl in red, dated 17. The settee occupies most of the canvas and extends beyond the right edge; its back of black wood is carved in geometric patterns, and its seat cushion is floral patterned; at left a girl in black clothes sits against a red and blue cushion, reading a large book held in both hands; at right another girl in creamy-pink clothes sits frontally looking at the viewer, her hands clasped in her lap. PL, 10 Mar 1987 (23 illus); DL, 14 June 2001 (454 illus cover, as *Sunday afternoon*).

315 | ***The blue gown*** | o/c 20 x 16; signed bl, dated 17. Gertrude stands facing left, before a cream chest of drawers, in a black hat and flowered shawl over a blue dress; she puts a glove onto her right hand. RA, 1917 (683); Pyms Gallery, autumn 1983 (22 illus, as *Woman in a blue gown*); Cross, p.169 (illus); McConkey, p.226 (illus); Fox/Greenacre, p.39 (illus) and p.130 (illus no.75); WL.

316 | ***Betty, shut the door*** | o/c 24 x 18; signed bl in red, dated 1917. A full length frontal standing view of a girl about 12 in dark blue clothes and stockings, with a long necklace (amber?) and long red-tinted hair over her left shoulder; on her right shoulder appears a coloured collar or fabric; her right hand is extended against a white door with brass knob; beneath her the floorboards shine; a rather stark image; she has a slightly apprehensive look; the girl may be the left girl in *Two girls on a settee*. SL, 13 Dec 2005 (72 illus).

317 | ***Summer*** | o/c 36 x 30; signed bl, in black, dated 17. Gertrude stands facing right in a long white dress and a green hat with a black ribbon, holding flowers in her right hand; she is viewed from a roughly paved path against a distant landscape of fields; the site may be the same garden as in *In the garden – summer*. *The Times* of 7 May 1918 said of it "the garden flowers are painted with real zest, though he fails over the bloom of the elder". RA, 1918 (106); perhaps Grosvenor Galleries 1921 (51, price £42); perhaps Grosvenor Galleries, winter 1922 (34); perhaps Venice 1924 (29, as *Estate*); perhaps LG, 1927 (19); perhaps NEAC, 1927 (197); SL, 10 June 1998 (94); CSK, 12 Mar 2014 (81 illus); BAL, 50735.

318 | ***Summer hoeing*** | o/c 40 x 30; signed bl, dated indis 17. Set among fields below a large blue sky; at right a woman in a red and black neck scarf, dark hat and cream skirt, stands looking down at a young girl who reaches up to her hands; in the front foreground is a basket of potatoes(?); in the middle distance at left is a man hoeing; at centre a man bends down to the plants, and at right is another figure. PL, 13 Nov 1984 (65 illus, prov QH); WL.

319 | ***Summer hours*** | o/c 14 x 22; signed. Two girls on a stone wall, the one at left sitting in a white hat and blue dress with a red scarf(?), facing right; the other girl at centre is lying down holding a white parasol, facing the viewer, and has a red hat; above the wall is blue sky. RA, 1917 (572); BAL, 65339; BL, 1 Dec 1993 (28).

320 | ***The maiden*** | oil. ISSPG, 22nd exhibition 1917 (33).

321 | ***In the garden – summer*** | o/c 16 x 20½; signed bl, dated 1918. Gertrude lies in a deck chair on a stone terrace, her head at left, facing the viewer; she wears a white dress, stockings and shoes; her right hand holds up a parasol; her head rests on a dark blue cushion; beyond are garden flowers, then fields and Castle-an-Dinas hill; at right a road leads towards a village; the upper frame intersects two pieces of foliage. LG, 1918 (30, as *The garden*); *Colour*, Nov 1918, p.73 (illus, as *The deck chair*); PL, 7 June 1994 (153 illus).

322 | ***In the kitchen*** | o/c 25½ x 22; signed br in red, dated 1918 but altered by the artist from 1917. A young woman seated at left facing right, in a dark blue coat and multi-coloured scarf, holds a hat in her right hand; her left hand rests on a fur in her lap; at right stands Gertrude with a yellow headscarf, pink cardigan with black edging, cream blouse and pale skirt with a large check pattern, resting her right hand on the ledge of a dresser set with colourful china, her left hand on hip; behind her is a wall of green panelling with glazing above; at far left is a large fireplace, with boxes on the mantel-shelf. Set in Maen Cottage. On the reverse is another painting, *The midday rest*. An LG label is affixed to the reverse of the frame. *Colour*, Oct 1918, p.55 (illus); LG, 1918 (9); PL, 6 Nov 1990 (69 illus); PL, 4 June 1991 (16 illus); PL, 25 Nov 1997 (11 illus); WL.

323 | ***Lunch*** | signed bl in red, dated 1918. In the foreground is a dining table; at left a seated young woman in a yellow hat and striped multi-coloured jacket (perhaps a Crysede fabric), holds a wineglass which is being filled with red wine by another woman standing centre, in a blue cardigan; a bowl of flowers and other items on the table; an Egyptian style textile is above the mantelpiece; at the right edge is a sideboard which also appears in *Woman by the sideboard*. LG, 1918 (19); *Morning Post*, 25 Oct 1918; BL, 7 Nov 1985 (100); BG, 1987 (13); BAL (BON50736).

324 | ***The reader*** | o/b 13 x 11; signed, dated 18. RA, 1918 (465); CL, 20 Dec 1990 (135, as *Reading by the fire*).

325 | ***Mother and child*** | o/c 24 x 24; signed br, dated 1918. A young woman in a white dress stands at left, facing right, her head turned towards us; she holds a child in her arms and looks at him, her lips open; the child has red clothes and gazes at something we cannot see; at tr is foliage. Done in a simplified style. The sitters have been identified as Nannie Pearce Tregenza and her son Joseph (b.1917), who lived next door to the Harveys from 1915 to c.1920. NMAG, 2001 (95); *The Western Mail*, 24 Aug 2002 (illus). National Museums and Galleries of Wales, Cardiff (A2092), given by Miss Lilian Howell of 251 Newport Road, Cardiff on 7 March 1919.

326 | ***Early spring*** | o/c 30 x 26; signed bl, dated 18. A young woman in a black blouse and hat and blue skirt holds a baby in a red shawl, standing in a green meadow with white flowers, facing the viewer; behind are leafless trees and a hill with hedged fields. The model looks similar to that in *In the kitchen* (1918) who has a similar hat. *Morning Post* of 25 Oct 1918 wrote "The beautiful landscape is blithely visualised and finely painted, and the women [*sic*] and child are pre-Raphaelite in elabor-ation. But there is no pictorial affinity between the figures and their setting. The landscape is harmonised by sun-warmed air, whereas the figures smack of studio artifice". LG, 1918 (12); SL, 11 May 1998 (18 illus); Sotheby's New York, 23 Oct 2007 (177 illus); WL.

327 | ***Gathering pussywillow*** | o/c 27 x 27; signed bl, dated 1918. At left foreground a young woman stands with a patterned smock and dark hat, left hand on hip; the right hand holds a bunch of pussywillow across her waist; behind rise hillsides with trees. Grant M. Waters, *A Dictionary of British Artists Working 1900–1950* (Eastbourne Fine Art, 1975), pl.194 (illus). LG, 1918 (20); SL, 2 Aug 1972 (311 ni); SL, 11 Apr 1973 (102 ni, as *The maiden*).

328 | ***Boy by the harbour*** | o/c 20 x 18; signed bl, dated 18. A close-up three-quarter length view of a teenage boy with red lips, in dark hat and clothes, with a brightly patterned neckscarf; he leans against a railing, looking to our right; beyond lies the Mousehole harbour wall and at left are two boats; the sea is very pale blue. CL, 21 Nov 1995 (95 illus); BL, 31 March 2021 (78 illus, as *Boy at the harbour, Mousehole*); BL, 30 March 2022 (105 illus, as *Boy at the harbour, Mousehole*); WL.

329 | *Young girl in a blue blouse* | o/c 13½ x 11½; signed br, dated 1918. A girl about 12 years old, shown to chest level, faces us; her long black hair is parted centrally and tied with a green bow on her right shoulder; she wears a mid-blue blouse with a curved neckline in dark blue; behind her is a calm, pale blue sea and above that a narrow band of whiter blue sky. The sitter has been identified as Mornie Birch by her son.

330 | *One summers day* | o/b 30 x 24; signed br in black, dated 18. At left a fair haired boy sits on a stone wall facing us, in blue jersey, brown shorts and bare feet; at right an older dark haired girl sits looking at us with her legs over the other side of the wall and her left hand resting on it, wearing a bright red and gold multi-coloured shawl over a purple dress with a glimpse of white chemise at her left thigh; beside the boy is a tall thin tree with ivy up it; the sky is cloudless blue. SL, 4 June 2003 (7 illus).

331 | *The yellow scarf* | LG, 1918 (7).
332 | *A game of cards* | LG, 1918 (8).
333 | *A woman and her child* | LG, 1918 (10).
334 | *Foxgloves* | LG, 1918 (13). *Morning Post*, 25 Oct 1918 mentioned its "over-emphasis of the cymbal notes".
335 | *In the studio* | a woman (Gertrude?) stands at left, her body turned towards the wall but her face turned left, with a pale blouse, dark skirt and shoes; her left hand is on her hip; at right is a console table bearing several glass objects including a flagon, wine glass and a large glass ball; below the table is a large vase holding brushes, and in the foreground is a palette with brushes. LG, 1918 (14); *The Studio*, vol.76 (1919), p.62 (illus).
336 | *Elms in sunlight* | LG, 1918 (17).
337 | *Black Gardens, spring* | LG, 1918 (21). *Morning Post* of 25 Oct 1918 said "The least pretentious but most perfect and charming painting is 'Black Gardens'. Here, vision, feeling and craft combine happily and make a picture of abiding truth".
338 | *The interior* | LG, 1918 (22).
339 | *The fisher boy* | LG, 1918 (23).
340 | *Children seated on a wall* | LG, 1918 (24).
341 | *Children sitting on a wall* | o/c 32 x 25¾; signed br in black, dated 18. At left a bare foot young boy with yellow hair sits on a stone wall topped with turf; he wears a blue jersey and greenish shorts; at right an older girl sits with her legs the far side of the wall, wearing a purple dress with a red and gold patterned shawl; both children look at us; behind the boy is a pollarded tree with foliage up its trunk; the sky is plain blue. CL, 15 Nov 2007 (45 illus); CSK, 20 June 2013 (125 illus). This is probably *Children seated on a wall*.
342 | *The blackberry gatherers* | perhaps referred to in the *Notebook* as 'Blackberry Pickers, 30 x 28'. LG, 1918 (25); WP, 8 June 1920 (102); perhaps Grosvenor Galleries, winter 1921 (39, price £52-10s).
343 | *On the cliff* | mentioned in the *Morning Post*, 25 Oct 1918. LG, 1918 (26).

344 | *Ash trees* | LG, 1918 (27).
345 | *The brocade skirt* | LG, 1918 (28).
346 | *A boy and girl* | LG, 1918 (29).
347 | *A cottage window* | a young woman stands facing left before a deep-cilled window, in a pale blouse and a white apron over a dark skirt; her left hand is on her left hip and her right hand reaches up to a small bird cage on the wall by the window; three paintings hang on the walls. This painting is very similar to *First Light* (1919). LG, 1918 (31); *The Studio*, vol.76, 1919, p.65 (illus).
348 | *The letter* | LG, 1918 (32).
349 | *The ribbon skirt* | Gertrude stands at centre, full length, looking at the viewer with head tilted slightly left, and leaning against a console table; she wears a dark hat, an embroidered black shawl and an ankle length dress made of many vertical strips of plain and flowered material; her left hand holds a single flower; her right hand rests on the table beside a small bunch of red flowers; the floor is polished wood; on the cream wall behind hangs at tl a framed picture. LG, 1918 (33); *The Studio*, vol.76, 1919, p.63 (illus); WL.
350 | *An interior* | o/c 24 x 20; signed br, dated 1919. A young woman wearing a black jacket over a grey dress with green trim, stands centre leaning against a dining table with a blue check cloth; her left foot rests on a footwarmer(?); the fruit bowl on the table is the same as in *Lunch* and *Woman by the sideboard*. On the reverse is a study of *Seaweed gatherers* (qv). LG, 1920 (32); *Colour*, Dec 1920, p.90 (illus); *Connoisseur*, June 1990, p.116 (illus); CL, 8 Mar 1990 (26 illus); BL, 22 Jan 2014 (104 illus); WL.
351 | *Coloured wools* | o/c 22 x 30; signed bl, in black, dated 1919; inscr on label on reverse of the frame. A young woman in a vertically striped skirt, blue blouse and black cardigan, sits centre beside a table with a round end on which is a basket overflowing with many balls of wool; a ball of red wool lies on the carpet, which has a blue-grey geometric pattern; behind is a wall with two pictures; the same carpet is in *An interior*. Done in a very clearly-defined style. In 1920, Frank Rutter wrote in the *Sunday Times*, "its clean bright colour is very welcome in an exhibition still too full of pictures in mournful drabs and dirty browns"; perhaps referred to in the *Daily News* of 3 May 1920 as *Red Wool*. The painting was caricatured in *Punch*, 12 May 1920, p.377, making a joke about a kitten. RA, 1920 (54); SWS, 20 Oct 1982 (1195 illus).
352 | *Mother and child* | o/c 9¾ x 7; signed bl, dated 1919. A young woman in a white blouse, her hair in a pigtail with a red bow, stands leaning left over a child in a wooden armchair with white hat, purple shirt and with a red blanket over its legs; the background is not clear. Perhaps Grosvenor Galleries, Exhibition of Modern Art 1922 (36, price £31-10s); perhaps Goupil Gallery, winter salon 1924 (124, price £52-10s); DMG, pub v (58 illus); PL, 7 May 1985 (14 ni, as *Mother and child by the sea*).
353 | *First light* | o/b 14 x 11; signed bl, in black, dated 1919. A three-quarter length view of a young woman with dark hair seen in profile and contre-jour standing facing left, wearing white clothes over a black skirt, her left hand on her hip; her right hand feeds foliage to a small bird in a cage at left at head height; behind her is a large window in a white

surround reaching the upper frame, with a net curtain at the bottom; beyond is pale blue calm sea and grey sky; at right is a vertical strip of papered wall and part of a painting; the overall effect is very pale. This painting is very similar to *A Cottage Window* (1918). SL, 28 Oct 2008 (231 illus).
354 | *Seaweed gatherers* | o/c 20 x 24. An unsigned and unfinished sketch on the reverse of *An Interior* (1919). In the foreground a laden cart drawn by a brown horse stands facing; at right is another with a man in a white shirt on top; behind at left is another with a white and a brown horse; at bl, seaweed lies on the beach; the sky is cloudy with pale blue streaks. BL, 22 Jan 2014 (104 ni).
355 | *Cornish farm* | o/c 16 x 12; signed bl, in purple, dated 1919. In the foreground a short path leads to a blue-green picket gate, with mainly leafless trees and farm buildings beyond; in the distance is a hill with trees on the crest, and the upper part of a large house is visible above the crest. The tonality is pale. CL, 23 June 1994 (3 illus); PL, 9 June 1998 (34 illus, as *The farm gate*); DL, 17 Feb 2000 (551 illus, as *The hillside farm*); CL, 24 Nov 2000 (4 illus, as *The farm in the valley*); WHL, 8 Feb 2001; PH, 2001 (59); WL.
356 | *Thatching the rick* | o/c 18 x 16; signed, dated 19; inscr verso. SWS, 24 Oct 1995 (268, ni). This may be the same work as that dated 1914, which has the same dimensions.
357 | *Wooded hillside near Newlyn* | o/c 21¾ x 26¾; signed, dated 1919. In the foreground many trees cover a hill rising centre, with a copse on the top; at bl, sit a woman in pale clothes and a man in dark clothes. SWS, 21 July 1987 (2956); Somerville Ltd London 1988 (11 illus, as *Pauls Hill, Newlyn*); WL.
358 | *Portrait of a girl* | o/c 20 x 16; signed tl, dated 1919. A head and shoulder study of a young woman with long brown hair, a green ribbon above her left ear, facing the viewer; she wears a red and blue patterned shawl over a dark blue blouse. *Colour*, Oct 1920, cover (illus); WL.
359 | *Girl with loose hair* | o/c 12 x 12; signed bl in red, dated illegible. Head of a young woman turned left but facing us, in a red blouse with black trim. The sitter is the same as in *Portrait of a girl* (1919).
360 | *The fisherman's courtship* | o/c 24 x 19; signed bl, dated 19. A couple lean against a rail alongside a harbour; the man at left has a cap, pale jersey and dark trousers, and holds nets in his hands; he looks right towards a young woman standing at right wearing a pale dress; in the foreground are two lobster pots, and the man rests his right foot on the crown of one. WL.
361 | *The gate, spring* | o/c 29½ x 24½; signed br in red, dated 19; signed and inscr verso. In the foreground is a five-bar gate; at left a boy in a green jersey sits on the gate playing a tin whistle; at right a boy in a striped shirt sits on the ground playing a whistle; further right a girl in a brown plaid dress half-sits on a stone holding a posy of white flowers; beyond are fields; at left, swifts are flying; the right edge is occupied mostly by the field wall. Perhaps LG, 1920 (29, as *The gate*); DL, 5 Sep 1985 (384 illus); NMAG, 2001 (56); MacConnal-Mason, March 2022.
362 | *The road (figures walking before a landscape)* | o/c 30 x 30; signed bl, in dark

brown, dated 1919. In the foreground a boy in working clothes with a sack over his shoulder followed by a girl and two women carrying pails, and a lean dog, walk left along a road; the girl wears a blue shirt, one woman a red headscarf, the other woman a mauve shirt; beyond is a simplified, extensive, landscape of rolling hills and clumps of trees done in cool, muted colours; at right is a gabled house; the sky is dull yellow-grey. The dog closely resembles that in *By the Sea* (1917). This work is probably *The Road* which was shown at LG, 1920 (20), qv. BL, 15 June 2004 (8 illus, as *The Road*).

363 | **On the sands** | o/c 16 x 15½; signed bl, in black, dated indis 19. On a pebbly beach two girls at right and two boys at left sit by a small fire; the right girl wears a red cap and blouse and looks at us; the central girl wears a white hat and dress; behind them at right are two girls in white smocks by the calm blue sea. BH, 1932; BL, 26 Sep 2018 (115 illus); WL.

364 | **Landscape** | o/c 19½ x 23½; signed br in red, dated 19. A view mostly of trees which fill half the canvas; at right centre is a glimpse of a large house with pink walls and tall grey slate roof which looks like Treriefe; the sky is clear blue. This may be the work exhibited at LG, 1920 (27) as *Tereiffe*.

365 | **Spring** | oil. ISSPG, 26th exhibition 1919 (94).

366 | **Portrait of Paul Jewill Hill as a boy** | o/c 12½ diam; signed, dated 1920. Stephen Paul Jewill Hill (1912-1985) also appears in *Laura and Paul Jewill Hill* (1916). DL, 12 Oct 2004 (455 illus).

367 | **Portrait of James Jewill Hill** | o/b 12½ diam; signed bl, dated 1920. Frontal head and shoulders of a small boy with dark brown hair cut neatly across his forehead, wearing a V-neck white jacket over a white vest; the background is plain dark red. James (1917–1940) was younger brother to Stephen and Laura Jewill Hill. Penlee House Gallery & Museum (2004.62).

368 | **Girl in a blue dress** | o/c 18 x 14; signed bl in red, dated 1920. Half-length view of a teenager in a blue dress with white spots and a white necklace; she sits with hands in her lap on a low wall with the bluish sea behind.

369 | **Leswidden pit** | o/cb 20 x 29½; signed bl in black, dated 1920. In the middle distance at left is a high slag-heap reaching a point, with equipment for carrying spoil up it; beside stretch extensive pits and heaps; in the foreground are telegraph poles, green scrub and men working; in the immediate foreground is a rail track; in the far distance are fields and a smoking chimney; beyond the land, at right, is sea with a lighthouse indicated by breaking waves. PL, 6 June 2000 (119 illus); WHL, 27 July 2000 (190 illus); PCF: C&SI, p.191 (illus, as *A china clay pit, Leswidden*); 'Amongst heroes', London, 2013; *Amongst heroes*, p.38 (illus). Royal Cornwall Museum, Truro (2000. 24).

370 | **Market day** | o/c 28 x 28; signed bl, dated 1920. In the foreground are horses and carts moving left into a street at the end of which is Penzance Market Hall; several figures stand and talk; at right are a woman and a girl; behind the carts is a shop whose sign says Newson(?). The work is crisply drawn and carefully painted.

371 | **Moored boats in Newlyn harbour** | o/c 29½ x 23½; signed br, dated 1920. Several boats are moored across the painting; at left is PZ49 in grey, and at centre is PZ37 in green; a large sailing ship is moored beyond; the town rises at right; the sky is grey and feature-less; the sea is blue and very calm. Perhaps LG, 1920 (22, as *Newlyn boats*); Bearne, Torquay, 29 June 1993 (761).

372 | **Lustre** | o/c 20 x 16; signed tl, dated 1920. A tall mirror above an ornate console table is set against a pale green wall; a glass chandelier stands on the table and is reflected in the mirror; also in the reflection is a woman (perhaps Gertrude) who stands resting her left hand on a chimney piece, above which hangs a painting in a deep frame; at the top of the reflection are dark pink flowers whose originals can just be seen at the tr edge of the painting. The *WMN* of 27 June 1922 gave a detailed description. LG, 1920 (24); Harris & Sons, Plymouth, June 1922; PL, 23 Apr 1985 (41 illus, as *The pier glass*, prov the owner's parents, from the artist).

373 | **At the dressing table** | o/c 16½ x 20; signed bl, dated 1920. Rear view of a woman (Gertrude) standing to the right of a dressing table by a window, adjusting her hair; the table bears a multi-coloured striped cover. Fox/Greenacre, p.130 (illus no.76); PH, 2001 (64); WL. Cyfarthfa Castle Museum, Merthyr Tydfil (CCM.23.991).

374 | **The tea table** | o/c 30 x 24; signed br, dated 1920. On a square table covered by a white cloth are several items of a teatime meal; at bl, sits a man, his back to the viewer, in blue jacket and brown trousers; opposite him sits an elderly woman clothed in black with a central parting to her hair; at right stands a middle-aged woman in a cream blouse and long dark blue skirt, cutting a large round of cheese; behind is a large kitchen range, and at right a dresser with plates, cups etc. CL, 5 Mar 1987 (46 illus); *PCF: C&SI*, p.191 (illus); WL. Royal Cornwall Museum, Truro (2001.12.2).

375 | **The excursion** | o/c 20 x 24; signed bl, dated indis 1920. A child with auburn hair, in a pale yellow jersey and blue socks, sits on a donkey moving right, led by a woman in a red hat with blue stripe and a dark overcoat; at left, following the donkey, is a girl with red hat, yellow jersey, blue skirt and dark stockings; at right is a small brown dog; in the distance are hills. *Colour*, Oct 1920, p.47 (illus); WL.

376 | **The new book** | o/c 20 x 19; signed, dated 1920. A woman in white blouse and blue skirt facing left holds a book open in both hands; she sits before a window with a deep seat; at tr is a picture on the wall; the overall tonality is very pale. RA, 1920 (1); BL, 14 June 2006 (80 illus).

377 | **The new book** | *The Cornishman* of 17 March 1920 said "Three ladies are in a drawing room, the elder seated at an occasional table evidently reading aloud to the others". PEAG, 1920.

378 | **A kitchen interior** | LG, 1920 (10).

379 | **September at Cape Cornwall** | LG, 1920 (11).

380 | **The cave** | LG, 1920 (12).

381 | **Evelyn** | LG, 1920 (13).

382 | **The sunlit room** | *The Connoisseur*, Nov 1920, mentioned its figure drawing; Benezit records 'Piece ensolleillee' sold for £11-11s in February 1927. LG, 1920 (14).

383 | **Planting potatoes** | *Colour*, Oct 1920, mentioned its "abstract rhythmic qualities"; Konody in the *Observer*, 3 Oct 1920, referred to its "Rare energy and concentration". LG, 1920 (15).

384 | **Mary** | LG, 1920 (16).

385 | **The inn yard** | LG 1920 (17).

386 | **Newlyn wagonettes** | LG, 1920 (18); *Sunday Times* wrote "an amusing example of Mr Harvey's genre painting and is analogous to some of Orpen's Irish pictures both in style and in the humour of the observation".

387 | **The potato harvest** | o/c 31 x 25½; signed bl, dated 1920. At left a woman stands facing us in white blouse and long dark skirt, resting her hands on a long rake (?); at right stands a man drinking from a cup held in both hands; between them is an earthen jug; beyond lies a wide expanse of deep blue sea, with a headland at right, and trees; the sky is pale blue. LG, 1920 (19). *PCF: West Yorkshire*, p.301 (illus) (as dated 1910). Kirklees Museums & Galleries (1983.733).

388 | **The road** | *Colour*, Oct 1920, mentioned its "beautiful realisation of distance". LG, 1920 (20);

389 | **China clay pit** | the *Notebook* refers to 'China Clay Pit St Just, 30 x 24'. LG, 1920 (21).

390 | **Newlyn boats** | *Connoisseur*, Nov 1920, referred to its "grey simplicity, unhampered by the intrusion of 'modern' figures, was restful in effect". LG, 1920 (22).

391 | **Newlyn** | LG, 1920 (23).

392 | **Cornish children** | o/c 14 x 18; signed bl in red, dated 1920. At left a teenage girl is seated facing right, her legs tucked beside her, wearing a blue hat, yellow and red scarf, grey and white checked jacket and blue skirt, with bare feet; her right hand rests on her right calf. At right a boy lies on his back looking at her, his right arm extended holding a daisy puff and his bare legs crossed; he wears a yellow jersey and grey shorts. The figures are on a grassy meadow with wild flowers. *Connoisseur*, Nov 1920, mentioned "its clever foreshortened passage". LG, 1920 (25); CL, 21 Nov 2003 (34 illus); CL, 8 June 2006 (289).

393 | **Mabel** | LG, 1920 (26).

394 | **Tereiffe** | a misprint for Trereife. *The Times*, 5 Feb 1932, wrote "good, sunny, landscape". LG, 1920 (27); BH, 1932.

395 | **A fisher boy** | LG, 1920 (28).

396 | **The gate** | see *The gate, spring* (1919). LG, 1920 (29).

397 | **Madonna** | Konody in the *Observer* on 3 Oct 1920 praised its "real self expression". LG, 1920 (30).

398 | **The kitchen** | LG, 1920 (31).

399 | **Blackberry gatherers** | o/c 21½ x 26¾; signed bl, dated 1921. At left a woman walks to the right, holding a baby over her left shoulder; she is preceded by a girl with a walking stick in her right hand; at right stands a young woman facing the viewer, legs astride, in dark hat and a dress with very large lapels; behind is the sea and the coast in the distance. Done in a very clear style. Grosvenor Galleries, 1921 (39); SL, 10 Mar 1982 (101 illus); WHL, 28 Sep 1989 (578 illus, as *Blackberry Pickers*); CL, 8 Mar 1990 (24a); WL.

400 | **Ploughing** | o/c 25 x 30; signed br, dated 1921. The foreground is a ploughed field; at right a man walks behind a white and a dark horse moving right; beyond are farm buildings; set in a large and detailed landscape. PL, 18 Sep 1990 (26 illus); DL, 10 Feb 1994 (313 illus); WL.

401 | *Portrait of a girl at Newlyn harbour* o/c 15½ x 13½; signed br, dated 21. Head and shoulder view of a young woman facing right, in a blue on white spotted dress and a red ribbon above each ear; behind her is a simplified view of Newlyn harbour with green dashes for the sea. SC, 20 Oct 1988 (3147 illus, as *Faraway fancies, Newlyn harbour*); DL, 8 Dec 1988 (397 illus, as *Portrait of a young woman in front of Newlyn harbour*); DMG, pub V (67 illus); Messum's (63 illus, as *Portrait of a girl at Newlyn harbour*).

402 | *Summer, girls on a beach* | o/c 18 x 22½; signed bl, dated 21. At left a girl in a white dress facing right sits on a square of white cloth with coloured edges on soft sand beside the blue sea, tending her long hair; at right a younger girl with short dark hair in a white dress stands with hands behind her back, facing left. RGG, RH2312.

403 | *Cottages in a landscape* | o/c 13 x 17; signed bl, dated 21. In the foreground is a row of cottages in pale tones; beyond at left are fields, and at right are trees. SL, 19 May 1982 (8 illus); PL, 28 June 1982 (9, as *Cottages near Dartmoor*); WL.

404 | *The boatyard* | o/p 11½ x 15; signed br, dated 1921. At left and centre are two boats with cream upper hulls raised up for repairs, and a man sits on a trestle, painting the underside of one; at right is a white shed with a red roof. PH, 2001 (81); WHL, 27 Sep 2007 (85 illus); Morphets, Harrogate 25 Nov 2010 (395 illus); Barnes Thomas, Penzance, 14 Feb 2011 (205 illus).

405 | *The balloon seller* | o/c 20 x 24; signed bl, in red, dated 21. At left stands a woman with a plumed black hat, orange shawl, purple blouse and white skirt, holding a large basket containing coloured feathers over her right arm, her left hand on hip; in the centre foreground a woman (perhaps Gertrude) is shown half length in a patterned headscarf and whitish blouse, blowing into a blue balloon, with several other balloons before her; at right stands a man with his back to the viewer, with a brown hat, holding a broom in his left hand, and with a red-bordered carpet over his right shoulder; behind at left is a green-blue gypsy caravan and at right a bright yellow one. The *Cornishman* of 23 March 1921 said "the vivid colouring is a feature". PEAG, 1921, as *Gypsies*; C. Glasgow, 17 Nov 1994 (839 illus).

406 | *Afternoon tea* | o/c 20 x 18; signed, dated 1921. Gertrude in a deckchair in a paved garden. WHL, 20 July 1974 (272 ni); DMG, autumn 1974 (26 ni).

407 | *An interior* | The *Cornishman* of 23 March 1921 said "A lady is standing in a room examining one of a number of coloured vases. The yellow jersey and colour scheme generally is admirably executed, while the light is perfect". This may be *The white room*. PEAG, 1921.

408 | *The white room* | the *WMN* of 3 May 1921 said "Plain cream walls, pepper and salt door, and a small mahogany table carrying some pieces of ornamental china are its attributes, and its more directly human interest is a pretty girl in a primrose jacket and red and grey check skirt, with a blue and red cap, who is engaged in dusting china". RA, 1921 (352). Harris & Sons, Plymouth, July 1923.

409 | *Gipsies* | oil. ISSPG, 27th exhibition, 1921 (76).

410 | *On the line* | oil; signed bl, dated 1922. In a kitchen, an older woman (Gertrude) stands at left on wooden steps to hang blue and white striped washing on a line; she wears an open yellow jacket with dark edges, a yellow headscarf, and pale blue skirt; at right a teenage girl stands facing left, with very long hair platted down her back, in a pale blouse and dark skirt, leaning against a table watching her; on the shelves behind is much coloured crockery. Konody in the *Observer* on 1 Oct 1922 wrote: "a domestic scene in a Cornish cottage interior, is another instance of pleasing subject interpreted in terms of pure art. He stands or falls by the strong emphasis of his pure colour notes set one against the other without intervening neutral passages of chiaroscuro, and yet sufficiently indicative of volume to escape the effect of poster-like flat decoration". *Drawing & Design*, 1923, commented: "In this picture Mr Harvey has managed to create an interesting and decorative piece of composition. A dexterous treatment of light effects and the clever poise of both figures have chiefly contributed to this result." Royal West of England Academy, Bristol, 1922 (price £84); Grosvenor Galleries, summer 1923 (125); *Drawing & Design*, Dec 1923, p.711 (illus); City Art Gallery, Manchester, 'Living British Artists', 1927 (no.128, price £50); RHA, 1928 (11); Brighton, autumn 1934. Brighton & Hove Museums (FA000333), bought in 1934 for £40.

411 | *Portrait of the artist's wife, Gertrude* o/c 29½ x 19½; signed br, dated 1922. Full length view of Gertrude wearing a multicoloured shawl, standing before a tall wardrobe with four levels of drawers; she stands on a pale carpet. The *Notebook* refers to 'Gert/Indian Shawl 30 x 20'. WHL, 27 June 1975 (45 ni); WHL, 5 Mar 1981 (235 illus, as *Gertrude in a Japanese Kimono standing before an 18th century linen press*); SL, 16 Sep 1981 (21 illus).

412 | *Clara* | o/c 24 x 18; signed br in brown, dated 22. A three-quarter length view of a young woman facing half-left standing leaning against a low stone wall, wearing a short sleeved blouse with vertical grey and dark brown stripes and a grey skirt; her left hand rests on the wall coping; her right hand holds a red rose with the flower turned down; her hair is parted but with a plait behind; beyond her is a brownish landscape with a slender blossoming tree at left and at right a mine head on the horizon; the sky is grey and cloudy; the down turned red flower may signify loss, and the white blossom hope, but in Cornish superstition red and white flowers are associated with death. This image is a larger version of another *Clara* from 1923. SL, 14 Sep 2006 (163 illus, unframed); CSK, 20 June 2013 (18 illus); CSK, 14 Nov 2013 (113 illus); SL, 15 July 2015 (69 illus); CSK, 1 Dec 2016 (52 illus).

413 | *Portrait of a girl in a checked blouse* | o/c 16 x 12; signed tr in red, dated 22. Bust length view of a teenage girl facing us, with cropped black hair and a blouse with round neck and a pattern of white and blue squares with red lines; the background is plain black; the hand-painted frame is said to be original. BL, 20 Feb 2019 (91 illus).

414 | *The critics* | o/c 23¾ x 29¾; signed bl, in red, dated 1922. Two women sit at a round table, the nearest holding a piece of paper; behind her a woman in a red jacket stands with her hands on the shoulders of the seated

woman; through the open door is the entrance hall of Maen Cottage. The figures are Ella Naper, standing, and Gertrude Harvey, seated. RA, 1922 (11); PAEE, 1938 (423); Fox/Greenacre, p.130-1 (illus no.77); Fox, p.77 (illus); PH, 2001 (65); *PCF: Birmingham*, p.112 (illus); WL. Birmingham City Museum & Art Gallery (1922P169), presented 1922 by Sir Barry Jackson, who owned and built the Birmingham Repertory Theatre which opened in 1913.

415 | *A windy day* | o/c 17 x 20½; signed bl, in black, dated 22. An expansive landscape of rounded green hills with some trees, leafless or brown; in the sunlit foreground at left two young women with red items of clothing walk leftwards bent against the wind; above the high horizon the sky is dark grey. Stockholm Auktionsverk 28 April 2014 (937 illus); CL, 23 Nov 2017 (125 illus).

416 | *Blackberries* | o/c 28½ x 36; signed, dated 22. At right Gertrude stands full length facing right in profile, her arms raised to pick fruit from a tall bush; she wears a red patterned headscarf, a dark blue blouse, an orange skirt with red horizontal stripes, and black shoes. At left stands a young woman facing right in profile, her head turned down towards a fruit held up in her right hand; her left arm carries a basket; she has a white blouse and a grey skirt; her plaited hair is tied with a red bow; behind are rolling fields, and a big cloudless blue sky. RA, 1927 (396). Atkinson Art Gallery, Southport (ref. 320), bought in 1928 for £42.

417 | *Lovers* | oil; signed bl, dated 1922. At right a man in a hat and suit with waistcoat or cardigan walks with a woman on his right who wears a beret, pale blouse and dark skirt; they move left towards a granite block stile in a turfed dry-stone wall; behind are farm buildings (or hayricks?). Grosvenor Galleries, winter 1922 (87); *Drawing & Design*, December 1923, p.713 (illus), which commented "Mr Harvey has here painted for us a simple but accurate conception of the peace and quiet of the sunset hours. So tranquil is the setting that we are almost startled by the intrusion of the two silhouetted figures"; British Empire Exhibition 1925 (Q.12) when an unidentified review described it as among works "that linger in the memory"; sold for £26-5s in December 1926 (Benezit); LG, 1927 (5); *Apollo*, 1927, said "as sentimental as any English painting of the eighties or nineties, but it combines a certain pre-Raphaelite acerbity with solid modelling and a subdued but engaging quality of tone"; WL.

418 | *A view of Mousehole* | o/c 16 x 24; signed bl in red, dated 22. A sunlit view of the harbour, with four dinghies in the foreground and a red one in the middle distance; the horizon is formed by a terrace of houses above the harbour wall; at far left is the Ship Inn. SL, 12 Nov 1986 (41 illus); PL, 6 Nov 1990 (60 illus, as *Mousehole harbour*); CL, 22 Nov 2006 (262 illus); SL, 11 Dec 2007 (77 illus); CL, 4 June 2009 (32, as *Mousehole harbour*, as 16 x 23); CL, 31 May 2012 (39, as *Mousehole harbour, Cornwall*); WL.

419 | *Man with a woman in a cart* | o/c 21¾ x 27; signed bl, dated 22. The setting is Mousehole. In the foreground stands a cart with two large wheels, in which sits a woman in a black hat with a white feather and a grey-black shawl; she looks at a bearded man standing between the viewer and the cart,

with a bowler hat and black waistcoat, a pipe
in his mouth; he holds something in his hands;
at left is a grey building with the sign 'Ship
Inn', and behind lie more houses and a jetty.
The man is probably a fish-seller. The *Notebook*
refers to 'The Donkey Cart (Barlow) 28 x 22'.
CL, 10 Nov 1988 (55 illus); DMG, autumn 2000
(21 illus, as *By the Ship Inn, Mousehole*); WL.

420 | *Chy-An-Mor* | o/c 18 x 24; signed bl
in red, dated 1922. Much of the picture is
of moorland; at top centre is a row of farm
buildings; at tr are a couple of green fields;
above is a thin stretch of pale blue sky. PL,
10 Nov 1987 (16 illus); PL, 14 June 1988 (17);
DMG, winter 2000 (10 illus, as *Near Zennor*);
CL, 22 Nov 2002 (38 illus, as *Near Zennor:
Chy-An-Mor*); WL.

421 | *St Paul* | o/b; signed br in black, dated
22. Set in a choir stall at St Hilary. On a sea
shore a tonsured monk kneels at left, hands
raised, facing right towards a cowled monk
who places a stone at the sea's edge; behind
them is a stylised shore landscape, and
St Michael's Mount is in the tr corner.

422 | *Marazion marshes* | oil. The *Observer*
of 18 June 1922 wrote "it has the merit of
serious formal interest together with colour".
Grosvenor Galleries, summer 1922 (50); Royal
West of England Academy, Bristol, 1924 (663).
The *Notebook* refers to 'Marazion Marshes
30 x 25'.

423 | *Marsh landscape* | o/c 30 x 36; signed bl,
dated 1922. The foreground is a large expanse
of watery marsh with yellowish reeds; at left
in the water is a line of wired posts and at
far left the grassy embankment of a road;
in the distance are three groups of white
cottages facing us, and more behind; beyond
is a rounded hill with fields and at far right a
copse of green trees; three ducks fly from right
to left across the middle of the picture; the
sky is cloudy pale blue. This work is similar to
Marazion marsh (1923). BL, 1 March 2017 (67).

424 | *The mackerel season, Newlyn* | oil. The
Cornishman of 22 March 1922 said "here is
a corner of the harbour cram full of fishing
boats with their various coloured funnels, the
men and the carts and everything that goes
to the making of the busy scene at Newlyn
on mornings when mackerel are landed"; also
noticed by the WMN of 18 March 1922. ISSPG,
28th exhibition, 1922 (194); Opie Gallery, 1922
(as *Newlyn mackerel season, Newlyn*).

425 | *A fisherman* | oil. CI, 1922 (257).

426 | *My kitchen* | o/c 39½ x 30½; signed br
in red, dated 23. A woman (Gertrude?) with a
black hat and black cardigan, sits at left holding a basket of fruit and vegetables on her lap;
another woman in a white dress stands centre,
her left hand resting on a kitchen table; the
floor is of black and white square tiles. RA,
1923 (364); WAGL, 1923 (67, price £157-10);
Fox/Greenacre, p.131 (illus no.78); BAL, 37298;
Hardie, opp. p.208 (illus); WL. Oldham Art
Gallery (OLDMS: 6.24), bought 1924 for £50.

427 | *An interior* | o/c 24 x 20; signed br, dated
1923. A woman sits in a rocking chair, wearing
a black cardigan and white skirt; her back is
to the viewer and she is talking to a woman at
right perched on an armchair, in a red jacket,
black hat and skirt, with a walking stick in
her hands; behind is a wooden cupboard with
china on it; a small dog is asleep before the
armchair. CL, 7 Mar 1997 (171).

428 | *Janie* | o/c; signed br, dated 1923.

A young woman turned to the left occupies
the whole height of the painting, facing the
viewer with hands on hips; she wears a V-neck
dress; behind her at right are rocks, with the
sea beyond and the coast in the distance. The
Notebook refers to 'Janie Kelynack 16 x 14'. An
unidentified reviewer wrote "a clean-drawn,
clean-coloured portrait inclining to the early
Italian style of Mr Brockhurst, but free from
black shadows on the flesh". The *Times* of
4 May 1925 said "Janie, rather scornful of
her Cornish landscape, does something more
(than satisfy expectations of an accomplished
painter) ... though here again ... the graduation
of colour is a bit too easy for the bold contours".
S.P.B. Mais in the *Daily Graphic* of 2 May 1925
said "Janie is a not unworthy companion to
The Model (by Dod Procter). Here we have a
brown eyed, buxom Cornish fisher girl, with
dark brown hair blown about her face by the
wind, dressed in a simple magenta dress,
standing with hands on hips, against a background of grey seas and blue mountains. The
look in her eyes is that of Eve, rudely healthy
in body, unwoken as yet in mind." RA, 1925
(4); RGI, 1925 (125); SWS, 9 June 1982 (1227 illus).

429 | *Clara* | o/c 13 x 13; signed bl, dated 1923.
Head and shoulders view of a pensive young
woman facing half-left, with straight dark
hair parted over her left eye, in a boldly
striped dress with sleeves and halter neck;
behind is an indistinct landscape with a mine
tower at bl; the sky is large and cloudy in dark
tones. A larger version of this image was done
in 1922, also titled *Clara*. The model was Clara
Matthews to whom the *Notebook* records a
later payment of £1-17-6d on 29 April 1928.
Drawing & Design, December 1923, p.710
(illus), commented "The background depicts
a grey and cloudy sky, and its cold colouring
does not attract the eye from the centre of
interest – the expression on the girl's face".
Goupil Gallery exhibition of Modern British
Art, summer 1924 (202, price £26-5s); PH,
2001 (55).

430 | *Mousehole harbour* | o/c 20 x 18; signed
br in red, dated 23. A view of the harbour with
town and hills beyond; in the left foreground a
man in a red jersey pushes a wheelbarrow along
the quay towards the right; two children sit on
the wall; at br the heads of two men sitting on
a bench are visible above the wall; several fishing boats are moored in the harbour in four
rows; the general tonality is dark. The *Notebook*
refers to 'Mousehole harbour, PEAG, 20 x 16'.
CL, 23 June 1994 (2 illus); WL.

431 | *The quay, Penzance harbour* | o/c 18 x 20;
signed bl, in black, dated 23. In the foreground
several dinghies are moored to a jetty, where
fishing nets hang to dry; beyond a steamer
with a black and red hull lies beside the quay;
in the distance is sea and land under a grey
cloudy sky; at far left is a yellow building
with a rounded roof; the scene is animated
by several figures such as a woman in a pink
dress and a horse and cart. Messum's, 2020.

432 | *The clay pit* | o/cb 22½ x 31¾; signed bl,
dated 23. In the foreground of a quarry two
men in a cream and a red shirt push a laden
rail wagon leftwards, helped by another man
at the front, far, side of the wagon; beyond are
cuttings and men working; the tonality is pale.
The scene is believed to be Leswidden china
clay works near St Just; the pit closed in the
early 1940s; some pencil underdrawing is

visible. There is a separate pencil sketch
showing the main figure moving right. PL,
7 June 1994 (11 illus); *NACF Review*, 1995 (4225
illus); PH, 2001 (95); *PCF: C&SI*, p.191 (illus);
'Amongst heroes', London, 2013; WL. Royal
Cornwall Museum, Truro (1995.29), acquired
2 June 1995.

433 | *A summer evening* | o/c 30 x 36; signed
br in red between parallel lines, dated 23; labels
on frame. A landscape with a man and woman
at bl, walking right; he has his arm round her
waist, and she wears a white dress; at centre
two tall trees reach the top edge, with a burst
of white sunlight shining through the foliage;
beyond are green fields and trees and hedges
seen contre-jour; the sky is green-blue; the
overall tones are green. New Chenil Galleries,
London, 1920s?; CSK, 9 June 2000 (135 illus);
CL, 11 Dec 2008 (3 illus, as *A summer night*).

434 | *Drift valley* | o/c 24 x 30; signed br,
dated 1923. A view across a wooded valley
towards the opposite hillside, with large
fields; on the left horizon are hills; on the
right horizon are farm buildings. CI, 1925 (155);
Apollo, 1927, p.213, referred to it in 'Living
British Artists', Leeds, March–April 1927
(100, price £40). Leeds City Art Gallery at
Lotherton Hall, bought 1927, ref. 751/1927; PH,
2001 (62). *Oil Paintings in Public Ownership:
West Yorkshire: Leeds* (The Public Foundation,
2004), p.97 (illus); WL.

435 | *Marazion marsh* | o/c 24 x 30; signed br
in red, dated 23 (the 2 is indis). The foreground
is green grass in a flat landscape; at right is
a road with telegraph poles; at centre left are
two groups of white farmhouses; at centre
right is a rounded hillside with fields bordered
by hedges; the cloudy sky occupies half the
canvas. PH, 2001 (49); *PCF: C&SI*, p.113 (illus); WL.
Penlee House Gallery & Museum (1989.68).

436 | *Time for idle gossip* | o/c 18 x 24; signed,
dated 1923. Four women stand in a line to
draw water from a red brick pump; beyond is
Mount's Bay; the far left woman is old, with
arms crossed, wears black clothes, and has a
large pitcher by her feet; the second left woman
wears a red blouse and dark blue skirt and has
both hands on hips; the third left woman wears
a yellow blouse and brown skirt and holds a
metal pail in her right hand, facing the second
woman; the far right woman wears a red headscarf, white blouse and black skirt, and stands
at the tap filling a large pitcher. The setting
appears to be above Bowjey in Newlyn.
The figures are like a frieze, and done in
a simplified style with blocks of colour. DL,
12 Dec 1985 (426 illus, as *A time for gossip*);
WHL, 27 Mar 1990 (500 illus); WHL, 28 Nov
1991 (160 illus); DL, 12 Feb 1998 (370 illus,
as *Village gossip*); *Laporte: A History in Art*
(Laporte, 2000), cover (illus, as *Village Gossip*).

437 | *Blackberries* | o/c 30 x 25; signed br in
red in a cartouche, dated 23. Six children are
shown; at centre a girl in a black dress faces us
with a full panier of berries over her left arm
and a pail handle in her right hand; behind
her a boy facing left reaches up to pick berries;
at left a small girl in a red and white dress
holds a full pail of berries; at far left is an
older girl in a blue dress and grey cap; at right
is a girl in red, and at far right a girl with two
plaits in a white spotted dress; in the distance
are rounded hills and a green meadow, and
at right a sapling. The central girl has been
identified as the later Mrs G. Luckwell, who

in 1923 was Greta Pollard and 10 years old, who married Ivor Luckwell in 1937; she is said to have modelled for other works by Harvey and for Stanhope Forbes and Dod Procter. Konody wrote (undated) "Among other pictures the Visitor to this year's academy should not miss". Mais said in the *Daily Graphic* on 3 May 1924 "(it) represents a group of children with baskets and tins picking blackberries". RGI, 1924 (454); RA, 1924 (629); RGG, 'Modern British Painters', 1986 (19 illus).

438 | *A billygoat* | o/c 18 x 24; signed br, dated 23. A close-up view of a feeding goat standing facing right; at left is a small tree. The paint is thickly applied. DL, 16 Apr 1982 (635 illus); DL, 9 July 1982 (917 ni).

439 | *St Fingar* | o/b; signed, dated 1924. Set in a choir stall at St Hilary. In a forest clearing, a well-dressed woman kneels at right beside a small pool; behind her a man holds the bridles of a black and a white horse; at left a dead stag lies on the ground, a dog standing beside it.

440 | *The road to market* | o/c 43 x 50; signed bl, in black, dated 24. A jig drawn by a brown horse moves right along a country road, accompanied by three figures, in a landscape of fields and hills. Konody wrote in the *Observer* of 4 May 1924 "'The Road to Market' is, in the order of hanging, the first example of a whole group of painters working in Cornwall, who have freed their palette from the greyness of the old Newlyn School, and revel in the brightness of pure, undefiled pigment used with a strong decorative sense of pattern, without transition of neutral tones. I am rather hazy of the origin of this new Cornish school, but think its run is largely due to the example of Mr Harold Knight. Mrs Dod Procter is the most intense member of the group." RA, 1924 (307); Royal West of England Academy, Bristol, 1925 (price £100); SL, 11 Mar 1992 (10, as *Going to market*); CL, 5 Mar 1999 (75 illus); PH, 2001 (60).

441 | *A country girl* | o/c 14 x 12; signed br, dated 24. A girl in a white shirt faces the viewer, her right hand supporting a bag carried over her right shoulder; beyond is a simplified landscape. SL, 25 May 1983 (55 illus); WL.

442 | *Coastal landscape with three girls on headland path* | o/c 14 x 16; signed, dated 1924. Morphets Harrogate 10 Apr 1986 (220).

443 | *Girl resting on a flower strewn bank* | o/c 14 x 12; signed bl, dated 1924. A young woman seated facing left, looking at the viewer; she wears a dark jacket over a short sleeved dress. DL, 12 Dec 1985 (400 illus); BG, 1986 (13, as *Girl in a meadow*); BAL, 37233 (as *A Gypsy girl*).

444 | *Midge Bruford* | o/c 11½ x 11½; signed br in red, dated 24. A young woman rests her elbows on a table with both hands raised to support her chin; she gazes directly at the viewer; she has fair hair parted centrally and wears a dark blue pullover with long sleeves, and on the right little finger is a ring with a large red stone; the background is plain, divided vertically into dark and pale areas.

445 | *Pelman patience* | o/c 20 x 24; signed br in red, dated 1924. A young woman in a dark patterned jacket and pale skirt sits by a round table on which are laid out a pack of cards with red backs upwards; at left a woman with a shawl, silver stockings and long necklace sits in a blue armchair watching; at right a man in a brown jacket and red muffler leans against a console table; at far left is a white fireplace. The *WMN* of 22 March 1924 recorded "… a dexterous interior scene of a girl dealing cards while a young man and a girl watch events". Newlyn Art Gallery, 1924.

446 | *The donkey meadow* | o/c 24 x 30; signed bl, dated 24. In a garden with wicker fences, three women bend to gather anemones; the nearest woman wears a bright red skirt; behind stands a girl with long plaits holding a large, full basket on her hip, looking at the viewer; beyond is another garden, and trees in the distance. The scene is Rough Lea Flower Farm at Stable Hobba in Newlyn Coombe, and the work was commissioned by the owners, Basil and Barbara Bond. PH, 2001 (77); WL.

447 | *Study of flowers in a garden* | o/c 18 x 16; signed, dated 1924. DMG, autumn 1974 (29 ni).

448 | *A tree at Trereife* | o/c 20 x 16; signed, dated 1924. PH, 2001 (53).

449 | *The flower gatherers* | o/c 36 x 25; signed bl, in white/yellow, dated 25. Two women and a man walking left bearing baskets of flowers on their heads; the middle woman wears a red skirt. Probably RA, 1925 (562, as *The flower farm*), of which Konody wrote in the *Observer* on 17 May 1925 "'The flower farm' has many bright colours, but they are not coordinated, and the result is rather crude". SL, 23 Nov 1994 (12 illus); WL.

450 | *In the garden* | o/c 17¼ x 17½; signed br, dated 25; inscr 'In the Garden' on the canvas overlap. The *Notebook* refers to 'Gert in Garden 16 x 16'. A woman sits in a garden, with a bright red skirt, blue-green short-sleeved top, and dark headscarf; her hands clasp her right knee. LG, 1927 (38); CL, 8 June 1989 (1 illus, as 1925); PH, 2001 (76, as *Portrait of Gertrude Harvey*, as 15½ x 17½, undated).

451 | *Girls outside the Gaiety cinema, Newlyn* | o/c 19¼ x 19¼; signed bl in red, dated 25. Head and shoulders view of two young women with cloche felt hats and heavy coats; the left figure looks at the viewer, the right figure applies her lipstick; behind is a building. The models have been identified as Helen Francis aged 24 (lt) and her friend Winifred. The cinema was located in The Coombe, Newlyn. Perhaps LG, 1927 (13, as *Matinee*); Fox/Greenacre, p.131 (illus no.79); PH, 1993 (64 ni, as *Gaiety girls*); PH, 2001 (68); WL.

452 | *Kate* | the *WMN* of 9 July 1925 said "a portrait of a young girl, fresh and virile in treatment". PEAG, 1925.

453 | *Ash trees at Drift, near Penzance, Cornwall* | o/c 20 x 24; signed bl, dated 25. In the foreground are drinking troughs, and a boy sitting on a stone wall; behind is a row of tall trees reaching the upper edge of the canvas. LG, 1927 (15, as *Ash trees, Drift*); WHL, 15 July 1988 (285 illus, as *Ash trees at Drift*); WHL, 1 Dec 1988 (415).

454 | *The flight* | o/c 30 x 25; signed bl in red, dated 25. The *Notebook* records 'The flight into Egypt 30 x 25'. A child in a white dress sits on a wall facing the viewer, his right hand raised in blessing; behind him his mother sits looking at him, leaning her left hand on the wall, wearing a blue short-sleeved dress; at right, the father in a white shirt feeds a donkey; at far left is an inn whose sign is a lamb; the sky is darkening, with stars visible. The *Daily Graphic* of 1 May 1926 wrote "The two outstanding pictures from the point of view of sheer power are 'The back bedroom' (594) by Dod Procter ... and 'The Flight' (550) by Harold Harvey ... a lusty mother in a blue gown is looking after her baby while her bearded husband is preparing the donkey for the flight from the inn that bears the sign of the Lamb. Here is a Biblical subject taken out of its context and translated to a wild Cornish moor. There is even the anachronism of a sign post. Yet one feels that if this picture is eventually placed in some church, as it ought to be, it will inspire devotion and reverence …" An unknown review described it as a "grave and dignified painting ... one of the few Biblical subjects treated both with modern freshness and an old-world seriousness. It will not please everybody, but it deserves respect". RA, 1926 (550); Leeds City Art Gallery, 'Living British Artists', 1927 (84, price £50); Fox/Greenacre p.83 (ni); PH, 2001 (90).

455 | *The shoemaker, Newlyn* | o/c 18 x 23; signed bl, dated 1925.

456 | *Girl with basket of tomatoes* | the *Sheffield Daily Telegraph* on 28 Aug 1925 said "a small work of distinction". Mappin Gallery, Sheffield, 1925 (6).

457 | *Woolwork* | oil. Perhaps the same as *Coloured Wools* (1919). Goupil Gallery, winter salon 1925 (128, price £100).

458 | *Girl on a cliff* | o/c 41 x 36; signed bl, in black, dated 26. A young woman with blonde hair is seated in an awkward pose upon a flat rock, her face turned to the viewer, and leaning on her left hand; she wears a pink short-sleeved blouse and a greenish skirt; beyond is a rocky outcrop and a blue-green sea; the horizon line goes between the eyes of her tilted face. The model was Cressida Wearne, then aged 16, painted in her backyard sitting on an oil drum; Porthcurno and Logan Rock were painted in afterwards. It appears she was painted again by Harvey as the *Notebook* records 'Cressida on the Cliffs 50 x 40' (a larger size than this work). *Apollo*, 1927, described it as "full of light, solid form, distance and good design". The *Daily Sketch* of 12 February 1927 (illus) wrote "this study on the Cornish coast is typical of the art of Harold Harvey, the Newlyn painter". *The Times* on 4 February 1927 wrote it "lolls out of the canvas in the most precarious manner". BH, 1932 (as *Youth*), which *The Times* of 5 February 1932 described as "a fair girl sitting on a rock and leaning out towards the spectator, and this is managed with a good deal of skill"; F&R, Sep 1932 (as *Youth*). *Western Daily Press Bristol*, 16 Sep 1932, pp.5 and 8 (illus), which described "grace of outline in the figure, an arresting expression on the face." PH, May 1993 (65 ni); PH, 2001 (75); *PCF: C&SI*, p.113 (illus); Wallace, p.60 (illus); WL. Penlee House Gallery & Museum (1989.66).

459 | *A summer evening* | o/c 24 x 20; signed br, dated 1926. The whole height of the painting is occupied by the full-length portrait of a young woman; she sits on the wall of Vivian House in Newlyn, facing the viewer, looking slightly right; she wears a blue sprigged blouse, open over a pale green chemise with pink edging, and a matching blue skirt; her hands clasp her right knee, over which is draped a patterned shawl; beyond and below her, at right, is St Peter's church, Newlyn and its lychgate, and other buildings below a rising hillside with fields and trees; at tr is a hazy

Penzance; the sky is mainly yellow. The lychgate has now gone. The *Notebook* records payment to Miss Evelyn Cole in June/July 1925. Mentioned in *Apollo* 1927. *The Connoisseur* 1927 wrote "the colour was more a matter of pre-Raphaelite craftsmanship, of tinted pattern, than of pure flowing colour". The *Morning Post* on 8 February 1927 wrote it "appeals strongly". LG, 1927 (16, as *A summer evening (Evelyn)*). King & Chasemore, Pulborough, 13 July 1976 (11); PL, 17 June 1986 (28 illus); W&H, 1986 (14 illus); WHL, 30 June 1988 (454 illus); PH, 2001 (73); WHL, 6 Dec 2007 (250 illus); WHL, 27 Sep 2012 (110 illus); WHL, 14 Mar 2013 (191 illus).

460 | *The girl (Zennor)* | o/c 18 x 18; signed br, dated 26; inscr 'The Girl Zennor' on the stretcher. A teenage girl stands centre, facing left, her left hand carrying a pail; she leans back against a large boulder which occupies the br corner; behind her is a landscape of cottages, bridge, allotments, and rocks set among grass; at centre left is the lane leading to the churchyard of St Senara; the background is not in full perspective and appears more as a flat pattern. *The Times* of 4 Feb 1927 said "the ground- pattern is tilted to provide an interesting back-ground". LG, 1927 (21). CL, 5 June 1992 (4 illus).

461 | *Mother and child above Zennor* | o/c 18 x 18; signed br in red, dated 26. In the foreground a mother sits facing right, wearing a pink short-sleeved blouse and holding in her lap a young child wearing a blue short-sleeved dress and with bare feet; behind and below them is a farm with cows at tl and a lane at far right leading to the stile to the churchyard of St Senara. Perhaps the same as *The mother (Zennor)*. PL, 18 June 1985 (54 illus); SL, 27 Mar 1991 (55 illus, as *Mother and child*); PH, 2001 (89); WL.

462 | *The red shawl, Portrait of Miss Alison Rose* | o/c 24 x 20; signed, dated 26; title inscr on stretcher. This may have been shown at LG, 1927 (31, as *Portrait of Miss Alison Rose*). PL, 2 May 1995 (76); WHL, 28 Sep 1995 (70 illus).

463 | *Seaweed gatherers* | o/c 25 x 30; signed br in black, dated 1926. In the foreground are three horses facing right, with carts being loaded by two men; another man in a blue jacket stands smoking by the horses; a white dog lies at bl; at the right edge a white and brown horse move left, behind the others. Perhaps LG, 1927 (30, as *Seaweed*). WHL, 10 June 1977 (83 illus); WHL, 27 Mar 1980 (93 illus); LWG, Mar 1982 (38 illus, as *Seaweed*); PL, 14 Nov 1983 (65 illus, as *Collecting seaweed*); SL, 15 May 1985 (39 illus, as *Gathering wrack*); CL, 12 June 1986 (91 illus); CL, 9 Nov 1989 (16, as *Gathering seaweed*); PL, 17 July 2001 (13, as *Gathering kelp at Newlyn*); DL, 18 Oct 2001 (450 as *The seaweed gatherers*); BAL, 2854I; WL.

464 | *Listening to the sea* | o/c 18 x 18; signed br, dated 26. A young woman looks at the viewer, holding a shell to her left ear, the right hand with forefinger raised for silence; set against a beach with wave patterns in the sand. The model may be the left girl in *On the sands*. Perhaps LG, 1927 (4, as *The shell*). SL, 25 May 1983 (54 illus); WL.

465 | *Shellfish gatherer* | o/c 15 x 12; signed br, dated 1926. A young woman stands full length in profile facing right, in a long dress and brimmed hat, a basket over her right arm, holding a long implement with both hands; behind her is beach, sea and sky. WHL, 17 May 1996 (305 illus); DL, 15 June 2004 (556 illus).

466 | *Logan's Rock, Porthcurno beach* | o/c 18 x 18; signed br, dated 26. A rocky headland, which visually almost reaches the pile of rocks at right; no figures are visible; the horizon is very high. Perhaps LG, 1927 (12, as *Treryn Dynas (Logan Rock)*), of which the *Morning Post* of 8 February 1927 said it "appeals strongly". CL, 7 Nov 1985 (14 illus).

467 | *The bridge at Newlyn* | o/c 18 x 20; signed br in red, dated 26. At left is the bridge with a central cut-water and five people standing on it, one in a green dress and another in pink; behind are buildings and at right two horse-drawn carts stand before the Kerris Dairy and other buildings; one horse wears a green cover; the stream flows briskly at bottom right; the scene is sunny and the sky is blue with white clouds. Messum's, 2020.

468 | *On the Cornish coast* | o/c 17½ x 17½; signed, dated 26. SC, 7 Oct 1983 (1246 ni).

469 | *Vessels in a harbour* | o/c 18 x 18; signed br, dated 26. Several small boats on still water in a harbour. SC, 7 Oct 1983 (1247 illus); WHL, 5 Dec 1989 (380 illus, as *Penzance fishing boats moored in Newlyn harbour*).

470 | *Anemones* | o/c 28 x 36; signed bl, dated 26. Two women seated amid flowers in a garden; the left figure wears a black blouse, white skirt and patterned headscarf and holds a posy of flowers in both hands; the right figure wears a white blouse and blue skirt and holds a red flower in her right hand. The models are said to be Miss Clarry and Miss Howell. RA, 1927 (726); FAG, 1927 (143); Bradford, 1928 (106); RHA, 1929 (214); WHL, 20 July 1974 (155 illus); DMG, autumn 1974 (31 illus); Wortley, p.269 (illus); Fox/Greenacre, pp.35 (illus) and 131 (illus no.80); SL, 1 Oct 1997 (13 illus); PH, 2001 (74); WL.

471 | *Iris pickers* | o/c 20 x 18; signed br in red, dated 26. Amid diagonal rows of blue and yellow flowers two women walk towards us, each carrying a laden basket of flowers on her shoulder; the first wears a red blouse and black skirt, the second a long creamy dress; there is no sky. BL, 2 March 2016 (92 illus).

472 | *Tulip pickers* | o/c 20 x 20; signed bl, dated 26 in red. Three young women facing left bend to pick tulips in a field which gently slopes towards the coast; the nearest woman wears a dark blue skirt and white short-sleeved blouse; the woman behind her wears a headscarf and whitish blouse and skirt; the woman at right wears a yellow headscarf, blue blouse and olive skirt; in the far distance is Penzance; most of the scene is of red and yellow tulips in bloom; the subject and style are similar to 'The donkey meadow' (1924). CL, 5 Mar 1976 (79 ni); SL, 23 May 2013 (35 illus); BL, 26 Sep 2019 (87 illus).

473 | *Summertime* | o/c 20 x 18; signed bl, dated 26. In a field a figure stands at left; beyond is a field of wheat(?) and farm buildings in a valley, under a large sky. *Apollo* in 1927 wrote "the girl's red petticoat has been the colouristic motif". LG, 1927 (19, as *Summer*) BH, 1932; WL.

474 | *The parrot picture* | o/c 18 x 18; signed, dated 26. The *Notebook* records 'The Parrot Picture 18 x 18'. LG, 1927 (6). Mentioned in *Apollo* 1927. PL, 12 Nov 1985 (126 ni, as *Pretty Polly*); PL, 28 Jan 1986 (51 ni, as *Pretty Polly*); P. Bath, 8 Dec 1986 (96, as *Pretty Polly*).

475 | *Rima* | oil; undated. The *Notebook* records 'Rima 40 x 30'. A young woman kneeling half-left, arms outstretched, a parrot on her right hand, a snake lying before her; the background is leafy. *The Cornishman* wrote on 31 Mar 1926: "You may be startled by his 'Rima', but you cannot deny the vitality of the flashing colours, the decorative charm of the brilliant birds, the arresting personality of the woman and the vivid background of green foliage." *Daily Sketch*, 23 March 1926 (illus) with caption "a very different conception from Epstein's sculptural figure". Mentioned in the *Daily Express* on 1 May 1926. RA, 1926 (408); *RAI*, 1926, p.112 (illus).

476 | *An interior* | undated. In a bedroom a woman in a white headscarf and dark dress kneels at left beside a large circular tin bath; her right hand touches the water; at right a small nude boy sits on a towel on a wooden chair, ready to be bathed; in the foreground at left is a large ceramic jug; behind the figures is a large bed with tall, dark head and foot rests. *The Times* (undated) wrote "... Apart from its grace of reserved colour, this ... is noteworthy as one of the very few pictures which attempt the pictorial – as distinct from the literary – invention advised by Reynolds". *The Cornishman* on 31 Mar 1926 said "(it) pleases by contrast and the skill of the artist, who is in his prime". An unknown reviewer wrote of its "evidence of aesthetic as distinct from technical interest in the third dimension". RA, 1926 (124); RGI, 1926 (218 illus); *The Studio*, vol.92, July 1926, p.41 (illus); WL.

477 | *Gertrude in the kitchen at Maen Cottage* | o/c 30 x 25; signed br in red, dated 27. Two labels on original stretchers. Gertrude stands facing left before the dresser on which many plates and bowls are displayed; she is drying a large bowl, and wears a green and black horizontally striped skirt and a dark short-sleeved blouse over it; the floor is black and brown tiles or lino; above her head cloths hang drying. Perhaps BH, 1932 (40, as per label). PL, 26 Nov 1996 (14 illus); WL.

478 | *Girl in a round-backed chair* | o/c 16 x 14; signed br in red, dated 27; label on reverse 'BH HH 15 ex.38', perhaps Barbizon House. Head and shoulders view of a teenager in a pale blue blouse with open collar, sitting in a wood-spindled round-backed chair; she has long dark hair and looks straight at us; the background is plain.

479 | *The elm tree* | o/c 20 x 16; signed bl, dated 27. A mature tree stands in the foreground at the edge of a ploughed field, its many branches showing yellow-green leaves in the sunshine; behind are green meadows, more trees, low hills and a grey farmhouse; the sky is pale blue. CL, 16 Dec 2021 (6).

480 | *Daffodils* | o/c 24 x 20; signed br, dated 1927. A young woman sits on a bank high above the coast; at bl, is a shed which may be the Mousehole lifeboat station; she has a prominent nose and wears a blue and white dress with round neck; her right hand holds a bunch of white daffodils, her left hand rests in her lap; at bl, is a basket of daffodils. Perhaps RA, 1931 (387). SWS, 25 May 2000 (2409 illus); DMG, autumn 2000 (26 illus); PH, 2001 (71); WL.

481 | *Siesta* | o/b 26 x 24; signed bl, dated 27. At right a young mother with short dark hair, in a white sleeveless blouse and dark skirt, leans left over a baby in white clothes lying on a cot with white bedding, resting its head on a red cushion; the background is plain white; the overall tonality is very pale. The mother has been identified as Elizabeth Jane Faull and the baby as Joan Faull (b.1925) who was then about one year old. The *Evening Standard* of 4 May 1928 wrote of "the tender joy of the mother and child". RA, 1928 (681). Royal Leamington Spa (A7.1928), donated 1928.

482 | *The mother (Zennor)* | perhaps the same as *Mother and child above Zennor*. *The Times* on 4 Feb 1927 referred to its "half-way house between realism and decoration"; the *Morning Post* of 8 Feb 1927 wrote "But all three contributory influences meet and merge to form the beauty of 'The Mother'. In sentiment, design and colour this picture is most attractive, and it is painted with rare skill and charm". LG, 1927 (1).

483 | *The bather* | LG, 1927 (2).

484 | *Schooner (Newlyn harbour)* | LG, 1927 (3).

485 | *Boats (Newlyn harbour)* | the *Notebook* records 'Boats Newlyn Harbour 18 x 16'. The *Morning Post* of 8 Feb 1927 said it "appeals strongly". LG, 1927 (7).

486 | *Marigolds* | LG, 1927 (8).

487 | *The dresser* | perhaps *Kitchen Still Life*, wrongly attributed to Gertrude Harvey (o/c 16 x 13) in *Laporte: A History in Art*, (Laporte, 2000), p.43 (illus), which shows a dresser with three shelves above the cupboard top, laden with coloured plates, jugs and cups hung on hooks, and a soup tureen. Mentioned in *Apollo* 1927; mentioned in an unidentified review of 1932 as among his most striking successes. A letter to Harvey from Sir George Clausen says "I liked much the Kitchen Dresser". LG, 1927 (9); City Art Gallery Manchester, 'Living British Artists', 1927 (no.136, price £50); RHA, 1932 (308); BH, 1932 (4); PL, 1 Oct 1996 (77 ni, as by Newlyn School).

488 | *A corner of my garden* | *The Times* of 4 Feb 1927 wrote "a well-composed study of foreground detail"; the *Morning Post* referred to the obvious influence of the pre-Raphaelite Brotherhood. LG, 1927 (10).

489 | *A maid of all work* | described by the *Birmingham Daily Gazette* of 20 November 1934 as "a particularly fine work". LG, 1927 (11); RHA, 1928 (3); Birmingham Repertory Theatre, 1934.

490 | *Matinee* | perhaps the same as *Girls outside the Gaiety cinema, Newlyn*. LG, 1927 (13).

491 | *Ethel* | the *Notebook* records 'Ethel 30 x 20' and payments to Ethel Green on 8 Sep 1923 and 26 Aug 1927, and to Ethel Chiffers in 1922. The *Connoisseur* in 1927 referred to the "self-conscious brightness of its colours". *The Aberdeen Journal* of 28 Oct 1927 recorded "a girl with a flower". LG 1927 (14); Goupil Gallery, winter salon 1927 (240, price £63).

492 | *Josephine* | the *Notebook* records 'Interior with Guitar (Josephine) 30 x 25'. The model was Gertrude's niece, Josephine Legate (1906–1988). LG, 1927 (17).

493 | *The scarecrow* | LG, 1927 (18).

494 | *Lilian* | the *Notebook* records payments to Lilian Gilbert (Mrs Brood) in 1923 and 1925-7. Dod Procter also painted a 'Lilian', RA, 1923. *Apollo* in 1927 wrote "he has the qualities of a portrait painter". The *Morning Post* of 8 Feb 1927 described it as being in "the Clausen-Forbes convention". LG, 1927 (22); RA, 1923.

495 | *The old bridge, Newlyn* | LG, 1927 (23).

496 | *A Newlyn fisherman* | *Apollo* in 1927 wrote "the painting of the fisherman's hands should not be overlooked". LG, 1927 (24).

497 | *Jane* | *The Times* of 4 Feb 1927 wrote "Jane is an excellent head". LG, 1927 (25).

498 | *Iris* | the *Notebook* records 'Iris Angove 16 x 14'. Mentioned in *Apollo* 1927; the *Connoisseur* 1927 referred to its colour; the *Morning Post* of 8 Feb 1927 referred to the obvious influence of the pre-Raphaelite Brotherhood. LG, 1927 (26).

499 | *Tol Carne* | Tol Carne is an area in the north of Newlyn. The *Connoisseur* in 1927 wrote "the latter the least worthy exhibit of all the forty included being rather like a coloured picture postcard". *The Times* on 5 Feb 1932 mentioned its fidelity. LG, 1927 (28); RHA, 1928 (48); BH, 1932.

500 | *Portrait of Miss Betty Rose* | Elizabeth Rose (Betty) was born in 1903, married in 1930 and died in 1998. She attended the Harvey-Procter School from April 1924. The *Morning Post* of 8 Feb 1927 said it "appeals strongly". LG, 1927 (29).

501 | *Sea-weed* | LG, 1927 (30).

502 | *Portrait of Miss Alison Rose* | Alison Helen Rose was born in 1900 at Edinburgh and studied at Heatherley's before coming to Newlyn; she attended the Harvey-Procter School from at least April 1922; she exhibited at Newlyn Gallery 1926/7 and elsewhere between 1924 and 1939; she died unmarried shortly after WWII. This may be work titled *The red shawl, portrait of Miss Alison Rose*, dated 26. LG, 1927 (31).

503 | *The bracken carriers* | the *Notebook* records 'Bracken Gatherers 24 x 20'. Mentioned in *Apollo* 1927; the *Morning Post* of 8 Feb 1927 mentioned its "Pre-Raphaelite realism and a touch of Jean Francois Millet's non-conformist poetry". LG, 1927 (32).

504 | *Zennor* | the *Notebook* records 'Zennor 40 x 30'. The *Connoisseur* 1927 mentioned its drawing; *The Times* on 5 Feb 1932 mentioned its fidelity. LG, 1927 (33); NEAC, 1927 (195); BH, 1932.

505 | *Through the mirror* | the *Morning Post* of 8 Feb 1927 referred to "the charming glimpse". LG 1927 (34); perhaps BH, 1932 (as *The mirror picture*).

506 | *The two bridges (winter morning)* | the *Notebook* records 'The two bridges 20 x 34'. LG, 1927 (35); perhaps RSA, 1930 (288, as *The bridges*).

507 | *Resting* | mentioned in *Connoisseur* April 1927 for its bright colours. LG, 1927 (36).

508 | *The marsh at Marazion* | perhaps the 1923 work. *The Times* on 4 Feb 1927 wrote "an almost heart breaking pre-Raphaelite appeal to anybody who knows the place"; the *Connoisseur* in 1927 wrote "the good sense of atmosphere shown … was a matter of colour". LG, 1927 (37).

509 | *A street in Newlyn* | LG, 1927 (39).

510 | *Greta* | the *Notebook* records 'Greta: girl with buttercups 20 x 22'. LG, 1927 (40).

511 | *Rainbow over rocks* | o/c 26 x 20; signed bl, dated 1928. A very rocky coast looking out to sea, with waves breaking; two tiny figures stand at br. WHL, 15 Aug 1985 (232 ni, as dated 1929, as *The rainbow*); SL, 22 July 1987 (6 illus); SL, 2 Mar 1988 (20 illus); WL.

512 | *Rocky tor with heather in the foreground* | wc 10 x 12½; signed, dated 1928. DL, 20 July 1974 (279 ni).

513 | *On the sands* | o/c 20 x 30; signed bl, dated 1928. Two girls lying full length on a yellow sandy beach, with sparkling sea and cliffs beyond; the right girl lies on her front reading a red-covered book; the left girl lies on her back looking at the other. The right girl was painted in *Two young girls with a butterfly* (1929) as the right hand girl. SL, 13 May 1987 (130 illus); CL, 27 Mar 1997 (169); WL.

514 | *Mounts Bay, Cornwall* | o/c 17 x 15; signed, dated 28. Bearnes, Torquay, 10 Jan 1990 (249).

515 | *The church bridge, Newlyn* | o/c 20 x 16; signed bl, in black, dated 28; title inscr on the stretcher. A view down the stream with a bridge at tr cut by the frame; at right foreground a man sieves into a barrel; on the bridge a woman in a red dress stands by a man with a blue shirt sitting on the parapet; at left are the stream bank, trees and St Peter's church. BH, 1932. PL, 8 Mar 1994 (9 illus); PL, 7 June 1994 (5 illus); WL.

516 | *Sennen Cove* | o/c 19¾ x 29; signed bl, dated 1928. At left is a large pile of rocks; in the centre, sea washes a sandy beach; beyond is a headland. WHL, 28 Nov 1985 (50 ni, as *Cornish coastal scene in spring time*); DL, 4 Dec 1986 (283 illus); PL, 15 Sep 1987 (35 illus); PL, 18 May 1988 (35 illus).

517 | *Silver sands* | Goupil Gallery, winter salon 1928 (218, price £60).

518 | *The Spanish guitar* | o/c. In a sitting room with a sideboard at left and a round table at right, a young woman sits facing us in a rocking chair; she holds a guitar on her lap and her right hand plucks the strings while her left hand adjusts the tension; the upper end of the guitar carries a tail of coloured ribbons; she wears a dark jacket, red dress and shoes; at br a cat lies in a circular basket. *Western Daily Press Bristol*, 16 Sep 1932, pp. 5 and 8 (illus), which said "the colouring is rich but well toned". RA, 1928 (526); WAGL, 1928 (251); F&R, Sep 1932.

519 | *The empty tomb* | *The Cornishman* of 28 March 1928 said "we find ourselves in sympathy with the bereaved who form the figures in the painting". Newlyn, 1928.

520 | *The lovers* | the *WMN* of 8 June 1928 recorded "A pale, consumptive-looking city youth is telling his love to a village girl, who listens with downcast eyes. The anxious expression and depth of feeling depicted on the youth's face is marvellously clever. They are sitting on a large rock, overlooking a dreary sea." Harris Galleries, Plymouth, 1928.

521 | *Titbits* | o/c 24 x 20; signed br in black, dated 1929. Two women stand in a dining room; at left Gertrude wears a cloche hat and and checked skirt, a small multi-coloured bag over her right arm; she removes a glove from her left hand; the right woman wears a multi-coloured scarf (in a Crysede fabric) and pink coat and leans against a chair and offers food to a small brown and white dog seated before her. Fox/Greenacre, p.131 (illus no.81); Berriman, pl.36; SWS, 15 Dec 1982 (1502); PL, 25 Mar 1986 (69 ni); WHL, 14 Apr 1988 (451 illus); PH, 2001 (69); BAL, 16592; WL.

522 | *The toilet* | o/c 21¼ x 18; signed br in red, dated 29. A woman seated in a rounded wooden armchair facing front-left, with both hands raised to her hair which has a yellow ornament over her left ear; she wears a white sleeveless chemise and dark skirt; before her, at bl, is a fragment of dressing table; behind at tl is a round table bearing two books. An unknown review (of 1932?) said "It is in 'The

Toilet' that he most closely approaches the solidity and firm plastic modelling of Mr Harold Knight". Described by the *Birmingham Daily Gazette* of 20 November 1934 as "a particularly fine work." BH, 1932; Birmingham Repertory Theatre, 1934; RHA, 1937 (105); PL, 29 Jan 1991 (33a illus); PL, 7 June 1994 (129 illus, as *La toilette*); PL, 17 June 1997 (17 illus, as *The dressing table*); PH, 2001 (94, as *The dressing table*); WL.

523 | *Gertrude in an interior* | o/c 30 x 24; signed bl in red, dated 29. Gertrude stands facing left, adjusting her skirt of horizontally striped fabric in green and purple; she wears a purple headscarf, and a green blouse or cardigan; at left is a tallboy and at right a chair; below a window is a dressing table with mirror; the carpet is green. CL, 28 Nov 1996 (158 illus); CL, 6 Nov 1998 (119).

524 | *Mother and child* | oil 70 x 60; signed bl, dated 1929. A seated woman facing left, in an embroidered cape, holding on her lap a baby in a long white dress; behind is sunny pasture. Perhaps Goupil Galleries, *c.*1930, when Wilenski wrote "'Mother and Child' as a neo-Renaissance 'Madonna of the Bridges' is intelligently planned and painted, and has an unassuming charm". RA, 1930 (617); *RAI*, 1930, p.109 (illus).

525 | *Two young girls with a butterfly* | o/c 24 x 22; signed bl in red, dated 29. Two young teenage girls kneel facing each other in a sunlit hill-top meadow; the right girl wears a white short-sleeve dress and has bare feet, and holds a red and black butterfly in her outstretched hands; the left girl wears a reddish blouse matching her hair and a creamy skirt, and she looks at the butterfly; beyond are green hills and at far right a patch of coast; the sky is cloudy with blue patches. The right hand girl was painted in *On the sands* (1928) as the right hand girl. CL, 7 June 2007 (137 illus); CL, July 2020 (51 illus).

526 | *Cottages beneath the hills* | o/c 19½ x 23½; signed bl, dated 29. At bl, two cottages lie in the dip of a grassy field; the middle distance is mainly leafy trees, with green hills beyond. CL, 7 Nov 1991 (3); CL, 1 July 1993 (38 illus); WL.

527 | *The little farm* | o/c 24 x 22; signed bl, dated 29. A sunny coastal hillside strewn with boulders; in the centre is a farmhouse with outbuildings; washing hangs to dry in a ruin; the blue sea is visible at upper right. The site has been identified as Greeb Farm, Lands End. Towneley Hall Art Gallery & Museum, Burnley (paoil263).

528 | *The flower painter* | o/c 22½ x 27; signed br, dated 1930. Gertrude sits at right, wearing a headscarf and dark clothes over a creamy blouse, holding a painter's brush in her right hand and palette in her left, facing a painting on an easel; in the foreground is a green table with a bowl of flowers placed on a mirror. RA, 1930 (47); PL, 12 Nov 1985 (125 illus, as *Gertrude painting*); SL, 13 May 1987 (129 illus); WL.

529 | *Kitchen interior* | o/c 21 x 18; signed bl, dated 1930. Gertrude stands at left, in a patterned headscarf and a dark jacket over a white blouse; she works at a table, pouring into a bowl from a jug in her left hand, and mixing the bowl's contents with her right hand; on the near edge of the table lies a large fish, and behind it are several bottles and bowls; on a shelf above the table are several cups, jugs and plates. DMG (as *Gertrude in the kitchen*).

530 | *Peter Kitchen* | o/c 18 x 18; signed, dated 30. The subject may be related to Sarah Kitchen painted by Jill Garnier. *The Times* of 5 Feb 1932 wrote "an excellent painting of a boy eating an orange by Newlyn harbour". BH, 1932; SWS, 22 Oct 1985 (2823 ni).

531 | *Portrait of a seated gentleman* | o/c 25½ x 21½; signed, dated 30. DL, 9 May 1985 (57 ni).

532 | *Kitty* | o/c 24 x 20; signed bl, dated 30. The *Notebook* records 'Kitty Batten 24 x 18'. A young woman sits on a green dining chair, facing front, in a pink open-neck blouse with long sleeves, and dark blue skirt, with hands clasped in her lap holding a daisy; the floor is plain dark brown; behind her the wall is white with a pale brown strip at far right. She may have modelled for *Rima* and for the maid in *The young menage*. RA, 1931 (738); *RAI*, 1931, p.95 (illus); BH, 1932; F&R, Sep 1932; *Western Daily Press Bristol*, 16 Sep 1932, p.5; Fox/Greenacre, p.83 (ni). Frank Rutter in the *Sunday Times*, 3 May 1931, p.13 said it "has an intensity and vital quality sadly lacking in most of the larger portraits". *The Times* of 5 Feb 1932, p.10, wrote "a charming head". The *Western Daily Press Bristol*, 16 Sep 1932, p.5 described it as "one of the most outstanding" of the life studies, with "a wonderful life-like expression." Philip Mould, London, summer 2021.

533 | *Newlyn bridge* | o/c 19½ x 19½; signed br, dated 1930. The stream leads towards the bridge, on which several people stand; at left are buildings, at right a road with railings by the stream edge; beyond the bridge are more buildings. PH, 2001 (87).

534 | *French crabbers* | o/c 18 x 21; signed bl in red, dated 30. Label on reverse 'BH, HH 31 EX 33'. In the foreground are several rows of small fishing boats with Penzance numbers, lined up in threes; behind them a boat leaves harbour, and above rises the town; the water is flat calm; done in a rather crisp style. RHA, 1931 (177); perhaps BH, 1932; PH, 2001 (82); *PCF: C&SI*, p.113 (illus). Penlee House Gallery & Museum (2002.L5P).

535 | *Harbour scene* | o/c 20 x 24; signed bl, dated indis 30 or 34. A label on reverse gives title as 'Harbour Scene' and another (later) as 'The Harbour at Newlyn, Cornwall'. A sunny view of Newlyn towards the Old Harbour, with the hill of Fore Street at right; at the jetty is a two-masted boat beside which is a cart pulled by two horses, and a dinghy on the jetty surface; the sea is blue and calm, and the sky is mostly blue with white cloud gathering on the horizon.

536 | *After the fair* | Fox/Greenacre, p.41 (ni), which dates it 1930 and comments "the return of a family from a fair laden with balloons and gifts".

537 | *A summer afternoon* | RSA, 1930 (275).

538 | *Boats, Newlyn harbour* | o/c 20 x 20; signed bl in red, dated 31; signed and dated on a label on the frame. In the foreground are six small fishing boats side by side; behind them is a jetty (from right to left) with a boat alongside, and behind that another jetty (from left to right); the coast forms the horizon. CL, 5 June 1992 (17a illus); PH, 2001 (83).

539 | *The blue door* | o/c 30 x 25; signed bl, dated indis 31. At left a blue front door opens onto a sunny terrace with a round table bearing a white cloth and breakfast crockery; left of the table sits a young woman in a yellow blouse and dark blue skirt; she talks to another young woman standing further left leaning against a round column, wearing a long green dress and holding a cup and saucer in both hands; above the terrace a plant grows across the door-space, and a black cat sits at br; beyond is Mount's Bay with a ship moored at the quay and St Michael's Mount in the distance. The setting is the front of Harvey's home, Maen Cottage. This is the first of four treatments of the terrace, the others being *The blue door, Newlyn* (1934), *The breakfast table* (1938) and *A balcony, Penzance* (1940). The *Observer* of 7 Feb 1932 described it as "among his most striking successes"; *Western Daily Press Bristol* 16 Sep, 1932, pp.5 and 8 (illus). SL, 12 July 2007 (92 illus). BH, 1932 and F&R, Sep 1932 (both as *The doorstep picture*). Bangor University (0B00257), bequeathed 2009.

540 | *St Peter's church* | o/c 18 x 14; signed bl, dated 31. A footpath leads to a gate beside the east end of the church, with three pointed windows; around are several secular buildings; behind, a row of trees runs along an elevated ridge.

541 | *View of Treriefe, Cornwall* | o/c 18 x 24; signed bl in red, dated 1931. Treriefe house is at left, set in its grassy park with cattle; a lopsided tree stands at centre and tall trees are at far right; an iron 5-bar fence runs across the width of the painting near the lower edge; the sky is blue and cloudy; the dominant colour is the green grass. CL, 21 Mar 1996 (35 illus).

542 | *The model* | o/c 19¼ x 17; signed bl, dated 31. Head and shoulders view of a teenage girl seated facing the viewer, with fair complexion and dark hair to her shoulders; she wears an open neck, sleeveless, bright red dress; behind at left are frames and papers; at right are bottles and containers. BH, 1932; S. Leverhulme sale, 26 June 2001 (462 illus); WL.

543 | *Study in green* | o/c 20 x 18; signed tr in red, dated 1931. A young woman with short brown hair, facing right, seated sideways on a green wooden chair, wearing a green and white checked dress with short sleeves and round neck; her left arm extends along the top chair rail and her right hand holds a small white and black china dog on her lap; the background is plain green-brown. CSK, 22 March 2017 (40); Bellman's, Billingshurst, Sussex, 5 Sep 2017 (1607, as attributed to Harold Harvey).

544 | *Sketch of Rhoda* | pencil on paper 7 x 4½; signed at top, dated 1931. Head and shoulder view of a teenage girl facing left, with short hair and open-neck blouse. The sitter is Rhoda Harvey, Harold's niece. PH, 2001 (102).

545 | *The Gull Rock* | there's a Gull Rock near Portscatho and another at Dodman Point, south of Mevagissey. RHA, 1931 (170).

546 | *Daffodils* | the *WMN* of 24 March 1931 recorded "… a typical Cornish lass and a young farm hand returning to the packing shed with baskets of the early spring flowers … the baskets of flowers, and even the gate through which they are passing, are treated with completeness." Exhibited at Harvey's own house.

547 | *The young menage* | o/c 36 x 30; signed br, dated 1932. A young couple drinking coffee sit at a dining table bearing a white cloth, set with bowls of fruit and a water jug; behind is a corner cupboard with decorated china; at right a maid in a blue dress stands holding a tray, looking at the woman. RA, 1932 (403);

RAI, 1932, p.102 (illus). Royal Leamington Spa (A141.1933), donated 1933.

548 | *The idler* | o/c 33 x 26; signed br in red, dated 32. A young woman in a white-on-red dress and white stockings stands facing us, looking into a mirror in her left hand; behind her is a chest of drawers with a white cloth on top; at left is a table with a striped cloth and a round bowl. *The Cornishman* of 23 March 1933 noted "a girl looking in a hand mirror and neglecting her housemaid's work". RHA, 1934 (40).

549 | *A study in greens* | o/c 24 x 18; signed br, dated 1932. A young woman, shown half-length, with her left hand on hip, looks at the viewer, standing before a mantelpiece on which are glass candleholders. The same mantelpiece appears in *The young menage*. The pose is almost identical to *Janie* (1923). The model has been identified as Isabel Drew. RA, 1933 (313); *RAI*, 1933, p.88 (illus); *The Times*, 2 May 1933, p.18 (illus); RGI, 1933 (442); RHA, 1939 (157, as *A study in green*); PL, 5 Mar 1991 (15 illus); WL.

550 | *The red silk shawl* | o/c 30 x 25; signed bl, in black, dated 1932. At right a young woman with dark hair sits in an armless rocking chair, facing left, in a blue-grey jacket, pale green blouse, black skirt and green shoes; she is sewing the red shawl spread over her lap, but looks at the viewer; at left is a lit fireplace; on the mantelshelf and the fitted cupboard are pieces of china and glass; at far right is a console table with a candelabra. The scene is the sitting room at Maen Cottage. Probably BH, 1932 (26, as *The shawl*). Clevedon Sale Rooms, 7 May 1998 (175, as *Red silk shawl – lady in parlour at Maen Cottage, Newlyn*); SL, 3 Dec 1998 (43 illus); CL, 5 Nov 99 (190 illus); CL, 21 Nov 2003 (36 illus); WL.

551 | *Portrait of Miss Sue Palmer* | o/c 20 x 16; signed bl in red-brown, dated 32; title inscr in pencil on frame verso. A head and shoulder frontal view of a young woman with light brown hair in a green open-necked blouse; the background is plain off-white; the light falls from the left. SWS, 25 May 2000 (2399 illus, as *Portrait of a lady*); DMG, winter 2000 (7 illus, as *Portrait of a lady*); PH, 2001 (93); BL, 21 Jan 2015 (113 illus).

552 | *Laura Jewill Hill – the unwilling sitter* | o/c 20 x 24; signed bl, dated 32 in dull brown; title inscr on frame. At centre, before a three-part screen, Laura faces us sitting with hands in her lap on a gold day-bed with raised head-piece, wearing a large pale blue skirt and red blouse; at right we see the back of a male artist painting her, seated on a chair with an open round back; in the foreground is a table with a red and white striped cloth set with yellow, blue and white cups and tea pot, a bottle of liquid, and an ornamental white jar. Laura Challen Jewill Hill (1907-2004) also appears in *Laura and Paul Jewill Hill* (1916). BL, 9 June 2015 (114 illus).

553 | *Woman in a white blouse* | o/c 18 x 15; signed bl in red, dated 32. Head and shoulders view of a young woman facing us but looking to our right; she wears a white blouse with embroidered collar; her eyes are downcast.

554 | *Boys bathing* | o/c 20 x 18; signed br, dated 32; inscr 'Boys Bathing' on the canvas overlap. Seven boys, of whom five are sitting and two standing, on the steps of a stone jetty with water to the left; another is swimming; the tonality is bright. PL, 11 Nov 1986 (30

illus); CL, 18 Dec 1991 (115 illus).

555 | *Stream in the woods* | o/c 19½ x 17½; signed bl in red, dated 32. A stream runs from tr to bl, between green and wooded banks – perhaps Newlyn Coombe; the season may be early autumn.

556 | *Tolcarne bridge, Newlyn* | o/c 17½ x 19½; signed bl, dated 32. The stream runs under a sunlit round-arched bridge with figures on it; buildings flank the stream and seagulls fly over it; beyond is the town. DL, 12 Dec 1985 (140 illus); PH, 2001 (85, as *Newlyn bridge*).

557 | *A Cornish farm* | o/c 24 x 20; signed, dated 32. PL, 12 Nov 1985 (55 illus).

558 | *Herring boats, the Slip, Newlyn* | o/c 16 x 18; signed bl, dated 1932. Boats in the foreground parallel to the lower edge; at left is the quay; beyond are other boats and Newlyn. DL, 28 Aug 1986 (399 illus).

559 | *Gypsies* | *The Times* of 5 Feb 1932 wrote "he brings everything into the same plane in a decorative pattern". BH, 1932.

560 | *Nancharro* | *The Times* of 5 Feb 1932 made the same comment as for Gypsies. Nancherrow is a hamlet slightly north of St Just. BH, 1932.

561 | *Ploughing above Lamorna under a big sky* | o/c 20 x 18; signed, dated 1932. In the foreground horses pull a plough to the right; beyond are rolling hills and fields, under a cloudy sky which fills much of the canvas. WHL, 20 April 2006 (315).

562 | *The harbour office, Penzance* | o/c 18 x 19; signed, dated 1932. At centre is a green-roofed building, at right a pink-faced building; behind is the church and other buildings; the foreground is open space, with a man standing at far left. WHL, 29 Sep 2005 (95); WHL, 27 Sep 2012 (480 illus, as *The Custom House, quayside Penzance*).

563 | *Spring, Drift* | *The Times* of 5 Feb 1932 said it was "a good, sunny, landscape". BH, 1932.

564 | *Newlyn Coombe* | mentioned in *The Times*, 5 Feb 1932. BH, 1932.

565 | *Buryas bridge* | mentioned in *The Times*, 5 Feb 1932. BH, 1932.

566 | *The shawl* | this is probably *The red silk shawl* (1932). *The Observer* of 7 Feb 1932 described it as among "his most striking successes". BH, 1932 (26).

567 | *Newlyn* | RHA, 1932 (41).

568 | *The window* | described by the *Birmingham Daily Gazette* of 20 November 1934 as a "particularly fine work". RHA, 1932 (126); Birmingham Repertory Theatre, 1934.

569 | *The top of the bus* | wc & pencil on paper 8¼ x 6¾; not signed or dated. A study for the oil painting of the same title. On the yellow wooden benches of an open-top bus, a man in grey clothes and cap, a mother in blue dress and green bonnet and her child, and another man sit on the far side; on the near side sits a young woman with a make-up compact, and an older woman; beyond is countryside with the suggestion of a church spire. CSK, 15 April 2008 (50 illus).

570 | *The top of the bus* | o/c 40 x 30; signed br in white, dated 32 indis; label on reverse for Centenary Exhibition Wellington New Zealand 1939–40. On an open-top bus moving left, in the far seats sit an old man at left, a young mother with baby, a man reading a newspaper at right, and part of the conductor standing at far right; on the near seats are

a young boy eating and at right his mother; behind is a shop sign in gold on red, Michell & Sons. (On canvas reverse is an unfinished portrait of a woman). RA, 1932 (657).

571 | *A Cornish mining valley* | *Western Daily Press Bristol*, 16 Sep 1932, p.5, wrote "the whole picture gives the viewer an impression of a hot day with a clear atmosphere, despite the absence of sky". F&R, Sep 1932.

572 | *The Market House* | signed bl. A street scene at Penzance with at centre the Davy statue in front of the Market Hall; many people walk about, and a couple ride a motorbike. F&R, Sep 1932; *Western Daily Press Bristol*, 16 Sep 1932, pp.5 and 8 (illus).

573 | *The Davy statue, Penzance* | o/c 24 x 20; signed br in red, dated 33 indis. At left is the statue in pale stone; at right is the tall colonnaded Market building; between are shops, several people and a horse drawn cart; the large sky is cloudy grey.

574 | *The patchwork quilt* | o/c; signed bl, dated 33. A woman seated centre in a wooden rocking chair facing left, with a large patchwork quilt spread over her lap and occupying the whole foreground; her left hand holds the fabric and her right hand is raised as if sewing; behind her at left is a fireplace and a wooden cupboard; at right is a console table beneath a circular mirror; in the right foreground is a small table with sewing equipment. RA, 1933 (382); CI, 31st International Exhibition (158); RHA, 1936 (175); *Apollo*, March 1969; WL.

575 | *Zena* | o/c 20 x 18; signed br in red, dated 33. A frontal half-length portrait of a young girl; she has short hair and wears a pink short-sleeved shirt; she sits in a wooden chair with her head against the top back rail; her right arm is in a sling of dark patterned fabric; her hands are clasped at the lower edge; the background is plain grey-pink. The *Notebook* records 'Zena: girl with arm in a sling, 20 x 18'. DL, 14 Dec 1989 (455 illus); PL, 17 Nov 1998 (2 illus).

576 | *Portrait of a gentleman* | o/c 26 x 21½; signed bl, dated 33. A man with a moustache sits facing the viewer, in a suit; his left hand holds a cigarette and has a ring on the little finger; his right hand is on his lap holding a monocle on a string; the background is plain. The 1988 identification of the sitter as the artist's father is uncertain. DL, 26 Feb 1987 (336 ni); CL, 18 Feb 1988 (133 illus, as *Portrait of the artist's father*); Woolley & Walling, Salisbury, 9 Nov 1988 (112, as *Portrait of the artist's father, Francis Harvey*); PL, 2 Dec 1988 (243, as *Portrait of a gentleman smoking a cigarette*); SWS, 29 Jan 2001 (1702, as *Portrait of the artist's father, Francis Harvey*).

577 | *Study for Portrait of a gentleman* | charcoal, 22 x 12; signed, dated 1933. Three-quarter length view of a mature man in jacket and tie seated facing right, looking at us, with a sketch pad in his lap; his raised left hand holds a cigarette, his right hand a pencil. Matthews, Oldcastle, Eire, 30 Dec 2016 (140 illus).

578 | *Walkers* | o/c 40 x 36; signed bl, dated 33; label on reverse for Britain at Play exhibition, price £100. On a hill path two young women walk in front of a man with a pipe, all moving left; the left girl wears a pink dress, the other a dress of blue spots on white; the man wears a white shirt and blue-grey trousers; all carry rucksacks; behind are hills; the sky is vast and full of white clouds. *WMN* of 24 March 1933 said it "shows two girls and a man on a walking tour equipped with hikers paraphernalia". PEAG, March 1933.

579 | *Marazion marshes* | o/c 29½ x 24½; signed bl, in black, dated indis 33. A view inland towards Ludgvan church at tl; a pair of ducks fly over the reeds in the lower half of the picture.

580 | *Mousehole harbour* | o/c 20 x 24; signed br in black, dated 1933. In the foreground several dinghies and a small fishing boat are moored in calm water, bows to the left; in the middle ground is a beach with three dinghies and two figures standing by the red one; above are houses along the harbour front; at bl, are dark rocks. WHL, 14 Feb 1975 (141 illus); BL, 22 July 1993 (16).

581 | *Newlyn Coombe* | o/c 20 x 18; signed bl, dated 33. An upstream view of water flowing over small rocks toward the viewer; at right are trees and foliage; at left is the stream bank with shrubs and a railing on which lean three figures; further left are fish warehouses which reach the upper frame; a figure sits on a window sill; the tonality is sunny and light. PL, 10 Nov 1987 (19 illus, prov the artist's family); PL, 13 Sep 1988 (10 ni); WL.

582 | *Fish stores, Newlyn* | o/c 17 x 19; signed bl, dated 1933.

583 | *The stream in winter* | o/c 18 x 16; signed bl, dated 33; inscr on the stretcher. A view up a full stream between close banks with trees; the colours are mainly yellowish, indicating sunlight on foliage and water. PL, 10 May 1988 (12 illus, prov given to the present owner by the artist as a wedding present); CSK, 18 Nov 2009 (109 illus); Newlyn School Gallery, Penzance, 2010 (as *Lamorna River*).

584 | *Trewoofe farm, a man ploughing beneath trees* | o/c 19 x 17½; signed bl, dated 33. In the foreground is a ploughed field; at right a man ploughs with a pale horse moving left; beyond are trees and farm buildings. DL, 12 Dec 1985 (398 illus).

585 | *Rhododendron* | o/c 14 x 14; signed bl, dated 33. A group of several large reddish-pink blooms occupies much of the centre, surrounded by foliage. WHL, 1 Dec 1983 (268 ni, as 14 x 13); DL, 9 Feb 1995 (214 illus); PL, 6 June 1995 (18 illus).

586 | *A sunlit room* | oil 30 x 25; signed, dated 1933. Gertrude sits on a ladder-back chair, facing left, in a striped skirt, sleeveless white bodice and patterned headscarf, about to remove her left shoe; behind is an oval mirror and at left a wardrobe; the floor is sunlit. RA, 1934 (219); *WMN*, 17 Mar 1934 (illus) in report on the NSA spring exhibition; *The Studio* March 1942, p.70 (illus, as *In the bedroom*).

587 | *The kitchen through an arch* | o/c 24 x 20; signed, dated 1933. A tall rounded arch in a white wall leads to a kitchen where a woman in a red skirt and blue top sits by a table with a white cloth; she works at a bowl on her lap; behind is a tall dresser with many plates etc.

588 | *Wheelbarrow in garden* | o/c 16½ x 12½; initialled, dated 1933. SL, 30 Apr 1986 (484 ni).

589 | *Rhoda* | o/c 22 x 20; signed br in red, dated 34; title inscr in red below the image. A young woman with fair hair faces half-right, wearing a pale open-neck blouse; behind is a green curtain. This portrays Rhoda Harvey (1914–2005), a niece of Harold's who was a lover of Ben Nicholson's in the 1950s. PH,

2001 (92, as dated 1931); *PCF: C&SI*, p.113 (illus). Penlee House Gallery & Museum (2003.35).

590 | *Girl with a toy parrot* | o/c 20 x 18; signed br, dated 34. A girl in a white dress, facing right, with a white parrot sitting in a tree at eye level. WHL, 20 July 1974 (271, as *The toy parrot*); SL, 6 Feb 1985 (392 illus, as *Girl with cockatoo*); CL, 12 June 1986 (92 illus, as *The toy parrot*); CL, 29 July 1988 (141 illus, as *Girl with a parrot*); BAL, 37921 (ni).

591 | *The little maiden* | o/c 20 x 18; 1934. An adolescent girl shown 3/4 length, stands facing left, her left hand on hip, wearing a white blouse; she is on a hill overlooking Newlyn town and harbour, and pale blue sea. RA, 1935 (515); *RAI*, 1935, p.78 (illus); PH, 2001 (70); *PCF: Staffordshire*, pp. 101 and 279 (illus). Wolverhampton Art Gallery (OP.294), donated 1935.

592 | *The window* | o/c 24 x 20; signed bl in red, dated 34; inscr on reverse The Window and 'Mary'. A woman in a blue top and floral skirt stands facing right at a daylit window; she pulls aside the blue and white striped curtain; at left is a similar window and curtain; at far right a glass bowl of flowers stands on a polished round table.

593 | *The blue door, Newlyn* | o/c 30 x 25; signed br, dated 34. At left a blue door opens onto a terrace above the harbour; on the terrace sits a man facing the viewer and holding an open accordion; at left stands a woman in a pink blouse, knitting. The setting is the porch at Maen Cottage. The models have been identified as Kitty Batten and Arthur Chiffers. F&R, 1938; SL, 12 Nov 1986 (42 illus); PH, 2001 (72); Hardie, p.102 (illus); WL.

594 | *Study for 'The blue door'* | pencil and wc 8½ x 5¾; initialled. PL, 12 Nov 1985 (56 ni).

595 | *The accordionist: study for 'The blue door'* | pencil sketch on paper *c*.15 x 19. Full-length view of a man on a chair, in a hat, jacket and muffler; his legs apart, the right foot rests on something on the ground; he holds an extended accordion and his left hand is not visible; at tr is a slight sketch for the right end of the accordion and his left hand. PL, 6 June 2000 (202 ni).

596 | *Fête champêtre* | o/c 40 x 36; signed br, dated 34. A drummer and three brass players stand at bl; at right is a marquee and four figures; beyond are Trereife House and many people. This shows the Whit Monday Newlyn Gala in the grounds of Trereife House, when villagers processed with the banner designed by Frank Bramley and John Mackenzie, and two brass bands. RA, 1934 (399); *RAI*, 1934, p.90 (illus, as *A fête champêtre*); CI, 1934 (110); RHA, 1936 (126); *The Studio*, March 1942, p.71 (illus); PL, 23 Apr 1985 (43 illus); SL, 13 May 1987 (132 illus); WL.

597 | *A haywain near Lamorna* | o/c 20 x 20; signed br in black, dated 34. A narrow country lane of reddish earth is shaded by trees on both sides, through which the sun shines from the right; in the distance at left a cart laden with hay and drawn by a white horse attended by a walking man moves towards us. BL, 26 Sep 2018 (116 illus).

598 | *Lady Gwen Cornish tin mine* | o/c 34 x 50; signed br, dated 34. Industrial machinery and buildings in a rolling landscape, under a large blue sky. The mine was at Breage, near Helston. CL, 4 Mar 1983 (218 ni, as *The pit head*); WHL, 13 Dec 1984 (214 illus); PL, 25 Mar 1986

(46 ni, as *Lady Gwen tin mine*); CL, 13 Nov 1986 (49 illus, as *The Lady, a Cornish tin mine*); WHL, 28 Feb 1989 (450 illus); WHL, 3 May 1989 (375 illus); CL, 8 June 2001 (126 illus, as *The Lady, Wheal Reeth Tin Mine, Breage, Cornwall*); WL.

599 | *Penberth Cove* | o/c 15½ x 13½; signed br in black, dated 34. A narrow stream runs under a flat stone bridge; beyond are huts and at left boats are beached; a figure stands close to the bridge. Light tones predominate. Penberth is a little north of Treryn Dinas. PH, 2001 (88).

600 | *Hikers* | oil. This may be *Walkers* of 1933. Atkinson Art Gallery Southport, 49th spring exhn of Modern Art 1934 (388, price £100).

601 | *A May procession* | o/c 72 x 36; signed br, dated 35. A procession of girls in white robes and head veils with garlands moves left towards the viewer; the three girls in the foreground have their hands clasped in prayer, whilst the two behind carry a statue of the Virgin Mary on a blue cushion. The setting is an unknown church with Byzantine arches; the perspective is flat; the girls' faces are painted in detail. RA, 1935 (163); CI, 1935 (92); *The Times* 4 May 1935 (illus); WHL, 4 Dec 1980 (339 ni); CL, 12 Mar 1982 (78 illus); PL, 10 Nov 1987 (41 illus); Fox/Greenacre, p.83 (ni); PH, 2001 (91); WHL, 10 Sep 2009 (200 illus); CL, 14 Dec 2016 (86 illus); WL.

602 | *Cornish miners* | o/c 30 x 25; signed bl, dated 1935; inscr on the stretcher. Several miners in helmets with lamps move toward the viewer; the central man looks at the viewer; the right hand man smokes a cigarette; behind, at right stands a horse and cart; at tl are the struts of a mine shaft. Said to have been done in a studio against a painted backdrop of a mine in Manila or Malaya. The two main figures have been identified as Sidney Angrove (left) and Nicholas Grenfell (right). RA, 1936 (735); Southport, 1938; PL, 25 Mar 1986 (45 ni); PL, 11 Nov 1986 (106 illus); WHL, 3 May 1989 (588); WHL, 28 Sep 1989 (480 illus); PH, May 1993 (66 illus, as *Tin Miners*); PH, 2001 (96, as *St Just tin miners*); *PCF: C&SI*, p.191 (illus); Wallace, p.63 (illus); 'Amongst heroes', London, 2013; *Amongst heroes*, p.50 (illus); WL. Royal Cornwall Museum, Truro (1991.94), as *St Just tin miners*, acquired 22 Oct 1991.

603 | *Portrait of a man* | o/c 20 x 12; signed br, dated 35. Head and shoulder portrait of a mature man with receding hair facing half left, wearing a red bow tie and pale jacket over a white shirt; the background is plain green. On the reverse is an unfinished townscape of houses beside a steeply descending hill. BL, 22 Sep 2015 (125, as *Portrait of a man wearing a red bow tie*).

604 | *Portrait of Stella Mary Burdett* | o/c 20 x 16; signed br in red, dated 35. Half length view of a young woman with blue eyes and blonde hair, wearing a green-blue cardigan over a pale spotted dress, facing half-left, seated in an armchair, her head on a pale blue cushion and holding a red-covered book in her right hand. The sitter (1916–1996) studied at the Slade School of Art and exhibited at Bristol etc. BL, 25 Jan 2012 (174 illus); Bonhams New York, 4 May 2016 (83 illus).

605 | *A Cornish homestead* | o/c 25 x 30; signed br, dated 35. Several farm buildings occupy the middle ground; in the foreground a man sits on a white horse which drinks from a pond, a brown horse alongside; beyond are green fields and hills. F&R, 1938; CL, 13 Nov 1986 (47 illus); WL.

606 | ***Woman herding cows before a farmstead*** o/c 16 x 18; signed bl in red, dated 35. A broad landscape of small green fields with a large rocky outcrop in the centre distance; at left a woman with two white cows moves right towards a farmhouse with a smoking chimney; at br are pink foxgloves; the large sky is cloudy. WHL, 30 July 1987 (140 illus); CL, 23 Nov 2017 (124 illus, as *Herding cows before a farmstead*, withdrawn).

607 | ***The land's end*** | o/b 21 x 18; signed br in red, dated 1934 or 35. RA, label on reverse. The left foreground is occupied by rocks and a grassy ledge, with pink flowers at far left, overlooking blue-grey sea; in the distance are rocky islands. RA, 1936 (326); perhaps CI, 1936 (146); RHA, 1938 (151); PH, 2001 (43, as *Rocks off Land's End*).

608 | ***The road to the moor*** | o/c 14 x 18; signed, dated 35. SL, 28 Sep 1993 (1056 ni).

609 | ***Stream at Lamorna Cove*** | o/c 20 x 18; signed bl, dated indis 35. At left a narrow path runs beside trees overhanging a wide stream; there is much shadowy greenery on both banks.

610 | ***Old Newlyn*** | o/c 24 x 20; signed br in brown, dated 35. High up on a steep village road with whitewashed houses on both sides, a donkey cart approaches carrying goods; a woman selects items from the cart; at left are telegraph poles, a woman carries a pail in each hand, and washing hangs in the sunshine; at right figures stand in the doorways and a girl in a red dress pets a seated dog; beside her is an empty rocking cradle; the light is sunny and the sky misty with thin clouds. The scene prefigures *Old Paul Hill* of 1940. BL, 23 Jan 2013 (106 illus); BL, 10 July 2013 (130 illus).

611 | ***Morning, Newlyn harbour*** | o/c 13 x 17; signed bl, dated 35. Several small boats moored by the shore in calm water, a man sitting in a red one; at right rises the Macgrigor monument with houses beyond. SL, 17 Dec 2015 (64 illus).

612 | ***Portrait of a lady*** | o/c 12½ x 10½; signed bl in red, dated 36. A young woman smiling, facing the viewer, in a grey rollneck jumper and brown jacket and hat; behind is an expansive landscape with a wide blue river or lake and green meadow in the foreground, and steep hills beyond; the sky is yellow above the hill tops. sws, 26 Jan 1993 (260 illus).

613 | ***Study of a little girl*** | o/c 18 x 16; signed br, dated 36. A girl facing the viewer, in a spotted dress with a plain dark blue collar. The design is the same as in *A daughter of Newlyn*. SL, 13 May 1987 (136 illus); (85 illus, as *Study of a child*); WL.

614 | ***A daughter of Newlyn*** | o/p 17½ x 15½; signed br in red, dated 36; inscr rev title and dated 1936. Head and shoulder frontal view of a young girl with parted brown hair and red lips, in a pale green/blue dress with a dark blue collar, against a plain pale blue ground. sc, 20 Oct 1988 (3149 illus); DL, 8 Dec 1988 (398 illus, as *Portrait of a girl*); sws, 26 Jan 1993 (267); SL, 13 Dec 2005 (74 illus); CL, 22 Nov 2006 (286 illus); WHL, 27 Sep 2007 (310 illus, as *The daughter of Newlyn*).

615 | ***Doing her hair*** | o/c 30 x 25; signed bl, dated 36. A young woman stands facing our right before a dressing table, wearing a white camisole and striped underwear; both

hands are raised to her hair; on the table is a tilting mirror, a hair brush and a small red box; behind are muslin curtains lit by daylight.

616 | ***Girl in a Green dress*** | o/c; signed br in red, dated 36. Half-length view of a young girl turned right but looking left, in a pale green dress; the background is a dark geometric shape. .

617 | ***St Michael's Mount*** | o/c 20 x 18; signed bl, dated 1936; inscr on the reverse 'St Michael's Mount'. Close-up view of the Mount, mainly in blue tones; a yacht with white sails moves left in the foreground. CL, 12 June 1987 (122 illus); DL, 10 Dec 1987 (183 illus); SL, 12 Oct 1988 (74 illus); SL, 11 Oct 1989 (210 illus); CL, 27 Nov 1997 (148); WL.

618 | ***The Longships lighthouse, Land's End*** o/c 47 x 59; signed bl, dated 36. The foreground comprises around 30 people close to the cliff edge; beyond is a wind-swept sea flecked with foam, breaking upon the rocks bearing the lighthouse; a steamer rides the rough waves in front of the lighthouse. A seagull steals from a litter bin bottom right.

619 | ***The Longships lighthouse, Land's End*** o/c 14 x 18; signed bl, dated 36. This may have been a study for the larger, very similar version of the same title (see above). This painting was given by the artist to Morgan Hosking as payment for use of his telephone. WHL, 3 May 1989 (604 illus); WHL, 28 Sep 1989 (250 illus); PH, 2001 (44); *PCF: C&SI*, p.113 (illus); WHL, 30 Sep 2010 (434 ni); WL. Penlee House & Gallery Museum.

620 | ***Marazion marsh*** | o/c 20 x 30; signed, dated 1936. WHL, 18 Mar 1982 (155 illus).

621 | ***The duck pond*** | o/c 18 x 16; signed bl, dated 36. In the foreground is a pond which flows out at br; several small white ducks swim at the far end; beyond them is a white gate and farm buildings; at left stands a figure. DL, 22 June 1989 (294 illus, as *A Cornish farm*); PL, 29 Jan 1991 (28 illus); SL, 3 Mar 1999 (34 illus); sws, 26 Oct 1999 (1215 illus); WL.

622 | ***Summer's afternoon, Tredavoe*** | o/c 19 x 24; signed, dated 36. sws, 22 Oct 1985 (2824).

623 | ***A Georgian house, Chywoone Hill, Newlyn*** | o/c 19½ x 17½; signed bl, dated 36. A double-fronted brick house with four bay windows; before it are tall palm trees. DL, 9 May 1985 (428 illus).

624 | ***A windy day*** | o/c 18 x 18; signed bl, in red, dated 36; title inscr on the frame reverse in pencil and 'Harold Harvey, Maen cottage, Newlyn, Penzance'. Label recording ownership by Elizabeth J Ollerhead 1942. Old trees grow at left, reaching the upper edge, sunlight falling from the left on their leaves and branches; at right an earth path leads into the distance past a few cattle and more trees; the small area of sky is cloudy with blue patches. The site has been identified as Newland Hill. Bath Auctioneers, 24 May 2017 (50 illus); WHL, 17 May 2018 (50).

625 | ***The shop window*** | o/c 18 x 16; signed br in black, dated 1936. Two young girls in a red and a white dress stand with back to the viewer looking at boxes of fruit etc at a greengrocer's shop; the taller right girl wears a white dress and has her left arm round the neck of the shorter left girl; both wear sandals; in the foreground are tubs and vases of flowers and vegetables, showing rare use of sgraffito. The work is strongly coloured. Bonhams

identified the shop as Elsie Boulden's green-grocers in Jack Lane, Newlyn. PH, 2001 (99); BL, 2 July 2002 (20 illus); BL, 25 March 2003 (10 illus); WL.

626 | ***Study of a young girl*** | o/c 19 x 16; signed bl, dated 37. A girl with dark brown hair parted centrally sits on a chair facing the viewer, wearing a white dress; her arms are folded in her lap, and her legs and feet are bare; behind is a plain cream wall; the floor is mid-brown. CL, 29 June 1989 (43 illus).

627 | ***Portrait of a young girl*** | o/c 20 x 17; signed bl in red, dated 37. Head and shoulders of a teenager with brown hair and eyes, a red band in her hair, with a brown-purple shawl with delicate stripes over a white V-neck blouse, facing the viewer; the background is plain yellow. The girl has been identified by her daughter as Joan James. DL, 15 June 1988 (15 illus, as *Head of a girl*); WHL, 27 Mar 1990 (220 illus, as *Head and shoulder portrait of a young girl*); Taylor, Honiton, 19 Mar 1992 (33); PH, 2001 (100, as *Girl in a shawl*); BL, 21 Nov 2007 (116 illus, as *The brown eyed girl: Portrait of Joan James*).

628 | ***The letter*** | o/c 24 x 20; signed bl, dated 37. A woman with a horizontally striped green skirt stands centre facing left, her left hand resting on a rounded console table beside her; her right hand is outstretched holding a letter she is reading; the envelope is on the table; above the table is a large mirror in a heavy frame; at left is a small dog looking at the woman; at the right edge is a yellow-seated chair and a door frame; at the left edge is a door. The dog was a neighbour's and was called Murty. SL, 3 Nov 1982 (45 illus); PL, 10 Nov 1987 (97 illus); PL, 3 Mar 1998 (37 illus); CL, 7 June 2002 (74 illus); WL.

629 | ***The favourite necklace*** | o/c 25 x 30; signed br in red, dated 37. A young woman stands at right by a console table and a circular mirror, wearing a black cardigan and a long pink skirt, holding a single-string pearl neck-lace at her throat. WHL, 26 Feb 2004 (150 illus, as *The string of pearls*); SL, 25 Nov 2004 (418 illus).

630 | ***St Peter's Square, Newlyn*** | o/c 18 x 20; signed br in red, dated 37. The small shady space is enclosed by low buildings; at left stands a woman in white carrying a pail, with a white cat beside her; a washing line dries several white items; at right are two people by a single-storey building; beyond is a pink brick house with a man and a child walking past; the sky is pale blue, above a wooded hill in autumn colours. DMG, 2004.

631 | ***A wooded lane*** | o/c 20 x 16; signed br, dated 37. A lane leads into the picture, flanked by trees; at right a figure sits on a bank. DL, 12 Dec 1985 (399 illus, as *Summer sunlight, a man resting at the roadside*); CL, 12 June 1987 (123 illus, as *By the wayside*); SL, 1 Mar 1989 (42 illus); WHL, 27 Sep 1990 (55 illus, as *A rest by the wayside*); WL.

632 | ***Children by a stile*** | o/c 18 x 20; signed bl in red, dated 37. In the left foreground is a stone stile and a path leading across a meadow; at right are two children on the field wall; the left child lies prone and looks at the viewer; the right child sits looking left; beyond are gentle hills. DL, 26 July 1990 (546 illus).

633 | ***Farmstead among trees*** | o/c 19½ x 17½; signed bl in red, dated 37. Tall trees provide much of the subject matter, with a hint of early autumn in the colouring; below the trees are farm buildings; in the foreground a few cows grazing are watched by a man. Perhaps the same as *Farmstead, Drift*.

634 | *Tredavoe* | o/c 17½ x 19½; signed bl in red, dated 37. In the foreground is a sloping meadow with a few brown cows and a man seated at far left; in the centre are trees and houses; at right is a stream; the sky is grey. PH, 2001 (51).

635 | *Farm lad astride a pony* | o/c 18 x 20; signed bl, dated 37. A large horse moving left occupies most of the canvas, ridden by a young man in waistcoat and cap; behind is a landscape. DL, 17 Apr 1986 (329 illus).

636 | *The green boat* | o/b 22 x 24; signed, dated 37. PL, 23 Apr 1985 (27 ni).

637 | *Sailing Boats* | o/c 36 x 33; signed bl in red, dated 37. Several sailing and rowing boats on a blue sea; in the foreground are two toy boats, and in the background are two large yachts; at far left is St Michael's Mount.

638 | *Joan James* | o/c 35 x 30; dated 37. Half-length view of a girl standing facing us but looking right, leaning on a wood fence, in a white sleeveless blouse and a blue skirt; her right hand rests on her chest, her left hand is on the fence; behind are fields of many colours. The *Notebook* records 'Joan James 16 x 14'. The model was also painted by Dod Procter as *Girl in a chair* (*c.*1934) and *Blue* (1938); Joan James was born in 1923 and was later Joan Denton. *The Cornishman* in 1937 said "It ... portrays a girl simply dressed as the main subject of the picture, while the background is of hills". PEAG, March 1937; RA, 1937 (131).

639 | *Joan* | o/c 18 x 40; signed br in red, dated 37; inscr Joan on reverse. Head and shoulders frontal view of a young woman looking left, wearing a hair band, a blue blouse with white lace neck, and blue scarf with white spots.

640 | *The vision* | o/c; signed bl. A young woman with blonde hair, wearing a light blue dress sits facing us but looking left; both hands are raised level with her shoulders; at left are white lilies; at right is part of a lectern with a book; a bright light enters from the left. The *Notebook* records 'Vision'. *The Cornishman* of March 1937 reported "Another very effective piece of work is 'Vision', a study of a young woman with a startled expression on her face. This emotion is very well conveyed". RA, 1937 (621); PEAG, March 1937.

641 | *Drift farm* | perhaps the same as *Farmstead, Drift*. WAGB, 'Pictures of Cornwall and Devon by Modern Artists', 1937 (30, price £52-10s).

642 | *The brook, Lamorna* | o/c 22 x 19½; signed bl, dated 38. A stream runs towards the viewer; at left is a grassy bank; at right are trees and shrubs. This is a rare depiction of the Lamorna area, and was painted from the studio of S.J. Lamorna Birch. WHL, 15 Mar 1984 (130 illus); CL, 6 Mar 1986 (78 illus); WHL, 27 Mar 1990 (405 illus, as *Wooded stream, Lamorna*); WL.

643 | *St Michael's Mount from Marazion* | o/c 14 x 18; signed br, dated 1938. In the foreground are houses with a gate in a wall; a house fills much of the right edge; above is the Mount. WHL, 10 June 1977 (84 illus).

644 | *The market gardener* | o/c 20 x 18; signed bl in red, dated 38. Three-quarter length view of a man standing facing half-left, hands resting on the hoe handle, in a cap, grey pullover, yellow shirt with rolled sleeves and dark trousers. The model is Vivian Pearce who owned land in front of Maen Cottage. DL, 8 Oct 1998 (375 illus, as *The market gardener, in an anemone field*); DL, 18 Feb 1999 (52 illus, as before); CL, 4 June 1999 (234 illus).

645 | *John Humphreys* | o/c 30 x 25; dated 1938. Frontal head and shoulders of an elderly bald man in round glasses, with white moustache, wearing a dark jacket over waistcoat and white shirt; his right elbow rests on his desk, his hand on his jaw; on the desk is a silver container, a book(?), and a small animal's skull. Humphreys (1850–1937) was professor of dentistry. Commissioned by the University. University of Birmingham (A0.634).

646 | *Portrait of Mr Brash* | o/c 20 x 18; signed bl in red, dated 38. Head and shoulder view of a mature man facing us, with receding grey hair and a full face, wearing a brown jacket with white shirt and green tie; in the breast pocket is a dark green handkerchief; over his right lapel is a string securing a small object (eg monocle, watch or medal) obscured by the lower frame; the background is plain dark green. BL, 14 June 2005 (38 illus).

647 | *The young artist* | o/c 19 x 17; signed bl in red, dated 38. At left is a boy about eight years old with fair hair, facing right, in a pale brown cardigan, seated in a wood armchair at a circular dark wood table on which are a watercolour paint box, colouring book, a decorated mug, and magazines, the foremost of which is entitled 'Coal'; behind is a window with shrubs beyond; at tr is a green curtain and a chair back. *The Cornishman* 1938 described it as "… a simple domestic composition depicting a small boy with his box of paints intently painting, while [Harvey] has ingeniously conveyed the presence of the mother by a pair of hands knitting in the background". The painting has been altered in that originally at tr there was a female figure knitting, visible in *The Studio* illustration, that has been replaced by the back of a dining chair; it is not known who carried out this alteration. PEAG, Mar 1938; RA, 1938 (683); PEAG, summer 1941; *The Studio*, March 1942, p.70 (illus); WHL, 20 July 1974 (80).

648 | *Bog farm* | o/c 24 x 36; signed bl, dated 38. A row of buildings occupies the centre middle distance; in the foreground a path leads left among low trees; beyond the farm are hills with trees; a copse stands on the horizon at right. RA, 1938 (742); *The Studio*, March 1942, p.71 (illus); DL, 4 Dec 1986 (382 illus, as *Farm near Marazion*); SL, 2 Oct 1996 (35 illus, as *Farm in Marazion*).

649 | *A summer morning* | o/c 30 x 25; signed, dated 38. *The Cornishman* of March 1939 wrote: "It shows three girls on a sunlit flooded terrace after breakfast, with the blue of Mounts Bay stretching away in the distance". An unknown review said "poetry is less inherent in the subject, but what a matter-of-fact piece of prose most painters would have made of it and how many subtle undertones Mr Harvey has got into it". PEAG, Mar 1939; RA, 1939 (362); SL, 13 May 1992 (39).

650 | *The breakfast table* | o/c 30 x 25; signed bl in red, dated indis 38. On a terrace above Mounts Bay, at left a woman stands leaning against a round column, facing right and in a pale dress, her left hand behind her head and her right hand holding a tea cup; at right is a round table with green legs, set with a blue and white checked cloth, tea things and a vase of yellow flowers; behind it sits a young woman in a blue dress, her left hand resting on the table; a parrot perches on her right hand; in the foreground a girl in a white dress sits on the threshold, facing left and holding a tea cup in both hands; the terrace is decorated with foliage and flowers. The setting is the porch of Maen Cottage. RA, 1939 (362); F&R, 1946 (reproduced in reverse, as *Tea-Time Newlyn*). SL, 5 Mar 1997 (32 illus); WL.

651 | *My kitchen* | RHA 1938 (171).

652 | *Farmstead, Drift* | RHA, 1938 (184).

653 | *Ancilla Domini* | oil. An unknown review said "a rustic version of the Annunciation in much the same manner as Dod Procter [a reference to her *Blue*], is more sensitive in attitude and gesture and less sensitive in colour and modelling". RA, 1938 (378).

654 | *The yellow blouse* | o/c 19¼ x 15; signed bl, dated 39. A young girl with blonde hair faces the viewer, in a pinkish jacket open over a yellow blouse, both with large buttons; the background is plain dark brown. The sitter has been identified as Betty Pollard. PL, 23 Apr 1985 (31 illus); CL, 13 Nov 1986 (48 illus); CSK, 18 Dec 2012 (120 illus); *The Cornishman*, 10 July 2014; WL.

655 | *Kitchen interior* | o/c 20 x 20; signed bl in red, dated 39. In the kitchen of Maen Cottage, Gertrude stands at left in a red headscarf, yellow and green striped skirt, and pale green blouse, leaning against the dresser; before her stands a young girl with reddish hair in a blue blouse and dark skirt holding in both hands a basket of produce; many kitchen utensils and chinaware are shown on shelves; the kitchen is filled with sunlight from an unseen window at far right. DMG 2024.

656 | *The garden seat* | o/c 20 x 18; signed br in red, dated 39. A girl facing left sits on a blue backless bench sited on grass, in a white dress, her hands on the bench; by her right foot is a basket of greenery; behind are flowers and a piece of wall. The same girl, bench and basket also appear in *Allotments* (1939). SL, 27 Mar 1991 (56 illus); Messum's, Dec 2018; WL.

657 | *Cornish lane* | o/c 16 x 12; signed bl, dated 39. A sunlit view of a country path leading into the middle distance between hedges and trees; behind is a red field being worked. SL 30 Apr 1986 (480 illus, as *A country lane*); WHL, 30 July 1987 (320 illus).

658 | *Farm at Tredavoe* | o/c 18 x 20; signed bl, dated 1939. At left a vast tree in leaf spreads over sunlit farm buildings; at centre a metal barred gate leads away from a grassy meadow; at right a cow stands by a building. PL, 8 Mar 1988 (7 illus); P. Exeter, 30 Mar 1994 (559, as *Tredavoe farm Cornwall*, as 18 x 19); CL, 21 Mar 1996 (36 illus, as *Tredavoe farm, Newlyn*, in a frame hand painted by the artist).

659 | *Girl in a red dress* | o/c 18 x 14; signed bl, in black, dated 39. A full length view of a young girl in a pale red dress and sandals walking up a set of stone stairs; she moves left and faces us; she carries a bag with a white towel over her left shoulder; at far right part of a young man is seen following her up the stairs; the sky is pale blue. This figures also appears in smaller scale in the expansive beach scene of *August 1939* (1940).

660 | *Mousehole* | o/c 18 x 20; signed br in

dark brown, dated 39. A sunlit view along the western harbour mole, facing east; several small boats are moored in the harbour at left; at right a simple crane is working; beyond, on the headland several buildings catch the sun, a hill rising behind them. Gorringes, Lewes, 29 Nov 2005 (2535); CL, 7 June 2007 (144 illus); Barnes Thomas, Penzance, 14 Feb 2011 (71 illus); BL, 23 June 2015 (109 illus).

661 | *Newlyn harbour* | o/c 12 x 16; signed bl, dated 39. Several men look towards the market building at right, with boats alongside; beyond, the town rises up the hill; at far left is an iron gate with a boat beyond; the sky is cloudy; the work is loosely painted. PL, 12 Nov 1985 (88 ni); PL, 28 Jan 1986 (50 illus); WHL, 4 May 2000 (200 illus, as *Newlyn harbour and fish market*); WHL, 24 Apr 2001 (275, as *Newlyn fishmarket and harbour*); WHL, 15 Dec 2016 (175 illus, as *The fish market, Newlyn harbour*).

662 | *Washing fish boxes, Newlyn* | o/c 22 x 20; signed br in red, dated 39. The Newlyn stream flows towards us down the centre of the canvas; in the distance a man washes boxes in the water; beyond is a building with a horse and cart standing before it. SL, 1 Oct 1997 (18 illus); PH, 2001 (86); CL, 7 June 2002 (62 illus, as 22 x 20); DMG, spring 2009 (12 illus, as *Washing fish boxes, Newlyn River*); WL.

663 | *Boy on a donkey* | o/c 14 x 18; signed bl in red, dated 39. In a green meadow a young boy sits on a pale brown donkey walking right, his left hand on the reins and his right on his hip; at left another donkey follows; beyond are several small white houses and at far right is a very tall thin building; on the horizon are brown hills; the sky is blue-grey. Seen by Bonhams New York, late 2016.

664 | *Butterflies* | RHA, 1939 (30).

665 | *Tin miners* | o/c 40 x 30; signed br in red, dated 1939. Two young men stand in the foreground, wearing helmets with lamps. The left man is frontal, with a pipe in his mouth and a roll of wire over his right arm; the right man faces left in profile with his left hand in his pocket, and his right hand on his right lapel. Behind are mine buildings. The figures are Sidney Angrove (right) and Nicholas Grenfell (left). RA, 1939 (383). BL, 25 Jan 2012 (173 illus).

666 | *Allotments* | oil; signed bl. In the left foreground a woman picks beans, and at right a man stands leaning on an implement; before them sits a girl facing left, in a pale dress; beyond is a distant landscape. There were allotments just below Maen Cottage. *The Cornishman* in March 1939 reported "The whole composition of 'Allotments' is an extraordinarily fine piece of work. The drawing of the three figures who occupy the centre of the picture is very well done, while the draughtsmanship shown in the drawing of the patchwork of allotments in the background calls for special praise". An early stage of this work in Harvey's studio is illustrated in *Picture Post*, 15 Oct 1938. The same girl, bench and basket also appear in *The garden seat* (1939). PEAG, Mar 1939; RA, 1939 (625); *RAI*, 1939, p.9 (illus).

667 | *Portrait of Michael Spring* | o/c 23½ x 19; signed br, dated 1940. Head and upper torso view of a young man with thick hair facing half left; his hands hold the lapels of his open jacket. He is shown aged about 17, and is the second son of writer (Robert) Howard Spring (1889–1965) whose famous novel *Fame is the spur* was published in 1940. The Spring family lived at Mylor, near Falmouth, at this time. Michael lodged with the Harveys in Newlyn while taking painting lessons from Dod Procter. PH, 2001 (45).

668 | *Portrait of a girl in riding dress* | o/c 19½ x 17½; signed br, dated 1940. Full length portrait of a girl facing left, standing by a bay window; her left hand is in her pocket, the right hand holds a whip; her right leg is bent at the knee, the foot resting on a chair. WHL, 7 Oct 1977 (34 illus).

669 | *The onion boy* | o/c 24 x 20; signed br in red, dated 1940. A half-length portrait filling the height of the canvas; a teenage boy faces the viewer in black beret and dark blue jersey with short sleeves; he stands by a railing with a string of onions over his right shoulder; behind is the harbour at Newlyn with several boats. The model has been identified as an evacuee, Samuel Richard Kemp (1927–1996). PL, 23 Apr 1985 (42 illus, prov a wedding gift to the owner from Harvey's widow).

670 | *A balcony, Penzance* | o/c 24 x 18; signed bl, dated 1940. A view onto a stone balcony, a blue door at left; the balcony has a column at left, and a circular table and chair; a cat sits on the threshold; beyond is the harbour and St Michael's Mount. The setting is the same as in *The blue door, Newlyn* (1934) and *The breakfast table* (1938). SL, 13 Nov 1985 (123 illus); WL.

671 | *An old street in Newlyn* | o/c 23½ x 19¾; signed bl, dated 1940. A view down the hill, flanked at right by a terrace of creamy yellow houses; at left a man leans on a low stone wall; in the distance is the harbour. The houses are still there, and Harvey has shown them in morning sunshine. DL, 12 Dec 1985 (397 illus); SWS, 25 June 1986 (555 illus, as *Old Paul Hill, Newlyn*); PL, 15 Nov 1988 (51 illus).

672 | *Newlyn harbour* | o/c 30 x 16; signed bl, dated 1940. At right a tree rises the full height of the canvas and frames a view of Newlyn harbour; the south pier and lighthouse are visible; in the foreground is sloping ground with a man leaning on a hoe. PH, 1993 (67 illus); DL, 27 Oct 2016 (380, as *Looking down to Newlyn harbour*).

673 | *August 1939* | oil 70 x 60; signed bl, dated 1940. A beach scene with eight figures in the foreground; a girl in a red dress walks up the stone stairs to the promenade above, with more figures standing. RA, 1940 (348); *RAI*, 1940, p.72 (illus).

674 | *The corner pool, Lamorna* | o/c 23 x 19; signed, dated 1940. A stream flows up the centre of the picture, flanked at left by trees on the bank. The *Notebook* records 'The corner pool, 20 x 24'. DL, 5 Oct 1989 (532 illus); DL, 14 Dec 1989 (181 ni); DL, 31 July 2008 (207 illus).

675 | *The gate* | o/c 24 x 21; signed 'H Harvey' in red, dated 1940. In the foreground is a white wooden garden gate; it is joined at left by red chain-link mesh; behind are white houses and gardens with trees; the lower half of the gate is in shadow but the rest of the scene is sunny. NSA, summer 1941. *PCF: C&SI*, p.191 (illus); WL. Royal Cornwall Museum, Truro (1941.78), acquired 5 Nov 1941, presented by NSA and friends of Harold Harvey.

676 | *In the garden* | o/c 20 x 16; signed br, dated 1940. A full-length view of a young woman in pale clothes and red headscarf, sitting with knees bent in a flowery garden; she reads a book on her lap. PH, 2001 (98).

677 | *Apple blossom* | o/c 20 x 15; signed in red br, dated 1940. In a grassy meadow a single tree stands laden with white blossom; above is a thin strip of blue sky. Probably exhibited Newlyn 1945, where noted by *The Cornishman* of 29 March. SL, 17 Dec 2015 (70 illus).

678 | *Sleeping cat* | o/c 16 x 18; signed, dated 1940. DL, 12 Oct 2004 (454 illus).

679 | *Ailsa* | oil. RA, 1940 (659). The *Notebook* records 'Ailsa'. Probably a portrait of Ailsa Morley Rae, who married Harold's nephew Raymond Vigurs Harvey in the summer of 1937.

680 | *Bridge over a river in a Cornish village* | o/c 20 x 18; signed, dated 1941. PL, 9 Jan 1987 (279).

681 | *Mine workings* | o/c 18 x 20; signed, dated 1941. In the foreground are two mine pumps; the background is fields and hills with a blue sky. PH, 2001 (97).

682 | *The fishing wharf, Newlyn* | o/c 18 x 18; signed bl in red, dated 1941(?). A busy scene with several figures; at left two men carry a full basket of fish, and a man sits on a wall beside a full basket; at right a group of men stand talking; at far right is part of a brown horse; beyond is a wharf with a covered wooden walkway; many seagulls overlay the scene; in the distance is the hill above Newlyn, with a thin strip of cloudy sky; four boats lie on the calm harbour water. DMG 2024.

683 | *The Mantelpiece* | o/c 14 x 10; signed br in red, dated 1941. The white mantelpiece of the sitting room at Maen Cottage; above is a facetted mirror; above the copper fire-cover hangs a small white (cameo?) portrait on a blue ground, set on a grey mount; on the mantelshelf are two green glass candlesticks and a large plain glass candleholder, and two small items; at right a colourful ceramic figurine stands on a low cupboard, beside a large vertical plate; the walls are white. The mirror and both types of candlestick, the figurine and the cameo all appear in earlier paintings by Harvey. Known to have been owned by Wallace Nichols until his death 1967.

684 | *Joan* | oil. Perhaps a portrait of Joan Manning-Sanders or Joan James. RA, 1941 (34); RGI, 1941 (93).

685 | *A window in Newlyn* | oil. *The Cornishman* of 6 May 1941 recorded "… a mother and her young child sitting at a window with a rainbow across the middle background. The woman is sewing and the child playing. Both are absorbed in their interests." RA, 1941 (135).

UNDATED WORKS

Listed in alphabetical order with estimated dates where possible.

1 | *A boy and two horses* | o/c 14½ x 17½; signed bl. A boy on a dark horse moving left, with a white horse on his far side; at left is a gabled farm building. DL, 6 June 1996 (145 illus).

2 | *A Cornish landscape* | WP, 8 June 1920 (81).

3 | *A girl in a red dress* | o/c 19 x 15; signed, perhaps mid-1930s. Head and shoulder view of a young woman in a sleeveless blouse with wide-open collar, looking left, her arms folded. The *Notebook* records 'The Red Dress (Joan) 20 x 16'. SL, 1 Mar 1989 (76 illus); WHL, 12 July 1990 (209 ni, as *Portrait of a girl in a red dress*); Tennants, Leyburn 22 Nov 2002 (746 illus, as *Portrait of a woman half length in a red* *blouse)*; WL.

4 | *A seated gentleman* | pencil sketch 18½ x 11½. DL, 6 Oct 1988 (29 ni).

5 | *A sheltered corner* | WP, 8 June 1920 (75).

6 | *After a storm* | o/c 25 x 30; signed br in black; 1930s. Damaged trees in a park-landscape, and farm buildings in the distance at right. CL, 28 Nov 1996 (75 illus).

7 | *An afternoon walk* | o/c 20 x 18; signed. A woman walks away from us in a white dress and black hat and shawl, along a rural path with hedges at left and trees at right; the sky is blue. Bamfords, Derby, 13 Oct 2010 (1322 illus).

8 | *April showers* | WP, 8 June 1920 (91).

9 | *At the watering hole* | o/c 16 x 12; signed bl. In the foreground a boy on a white horse moving towards us rides through a pool; behind at left are more horses, and beyond them are trees and buildings. SL, 13 May 1992 (1); PH, 2001 (24).

10 | *Betty, Countess of Denbigh* | o/c size not known (portrait format). Said to be of *c.*1931 or 1936. Wife of the 10th Earl Denbigh. A lady seated turned half-left on an armchair and looking at us, with both hands on her lap; she wears a shimmering open blouse over a long black dress with v-neck, and silver shoes and long earrings; behind at left is a large oriental cupboard and at right a round-back chair; on the floor are two patterned rugs, the right one in bright colours; the walls are plain whiteish with deep skirting boards.

11 | *Blackberry harvest* | WP, 8 June 1920 (116).

12 | *Blowing dandelions* | o/c 18 x 16¼; signed br; indis date; *c.*1902. In the foreground a young girl sits on a grassy hillside, facing left, in a white smock over a black dress and with a red bow tied to her left plait; to the left sits another child wearing a blue striped hat and blue jacket; behind lies a distant landscape of fields and hills. CL, 9 June 1988 (13 illus).

13 | *Bubbles* | WP, 8 June 1920 (15).

14 | *By the sea* | o/c 22 x 26; signed. A different size to the 1917 work of this title. BL, 1 May 1975 (27 ni).

15 | *Children on the quay, Newlyn* | o/c 15 x 18, early style. In the foreground at left a boy in a white shirt sits facing half-right, his left leg outstretched with bare foot, pulling a sock onto his right foot; at right a young girl in a white cap and red shirt under a dark dress leans against something, looking left at the boy; in the middle distance are several figures along the quay edge; at tl is the lighthouse and at tr the Old Quay. DL, 17 Apr 1986 (322 illus, as *Children on the beach*); PL, 8 Mar 1988 (5 illus).

16 | *Children swinging on the gate* | o/c 16 x 18; signed br. In bright sunshine three children play with a five-bar gate. At left a girl in a red dress over a white blouse faces right, pushing the gate open; another girl in white dress and bonnet sits on the top bar; at right a boy in a blue shirt leans over the top bar. Behind is Mounts Bay with St Michael's Mount at right. The girl in red is similar to that in other paintings of 1912–14. This may be *The gate* recorded in 1912. Gorringe's, Lewis, 7 Dec 2011 (2177).

17 | *Cornish cottages* | o/c 14½ x 17½; signed bl in red; *c.*1905 or earlier. At right is a row of cottages in sunlight; in a doorway a woman in pink dress and red cap stands knitting and a young girl sits in the road before her; at left, in the distance, are a woman at a pump and a man standing. PH, 2001 (39).

18 | *Cows above Newlyn* | o/c 12 x 16; signed.

In a green meadow stand four cows facing left; the foreground cow is white and black; beyond at left a brown and white cow is seen from the rear; beyond at right are two brown and white cows; the sky is cloudy with blue patches. DL, 27 Oct 2016 (138).

19 | *Daffodils* | o/c 30 x 25; signed. A larger work than the 1917 and 1927 works of this title. Debenham Coe, London, 10 May 1972 (45).

20 | *Daffodils* | o/c 32 x 26; signed br. In a sunny meadow with many flowering white and yellow daffodils, a young woman with light hair stands wearing a pale blue blouse and a white apron; her left hand holds a bunch of white flowers, her right hand touches her forehead; before her at far left is a basket with many cut flowers; behind at left is a woman in a pink blouse kneeling, and another woman standing in blue clothes; in the distance the trees are bare. This may be the *Daffodils* recorded by Debenham & Coe in 1972 (45). RGG.

21 | *Daisies* | signed br; *c.*1902. In the foreground centre, a young girl in white dress, bare feet, sits in shade on a pebble shore; behind at left, in sunshine, are girls in yellow and red dresses; in the distance is blue sea with a rowing boat at tr. Wortley, p.282 (illus).

22 | *Family with an accordion* | o/c 36 x 30; not signed, dated or titled. On a rocky hilltop a family rests; at left a woman with a baby sits on a boulder; at right a man in a hat plays a green accordion; two girls are beside the man and a boy lies of the grass, playing with a dog; behind is a large landscape of hills and mine workings; further is a slice of sea.

23 | *Feeding chickens* | o/c 16 x 12; signed bl; *c.*1912. In the right foreground a man in a cap and white shirt, facing left, holds a bowl in his left hand; with his right hand he gives food to a chicken and many chicks; beyond a girl sits on a picket fence; at left is a farmhouse with two chimney stacks. PL, 13 Nov 1984 (59 illus, prov QH); WL.

24 | *Feeding time* | o/c 12 x 16, early style; signed bl. In a sunny meadow a young man at left wearing a pointed cap and white shirt sits on an upturned basket; before him is a trough into which he pours feed from a metal pail; several pigs eat at the trough and more approach from centre-right. WHL, 6 Oct 2011 (200, as of 1906); SL, 10 May 2012 (53); WL.

25 | *Figures on The Cliff, Newlyn* | o/c 12 x 16; signed bl, in black. At left a man approaches carrying a fish in his left hand, an oar over his right shoulder; at right two men lean over a metal railing beside a rising road; beyond are buildings. CL, 11 July 2013 (107 illus, originally as *Figures on a quay, Mousehole*); CL, 23 Nov 2017 (108 illus).

26 | *Fine morning, Sennen* | o/c 24 x 31½; signed br. An extensive view of the beach at Whitesand Bay, with Aire Point on the horizon; in the foreground, seagulls walk on the sand or fly over the surf.

27 | *Flowers before a window* | o/p 6 x 4; a pair, each signed. DL, 2 Sep 1987 (156 ni); DL, 14 Dec 1989 (83 ni); DL, 29 Mar 1990 (134 ni).

28 | *Four fishing boats in harbour* | o/c; signed bl, in black. At left are four boats, two numbered PZ476 and (indis) PZ206.

29 | *Friendly overtures* | WP, 8 June 1920 (121).

30 | *Gathering snowdrops* | o/c 19¾ x 23¾, early style; signed bl. Three girls in an open woodland; the right girl wears a purple smock

over a pale blouse, holding a basket on her left arm, her two hands clasping a small bunch of flowers; the centre girl has a red hat (or red hair?) lies on the ground leaning on her elbows, hands cupping her face, looking at the left girl; the left girl has a pale smock over an olive-brown dress and sits on the ground looking at the centre girl. Perhaps MG, 1913 (as *First snowdrops of the year*); SC, 12 July 1985 (3301).

31 | *Gertrude Harvey* | pencil 14 x 19; signed bl. Full length standing view facing right, head down, hands behind back, left leg crossed over the right, in head band and light clothes; there is no background. PL, 6 June 2000 (204 illus).

32 | *Gertrude in the garden* | o/cb 9½ x 13½; signed bl. This sketch may be related to *Portrait of the artist's wife* (1916). A woman seated in a deck chair, with a blue hat and green dress, facing right, with foliage behind; painted loosely. SWS, 23 May 1989 (588 illus).

33 | *Girl at prayer* | pencil drawing on paper 10 x 6; not signed. A three-quarter length view of a girl standing facing slightly left, hands raised and palms together as in prayer, eyes open; she wears a short-sleeved dress with a collar; her hair reaches just below her ears. The girl resembles the foremost girl in *A May procession* (1935), and this may be a preparatory sketch. On the reverse is a pencil sketch of *Treriefe*, a house near Newlyn (QV). Bearnes, Hampton & Littlewood, Exeter, 9 Oct 2018 (393 illus).

34 | *Girl in a green scarf* | signed br. Head and shoulders view of a girl with an oval face and curly hair facing our right; she wears a green scarf over a grey top; behind her is part of a chair rail.

35 | *Girl in a landscape* | o/c 11 x 17; signed bl, in black, *c.*1910. A woman standing right faces the viewer, her left hand on hip, holding a bucket in her right hand; at left is a white and black horse; behind it is a fire with figures round it and a gypsy caravan. Whitford Fine Art.

36 | *Girl in a meadow* | o/c 21 x 17. PL, 16 May 1986 (249).

37 | *Girl with goats, Newlyn* | o/c 25 x 30; signed bl, indis date 90(?). In a meadow overlooking the dark blue sea, a young woman stands at right facing right, holding in her arms a kid goat; a young goat stands by her right foot, and an older goat stands at left.

38 | *Girl with goats* | o/c 15 x 18; signed bl, *c.*1905. In a meadow overlooking the dark blue sea, a young woman stands at right facing right, holding in her arms a kid goat; a young goat stands by her right foot, and an older goat stands at left. This appears to be a smaller version of *Girl with goats, Newlyn*. The woman is Adeline Mary Harvey; given by the artist to her. CL, 11 Mar 1994 (1 illus); WL.

39 | *Gretchen at the duckpond* | o/c 15 x 18; signed bl, inscr with title on the frame, *c.*1902. Probably painted at Tredavoe duck pond. At right a young girl in a purple dress sits on the stream bank facing left, watching ducks swimming. Mentioned in the *Western Daily Mercury* of 23 Aug 1912 as "a favourite subject delicately interpreted." HSG, Aug 1912 (18, as *Gretchen at the duck pond*); SL, 11 Nov 1987 (21 illus, as *Gretcha at the duck pond*); Messum's (88 illus, as *Greta at the duckpond*); WL.

40 | *Grey autumn, Mousehole* | o/b 20½ x 28; signed. WHL, 28 Nov 1978 (231 ni).

41 | *Half portrait of an attractive young lady*
o/c 19 x 15; signed. WHL, 5 Dec 1989 (243 ni).
42 | *Harrowing* | o/c 12 x 16; signed bl, *c.*1912; title inscr on the stretcher. At right a man in a white hat and shirt and dark clothes follows two brown horses moving left pulling a harrow; crows fly over the field; beyond are fields and trees below a dark grey sky. PL, 13 Nov 1984 (61 illus, prov QH); PL, 2 June 1992 (25 illus); BL, 30 Nov 2004 (9 illus); WL.
43 | *Harvest time* | o/c 12 x 16; signed br; title inscr on stretcher. CL, 20 June 1996 (59).
44 | *Haulers on a country road, Newlyn* | o/c 30 x 36. Apparently not signed; *c.*1920. A rutted road with telegraph poles occupies the centre foreground and rises towards us; a cart pulled by two horses led by a man, with a dog alongside, comes up the hill; another cart follows; both carts carry a white cargo; at left is a field with a stone gate pillar; the scene is sunlit but wintry, the trees leafless, and signs of snow on the road; in the background fields rise up the opposite slope of the valley, a hamlet at left; the sky is cloudy with blue patches. CL, 5 Mar 1999 (77 illus, prov sold CL, 10 Dec 1926 (19) for £26-5s).
45 | *Homewards, Buryas bridge* | o/c 12 x 14; *c.*1908. A full stream occupies the left foreground; at right a man on a white horse moves away left; a dog follows by the nearside rear hoof; they have just passed a white gate by which a figure stands at right. DMG, 1988 (99 illus).
46 | *How tempting* | WP, 8 June 1920 (129).
47 | *In the stable yard* | o/c 14 x 12; signed bl. A man on a white horse moving right; farm buildings are behind and at right; beyond are trees. LWG, Mar 1982 (37 illus); CL, 15 Apr 1981 (202 ni, as *Horseman in farmyard*).
48 | *In the whiting grounds* | o/c 30 x 24; signed br, *c.*1900. In a small dinghy at sea, seen stern on, a young man facing left stands at the stern with line in his hands; an older man with beard and pale jersey leans against the starboard side with a line in his hands; behind him an oar lies over the side; the stern is inscribed PZ532; there are sailing boats at tl. BBC Antiques Roadshow, Barnstable, Oct 2000; *Homes & Antiques*, Nov 2000, p.69 (illus); PH, 2001 (1); *PCF: C&SI*, p.112 (illus); Hardie, p.102 (illus); Wallace, p.64 (illus); 'Amongst heroes', London, 2013; *Amongst heroes*, p.17 (illus). Penlee House Museum & Gallery (2006.18).
49 | *Interior study of a young girl sitting on a wooden Cornish window seat* | o/c 14 x 17; signed. Peter Wilson, Nantwich 30 April 2003 (56).
50 | *Interior* | o/b 18 x 22; signed br. A bowl of mainly yellow flowers upon a table before an open window looking onto a tiled roof. Perhaps RA, 1935 (410); SL, 22 July 1987 (13 illus).
51 | *Jug of spring flowers* | o/c 19 x 15; signed. WHL, 5 Oct 2006 (35).
52 | *Landing the catch* | o/c 12 x 18; signed bl, said to be dated but none given. Many figures occupy the right foreground; at left is a dinghy; in the distance is a sailing boat and at right the Nor'rad Slip. DMG, autumn 1974 (30 illus).
53 | *Lands End* | o/b 21½ x 18; signed. In the foreground is a rocky headland, the sea at left; at tr is a suggestion of the Longships lighthouse. WHL, 6 Apr 1978 (221 illus); WHL, 4 Dec 1980 (382 ni).
54 | *Lilac doll* | o/c 15 x 18; signed bl, *c.*1904.

Plymouth Gallery label on reverse. Three children in a meadow; at left foreground sits a young girl with plaits, in cap, blue coat and purple skirt, sits on the grass looking out; her left hand holds the lilac doll; behind, at right, are two other girls, one in blue clothes sitting with flowers in her hands, the other lying with face cupped in her hands. The *Western Daily Mercury* of 23 Aug 1912 said "We do not quite like the drawing of the little maidens in 'The Lilac Doll' but have no doubt they are just as the artist saw them judging by his faithfulness to nature in the other works." HSG, Aug 1912 (22); DL, 15 June 2000 (570 illus); Hardie, p.13 (illus in Lays advert); SL, 15 Dec 2016 (51 illus, as *The lilac doll*).
55 | *Little brother* | o/c 14 x 18; *c.*1905–12. At right a girl in a white smock over a dark dress and with a blue ribbon in her hair faces left holding a small child with blonde hair and pale dress who is eating something; at left a child with a red headscarf watches them; behind are indications of a house. The Court House, West Quantoxhead, 2012.
56 | *Looking inland: a view near Penzance* o/c 15¾ x 21¾; signed, 1920s; inscr on the stretcher. A path leads out of a field through an open gate, past trees at right, into a distant landscape of fields. SL, 14 July 1982 (30 illus); WL.
57 | *Low tide* | o/p 19 x 24. Bearnes, Torquay, 1 Sep 1989 (294).
58 | *Low tide with vessel 'We'll Try', Newlyn harbour* | o/b 19 x 24; not signed, inscr verso 'Harold Harvey, given to Mrs Mary Parker of Baycliffe by Oliver Hall of Bardsea 1954'. A small fishing boat with blue sides over a red keel and orange cabin, inscribed PZ198 on her bow, is hauled up onto the beach, seen bow-on; at left is a white rowing boat and 3 seagulls; behind at left is a larger ship's bow; at far right is a small boat; in the distance are buildings; the sky is cloudy. Lane's notes say 'We'll Try' was registered PZ198 and based at Newlyn; Oliver Hall (1869–1957) was a painter and etcher, RA, 1927, Senior Academician 1945. WHL, 13 Sep 2018 (100 illus).
59 | *Madonna of the bridges* | Fox/Greenacre, p.83 (ni), which describes it as in neo-Renaissance style showing a madonna and child with Newlyn Coombe in the background.
60 | *Man with cap* | pencil sketch on paper *c.*15 x 19. Three-quarter length view of a man facing half-left, in a buttoned jacket, seated with his left hand on knee; he smokes a cigarette; the head is the most detailed area. PL, 6 June 2000 (202 ni).
61 | *Mending the nets, Newlyn* | o/c 14 x 17; signed bl, *c.*1909. A man sits on a lobster pot with his back to the viewer; at right another man holds a red-brown net; at left a man in a white smock sits on the rim of a dinghy; behind is a harbour scene. BAL (TAY45180, as *Newlyn harbour: mending the nets*); DL, 17 Apr 1986 (321 illus, as *Fishermen mending nets at Newlyn*); CL, 5 Mar 1987 (44 illus); WL.
62 | *Midge Bruford and fiancé, Coombe Hill, Newlyn* | o/c 28 x 24½; signed bl in red, early 1920s. In the foreground a woman in a white dress stands this side of a broad metal gate, her back to the viewer and facing right; on the other side of the gate, a man in dark clothes stands at left and faces the woman; beyond are many trees rising up the hillside, with blue sky above; the top frame intersects two patches

of foliage. Marjorie Frances Bruford was a close friend of Mornie Birch, and was known as Midge. She attended the Harvey-Procter School from August 1923. She was painted by Dod Procter as *Indolence* (RA 1932, no.643). The fiancé was the artist Richard Copeland Weatherby (1881–1953), who exhibited at RA, NEAC and Alpine Gallery 1922–1953; he lived several years in Cornwall, and was of the famous horse racing family. PL, 14 June 1988 (16 illus); Sworder, Bishops Stortford, 11 June 2002 (1252); CL, 21 Nov 2003 (35 illus); BL, 14 Nov 2006 (221 illus, as *Midge Bruford and her fiancé at Chywoone Hill, Newlyn*).
63 | *Monnow mill* | o/c 20 x 26; signed bl, in red, perhaps 1930s. A calm stream flows in the foreground, the left bank filled with trees; a weir breaches the right bank and behind is the mill house; at the right edge are tall trees. The river Monnow flows through Monmouth, and this work was perhaps done at the same time as *The poplars, Monmouth*. Reproduced by F&R, 1939.
64 | *Mother and child* | o/c 14 x 12; signed, indis dated, *c.*1905. A woman sits on a field wall facing left, in a blue blouse and white apron, holding a child on her lap; the child faces the viewer and wears a whitish bonnet and clothing; behind is a green meadow with trees. SL, 11 Mar 1992 (31).
65 | *Mother and child* | o/c 23 x 19. CL, 25 Jan 1978 (79).
66 | *Mother and child* | o/c 27 x 20; signed bl, in black. At left a young woman in a green dress leans over an awake baby lying in a cradle with finials at head and foot and a pitched roof at the head; the cradle covers are white; behind are shadowy indications of a room, and perhaps the parents' bed; the colours are mostly dark brown. The woman resembles that in *Tired out*. SL, 3 July 2002 (10 illus); Online Gallery, June 2008 (as *At the end of the day*); BL, 19 November 2008 (28 illus).
67 | *Mrs Algernon Newton* | o/p 8 x 4½; signed br, *c.*1913. A half-length figure facing slightly right, in an olive-green dress, reading a book held in both hands. The sitter was the first wife of Algernon Cecil Newton (1880–1968) who was a successful landscape painter (RA, 1943); he married Marjorie Emelia Balfour Rider in 1903, and their four children included Robert Guy Newton (1905–1956), a famous actor. In 1918 Newton lived at Bodrigy, near Lamorna. PH, 2001 (101).
68 | *Newlyn harbour looking towards Penzance* | o/b 12 x 13¾; signed bl, in black, perhaps *c.*1900. In the foreground a small steam ship lies within the Old Quay; beyond are sailing ships moored in calm waters; the dominant colour is the pale blue water. PL, 17 June 1997 (8 illus); WL.
69 | *Newlyn old harbour* | o/c 11½ x 15½; undated. At right is the old quay, with Penzance fishing boats in the foreground; beyond is Tolcarne and the Lidden. WHL, 22 Oct 1976 (100 illus).
70 | *On the front, Newlyn* | WP, 8 June 1920 (5).
71 | *On the quayside* | o/c 14 x 17; signed bl. In the foreground is a brown horse in a cart with red shafts; a boy sits on the driving seat, holding the reins, talking to a young woman standing at left, who wears a yellow blouse, black skirt and white apron; she holds a large child in her arms; beyond is a harbour, and at right three men lean against railings; the sky

is blue; the brush strokes are fluid, sometimes thickly applied. SL, 4 July 2001 (5 illus); SL, 10 May 2012 (54, as *The quayside, Newlyn*).

72 | *Paul, near Penzance* | o/c 18 x 22; signed bl, in brown. At bl, a brown and white calf grazes at the edge of a lane; behind it a man lying on the wall-hedge talks to a woman with a blue blouse in the lane with a child in blue clothes beside her; beyond her is an older man; at tl is the tower of Paul church; the sky is pale blue. Church Street Gallery, Stow on the Wold, 1979; SL, 13 Dec 2005 (70 illus).

73 | *Picking cauliflowers* | o/c 20 x 18; signed bl, *c.*1914. In a field of cauliflowers, at right is a horse and two-wheeled cart being loaded by two figures; at left a man carries a laden basket on his back toward the cart; in the distance are fields and farmhouses; the cloudy sky fills more than half the picture. PL, 14 June 1988 (15 illus); DMG, 1988 (98 illus).

74 | *Picking daffodils* | o/c 17½ x 13¾; signed br in black, *c.*1910–12. At left stands a young girl in a white dress and green bonnet holding a basket laden with flowers; at right her mother(?) in a white dress and red head-scarf bends down to pick them; white and yellow daffodils are all around them. SL, 27 June 2006 (70 illus); RGG, May 2008 (SP4391, as *Spring in the orchard, narcissus*, as *c.*1912).

75 | *Playtime at Carnyorth near St Just, Cornwall* | o/c 14 x 12; signed. Four girls are by a path; the left girl has a skipping rope; in front a girl half lies on the grass; at right stand two others; beyond are houses. WHL, 9 June 2005 (70 illus); WHL, 17 May 2007 (380 illus).

76 | *Ploughing* | o/c 11 x 17. Bearnes, Exeter, 4 July 2006 (363).

77 | *Ploughing* | 25¼ x 30. Perhaps the same as *Ploughing* (1921). PL, 18 Sep 1990 (26).

78 | *Polperro* | WP, 8 June 1920 (80).

79 | *Portrait of a girl* | Head and shoulder view of a girl facing left with shoulder-length brown hair and a dark dress or jacket with white markings. BAL (JDV37138).

80 | *Portrait of a woman reading* | o/c 22 x 17¾; signed br in red, late 1930s. At left a woman in a green dress and red neck scarf sits facing right reading a book open on her lap; above her is a mirror reflecting her head; at right a tankard holding brushes is on a window sill, suggesting she is an artist or a model; through the window is a yellowish house. On the verso is *Woman in an armchair*, similar to the recto work. PL, 10 Mar 1987 (35 illus); PL, 15 Sep 1987 (36 ni); DL, 2 June 1994 (300 illus, as *Gertrude reading*); PH, 2001 (56, as *Gertrude Harvey – the artist's wife*); WHL, 14 July 2011 (80 illus, as *Gertrude Harvey seated by the studio window reading a book*).

81 | *Portrait study of a lady in red* | o/c 20 x 15; signed; perhaps mid-1930s. Perhaps related to *A girl in a red dress*. Biddle & Wells, Birmingham, 1 May 1992 (406b).

82 | *Potato planting, Mount's Bay* | WP, 8 June 1920 (138).

83 | *Preliminary sketch for a portrait of a gentleman* | o/p 18 x 12. DL, 26 Feb 1987 (337 ni).

84 | *Sandy Cove* | o/c 12 x 16; signed bl, in black, underlined. At left a young man in a pale jacket and dark trousers leans against the railing alongside a rising road, speaking to two standing young women; the left woman has hands on her hips and wears a pink blouse, and the right woman wears a blue blouse; both have a white apron; the right woman leans back against a large iron hoop, and beside her on the ground is a large terracotta water pitcher; in the distance are houses and people, with a hill above; at far left is a strip of sea; the sky is pale grey clouds. Sandy Cove is on the edge of Newlyn towards Mousehole. The decorated wooden frame is carved and painted to resemble Newlyn metal-work. BBC Antiques Roadshow, Leicester, 30 Sep 2018; BL, 20 Feb 2019 (79 illus, as *Sandy Bay*).

85 | *Sculling* | o/c 14 x 18; signed bl in red, dated but illegible. In a white dinghy moving away from us are three seated men; the two in the prow are elderly and wear white jackets; a young man sits at the side in a blue jacket; a fourth man stands in the stern using an oar, wearing brown clothes; beyond are several ships moored at the quay; the sea is calm and blue; the sky is pale purple. The title is not inscribed and is probably not original.

86 | *Seaweed gatherers* | o/c 18 x 20; signed bl, in black. Perhaps 1918-22. At centre two brown horses in single file stand before a two wheeled cart heavily laden with seaweed; a young man with a red scarf stands on top of the pile, raking; at left stands another young man holding up a gathering on a pole or rake; a patch of greenery is at bl, above the signature; the blue sea laps on the beach; in the distance at left is a town with a pink tower under a blue spire or cupola; at right is St Michael's Mount and hazy land on the horizon; the sky is clear blue. BL, 30 Nov 2004 (8 illus).

87 | *Siesta* | o/b 21 x 21. A smaller work than the 'Siesta' at Royal Leamington Spa; perhaps a study for it. SWS, 15 Dec 1982 (1502a, ni).

88 | *Sketching on the quay* | Black chalk and wc 9½ x 6¼; signed br. At bl, a man in hat and belted jacket sits facing left with his back to the viewer; a brush is visible; at right stands a girl in a pale dress with square neck, watching the man. PL, 17 June 1986 (25a); PL, 16 June 1987 (22).

89 | *Sport on the shore, a crab race* | o/c 12 x 16; signed bl; inscr on the stretcher 'Sport on the Shore by Harold Harvey'. Date estimated as 1890 by Cross. Two boys wearing hats half lying on the jetty watch two crabs; beyond is blue sea with children paddling. Cross, p.170 (illus); PH, 2001 (2); Wallace, p.61 (illus). The Box, Plymouth (1964.21), donated from a private collection in 1964.

90 | *Spreading the nets* | o/c 15 x 18; signed br in yellow, perhaps 1905–15. On a sunlit grassy meadow beside the sea a white horse moving left pulls a cart laden with nets, led by a walking man; two more men attend to the cart; in the left foreground two boys in blue jerseys sit on the grass; in the right fore-ground is part of a ploughed field; in the distance is the sea and St Michael's Mount with land beyond; the thin strip of sky is grey. WP, 8 June 1920 (36, sold for £5); BL, 21 Jan 2015 (111 illus); BL, 23 June 2015 (107 illus).

91 | *St Peter's church, Newlyn* | A footpath leads to a gate beside the east end of the church, with three pointed windows; around are several secular buildings; behind a row of trees runs along an elevated ridge.

92 | *Steady – boys fishing off Newlyn* | o/c 40 x 50; signed br, and inscr. Three boys in a dinghy off Newlyn; the left boy sits at the stern holding the rudder; the centre boy stands with a line in his left hand; the right boy kneels with a grappling hook in his right hand; in the boat is a basket of fish. DL, 22 June 1989 (519 illus,

prov purchased from the artist *c.*1906).

93 | *Still life of daffodils and narcissi in a white jug* | o/c 20 x 16; signed br in red, *c.*1930. A pale blue-grey jug with a floral motif on its side and handle to the left, stands on a circular greenish table; the background is pale blue-grey; the white and yellow flowers touch the right edge of the frame and almost touch the left and top edges; the light comes from the left. CL, 19 June 1997 (169 illus); BL, 12 Mar 2002 (7 illus as *Daffodils and narcissi*); WL.

94 | *Still life, a vase of flowers* | o/p 5½ x 4; a pair, signed. DL, 26 Feb 1987 (496, 497 ni).

95 | *Taking a rest* | o/c 20 x 24; signed. PL, 23 Apr 1985 (28 ni).

96 | *Tea time* | o/c 30 x 25; signed bl, *c.*1920. A view of a room; at left is a table against the wall, set for tea; at centre a woman in a long yellow cardigan starts a gramophone; at left, beyond the table, a maid appears in a doorway; in the foreground a stool is on a striped a carpet; at right a cat sits by French windows; the colours are muted. DMG, pub v (62 illus); SWS, 28 July 1983 (2802a); SL, 23 May 1984 (28 illus); CL, 7 June 1985 (9); WL.

97 | *Team ploughing* | o/b 11 x 18. Joel, Melbourne, 7 Nov 1980 (1266).

98 | *The apple orchard* | o/c 18 x 20; signed. A girl in the foreground of an orchard, and several others at right. DMG, autumn 1974 (27 illus).

99 | *The balcony, Newlyn* | o/c 10 x 12; signed bl. At the top of open, sloping ground is a terrace of houses; at centre of these a large storey with one window projects and is supported by two brick and plaster pillars; in the foreground is a young child facing right and in a white smock. The building was demolished in the pre-war slum clearance. PH, 2001 (29).

100 | *The blackberry harvest* | o/c 16 x 14; signed br in black (inscr on the canvas overlap 'Blackberry Harvest Harold Harvey'), *c.*1908. In the left foreground of a grassy meadow, two women move right with a young girl between them; the nearest figure has a blue sleeve and a red headscarf; the child wears a cream hat; behind at left is another woman; each woman carries a basket; behind them are trees and blue sky (or sea?). The *Western Daily Mercury* of 23 Aug 1912 said "No one could wish for a prettier picture than 'The Blackberry Harvest'". HSG, Aug 1912 (29); CL, 21 Nov 1995 (96 illus); CL, 22 Nov 2006 (278 illus); CL, 5 June 2008 (21 illus); WL.

101 | *The carpenter's shop* | o/c 12 x 14; signed bl in red and verso. In a dark room a man facing us, wearing cap and rolled shirt sleeves, planes a length of wood on a bench; on the bench are tools and shavings; behind him is a window. Ritchie, Toronto 28 May 1996 (164a); Lawrence, Crewkerne, 10 Oct 1996 (191, as *Carpenter's workshop*); PH, 2001 (34); WHL, 27 Sep 2007 (200).

102 | *The family* | *The Studio*, March 1942, where Nichols described it as "a modernised version of the flight into Egypt is more than noteworthy".

103 | *The farmer's boy* | o/c 18 x 18; signed br in red. A boy in white shirt and khaki shorts, grey socks and brown boots rests on a horizontal tree trunk; behind is a meadow and at left a metal gate; the boy almost fills the height of the canvas. PL, 11 Nov 1986 (115 illus, as *A corner of the garden*); DL, 2 Sep 1987

(338 illus, as *A corner of the green*); WHL, 14 Apr 1988 (30 illus).

104 | *The fishmarket, Newlyn* | The *Notebook* records 'Fishmarket, Newlyn, 30 x 25'. Mentioned in *The Studio*, March 1942.

105 | *The fleeting joys of childhood* | WP, 8 June 1920 (14).

106 | *The fond farewell* | o/c 30 x 25; initialled HH, bl, *c.*1902. On a sunny shore, at left a young woman in a white dress stands facing right waving a handkerchief; at right a young woman in white sits with hands clasped round her knees looking at the other woman. CL, 12 Nov 1987 (92 illus); Messum's (89 illus as *Out to sea*); DMG, autumn 2010 (10 illus, as *Out to sea*); DMG, May 2012 (8 illus, as *Out to sea*); WL.

107 | *The front, Newlyn* | o/c 15 x 18; signed bl, *c.*1905 or earlier. A view of Fore Street, Newlyn. A wet road leads to the centre of the painting, flanked at left by shops; one advertises Lyons Tea and four small children look through its window. At right is a railing, to the right of which is the sea; in the middle distance people walk or stand in the road. PL, 29 Jan 1991 (30 illus).

108 | *The kitchen through an arch* | A tall rounded arch in a white wall leads to a kitchen where a woman in a red skirt and blue top sits by a table with a white cloth; on her lap is a bowl which she is working at; behind her is a tall dresser with many plates etc.

109 | *The little mother* | o/c 18 x 21½; signed br, title inscr on verso. A girl in a large straw hat with a dark blue band looks at the viewer; her arms hold a baby facing left with white clothes; behind is a whitewashed wall with a doorjamb at far right. WP, 8 June 1920 (141); NMAG, 2001 (47).

110 | *The midday rest* | o/c approx 20 x 24, on the reverse of *In the kitchen* (1918); *c.*1905-1910. At centre-left a young woman sits on grass facing right, in black feathered hat, red scarf, white blouse and dark blue skirt; at tr sits a boy; at far left are elements of another figure; the tone is dark. PL, 25 Nov 1997 (11 ni).

111 | *The old forge* | o/c 24 x 20; signed bl, *c.*1900. Inside a forge the blacksmith works at the anvil; two men stand at right beneath two windows; the overall tone is dark. PL, 12 Nov 1985 (89 illus); CL, 12 June 1986 (90 illus).

112 | *The orange sellers, Newlyn harbour* o/c 12 x 16; signed br. Two girls in pale clothes walking left each holds a full basket of oranges over their left arm; the left girl wears a blue hat and holds out her right hand to a sailor in a blue shirt and a cap seated on a box, perhaps taking payment for an orange; behind are boats alongside the quay, and across the harbour are the town and Paul Hill. BL, 29 Sep 2010 (167 illus).

113 | *The pipe* | o/c 11½ x 15½; signed bl. Three-quarter length view of an old bearded man seated frontally in an interior, wearing a cap and brown waistcoat and coat, holding a pipe in his right hand, and resting his right elbow on a table at left; on the table is a glass tankard full of beer and a stubby bottle; his left hand is just visible at br. WHL, 8 April 2010 (250 illus, as of 1902).

114 | *The rushing stream* | o/c 18 x 16; signed bl. In the foreground a stream flows at great force; behind is the bank with leafless trees. PH, 2001 (27); WHL, 27 Sep 2012 (98).

115 | *The shop (Dolphin Hotel)* | A village street where a tall building with a large shop window faces us; beside it is a horse and cart; at far right is part of a sign, DOLP … HO.

116 | *The sunbathers* | o/c 20 x 22; signed bl. On a grey beach a boy lies stretched out, his head at left, in white hat and shorts, his right knee raised; at right a younger nude boy sits facing the viewer, his hands clasping his left knee; beyond are large rocks and blue sea. PL, 14 June 1988 (17 illus); WHL, 28 Feb 1989 (240 illus, as *Two boys sunbathing on rocky Cornish shore*); SL, 8 Nov 1989 (23 illus, as 18 x 20, as *Boys on a beach*); WL.

117 | *The tired girl* | Shown at Newlyn, November 1937. *The Cornishman* of 18 Nov 1937 wrote "Mr Harvey has excelled himself again as a portrait painter, and there can be nothing but admiration for his 'The tired girl'".

118 | *The turnip cart* | o/c 24 x 30. On the reverse is a still life of flowers attributed to Gertrude Harvey. SWS, 24 Oct 1995 (280).

119 | *The village cobbler* | o/c 18 x 16. In a dark interior an old man sits at a table piled with tools and shoes, under a large window with a garden beyond; an unlit oil lamp hangs at top right. Hindman, Chicago, 11 Dec 2011 (322 illus).

120 | *The watering place* | o/c 32 x 22; inscr in pencil on stretcher reverse, *c.*1905. A man sits on a horse facing left, which crosses a small pool; behind are ducks at left and fields at right. Bonhams West, 28 Nov 1991 (444 illus).

121 | *The watering place* | o/c 20 x 18; signed br, *c.*1905. A man in white shirt and dark cap sits on a brown horse drinking from a pool, with another horse behind. CL, 15 Mar 1985 (27 illus); BL, 22 July 1993 (1); SL, 13 July 2017 (68 illus); WL.

122 | *The young ploughman* | o/c 25¼ x 30; signed br in dark brown, *c.*1905. At left two brown horses pull a plough guided by a boy at right; the field at left is ploughed and a broad strip of green meadow remains to be worked; a few gulls follow the plough; the sky is cloudy with darker patches. BL, 23 Jan 2013 (104 illus).

123 | *Thomas Harvey* | o/c 14 x 12. Head and shoulder view of a boy, who lived at 3 Lynn Terrace, Newlyn. WHL, 27 Mar 1990 (527 ni); WHL, 2 July 1990 (626 ni); CL, 15 July 1998 (15 illus); WHL, 25 Oct 2001 (160).

124 | *Three boys with pumpkin lantern* | small size. Shown at the BBC Antiques Roadshow, Salisbury, 1990.

125 | *Treriefe* | pencil drawing on paper 5½ x 10; not signed. An angled view of the house near Newlyn, with two storeys and attic, showing the front side with windows and main door; tall chimneys rise on both short sides; other buildings are visible on both sides. On the reverse is *Girl at prayer* (QV). Bearnes, Hampton & Littlewood, Exeter, 9 Oct 2018 (393 illus).

126 | *Trout stream* | o/c 20 x 19. Lawrence, Crewkerne, 4 Nov 1982 (264).

127 | *Tug of war* | o/c 12 x 15; signed bl (inscr on a label on the frame), *c.*1909. At centre right, sits a girl in a cream hat, white smock and red dress, holding one end of a rope; another girl is beside her at right; at left sits a boy in white hat and clothes, holding the other end of the rope; behind him are two boys, one with fair hair; the scene is a grassy area before a beach, with the sea and coast beyond. Perhaps RA, 1910 (727) and WAGL, 1910 (1057, price £150); PL, 14 June 1988 (13 illus, as *A test of strength*); DMG, 1988 (100 illus, as *A trial of strength*).

128 | *Two girls gathering faggots* | o/c 20 x 22, early style; signed bl. In a copse, a girl in the foreground faces left wearing a white blouse and a coloured headscarf, holding a bundle of wood wrapped in a cloth; behind her, at left, another girl bends to the ground, her right arm outstretched. The woods at Higher Faughan were a source of faggots. Perhaps shown at the Mendoza Galleries 1913 as *Faggot gatherers*, which was reviewed as among the best of his pictures there. CL, 11 June 1982 (5 illus).

129 | *Unloading the catch, Newlyn* | o/c 12 x 14; signed br, *c.*1905. Several fishing boats are tied up at the quay on the left, with sails furled; at left two men in white jackets secure a boat; behind are more men in blue with barrels, and a horse and cart. RGG.

130 | *View from a meadow* | o/c 18 x 24; signed br(?) and indis dated; perhaps mid-1930s. A meadow with many wild flowers; at right is a house and well-head; very diffusely painted. SL, 13 May 1987 (133 illus); WL.

131 | *View of a Cornish village* | o/c 15½ x 17½; signed indis bl, *c.*1915. In the right foreground a narrow lane bordered by reddish hedges leads over a hillside towards autumnal trees; a house lies at left and at far left is a tall red chimney; in the middle distance rises the tower of St Pol de Leon at Paul, which has a corner beacon tower; above is a large pale blue cloudscape; the landscape is in muted colours. St Pol de Leon is the parish church of Mousehole; the tower rises 86 feet. CL, 12 June 1987 (123a illus); WHL, 12 July 1990 (360 illus, as *Farmstead above Paul village, Newlyn*); WHL, 27 Sep 1990 (252 illus); CL, 24 Nov 2000 (5 illus, as *A view of Paul, Newlyn, Cornwall*); WL.

132 | *Village of Eggbuckland, Devon* | o/c 19 x 24. WHL, 17 May 1996 (205 ni).

133 | *When day's end is nigh* | o/c 15¾ x 17¾, early style; signed bl, indis. At left in a meadow a young woman in a white smock moves right carrying a young child in red cap, white dress and brown shoes; right of her walks an older girl in white cap, blouse and dark skirt carrying a bunch of flowers in her left hand; behind at right are three small figures, one in a yellow hat. SWS, 25 July 1989 (600 illus).

134 | *Winter sunshine* | o/c 11½ x 11½; signed bl. A young man on a white horse approaching the viewer across a pool; beyond are farm buildings and trees; at left is a man with two horses at the edge of the pool. DL, 8 Nov 1990 (390 illus).

135 | *With day dreams of fairies to charm every hour* | WP, 8 June 1920 (128).

136 | *Woman reading in a garden* | o/c 14 x 18; not signed, *c.*1900. At right, a woman wearing a hat and striped dress sits reading a book in a sunny, colourful garden beside a pale house. Fox/Greenacre, p.128, illus no.65; PL, 21 Nov 2000 (10 illus); PH, 2001 (79); CL, 13 Dec 2012 (59); WL.

137 | *Woodcutters* | o/c 25 x 30; signed. BL, 22 July 1993 (17).

138 | *Young girl looking out to sea* | o/c 20 x 16; initialled, late 1920s. In the foreground a girl with a long plait down her back tied with a ribbon, sits on rocks facing right, her right hand resting on the rock; beyond are the sea and coast; the sky is cloudy. All the motifs are thickly painted and lack detail, like a sketch.

CL, 7 June 1990 (157 illus); WHL, 12 July 1990 (410 ni, as *Girl seated on the rocks overlooking Mounts Bay, Cornwall*); WHL, 27 Sep 1990 (45 illus); WHL, 10 Oct 1991 (212 ni, as *Young girl seated on rocks*).

139 | *Young girls on a cliff top* | o/c 18 x 15; signed bl, *c.*1910. In a meadow with white flowers, a young girl reclines in the foreground on her left side, facing the viewer, her right arm covering her face; behind her at left sits an older woman in a white dress, her left arm supporting her, looking at the reclining girl; beyond at right a very young girl in white smock and red hat stands looking at the others; in the background at left is a pale flowering shrub; beyond are the sea and coast. CL, 6 Mar 1992 (1 illus); WL.

140 | *Young girls on seashore* | o/c 19½ x 17½. Perhaps the same as *A quiet paddle* or *Children on the surf.* PL, 16 June 1969 (64).

141 | *Young sailors* | o/c 14 x 16; signed br. In a white dinghy are three boys; the left boy with white hat holds an oar as a rudder over the stern; the middle boy is in the prow, watching the right boy who leans over the side holding a toy sailing boat in the water; beyond are two sailing boats with red sails, and a low coast; the sea is calm with clear reflections of the dinghy. WP, 8 June 1920 (130); Christies New York, 7 April 2006 (102 illus).

ATTRIBUTED WORKS

1 | *A seated man* | o/b 12 x 10; signed, dated 10. DL, 9 Oct 1997 (88 ni, as by H... Harvey).

2 | *An old man picking apples in a sunny Cornish orchard* | o/c 20 x 16. In the foreground a man with a long pole takes apples from a tall tree at right; at bl, is a basket of apples. DL, 16 Apr 1982 (634 illus); DL, 26 Feb 1987 (116 illus, as 'in the style of H Harvey'); DL, 30 Jan 1995 (137 illus, as *The apple picker*).

3 | *Broody hen and ducklings* | o/c 20 x 14. WHL, 19 May 1987 (314 ni).

4 | *Ducks swimming and seated at the edge of a pond* | o/c 10 x 14. WHL, 19 May 1987 (316 illus).

5 | *Friends sailing in the harbour* | o/b 12 x 16; initialed. CL, 19 Feb 2004 (121).

6 | *Hen and ducklings basking in the sun* | o/c 10 x 14. WHL, 19 May 1987 (315 illus).

7 | *Hen and ducklings beneath the boughs of a flowering apple tree* | o/c 14 x 18. WHL, 19 May 1987 (313 illus); WHL, 30 July 1987 (271 ni).

8 | *Japanese dolls* | o/c 14 x 10. In the foreground two dolls in Oriental costume are seated looking at each other, the female at left and the male at right; they sit in a landscape with many trees and colourful flowers. BL, 20 Mar 2007 (54 illus, title 'amended from *Chinese dolls*, as attributed to Harold Harvey').

9 | *Penzance harbour* | o/c 14 x 18; not signed. In mid-field is a sailing vessel facing left, with other boats beyond. DL, 8 Feb 1996 (84 illus).

10 | *Sharpening the scythe* | o/c 16 x 13. DL, 2 Sep 1987 (56 illus, as 'in the style of Harold Harvey').

11 | *Sketch of a farm boy* | o/p 11 x 8. DL, 16 June 2005 (564 illus).

12 | *Study of a horse and rider in a landscape* | o/c 19 x 23. P. Bath, 17 Nov 1997 (59).

13 | *The Great Work at Ashton* | o/c 33½ x 50. There are two Ashtons in Cornwall; one is near Breage, north of Porthleven; the other is near the junction of the A390 and A388. WHL, 29 Mar 1979 (202 ni).

14 | *View of Newlyn* | o/c 13 x 9. In the foreground is foliage; behind are sunlit buildings with steep roofs and tall chimneys; a pier of the harbour and a sailing boat are at left; the horizon is of rolling hills.

15 | *Woman in a garden above a harbour* | o/c 18 x 22. At left a path leads through a green garden to an arbour where a woman sits facing right; she wears a white dress and hat; beyond are gabled houses; at right is the sea. DL, 22 June 1989 (365 illus).

16 | *Woman in a studio* | o/c 20 x 25. A woman sits facing the viewer, in hat and dark coat over a pale blouse, with a pearl necklace. DL, 6 Oct 1988 (51 illus).

List of models

Angove, Iris | *A Daughter of Newlyn* (1936) and *Iris* (undated *c.*1927; identity not certain)
Angove, Sidney | *Cornish Miners* (1935)
Batten, Kitty | *Kitty* (1930) and *The Blue Door, Newlyn* (1934). Perhaps also for *Rima* and the maid in *The Young Menage*
Becket, Emma | title unknown
Bickersteth, Helen | *The White House*
Birch, Mornie | *The Girl and the Frog* (1908) and *Winding Wool* (1914; identity not certain)
Bruford, Marjorie Frances | *Midge Bruford and fiancé* (undated, early 1920s)
Chiffers, Arthur | *The Blue Door, Newlyn* (1934)
Chiffers, Ethel | *Ethel* (undated *c.*1927); identity not certain
Cole, Evelyn | *A Summer Evening – Evelyn* (1926) identity not certain
Drew, Isabel | *A Study in Green* (1932)
Francis, Helen | The left-hand girl in *Girls outside the Gaiety Cinema, Newlyn* (1925)
Gilbert, Lilian (Mrs Brood) | *Lilian* (undated *c.*1927; identity not certain)
Green, Ethel | *Ethel* (undated *c.*1927; identity not certain)
Grenfell, Nicholas | *Cornish Miners* (1935)
Harvey, Adeline Mary | *Girl with Goats* (undated)
Harvey, Rhoda | *Rhoda* (1934)
Harvey, Thomas | *Thomas Harvey* (undated)
James, Joan | *Joan James* (undated *c.*1937)
Jewill Hill, Laura, Paul and James Junior *Laura and Paul Jewill Hill* (1916) and *James Jewill Hill Junior* (1920)
Kelynack, Janie | *Janie* (1923) and *Siesta* (1925)
Kemp, Sam | *The Onion Boy* (1940)
Kitchen, Peter | *Peter Kitchen* (1930)
Legate, Josephine | *Josephine* (undated *c.*1927)
Mathews, Clara | *Clara* (1923)
Miss Clarry | *Anemones* (1926)
Miss Howell | *Anemones* (1926)
Naper, Ella | *The Critics* (1922)
Pearce, Vivian | *The Market Gardener* (1938)
Pollard, Betty | *Girl in a yellow blouse* (1939)
Pollard, Greta | *Blackberries* (1923)
Rae, Ailsa Morley | *Ailsa* (undated *c.*1940)
Rose, Alison Helen | *Portrait of Miss Alison Rose* (undated *c.*1927)
Rose, Betty | *Portrait of Miss Betty Rose* (undated *c.*1927)
Symons, Zena Crawshaw | *Zena* (1933)
Tregenza, Nannie Pearce (née Berriman) *Mother and Child* (1918)
Wearne, Cressida | *Girl on a Cliff* (1926)
Willis, Evelyn | *A Summer Evening – Evelyn* (1926; identity not certain)

Bibliography

Apollo, 1927, vol. 5

Art News, 15 April 1911

Balchin, W.G.V., *The Making of the English Landscape: The Cornish Landscape* (Hodder & Stoughton Ltd, 1983)

Barbizon House Record, 1932

Bedford, Hugh, *Frank Gascoigne Heath and his 'Newlyn School' Friends at Lamorna* (Hugh Bedford, 1995)

Bénézit, E. (ed.), *Dictionnaire critique et documentaire des Peintres, Sculpteurs, Dessinateurs et Graveurs* (Librarie Grund, 1976 and 2006)

Berriman, Hazel, *Arts and Crafts in Newlyn 1890–1939* (Newlyn Orion, 1986)

Berriman, Hazel, *Cryséde: The Unique Textile Designs of Alec Walker* (The Royal Institution of Cornwall, 1993)

Billcliffe, R., *The Royal Glasgow Institute of the Fine Arts 1861–1989: Dictionary of Exhibitors at the Annual Exhibitions of the Royal Glasgow Institute of the Fine Arts* (The Woodend Press, 1991)

Birch, Elizabeth Lamorna, *In Time and Place, Lamorna* (Patten Press, 1990)

Bird, Sheila, *Bygone Penzance and Newlyn* (Phillimore & Co., 1987)

Bonhams, sales catalogues

Bowness, S. & Phillpot C. (eds), *Britain and the Venice Biennale 1895-1995* (British Council, 1995)

Branfield, John, *Ella and Charles Naper: Art and life at Lamorna* (Sansom & Co., 2003)

Branfield, John, *Geoffrey and Jill Garnier: A marriage of the arts* (Sansom & Co., 2010)

British Impressions: The Progress of Impressionism 1880–1940, sales catalogue David Messum Gallery, London (The Studio, 1995)

Burlington Magazine, October 1985

A Checklist of Painters, c.1200–1994, Represented in the Witt Library, Courtauld Institute of Art, London (Continuum International Publishing Group Ltd.; 2nd edition, 1995)

Christies, sales catalogues

Colour, October 1918; November 1918; January 1919; October 1920, December 1920; January 1926

The Connoisseur, November 1920; April 1927; June 1990

Corin, John, *Fishermen's Conflict: The Story of Newlyn* (David & Charles, 1988)

Cornishman and Cornish Telegraph, 31 March 1926; 30 June 1926; 31 October 1935; 25 March 1937; 8 July 1937; 18 November 1937; 24 March 1938; 23 March 1939; 8 May 1941; 22 May 1941; 29 May 1941

Cross, Tom, *The Shining Sands: Artists in Newlyn and St Ives 1880–1930* (Westcountry Books, 1994)

Daily Express, 1 May 1926

Daily Graphic, 3 May 1924; 2 May 1925; 1 May 1926

Daily Mail, 7 May 1917

Daily News, 3 May 1920

Daily Sketch, 23 March 1926; 12 February 1927

David Lay, Penzance, sales catalogues

Davies, Peter, *Art in Poole and Dorset* (Poole Historical Trust, 1987)

Davies, Peter, *St. Ives Revisited: Innovators and Followers* (Old Bakehouse Publications, 1994)

Desmond, Ray, *Dictionary of British and Irish botanists and horticulturalists* (Taylor & Francis and the Natural History Museum, 1994)

Dolman, Bernard (ed.), *A Dictionary of Contemporary British Artists, 1929* (Antique Collectors' Club, reprint 1981)

Dolman, Bernard (ed.), *Who's Who in Art* (The Art Trade Press Ltd, 1927, 1929 and 1934 editions)

Drawing and Design, November 1922; December 1923

Dunbar, Janet, *Laura Knight* (HarperCollins, 1975)

Evening Standard, 4 May 1928

Fox, Caroline, *Stanhope Forbes and the Newlyn School* (David & Charles, 1993)

Fox, Caroline & Greenacre, Francis, *Painting in Newlyn 1880-1930* (Barbican Art Gallery, 1985)

Garstin, Norman, 'West Cornwall as a Sketching Ground', *The Studio*, 1909, vol. 47, pp. 109–121

Garstin, Norman, 'Studio Talk – Newlyn', *The Studio*, 1919, vol. 76, pp. 62–67

Goodman, J., *What a Go! The Life of Alfred Munnings* (Collins, 1988)

Graves, Algernon, *The Royal Academy of Arts: a complete dictionary of contributors and their work from its foundation in 1769 to 1904* (S.R. Publishers Ltd, 1970)

Green, Iris M., *Artists at Home, Newlyn 1870–1900* (privately published, 1995)

Grosvenor Galleries, London, exhibition catalogues

Gunzi, Roo et al., *Amongst Heroes : The Artist in Working Cornwall* (Two Temple Place, 2013)

Hale, Nic, *Norman and Alethea Garstin: A brief biography of two painters* (An Lyverji Kernewek, 1999)

Hamilton Davey, Frederick, *The Flora of Cornwall: Being an Account of the Flowering Plants and Ferns Found in the County of Cornwall Including the Scilly Isles* (F. Chegwidden, 1909)

The Handbook of Western Cornwall, Penzance, Falmouth and Neighbourhoods; St. Michael's Mount, The Land's End, The Logan Stone; etc. (Henry Besley, 1865)

Hardie, Dr Melissa (ed.), *100 Years in Newlyn: Diary of a Gallery* (Patten Press with Newlyn Art Gallery, 1995)

Hislop, R. (ed.), *Annual Art Sales Index* (Art Sales Index Ltd, Surrey)

The Homelovers' Book of Etching, Engravings and Colour Prints (Frost & Reed Ltd, 23rd–29th Editions, 1938–1961)

Homes and Antiques (BBC), November (2000)

Jesse, Fryniwed Tennyson *Her intermittent diary* (private collection)

Jesse, F. Tennyson (ed.), *The Paper Chase* (Elizabeth Forbes, 1909)

Johnson, J. & Greutzner, A., *The Dictionary of British Artists 1880–1940* (Antique Collectors' Club, 1976)

Keast, H., *Saint Hilary of Cornwall: The Story of a Cornish Parish and its Church* (Friends of St Hilary, 1986)

Kelly's Directory for Cornwall (1893)

Knight, Laura, *Oil Paint and Grease Paint* (Nicholson & Watson, 1936)

Langley, Roger, *Walter Langley: Pioneer of the Newlyn art colony* (Sansom & Co., 1997)

Laperriere, C.B. (ed.), *The Royal Scottish Academy Exhibitors 1826–1990* (Hilmarton Manor Press, 1991)

Laporte: A History in Art (Laporte plc, 2000)

Leicester Galleries, London, exhibition catalogues

Lomax, Pamela, *The Golden Dream: A biography of Thomas Cooper Gotch* (Sansom & Co., 2004)

Mais, S.B.P., *The Cornish Riviera* (Great Western Railway Company, 1928)

McConkey, Kenneth, *Edwardian Portraits: Images of an Age of Opulence* (Antique Collectors' Club, 1988)

Milner J., *The Studios of Paris: The Capital of Art in the Late Nineteenth Century* (Yale University Press, 1988)

Morning Post, 30 May 1913; 25 October 1918; 8 February 1927

National Art Collections Fund Review (1995)

The Observer, 3 October 1920; 18 June 1922; 1 October 1922; 4 May 1924; 17 May 1925; 7 February 1932

The Official Guide to Penzance (Beare and Son, 1876)

Parker, Simon, *A Star on the Mizzen: The story of the 1896 Newlyn fishing riots* (Giss'on Books, 1996)

Petteys, Chris, *Dictionary of Women Artists: An International Dictionary of Women Artists Born Before 1900* (G.K. Hall & Co, Boston, Mass, USA, 1985)

Phillips, sales catalogues

Phillipps, K.C. (ed.), *The Cornish Journal of Charles Lee* (Tabb House, 1995)

Picture Post, 'A Colony of Artists' pp. 50–2, 15 October 1938

The Pocket Price Guide to British Painting 1830–1980 (Antique Collectors' Club, 1990)

Public Catalogue Foundation: Birmingham, London (2008)

Public Catalogue Foundation: Cornwall & The Scilly Isles, London (2007)

Public Catalogue Foundation: Staffordshire, London (2009)

Public Catalogue Foundation: Tyne & Wear Museums, London (2008)

The Queen, 24 May 1913

Richards, Frank, 'Newlyn as a Sketching Ground', *The Studio*, 1895

Robins, A.G., *Modern Art in Britain 1910–1914* (Merrill Holberton Ltd, 1997)

Royal Academy, London, exhibition catalogues

Royal Academy Exhibitors 1905–1970 (E.P. Publishing Ltd, 1977)

The Royal Academy Illustrated, London 1925, 1929, 1931, 1932, 1933, 1934, 1939, 1940

Rutter, Frank, *Art in My Time* (Rich & Cowan, 1933)

Sheffield Daily Telegraph, 28 August 1925 (Review of Mappin Gallery Exhibition)

Smith, Father Christopher, *150 Years of Catholicism in Penzance* (Church of the Immaculate Conception, Penzance)

Smith, Jonathan, *Summer in February* (Little, Brown & Co., 1995)

Smith, Marcella, *Flower Painting in Water Colour* (Seeley, Service & Co., 1955)

Sotheby's, sales catalogues

Spalding, Frances, *Dictionary of British Art*, vol. VI (Antique Collectors' Club, 1990)

Stewart, A.M., *Royal Hibernian Academy of Arts: Index of Exhibitors and Their Works 1826–1979* (Manton Publishing, 1986)

The Studio, July 1926; March 1942

The Sunday Times, 30 April 1916

Thornton, A.H.R., *Fifty Years of the New English Art Club* (NEAC, London, 1935)

The Times, 10 May 1917; 7 May 1918; 4 May 1925; 4 February 1927; 5 February 1932; 2 May 1933; 4 May 1935; 31 May 2002

Tourist's Guide to Penzance (F. Rodda, Penzance, 1875)

Tregarthen, J.C. et al., *Cornwall, England's Riviera: A Guide to the Charm, Lure, Industry and Residential Advantages of the Duchy of Cornwall* (The Homeland Association Ltd, c.1930)

Vulliamy, Colwyn Edward, *Calico Pie: An Autobiography* (Michael Joseph, 1940)

Walke, Bernard, *Twenty Years at St Hilary* (Methuen, 1935; repub. Anthony Mott Ltd, London, 1982, and Truran Books, Truro, 2002)

Wallace, Catherine, *Under the Open Sky: The paintings of the Newlyn and Lamorna artists 1880–1940 in the public collections of Cornwall and Plymouth* (Truran Books Ltd, 2002)

Wallace, Caroline, *Women Artists in Cornwall 1880–1940* (Falmouth Art Gallery, 1996)

A Century of Art in Cornwall 1889–1989, exhibition catalogue (Cornwall County Council, 1989)

Waters, Grant M., *Dictionary of British Artists working 1900–1950*, vol. I (text) and vol. II (plate 194, *Gathering Pussywillows*) (Eastbourne Fine Arts, 1975)

Western Daily Mercury, 23 August 1912

Western Daily Press, 25 November 1915

Western Daily Press, Bristol and Bristol Mirror, 16 September 1932

Western Mail, 24 August 2002

Western Morning News, 3 December 1924; 17 March 1934; 22 May 1941; 26 May 1941; 26 March 1966

W.H. Lane, Penzance, sales catalogues

Who Was Who (A&C Black, 1967)

Whybrow, M., *St Ives 1883–1993: Portrait of an Art Colony* (Antique Collectors' Club Ltd, 1994)

Wilcox, Timothy, *A Day in the Sun Outdoor Pursuits in the Art of the 1930s* (Philip Wilson, 2006)

Wilenski, R.H., *Drawings and Paintings by Joan Manning-Sanders* (Faber & Faber, 1929)

Wood, Christopher, *The Dictionary of Victorian Painters* (Antique Collectors' Club, second edition 1978)

Wood, Christopher, *Paradise Lost: Paintings of English country life and landscape 1850-1914* (Barrie & Jenkins, 1988)

Wormleighton, Austin, *A Painter Laureate: Lamorna Birch and his Circle* (Sansom & Co., 1995)

Wortley, Laura, *British Impressionism, A Garden of Bright Images* (The Studio, 1988)

Index

Numbers in **bold** indicate works illustrated

Acknowledgements

This book could not have been written without the assistance of Mr A.G. Harvey, great-nephew of Harold, who made available an extensive collection of archive material including newspaper reviews, letters and a notebook kept by Harold. Other most helpful members of the family were Brian Harvey, another great-nephew, and Mrs Rhoda Littler, Harold Harvey's niece. Mrs Lorna Sullivan provided information about Gertrude Bodinnar's family. Invaluable help and information has also been received from a number of individuals, art dealers, auction houses and art organisations.

Penlee House Gallery & Museum would like to thank the following individuals and organisations who have given invaluable assistance in the preparation of both this book and the latest exhibition:

- Kenneth McConkey, Peter Risdon, Pauline Sheppard, Clara Hudson and Ian Parfitt for their roles in the production of this book.
- Richard Green of Richard Green Gallery, London, for sponsoring this publication.
- The Bowerman Charitable Trust and all the private collectors who have generously lent their much-loved works to the exhibition.
- Staff at all the public galleries and museums lending works to the exhibition: Brighton & Hove Museums; Cyfarthfa Castle Museum & Art Gallery; Gallery Oldham; Leamington Spa Art Gallery & Museum; National Museums and Galleries of Wales; Royal Institution of Cornwall, Royal Cornwall Museum, Truro; South Shields Museum & Art Gallery, Tyne & Wear Archives & Museums; The Atkinson, Southport; Wolverhampton Art Gallery.
- Staff at the many auction houses and art dealerships for providing images for the publication, and without whose vital assistance we wouldn't have been able to track down works for inclusion in the exhibition: Bagshawe Fine Art; Bonhams; Christie's; David Messum Fine Art; Grant Ford Limited; MacConnal-Mason Gallery, London; Messums Wiltshire; Richard Green Gallery, London; Sotheby's; The Nine British Art.
- The many people who have given us help and support, including Lucy Lillicrap and Tom Lillicrap.
- Penzance Council, which owns and operates Penlee House Gallery & Museum.
- And finally, the team at Penlee House, particularly Anna Renton, Katie Herbert, Richard Nesham, David Trevivian and Sandra Paternotte, and also Verity Anthony, Zoe Burkett, Maisy-Sky Lumbers, Katie Smith, Ewan Wilson, Myriam Gautier and Jamie Goldie.

About the authors

Kenneth McConkey is Emeritus Professor of Art History and former Dean of Arts at the University of Northumbria. In the 1970s he conducted pioneering research on late nineteenth- and early twentieth-century British and French art, looking particularly at the followers of Bastien-Lepage. He organised monograph exhibitions on the work of La Thangue (1978), Clausen (1980) and Lavery (1984), and worked on the revisionist reconsideration of French realism, *The Realist Tradition* (Cleveland, Brooklyn and Glasgow, 1980). He selected the British section of the Impressionist landscape exhibition at Cologne and Zurich in 1989 and organized *Impressionism in Britain* at the Barbican Art Gallery in 1995. In addition to co-authoring works on Sir Alfred East and Arthur Melville, his more recent books include *The New English, A History of the New English Art Club* (2006), *John Lavery, A Painter and his World* (2010) and *George Clausen and the picture of English rural life* (2012). He was awarded a Leverhulme Research Fellowship in 2020 to complete *Towards the Sun, The Artist-Traveller at the turn of the Twentieth Century* (2021). Currently he is guest-curator of *Lavery: On Location*, a major touring exhibition which opened at the National Gallery of Ireland, Dublin, in October 2023, before travelling to Belfast and Edinburgh.

Peter Risdon worked for the British Library for over 30 years. On retirement, he chose Harold Harvey as the subject for a 'life and work' biography; no full-length account of Harvey had been published before, and he had remained less well-known than was merited by his sustained achievements in colour, subject matter, and composition over nearly half a century. Since the first edition of this book, Harvey has become better known by a wider audience than ever before, enriching the story of British art and that of his native Cornwall. Peter has also published essays on art history in the *British Art Journal* and *The Burlington Magazine*. Now 80, he is researching the Life Reform Movement as reflected in European art of 1900–1950.

Pauline Sheppard has lived and worked in Cornwall since 1969. A founder member of Cornwall Theatre Company, her work has been seen as far afield as Berlin and as close as The Minack Theatre, where her adaptations of classic stories for the Minack Schools Fortnight in the 1970s and 80s became an important part of the season's calendar. As a writer her concerns are universal issues set in Cornwall. *Dogs* (1992) deals with the philosophy of freedom and crossing borders when a group of travellers are evicted from wasteland; and *Dressing Granite* (1997), about the survival of the individual. In 1998 she adapted Charles Lee's *Our Little Town*. Charles Lee was writing in Newlyn in the late 1890s and rubbed shoulders with the artists. In 2000 she adapted *The Ordinalia (The Cornish Mystery Cycle)* for the community of St Just. She also wrote educational story plays for the Maritime Museum in Falmouth; as well as Penlee House Gallery & Museum and for Geevor Mine. In 2005 she wrote *Tin & Fishes*, with St Just Miners wives and their families. She has written for Radio 4; and in 2008 toured with guitarist Pete Berryman with *Ghosts of May*. Pauline is also a bard of the *Gorsedh (Skrifores Gwari)*. Her first book, *Through The Granite Mirror*, published by United Writers publications, won the Gorsedh Kernow Holyer an Gof Cup for literature in 2021. She is currently working on another book entitled *Ffannett's Yard*.